RECONSTRUCTION

An Anthology of Revisionist Writings

RECONSTRUCTION

An Anthology
of Revisionist Writings

‖‖‖

EDITED BY
KENNETH M. STAMPP
AND
LEON F. LITWACK

LOUISIANA STATE UNIVERSITY PRESS · BATON ROUGE

To W. E. B. DuBois, Alrutheus A. Taylor,
and Howard K. Beale,
three pioneer revisionists.

ACKNOWLEDGMENTS

The essay by Kenneth M. Stampp which introduces this anthology was originally published as a chapter in his book *The Era of Reconstruction, 1865–1877* (New York: Alfred A. Knopf, 1965), and is reprinted here with the kind permission of the publisher. Grateful acknowledgment is also made to the following authors and publishers in whose books or journals these essays first appeared:

Richard N. Current, "The Friend of Freedom," from *The Lincoln Nobody Knows* (New York: McGraw-Hill, 1958).

Eric L. McKitrick, "Andrew Johnson, Outsider," from *Andrew Johnson and Reconstruction* (Chicago: University of Chicago Press, 1960).

LaWanda and John H. Cox, "Johnson and the Negro," from *Politics, Principle, & Prejudice, 1865–66: Dilemma of Reconstruction America* (New York: Free Press of Glencoe, 1963).

Stanley Coben, "Northeastern Business and Radical Reconstruction: A Re-examination," from *Mississippi Valley Historical Review*, XLVI (1959).

Howard Jay Graham, "The 'Conspiracy Theory' of the Fourteenth Amendment," from *Yale Law Journal*, XLVII (1938).

James M. McPherson, "The Ballot and Land for the Freedmen, 1861–1865," from *The Struggle for Equality: Abolitionists and the Negro in the Civil War and Reconstruction* (Princeton: Princeton University Press, 1964).

LaWanda and John H. Cox, "Negro Suffrage and Republican Politics: The Problem of Motivation in Reconstruction Historiography," from *Journal of Southern History*, XXXIII (1967).

Willie Lee Rose, "The Old Allegiance," from *Rehearsal for Reconstruction: The Port Royal Experiment* (Indianapolis: Bobbs-Merrill, 1964).

Joel Williamson, "The Meaning of Freedom," from *After Slavery: The Negro in South Carolina During Reconstruction, 1861–1877* (Chapel Hill: University of North Carolina Press, 1965).

[v]

ACKNOWLEDGMENTS

Richard N. Current, "Carpetbaggers Reconsidered," from *A Festschrift for Frederick B. Artz* (Durham: Duke University Press, 1964).

Richard N. Current, "The Carpetbagger as Corruptionist: Henry Clay Warmoth," from *Three Carpetbag Governors* (Baton Rouge: Louisiana State University Press, 1967).

David Donald, "The Scalawag in Mississippi Reconstruction," from *Journal of Southern History*, X (1944).

Thomas B. Alexander, "Persistent Whiggery in the Confederate South, 1860–1877," from *Journal of Southern History*, XXVII (1961).

Allen W. Trelease, "Who Were the Scalawags?" from *Journal of Southern History*, XXIX (1963).

Louis R. Harlan, "Desegregation in New Orleans Public Schools during Reconstruction," from *American Historical Review*, LXVII (1962).

Vernon Lane Wharton, "The Negro and Politics, 1870–1875," from *The Negro in Mississippi, 1865–1890* (Chapel Hill: University of North Carolina Press, 1947).

Horace Mann Bond, "Social and Economic Forces in Alabama Reconstruction," from *Journal of Negro History*, XXIII (1938).

Jack B. Scroggs, "Southern Reconstruction: A Radical View," from *Journal of Southern History*, XXIV (1958).

W. E. B. DuBois, *Black Reconstruction: An Essay Toward a History of the Part Which Black Folk Played in the Attempt to Reconstruct Democracy in America, 1860–1880* (New York: Harcourt, Brace, 1935).

Vernon Lane Wharton, "The Revolution of 1875," from *The Negro in Mississippi, 1865–1890* (Chapel Hill: University of North Carolina Press, 1947).

W. R. Brock, "The Waning of Radicalism," from *An American Crisis: Congress and Reconstruction, 1865–67* (London: Macmillan, 1963).

C. Vann Woodward, "The Political Legacy of Reconstruction," from *The Burden of Southern History* Rev. ed. (Baton Rouge: Louisiana State University Press, 1968).

[vi]

FOREWORD

In the early twentieth century American historians generally agreed that the political reconstruction which followed the Civil War was a national tragedy. Most of them maintained that the Radical Republicans, who dominated the Congress of the United States, and the carpetbaggers, scalawags, and Negroes, who controlled the southern legislatures, by their corruption, political opportunism, and vindictiveness, made Reconstruction the most disgraceful episode in American political history. The historians of that period believed that the policies of Abraham Lincoln and Andrew Johnson were both generous and wise, and that if they had prevailed the country would have been spared this orgy of hatred and venality; the harmony of the sections would have been restored more easily; and the South would have found a just solution to its race problem more readily.

As recently as thirty years ago nearly all the American history textbooks still presented this point of view with scarcely a reservation, and even the more detailed and specialized studies of professional historians rarely challenged it. Within the last three decades, however, a group of historians has restudied the era of Reconstruction and subjected the old interpretation to critical scrutiny. These revisionists have by no means repudiated all of the traditional story, but they have corrected many errors and misconceptions. Moreover, the new picture of the period that has taken form from their investigations has greater variety, a richer texture, more subtlety of shading and nuance, and much better perspective.

At the present time it would be far from the truth to

describe the revisionists of Reconstruction history as a small band of martyrs struggling against an establishment of professional historians, for revisionism has won the day and bids fair to become the new orthodoxy. Revisionism draws its strength from three decades of hard research, from an impressive array of scholarly articles and monographs, from modified ideas about race, and from a changed social climate. Rarely does a present-day historian defend the traditional interpretation of Reconstruction. Perhaps the surest sign of the triumph of revisionism is that it is now finding its way into the textbooks and into the writings of nonprofessional historians.

This anthology, therefore, is not so much an attempt to plead the case for revisionism as it is to record what historians today generally accept as an accurate portrait of the Reconstruction years. We are aware that the portrait is not yet finished. For example, no satisfactory full-scale studies of the carpetbaggers, the scalawags, or the southern Negroes of the post-emancipation period have yet been published; Lincoln's role would bear further study; and some of the Radical Republicans still need biographers. Moreover, it would be folly to assume that the revisionism of today will altogether satisfy the historians of tomorrow, for as long as this period of American history is the subject of active historical inquiry revisionism will be an endless process. Nevertheless, a significant change of interpretation has taken place during the past generation, and the new body of historical literature is formidable enough to justify an anthology of revisionist writings.

Indeed, the corpus of revisionist literature is now so large that we are able to provide only a small, but we hope representative, sample. Even though the Louisiana State University Press generously permitted us to submit a manuscript considerably longer than the one originally contemplated, we were still unable to find room for all the selections we hoped to include. The resulting omissions will be painfully obvious to those familiar with recent Reconstruction historiography, and our explanation doubtless will not satisfy those who are disappointed by the omission of selections from their favorite books or articles.

Some of the omissions are the result of deliberate policy. Except for the introductory chapter we decided to exclude purely historiographical essays. Accordingly, we have not included Howard K. Beale's early protest against the traditional interpretation or Bernard Weisberger's excellent recent essay.* That we do not consider it necessary to include Beale's influential article indicates how much has been accomplished since its publication almost three decades ago. What Beale and a few others called for in early historiographical critiques of the old interpretation has now largely been achieved.

We have also decided to omit what appears now to be a rather primitive form of revisionism—one that offered an economic interpretation of Reconstruction as a substitute for the earlier emphasis on political opportunism and vindictiveness. We believe that the economic interpretation presented in the 1920's and 1930's by historians such as Charles A. Beard, Howard K. Beale (before he changed his mind), Matthew Josephson, and William B. Hesseltine is now as much discredited as the former political interpretation. We are not suggesting the absence of either political or economic motives, but only the insufficiency of an interpretation that excludes humanitarianism, ideals, and ideology. The appreciation of the complexity of motivation and a more sophisticated approach to problems of human behavior are the very essence of Reconstruction revisionism.

What follows, then, is what present-day historians have been saying about the Reconstruction roles of Abraham Lincoln and Andrew Johnson; about the character and motives of

---

* Howard K. Beale, "On Rewriting Reconstruction History," *American Historical Review*, XLV (1940), 807–27; Bernard Weisberger, "The Dark and Bloody Ground of Reconstruction Historiography," *Journal of Southern History*, XXV (1959), 427–47.

the Radical Republicans; about the behavior of Negroes in the years immediately after emancipation; about the southern "carpetbag governments"; and about the reasons for the eventual collapse of Radical Reconstruction. We have made our selections relatively long in order to give each historian space enough to make his case. Taken together we hope that they will form a reasonably coherent whole.

K.M.S.
L.F.L.

Berkeley, July, 1968

CONTENTS

INTRODUCTION *The Tragic Legend of Reconstruction*
Kenneth M. Stampp   3

PART I

LINCOLN, JOHNSON, AND RECONSTRUCTION   23

1 THE FRIEND OF FREEDOM   *Richard N. Current*   25

2 ANDREW JOHNSON, OUTSIDER   *Eric L. McKitrick*   48

3 JOHNSON AND THE NEGRO   *LaWanda and John H. Cox*   59

PART II

THE RADICAL REPUBLICANS   83

4 NORTHEASTERN BUSINESS AND RADICAL RECONSTRUCTION: A RE-EXAMINATION   *Stanley Coben*   85

5 THE "CONSPIRACY THEORY" OF THE FOURTEENTH AMENDMENT   *Howard Jay Graham*   107

6 THE BALLOT AND LAND FOR THE FREEDMEN, 1861–1865   *James M. McPherson*   132

7 NEGRO SUFFRAGE AND REPUBLICAN POLITICS: THE PROBLEM OF MOTIVATION IN RECONSTRUCTION HISTORIOGRAPHY   *LaWanda and John H. Cox*   156

PART III

THE FREEDMEN   173

8 "THE OLD ALLEGIANCE"   *Willie Lee Rose*   175

9 THE MEANING OF FREEDOM   *Joel Williamson*   193

[xi]

Part IV

RADICAL RECONSTRUCTION IN THE SOUTH   221

10 CARPETBAGGERS RECONSIDERED   *Richard N. Current*   223

11 THE CARPETBAGGER AS CORRUPTIONIST: HENRY CLAY
    WARMOTH   *Richard N. Current*   241

12 THE SCALAWAG IN MISSISSIPPI RECONSTRUCTION
    David Donald   264

13 PERSISTENT WHIGGERY IN THE CONFEDERATE SOUTH,
    1860–1877   *Thomas B. Alexander*   276

14 WHO WERE THE SCALAWAGS?   *Allen W. Trelease*   299

15 DESEGREGATION IN NEW ORLEANS PUBLIC SCHOOLS
    DURING RECONSTRUCTION   *Louis R. Harlan*   323

16 THE NEGRO AND POLITICS, 1870–1875
    Vernon Lane Wharton   338

17 SOCIAL AND ECONOMIC FORCES IN ALABAMA RECON-
    STRUCTION   *Horace Mann Bond*   370

18 SOUTHERN RECONSTRUCTION: A RADICAL VIEW
    Jack B. Scroggs   405

19 BLACK RECONSTRUCTION   *W. E. B. DuBois*   428

Part V

THE COLLAPSE OF RECONSTRUCTION   471

20 THE REVOLUTION OF 1875   *Vernon Lane Wharton*   473

21 THE WANING OF RADICALISM   *W. R. Brock*   496

22 THE POLITICAL LEGACY OF RECONSTRUCTION
    C. Vann Woodward   516

RECONSTRUCTION

An Anthology of Revisionist Writings

THE TRAGIC LEGEND
OF RECONSTRUCTION

Kenneth M. Stampp

In much serious history, as well as in a durable popular legend, two American epochs—the Civil War and the Reconstruction that followed—bear an odd relationship to one another. The Civil War, though admittedly a tragedy, is nevertheless often described as a glorious time of gallantry, noble self-sacrifice, and high idealism. Even historians who have considered the war "needless" and have condemned the politicians of the 1850's for blundering into it, once they passed the firing on Fort Sumter, have usually written with reverence about Civil War heroes—the martyred Lincoln, the Christlike Lee, the intrepid Stonewall Jackson, and many others in this galaxy of demigods.

Few, of course, are so innocent as not to know that the Civil War had its seamy side. One can hardly ignore the political opportunism, the graft and profiteering in the filling of war contracts, the military blundering and needless loss of lives, the horrors of army hospitals and prison camps, and the ugly depths as well as the nobility of human nature that the war exposed with a fine impartiality. These things cannot be ignored, but they can be, and frequently are, dismissed as something alien to the essence of the war years. What was real and fundamental was the idealism and the nobility of the two contending forces: the Yankees struggling to save the Union, dying to make men free; the Confederates fighting for great constitutional principles, defending their homes from invasion. Here, indeed, is one of the secrets of the spell the Civil War has cast: it involved high-minded Americans on both sides, and there was glory enough to go around. This, in fact, is the supreme synthesis of Civil War historiography and the great balm that has healed the nation's wounds: Yankees and Confederates alike fought bravely for what they believed to be just causes. There were few villains in the drama.

But when the historian reaches the year 1865, he must take leave of the war and turn to another epoch, Reconstruction, when the task was, in Lincoln's words, "to bind up the nation's wounds" and "to do all which may achieve and cherish a just and lasting peace." How, until recently, Reconstruction was portrayed in both history and legend, how sharply it was believed to contrast with the years of the Civil War, is evident in the terms that were used to identify it. Various historians have called this phase of American history "The Tragic Era," "The Dreadful Decade," "The Age of Hate," and "The Blackout of Honest Government." Reconstruction represented the ultimate shame of the American people—as one historian phrased it, "the nadir of national disgrace." It was the epoch that most Americans wanted to forget.

Claude Bowers, who divided his time between politics and history, has been the chief disseminator of the traditional picture of Reconstruction, for his book, *The Tragic Era*, published in 1929, has attracted more readers than any other dealing with this period. For Bowers Reconstruction was a time of almost unrelieved sordidness in public and private life. Whole regiments of villains march through his pages: the corrupt politicians who dominated the administration of Ulysses S. Grant; the crafty, scheming northern carpetbaggers who invaded the South after the war for political and economic plunder; the degraded and depraved southern scalawags who betrayed their own people and collaborated with the enemy; and the ignorant, barbarous, sensual Negroes who threatened to Africanize the South and destroy its Caucasian civilization.

Most of Bowers' key generalizations can be found in his preface. The years of Reconstruction, he wrote, "were years of revolutionary turmoil, with the elemental passions predominant. . . . The prevailing note was one of tragedy. . . . Never have American public men in responsible positions, directing the destiny of the nation, been so brutal, hypocritical, and corrupt. The constitution was treated as a doormat on which politicians and army officers wiped their feet after wading in the muck. . . . The southern people literally were put to the torture . . . [by] rugged conspirators . . . [who] assumed the pose of philanthropists and patriots." The popularity of Bowers' book stems in part from the simplicity of his characters. None are etched in shades of gray; none are confronted with complex moral decisions. Like characters in a Victorian romance, the Republican leaders of the Reconstruction era were evil through and through, and the helpless, innocent white men of the South were totally noble and pure.

If Bowers' prose is more vivid and his anger more intense, his general interpretation of Reconstruction is only a slight exaggeration of a point of view shared by most serious American historians from the late nineteenth century until very recently. Writing in the 1890's, James Ford Rhodes, author of a multivolumed history of the United States since the Compromise of 1850, branded the Republican scheme of reconstruction as "repressive" and "uncivilized," one that "pandered to the ignorant negroes, the knavish white natives and the vulturous adventurers who flocked from the North." About the same time Professor John W. Burgess, of Columbia University, called Reconstruction the "most soul-sickening spectacle that Americans had ever been called upon to behold." Early in the twentieth century Professor William A. Dunning, also of Columbia University, and a group of talented graduate students wrote a series of monographs that presented a crushing indictment of the Republican reconstruction program in the South—a series that made a deep and lasting impression on American historians. In the 1930's, Professor James G. Randall, of the University of Illinois, still writing in the spirit of the Dunningites, described the Reconstruction era "as a time of party abuse, of corruption, of vindictive bigotry." "To use a modern phrase," wrote Randall, "government under Radical Republican rule in the South had become a kind of 'racket.'" As late as 1947, Professor E. Merton Coulter, of the University of Georgia, reminded critics of the traditional interpretation that no "amount of revision can write away the grievous mistakes made in this abnormal period of American history." Thus, from Rhodes and Burgess and Dunning to Randall and Coulter the central emphasis of most historical writing about Reconstruction has been upon sordid motives and human depravity. Somehow, during the summer of 1865, the nobility and idealism of the war years had died.

A synopsis of the Dunning school's version of Reconstruction would run something like this: Abraham Lincoln, while the Civil War was still in progress, turned his thoughts to the great problem of reconciliation; and, "with malice toward none and charity for all," this gentle and compassionate man devised a plan that would restore the South to the Union with minimum humiliation and maximum speed. But there had already emerged in Congress a faction of Radical Republicans, sometimes called Jacobins or Vindictives, who sought to defeat Lincoln's generous program. Motivated by hatred of the South, by selfish political ambitions, and by crass economic interests, the Radicals tried to make the process of reconstruction as humiliating, as difficult, and as prolonged as they possibly could. Until Lincoln's tragic death, they poured their scorn upon him—and then used his coffin as a political stump to arouse the passions of the northern electorate.

The second chapter of the Dunning version begins with Andrew Johnson's succession to the Presidency. Johnson, the old Jacksonian Unionist from Tennessee, took advantage of the adjournment of Congress to put Lincoln's mild plan of reconstruction into operation, and it was a striking success. In the summer and fall of 1865, southerners organized loyal state governments, showed a willingness to deal fairly with their former slaves, and in general accepted the outcome of the Civil War in good faith. In December, when Congress assembled, President Johnson reported that the process of reconstruction was nearly completed and that the old Union had been restored. But the Radicals unfortunately had their own sinister purposes: they repudiated the governments Johnson had established in the South, refused to seat southern senators and representatives, and then directed their fury against the new President. After a year of bitter controversy and political stalemate, the Radicals, resorting to shamefully demagogic tactics, won an overwhelming victory in the congressional elections of 1866.

Now, the third chapter and the final tragedy. Riding roughshod over presidential vetoes and federal courts, the Radicals put the South under military occupation, gave the ballot to Negroes, and formed new southern state governments dominated by base and corrupt men, black and white. Not satisfied with reducing the South to political slavery and financial bankruptcy, the Radicals even laid their obscene hands on the pure fabric of the federal Constitution. They impeached President Johnson and came within one vote of removing him from office, though they had no legal grounds for such action. Next, they elected Ulysses S. Grant President, and during his two administrations they indulged in such an orgy of corruption and so prostituted the civil service as to make Grantism an enduring symbol of political immorality.

The last chapter is the story of ultimate redemption. Decent southern white Democrats, their patience exhausted, organized to drive the Negroes, carpetbaggers, and scalawags from power, peacefully if possible, forcefully if necessary. One by one the southern states were redeemed, honesty and virtue triumphed, and the South's natural leaders returned to power. In the spring of 1877, the Tragic Era finally came to an end when President Hayes withdrew the federal troops from the South and restored home rule. But the legacy of Radical Reconstruction remained in the form of a solidly Democratic South and embittered relations between the races.

This point of view was rarely challenged until the 1930's, when a small group of revisionist historians began to give new life and a new direction to the study of Reconstruction. The revisionists are a curious lot who sometimes quarrel with each other as much as they quarrel with the disciples of Dunning. At various times they have counted in their ranks Marxists of various degrees of orthodoxy, Negroes seeking historical vindication, skeptical white southerners, and latter-day northern abolitionists. But among them are numerous scholars who have the wisdom to know that the history of an age is seldom simple and clear-cut, seldom without its tragic aspects, seldom without its redeeming virtues.

Few revisionists would claim that the Dunning interpretation of Reconstruction is a pure fabrication. They recognize the shabby aspects of this era: the corruption was real, the failures obvious, the tragedy undeniable. Grant is not their idea of a model President, nor were the southern carpetbag governments worthy of their unqualified praise. They understand that the Radical Republicans were not all selfless patriots, and that southern white men were not all Negro-hating rebels. In short, they have not turned history on its head, but rather, they recognize that much of what Dunning's disciples have said about Reconstruction is true.

Revisionists, however, have discovered that the Dunningites overlooked a great deal, and they doubt that nobility and idealism suddenly died in 1865. They are neither surprised nor disillusioned to find that the Civil War, for all its nobility, revealed some of the ugliness of human nature as well. And they approach Reconstruction with the confident expectation that here, too, every facet of human nature will be exposed. They are not satisfied with the two-dimensional characters that Dunning's disciples have painted.

What is perhaps most puzzling in the legend of Reconstruction is the notion that the white people of the South were treated with unprecedented brutality, that their conquerors, in Bowers' colorful phrase, literally put them to the torture. How, in fact, *were* they treated after the failure of their rebellion against the authority of the federal government? The great mass of ordinary southerners who voluntarily took up arms, or in other ways supported the Confederacy, were required simply to take an oath of allegiance to obtain pardon and to regain their right to vote and hold public office. But what of the Confederate leaders—the men who held high civil offices, often after resigning similar federal offices; the military leaders who had graduated from West Point and had resigned commissions in the United States Army to take commissions in the Confederate army? Were there mass arrests, indictments for treason or conspiracy, trials and convictions, executions or imprisonments? Nothing of the sort. Officers of the Confederate army were paroled and sent home with their men. After surrendering at Appomattox, General Lee bid farewell to his troops and rode home to live his remaining years undisturbed. Only one officer, a Captain Henry Wirtz, was arrested; and he was tried, convicted, and executed, not for treason or conspiracy, but for "war crimes." Wirtz's alleged offense, for which the evidence was rather flimsy, was the mistreatment of prisoners of war in the military prison at Andersonville, Georgia.

Of the Confederate civil officers, a handful were arrested at the close of the war, and there was talk for a time of trying a few for treason. But none, actually, was ever brought to trial, and all but Jefferson Davis were released within a few months. The former Confederate President was held in prison for nearly two years, but in 1867 he too was released. With a few exceptions, even the property of Confederate leaders was untouched, save, of course, for the emancipation of their slaves. Indeed, the only penalty imposed on most Confederate leaders was a temporary political disability provided in the Fourteenth Amendment. But in 1872 Congress pardoned all but a handful of southerners; and soon former Confederate civil and military leaders were serving as state governors, as members of Congress, and even as Cabinet advisers of Presidents.

What, then, constituted the alleged brutality that white southerners endured? First, the freeing of their slaves; second, the brief incarceration of a few Confederate leaders; third, a political disability imposed for a few years on most Confederate leaders; fourth, a relatively weak military occupation terminated in 1877; and, last, an attempt to extend the rights and privileges of citizenship to southern Negroes. Mistakes there were in the implementation of these measures—some of them serious—but brutality almost none. In fact, it can be said that rarely in history have the participants in an unsuccessful rebellion endured penalties as mild as those Congress imposed upon the people of the South, and particularly upon their leaders. After four years of bitter struggle costing hundreds of thousands of lives, the generosity of the federal government's terms was quite remarkable.

If northern brutality is a myth, the scandals of the Grant administration and the peculations of some of the southern Reconstruction governments are sordid facts. Yet even here the Dunningites are guilty of distortion by exaggeration, by a lack of perspective, by superficial analysis, and by overemphasis. They make corruption a central theme of their narratives, but they overlook constructive accomplishments. They give insufficient attention to the men who transcended the greed of an age when, to be sure, self-serving politicians and irresponsible entrepreneurs were all too plentiful. Among these men were the humanitarians who organized Freedmen's Aid societies to help four million southern Negroes make the difficult transition from slavery to freedom, and the missionaries and teachers who went into the South on slender budgets to build churches and schools for the freedmen. Under their auspices the Negroes first began to learn the responsibilities and obligations of freedom. Thus the training of Negroes for citizenship had its successful beginnings in the years of Reconstruction.

In the nineteenth century most white Americans, North and South, had reservations about the Negro's potentialities —doubted that he had the innate intellectual capacity and moral fiber of the white man and assumed that after emancipation he would be relegated to an inferior caste. But some of the Radical Republicans refused to believe that the Negroes were innately inferior and hoped passionately that they would confound their critics. The Radicals then had little empirical evidence and no scientific evidence to support their belief— nothing, in fact, but faith. Their faith was derived mostly from their religion: all men, they said, are the sons of Adam and equal in the sight of God. And if Negroes are equal to white men in the sight of God, it is morally wrong for white men to withhold from Negroes the liberties and rights that white men enjoy. Here, surely, was a projection into the Reconstruction era of the idealism of the abolitionist crusade and of the Civil War.

Radical idealism was in part responsible for two of the most momentous enactments of the Reconstruction years: the Fourteenth Amendment to the federal Constitution which gave Negroes citizenship and promised them equal protection of the laws, and the Fifteenth Amendment which gave them the right to vote. The fact that these amendments could not have been adopted under any other circumstances, or at any other time, before or since, may suggest the crucial importance of the Reconstruction era in American history. Indeed, without Radical Reconstruction, it would be impossible to this day for the federal government to protect Negroes from legal and political discrimination.

If all of this is true, or even part of it, why was the Dunning legend born, and why has it been so durable? Southerners, of course, have contributed much to the legend of Reconstruction, but most northerners have found the legend quite acceptable. Many of the historians who helped to create it were northerners, among them James Ford Rhodes, William A. Dunning, Claude Bowers, and James G. Randall. Thus the legend cannot be explained simply in terms of a southern literary or historiographical conspiracy, satisfying as the legend has been to most white southerners. What we need to know is why it also satisfies northerners—how it became part of the intellectual baggage of so many northern historians. Why, in short, was there for so many years a kind of national, or inter-sectional, consensus that the Civil War was America's glory and Reconstruction her disgrace?

The Civil War won its place in the hearts of the American people because, by the end of the nineteenth century, northerners were willing to concede that southerners had fought bravely for a cause that they believed to be just; whereas southerners, with a few exceptions, were willing to concede that the outcome of the war was probably best for all concerned. In an era of intense nationalism, both northerners and southerners agreed that the preservation of the federal Union was essential to the future power of the American people. Southerners could even say now that the abolition of slavery was one of the war's great blessings—not so much, they insisted, because slavery was an injustice to the Negroes but because it was a grievous burden upon the whites. By 1886, Henry W. Grady, the great Georgia editor and spokesman for a New South, could confess to a New York audience: "I am glad that the omniscient God held the balance of battle in His Almighty hand, and that human slavery was swept forever from American soil—the American Union saved from the wreck of war." Soon Union and Confederate veterans were holding joint reunions, exchanging anecdotes, and sharing their sentimental memories of those glorious war years. The Civil War thus took its position in the center of American folk mythology.

That the Reconstruction era elicits neither pride nor sentimentality is due only in part to its moral delinquencies—remember, those of the Civil War years can be overlooked. It is also due to the white American's ambivalent attitude toward race and toward the steps that Radical Republicans took to protect the Negroes. Southern white men accepted the Thirteenth Amendment to the Constitution, which abolished slavery, with a minimum of complaint, but they expected federal intervention to proceed no further than that. They assumed that the regulation of the freedmen would be left to the individual states; and clearly most of them intended to replace slavery with a caste system that would keep the Negroes perpetually subordinate to the whites. Negroes were to remain a dependent laboring class; they were to be governed by a separate code of laws; they were to play no active part in the South's political life; and they were to be segregated socially. When Radical Republicans used federal power to interfere in these matters, the majority of southern white men formed a resistance movement to fight the Radical-dominated state governments until they were overthrown, after which southern whites established a caste system in defiance of federal statutes and constitutional amendments. For many decades thereafter the federal government simply admitted defeat and acquiesced; but the South refused to forget or forgive those years of humiliation when Negroes came close to winning equality. In southern mythology, then, Reconstruction was a horrid nightmare.

As for the majority of northern white men, it is hard to tell how deeply they were concerned about the welfare of the American Negro after the abolition of slavery. If one were to judge from the way they treated the small number of free Negroes who resided in the northern states, one might conclude that they were, at best, indifferent to the problem—and that a considerable number of them shared the racial attitudes of the South and preferred to keep Negroes in a subordinate caste. For a time after the Civil War the Radical Republicans, who were always a minority group, persuaded the northern electorate that the ultimate purpose of southern white men was to rob the North of the fruits of victory and to re-establish slavery and that federal intervention was therefore essential. In this manner Radicals won approval of, or acquiescence in, their program to give civil rights and the ballot to southern Negroes. Popular support for the Radical program waned rapidly, however, and by the middle of the 1870's it had all but vanished. In 1875 a Republican politician confessed that northern voters were tired of the "worn-out cry of 'southern outrages,'" and they wished that "the 'nigger' the 'everlasting nigger' were in—Africa." As northerners ceased to worry about the possibility of another southern rebellion, they became increasingly receptive to criticism of Radical Reconstruction.

The eventual disintegration of the Radical phalanx, those root-and-branch men who, for a time, seemed bent on engineering a sweeping reformation of southern society, was another important reason for the denigration of Reconstruction in American historiography. To be sure, some of the Radicals, especially those who had been abolitionists before the war, never lost faith in the Negro, and in the years after Reconstruction they stood by him as he struggled to break the intellectual and psychological fetters he had brought with him out of slavery. Other Radicals, however, lost interest in the cause—tired of reform and spent their declining years writing their memoirs. Still others retained their crusading zeal but became disenchanted with Radical Reconstruction and found other crusades more attractive: civil service reform, or tariff reform, or defense of the gold standard. In 1872 they repudiated Grant and joined the Liberal Republicans; in subsequent years they considered themselves to be political independents.

This latter group had been an important element in the original Radical coalition. Most of them were respectable, middle-class people in comfortable economic circumstances, well educated and highly articulate, and acutely conscious of their obligation to perform disinterested public service. They had looked upon Senator Charles Sumner of Massachusetts as their political spokesman, and upon Edwin L. Godkin of the New York *Nation* as their editorial spokesman. Like most Radicals they had believed that the Negro was what slavery had made him; give the Negro equal rights and he would be quickly transformed into an industrious and responsible citizen. With the Radical Reconstruction program fairly launched, they had looked forward to swift and dramatic results.

But Reconstruction was not as orderly and the Negro's progress was not nearly as swift and dramatic as these reformers had seemed to expect. The first signs of doubt came soon after the Radicals won control of reconstruction policy, when the *Nation* warned the Negroes that the government had already done all it could for them. They were now, said the *Nation*, "on the dusty and rugged highway of competition"; henceforth "the removal of white prejudice against the Negro depends almost entirely on the Negro himself." By 1870 this bellwether of the reformers viewed with alarm the disorders and irregularities in the states governed by Negroes and carpetbaggers; by 1871 it proclaimed: "The experiment has totally failed. . . . We owe it to human nature to say that worse governments have seldom been seen in a civilized country." And three years later, looking at South Carolina, the *Nation*

pronounced the ultimate epithet: "This is . . . socialism."
Among the former Radicals associated with the *Nation* in
these years of tragic disillusionment were three prewar abolitionists: Edmund Quincy of Massachusetts, James Miller
McKim of Pennsylvania, and the Reverend O. B. Froth-
ingham of New York.

Finally, in 1890, many years after the Reconstruction governments had collapsed, the *Nation*, still accurately reflecting
the state of mind of the disenchanted reformers, made a full
confession of its past errors. "There is," said the *Nation*, "a
rapidly growing sympathy at the North with Southern per-
plexity over the negro problem. . . . Even those who were
not shocked by the carpet-bag experiment . . . are beginning
to 'view with alarm' the political prospect created by the
increase of the negro population, and by the continued inability of southern society to absorb or assimilate them in any
sense, physical, social, or political. . . . The sudden admission
to the suffrage of a million of the recently emancipated slaves
belonging to the least civilized race in the world . . . was a
great leap in the dark, the ultimate consequences of which no
man now living can foresee. No nation has ever done this, or
anything like this for the benefit of aliens of any race or creed.
Who or what is . . . [the Negro] that we should put the
interests of the 55,000,000 whites on this continent in peril for
his sake?" Editor Godkin answered his own question in a
letter to another one-time Radical: "I do not see . . . how the
negro is ever to be worked into a system of government for
which you and I would have much respect."

Actually, neither the obvious shortcomings of Reconstruction nor an objective view of the Negro's progress in the years
after emancipation can wholly explain the disillusionment of
so many former Radicals. Rather, their changed attitude toward the Negro and the hostile historical interpretation of
Reconstruction that won their favor were in part the product
of social trends that severely affected the old American middle

classes with whom most of them were identified. These trends had their origin in the industrial revolution; they were evident in the early nineteenth century but were enormously accelerated after the Civil War. Their institutional symbols were the giant manufacturing and railroad corporations.

In the new age of industrial enterprise there seemed to be no place for the old families with their genteel culture and strong traditions of disinterested public service. On the one hand, they were overshadowed by new and powerful industrial capitalists whose economic strength brought with it vast political influence. Legislative bodies became arenas in which the political vassals of oil, steel, and railroad barons struggled for special favors, while the interests of the public —and the old middle classes liked to think of themselves as *the public*—counted for nothing. On the other hand, they were threatened by the immigrants who came to America to work in the mines and mills and on the railroads—Italians, Slavs, and Jews from Poland and Russia. The immigrants crowded into the tenements of eastern cities, responded to the friendly overtures of urban political bosses, and used their ballots to evict the old middle-class families from power. Here was a threat to the traditional America that these families had loved—and dominated—to that once vigorous American nationality that was Protestant, Anglo-Saxon, and pure. Henry James commented bitterly about the people he met on Boston Common during a stroll one Sunday afternoon: "No sound of English, in a single instance escaped their lips; the greater number spoke a rude form of Italian, the others some outland dialect unknown to me. . . . The types and faces bore them out; the people before me were gross aliens to a man, and they were in serene and triumphant possession."

Soon the new immigrant groups had become the victims of cruel racial stereotypes. Taken collectively it would appear that they were, among other things, innately inferior to the Anglo-Saxons in their intellectual and physical traits, dirty and immoral in their habits, inclined toward criminality, receptive to dangerous political beliefs, and shiftless and irresponsible.

In due time, those who repeated these stereotypes awoke to the realization that what they were saying was not really very original—that, as a matter of fact, these generalizations were *precisely* the ones that southern white men had been making about Negroes for years. And, in their extremity, the old middle classes of the North looked with new understanding upon the problems of the beleaguered white men of the South. Perhaps all along southerners had understood the problem better than they. Here, then, was a crucial part of the intellectual climate in which the Dunning interpretation of Reconstruction was written. It was written at a time when xenophobia had become almost a national disease, when the immigration restriction movement was getting into high gear, when numerous northern cities (among them Philadelphia and Chicago) were seriously considering the establishment of racially segregated schools, and when Negroes and immigrants were being lumped together in the category of unassimilable aliens.

Several other attitudes, prevalent in the late nineteenth century, encouraged an interpretation of Reconstruction that condemned Radical Republicans for meddling in southern race relations. The vogue of social Darwinism discouraged governmental intervention in behalf of Negroes as well as other underprivileged groups; it encouraged the belief that a solution to the race problem could only evolve slowly as the Negroes gradually improved themselves. A rising spirit of nationalism stimulated a desire for sectional reconciliation, and part of the price was a virtual abdication of federal responsibility for the protection of the Negro's civil and political rights. An outburst of imperialism manifested in the Spanish-American War and the annexation of the Hawaiian Islands found one of its principal justifications in the notion that Anglo-Saxons were superior to other peoples, especially when it came to politics. In the words of Senator Albert J. Beveridge of Indiana: "God has not been preparing the English-speaking and Teutonic people for a thousand years for nothing but vain and idle self-admiration. No! He has made us the master organizers of the world to establish system where chaos reigns. . . . He has made us adepts in government that we may administer government among savages and senile peoples." What folly, then, to expect Italians and Slavs to behave like Anglo-Saxons—or to accept the sentimental doctrine that Negroes deserve to be given the same political rights as white men!

Finally, at this critical juncture, sociologists, anthropologists, and psychologists presented what they regarded as convincing evidence of innate racial traits—evidence indicating that Negroes were intellectually inferior to whites and had distinctive emotional characteristics. The social scientists thus supplied the racists of the late nineteenth and early twentieth centuries with something that antebellum proslavery writers had always lacked: a respectable scientific argument. When, in 1916, Madison Grant, an amateur cultural anthropologist, published *The Passing of the Great Race*, his racism was only a mild caricature of a point of view shared by numerous social scientists. Examining the history of the United States, Grant easily detected her tragic blunder:

Race consciousness . . . in the United States, down to and including the Mexican War, seems to have been very strongly developed among native Americans, and it still remains in full vigor today in the South, where the presence of a large negro population forces this question upon the daily attention of the whites. . . . In New England, however . . . there appeared early in the last century a wave of sentimentalism, which at that time took up the cause of the negro, and in so doing apparently destroyed, to a large extent, pride and consciousness of race in the North. The agitation over slavery was inimical to the Nordic race, because it thrust aside all national opposition to the intrusion of hordes of immigrants of inferior racial value, and prevented the fixing of a definite American type. . . . The native American by the middle of the nineteenth century was rapidly becoming a distinct type. . . . The Civil War, however, put a severe, perhaps fatal, check to the development and expansion of this splendid type, by destroying great numbers of the best breeding stock on both sides, and by breaking up the home ties of many more. If the war had not occurred these same men with their descendants would have populated the Western States instead of the racial nondescripts who are now flocking there.

In this social atmosphere, armed with the knowledge of race that the social scientists had given them, historians exposed the folly of Radical Reconstruction. At the turn of the century, James Ford Rhodes, that intimate friend of New England Brahmins, gave his verdict on Negro suffrage—one that the Dunningites would soon develop into the central assumption, the controlling generalization, of the Reconstruction legend. "No large policy in our country," concluded Rhodes, "has ever been so conspicuous a failure as that of forcing universal negro suffrage upon the South. . . . From the Republican policy came no real good to the negroes. Most of them developed no political capacity, and the few who raised themselves above the mass did not reach a high order of intelligence. . . . The negro's political activity is rarely of a nature to identify him with any movement on a high plane. . . . [He] has been politically a failure and he could not have been otherwise."

In the course of time the social scientists drastically revised their notions about race, and in recent years most of them have been striving to destroy the errors in whose creation their predecessors played so crucial a part. As ideas about race have changed, historians have become increasingly critical of the Dunning interpretation of Reconstruction. These changes, together with a great deal of painstaking research, have produced the revisionist writing of the past generation. It is dangerous, of course, for a historian to label himself as a revisionist, for his ultimate and inevitable fate is one day to have his own revisions revised.

But that has never discouraged revisionists, and we may hope that it never will, especially those who have been rewriting the history of the Reconstruction era. One need not be disturbed about the romantic nonsense that still fills the minds of many Americans about their Civil War. This folklore is essentially harmless. But the legend of Reconstruction is another matter. It has had serious consequences, because it has exerted a powerful influence upon the political behavior of many white men, North and South.

PART I

LINCOLN, JOHNSON, AND RECONSTRUCTION

Long before the collapse of the Confederacy, President Lincoln and Congress had staked out independent claims to ultimate responsibility for reconstructing the South. What made this significant was that the President and members of his own party differed as to where political power should reside in the postwar South and how loyal state governments should be re-established. Generations of historians, caught up in the dramatic struggle between the President and Congress, tended to simplify these differences in terms of magnanimity (read Part I: Lincoln, Johnson, and Reconstruction) and vindictiveness (read Part II: The Radical Republicans). The tragedy was said to be that "Reconstruction came in harsh, non-Lincolnian terms, and with it an exploitive era of corruption, scandal, and low-grade politics." The fact remains, however, that the Reconstruction advocated by Lincoln and Johnson envisioned "loyal" state governments with full jurisdiction over local matters, including the right to determine the Negro's place in their society. To argue, as have many historians, that Lincoln and Johnson favored a middle way is to assume that there were *two* extremes and that the governments estab-

[23]

lished under presidential Reconstruction did not constitute one of them.

The ruthless and vindictive character which historians assigned to the Radical Republicans elevated by comparison the statesman-like qualities of Lincoln and Johnson, particularly the "sense of fair dealing" implicit in their conceptions of Reconstruction. More recently, however, historians have placed a much greater emphasis on civil rights as a central issue of Reconstruction. This has prompted them to question the restoration politics of Lincoln and Johnson, to examine more critically the racial attitudes of the Presidents, and to suggest that these may have affected their southern policies.

1

THE FRIEND OF
FREEDOM

Richard N. Current

At the unveiling of the Freedmen's Monument in
memory of Abraham Lincoln, some eleven years
after his assassination, Negro leader Frederick
Douglass observed that the martyred President was
"the man of our redemption" but a white man
nonetheless. Lincoln had been "ready and willing
at any time during the first years of his administration to deny, postpone, and sacrifice the rights
of humanity in the colored people to promote the
welfare of the white people of this country." Approaching Lincoln as "a paradoxical hero," historian
Richard N. Current evaluates the contradictions in
his antislavery career and assesses his reputation
as the "Great Emancipator."

Some of the admirers of Lincoln, viewing the Emancipation
Proclamation as the grand climax of his career, have thought
of him as at heart an abolitionist, one who from early manhood had been awaiting his chance to put an end to slavery.
This notion can be made to seem plausible enough if only a
part of the record is revealed.

There is, for instance, the story of his second flatboat voy-
age down the Mississippi. He was then twenty-two. In New
Orleans (the story goes) he with his companions attended a
slave auction at which a "vigorous and comely" mulatto girl

was being offered for sale. She was treated like a mare, the prospective bidders inspecting her up and down, pinching and feeling, and then watching while she was made to trot back and forth. To Lincoln the spectacle was so shameful it aroused in him at once an "unconquerable hate" toward the whole institution of slavery. "If I ever get a chance to hit that thing," he swore as he walked away, "I'll hit it hard."

Lincoln perhaps took a stand for freedom as a member of the Illinois Legislature in 1837, when resolutions were introduced in response to the mob murder of Elijah Lovejoy, the antislavery newspaperman of Alton. These resolutions, instead of denouncing lynch law, condemned abolitionist societies and upheld slavery within the southern states as "sacred" by virtue of the federal Constitution. Lincoln refused to vote for the resolutions. Not only that. Together with a fellow member he drew up a protest against them, declaring that slavery was "founded on both injustice and bad policy."

Interesting also are his reflections on his experience of 1841, when with his friend Joshua Speed he was returning from a Kentucky visit. He made part of the trip by steamboat down the Ohio. "You may remember, as I well do," he wrote to Speed fourteen years later, in 1855, "that from Louisville to the mouth of the Ohio there were, on board, ten or a dozen slaves, shackled together with irons. That sight was a continual torment to me; and I see something like it every time I touch the Ohio, or any other slave-border." Speed, having resettled in Kentucky, had come to differ with Lincoln on the slavery question, and Lincoln now was defending his own point of view. "It is hardly fair for you to assume," he wrote, "that I have no interest in a thing which has, and continually exercises, the power of making me miserable."

As a member of Congress, in 1850, Lincon drafted and introduced a bill for the abolition of slavery in the District of Columbia.

During the 1850's, in his arguments with Stephen A. Douglas, Lincoln spoke often and with eloquence against slavery. On one occasion, in 1854, he said he hated Douglas' attitude of indifference toward the spread of slavery to new areas. "I hate it because of the monstrous injustice of slavery itself," he declared. "I hate it because it deprives our republican example of its just influence in the world—enables the enemies of free institutions, with plausibility, to taunt us as hypocrites . . . ." On another occasion Lincoln made his oft-quoted remark that the nation could not long endure half slave and half free. No wonder many southerners considered him "all broke out" with abolitionism at the time he was elected President.

After he was in the White House, Lincoln continued to express himself eloquently for freedom. In a published reply to Horace Greeley, who was demanding action against slavery, he said (1862) it was his "oft-expressed *personal* wish that all men every where could be free." He confided in a private letter (1864): "I am naturally anti-slavery. If slavery is not wrong, nothing is wrong. I can not remember when I did not so think, and feel." And in a talk to Indiana soldiers (1865) he remarked: "Whenever I hear anyone arguing for slavery I feel a strong impulse to see it tried on him personally."

On the basis of these and other items from the record, Lincoln appears to have been a long-confirmed advocate of freedom, if not an outright abolitionist. But when the whole of the evidence is considered, the conclusion to be drawn is not so clear.

It is not even clear whether in fact Lincoln ever underwent the New Orleans experience which was supposed to have made him an eternal foe of slavery. John Hanks told the anecdote to Herndon in 1865. Hanks had been one of Lincoln's fellow voyagers on the flatboat, but did not go all the way with the others to New Orleans. So he could not have seen with his own eyes what happened at the slave auction he later described. Herndon said he also heard the story from

Lincoln himself. In the account of the journey he gave in his autobiography of 1860, however, Lincoln made no mention of slaves or the slave trade (though of course he intended the autobiography for campaign purposes and could not have been so indiscreet as to emphasize any abolitionist convictions). In the autobiography he also spoke of a previous trip to New Orleans. With regard to this trip, he said nothing about slaves but did refer to Negroes, recalling that he and his one companion "were attacked by seven Negroes with intent to kill and rob them" and were "hurt some in the melee, but succeeded in driving the Negroes from the boat."

As for his stand against the 1837 resolutions of the Illinois Legislature, it is enough to point out that he actually took a position against *both sides* of the controversy. Slavery was bad, he held, but he also contended that "the promulgation of abolition doctrines tends rather to increase than to abate its evils."

Regarding the shackled slaves on the Ohio river boat, he gave at the time, in 1841, an account very different from the one he gave fourteen years afterward to Joshua Speed. Writing to Speed's sister Mary (September 27, 1841) he described the scene on board the boat quite philosophically as exemplifying "the effect of *condition* upon human happiness." Here were a dozen slaves, "strung together like so many fish upon a trotline," who were being taken from their old Kentucky homes to be sold down the river, who were being separated from families and friends and carried off where slavery was reputed to be at its harshest. Yet, as Lincoln saw them, "they were the most cheerful and apparently happy creatures on board." He concluded that God "renders the worst of human conditions tolerable, while He permits the best, to be nothing better than tolerable."

The point is not that Lincoln was falsifying his emotions when, in the much later account to Speed, he wrote of the sight of those slaves in chains as having been a "continual torment" to him. Certainly he had not forgotten the scene, and very likely he had come to view it in retrospect with heightened feeling. His attitude toward slaves and slavery might well have changed with the passing years—especially the years after 1850, when the issue of slavery extension engrossed national politics.

As late as 1847 his torment apparently was not troublesome enough to deter him from accepting a slaveholder as a law client and arguing against a slave's claim to freedom. Though Illinois presumably was a free state, its laws still provided for Negro servitude of a sort. Under the laws slave labor could be used, provided the slaves were not kept permanently in the state. Slaves worked the Coles County farm of Robert Matson, who brought his blacks from Kentucky every spring and took them back to Kentucky every fall. One of them, Jane Bryant, aroused the ire of Matson's housekeeper and mistress, who demanded that she be sold and sent to the Deep South. Jane fled, enlisted the aid of antislavery people, was taken from them, and, lacking the required certificate of freedom, was held in accordance with the Illinois laws. Matson, claiming her as his property, appealed to Lincoln for legal aid. Lincoln took the case and lost.

In Congress, despite his bill for abolition in the District of Columbia, he took a yes-and-no attitude toward slavery. His bill was carefully hedged about, so as to offend no slaveholder. It provided for gradual emancipation, with payment to owners, and it was not to go into effect unless approved by the "free white citizens" of the District, in a referendum. The bill did not please abolitionists. One of them, Wendell Phillips, called Lincoln "the slave hound of Illinois."

As for his remarks on slavery during the 1850's, it should be borne in mind that Lincoln always was opposing the spread of the institution into the territories. He was not advocating its destruction in the southern states. When he said the nation could not long remain half slave and half free, but must eventually become all one or the other, he doubtless was thinking of the real danger that the country might become *all slave*—if slavery were allowed to spread. He resisted the aggressive proslavery forces not only because of his concern for the sufferings of the black man, but also because of his concern for the welfare of the white man. Again and again he indicated that the civil liberties of every American, white as well as black, were at stake. He insisted upon "keeping the territories free for the settlement of free laborers." He was a free-soil man.

"You enquire where I now stand," he wrote in his letter of 1855 to Joshua Speed. "That is a disputed point. I think I am a Whig; but others say there are no Whigs, and that I am an abolitionist." And then he stated the limits of his antislavery zeal as precisely as he could: "I now do no more than oppose the *extension* of slavery." That was where he stood in 1854, and there is no convincing evidence that he had moved beyond that position by 1860 or 1861.

In fact, in the most widely read of his pre-nomination speeches, the one at Cooper Union in New York on February 27, 1860, Lincoln said he agreed with Thomas Jefferson and other founding fathers that slavery should be merely contained, not directly attacked. *"This is all Republicans ask—all Republicans desire—in relation to slavery,"* he emphasized, underlining the words. *"As those fathers marked it, so let it be again marked, as an evil not to be extended, but to be tolerated and protected only because of and so far as its actual presence among us makes that toleration and protection a necessity."* Lincoln further said that emancipation should be most gradual and should be accompanied by deportation of the freed slaves. "In the language of Mr. Jefferson, uttered many years ago, 'It is still in our power to direct the process of emancipation, and deportation, peaceably, and in such slow degrees, as that the evil will wear off insensibly; and their places be, *pari passu*, filled up by free white laborers. If, on the contrary, it is left to force itself on, human nature must shudder at the prospect held up.' "

As President, even if he personally had desired immediate emancipation, Lincoln had reasons of policy for going slow with regard to slavery. At the outset of the war the border slave states—Maryland, Delaware, Missouri, and above all Kentucky—hung in the balance. It seemed to Lincoln essential that these states be kept loyal to the Union, and it also seemed to him that a forthright antislavery program might incline them toward the Confederacy.

Whatever the reasons, Lincoln in the beginning was most reluctant to use his presidential powers against slavery. During his first year and more in office he lagged well behind the majority of his party in the cause of freedom. If, as he said, General McClellan had "the slows" when it came to advancing against the Confederate army, he himself had the same affliction when it was a matter of attacking the institution which Alexander H. Stephens called the cornerstone of the Confederacy.

Lincoln held back while Congress and some of his generals went ahead. General John C. Frémont proclaimed freedom for the slaves of disloyal masters in Missouri, and General David Hunter did the same for those in Georgia, South Carolina, and Florida. Lincoln revoked the proclamations of Frémont and Hunter, much to the disgust of all antislavery people, who were growing fast in numbers and in earnestness throughout the North. In the summer of 1861 Congress passed a confiscation act which freed such slaves as the foe put to military use. The next summer Congress passed a second confiscation act, which declared "forever free" all slaves whose owners were in rebellion, whether or not the slaves were being used for military purposes. Lincoln did not veto these laws, but neither did he see that they faithfully were carried out. He considered vetoing the second one, because in his judgment it amounted to an unconstitutional bill of attainder. He did not sign it until it had been amended, and even then he expressed to Congress his dissatisfaction with it.

While hesitating to enforce these laws, Lincoln responded in his own way to the rising sentiment in favor of emancipation. He came forth with a characteristically Lincolnian solution to the slavery problem. His plan contained five elements. First, the states themselves must emancipate the slaves, for in his opinion slavery was a "domestic" institution, the concern of the states alone. Second, slaveowners must be paid for the chattels of which they were to be deprived. Third, the federal government must share the financial burden by providing federal bonds as grants-in-aid to the states. Fourth, the actual freeing of the slaves must not be hurried; the states must be given plenty of time, delaying final freedom until as late as 1900 if they wished. Fifth, the freed Negroes must be shipped out of the country and colonized abroad, but they must be persuaded to go willingly. State action, compensation, federal aid, gradual emancipation, and voluntary colonization—these were the indispensable features of the Lincoln plan.

To carry out this plan he had to gain the approval of Congress, the border slave states, and the leaders of the Negro race. Congress responded affirmatively but without enthusiasm, indicating its willingness to vote the necessary funds. None of the border politicians were won over to the scheme, however, and very few Negroes could be persuaded to leave their native land, the United States.

Three times in the spring of 1862 Lincoln appealed to the border state congressmen. He told them that, if their states would only act, the war soon would be over, for the Confederacy lived upon the hope of winning the border states, and, once these had declared for freedom, that hope would be gone. He warned the congressmen that, if their states refused to act, slavery in time would disappear anyhow. It would be destroyed "by mere friction and abrasion—by the mere incidents of war." The border states, he eloquently said, had before them the grand opportunity of saving the Union. But he made no headway whatsoever; again and again they turned the opportunity down.

Meanwhile he did not let up in his efforts to talk the free Negroes into leaving the country. Some of their own leaders advocated starting life anew in the Negro republic of Liberia or Haiti. Lincoln preferred Central America as their new home. In his eagerness he was taken in by a group of land speculators who offered to sell the Chiriqui territory on the Isthmus of Panama. They pictured Chiriqui as a land rich in coal, among other things, but eventually became so effusive in their praises of this tropical paradise it became clear that their title was dubious and the resources nonexistent.

He was nevertheless loath to give up the colonization idea itself. He invited to the White House a group of five prominent Negroes—the first of their race a President ever so honored—and he honored them further by saying frankly that there was no place for them and their people in the United States. Though they might be treated better in the North than in the South, they would suffer discrimination everywhere so long as they remained in this country. "The ban," he said, "is still upon you." From Negroes who heard of this interview, the response was most unfavorable. One wrote to Lincoln: "Pray tell us is our right to a home in this country less than your own?"

If, in the summer of 1862, Lincoln had had his way, the later history of this country would have been radically changed. For instance, if the states had adopted his plan, there would probably be few Negroes left in the country, North or South. By 1900 the slaves of the border states would have been set free and sent abroad. The slaves of the Confederate states, if these states too had chosen to adopt the Lincoln plan, would have enjoyed the same fortune or suffered the same fate.

[33]

If, on the other hand, the war had come to an early end, as Lincoln hoped, the slaves of the Confederate states could have been left in bondage indefinitely, or at least until they were freed by some hand other than his. Even in the border states, after emancipation, slavery might have been re-established by action of the states. What these states had done, they could undo, according to Lincoln's conception of states' rights. Indeed, in order to discourage this contingency, he drafted an emancipation bill containing the proviso that, if any state should abolish and then reintroduce the institution, it would have to return to the federal government the federal funds it had received as a grant-in-aid!

President Lincoln did not behave like a great emancipator during the first year and a half of his term of office. The question is, did he change his mind and his policy after that? More particularly, did he intend—with the preliminary proclamation of September 21, 1862, and the final one of January 1, 1863—to free the slaves?

According to most accounts, he did. Despite his campaign pledges and the constraints of the Constitution, argue supporters of this position, he decided that he must strike at slavery for reasons of military necessity. He came to this conclusion, and drafted a fitting proclamation, in July of 1862. When he read this draft to his Cabinet, Seward advised him to withhold the announcement till the Union armies had won a victory on the battlefield. Otherwise, Seward cautioned, the proclamation might sound like a confession of military failure, like "the last *shriek* on our retreat." So Lincoln stalled, awaiting the hoped-for victory. When a delegation of Chicago churchmen appealed to him, he asked them whether a proclamation would do any good, whether it would not be as futile as the Pope's legendary bull against the comet. Before they left, he assured them that he had not decided against a proclamation, but held the matter under advisement. When Horace Greeley in the

New York *Tribune* called upon him to make freedom a reality, he patiently replied (August 22, 1862): "My paramount object in this struggle *is* to save the Union, and is *not* either to save or to destroy slavery. If I could save the Union without freeing *any* slave I would do it, and if I could save it by freeing *all* the slaves I would do it; and if I could do it by freeing some and leaving others alone I would also do that." At last McClellan's checking of Lee at Antietam gave Lincoln at least a substitute for victory, and a few days later he accordingly issued the document he long since had decided upon.

This is a familiar story, and there is a certain amount of evidence to give it historical substance. There is, for example, the record Welles made of a conversation Lincoln had with him and Seward on Sunday, July 13, while on a carriage ride to a funeral. "It was on this occasion and on this ride that he first mentioned to Mr. Seward and myself the subject of emancipating the slaves by proclamation in case the Rebels did not cease to persist in their war on the Government and the Union, of which he saw no evidence," Welles wrote afterward. "He dwelt earnestly on the gravity, importance, and delicacy of the movement, said he had given it much thought and had about come to the conclusion that it was a military necessity absolutely essential for the salvation of the Union, that we must free the slaves or be ourselves subdued, etc., etc." Welles added this comment: "It was a new departure for the President, for until this time, in all our previous interviews, whenever the question of emancipation or the mitigation of slavery had been in any way alluded to, he had been prompt and emphatic in denouncing any interference by the General Government with the subject."

Welles may have remembered accurately what the President said on that Sunday, though the record of the conversation is not a regular diary entry but a reminiscence that the diarist put down after the lapse of considerable time. And

Lincoln, if Welles summarized his sentiments accurately, may have meant what he said. Yet in the ensuing weeks others who saw Lincoln reported him as saying things that seemed to belie his determination to proclaim freedom for the slaves. When Greeley visited the White House to repeat the plea of his *Tribune* editorial, Lincoln protested that he dared not antagonize Kentuckians and impel them to desert to the rebel side. He expressed this same concern to others, including the Chicago religious group. If he really had made his decision and only was waiting for the auspicious moment to proclaim it, he might have put off his tormenters by frankly telling them so. As it was, he left even some of his official advisers to wonder whether he ever would issue the proclamation he had read to the cabinet.

These inconsistencies of his have led to the suspicion that, till after the battle of Antietam, he made no irrevocable commitment, even to himself. Here and there he dropped hints that he might issue the proclamation—and then again might not. Apparently his purpose was to prepare his hearers for the possibility that he might call the whole thing off. He was waiting for a decisive victory, but if that kind of victory had come, he might have forgotten about the proclamation. Some historians claim that he dusted it off and gave it to the world only when he learned the true proportions of Antietam. McClellan, though he turned Lee back, had let him get away. If McClellan had administered a crushing defeat, the proclamation might have stayed in its pigeonhole.

This theory depends on the supposition that Lincoln at the time was not so much concerned about military necessity as about political necessity. He had to contend with a strong bloc of Republicans in Congress, headed by Thaddeus Stevens in the House and Charles Sumner and Henry Wilson in the Senate, backed by a majority of the party, who had become Radicals on the slave question. They were demanding that the President carry out the laws, the confiscation acts, the act for

the enrollment of Negro troops. They held the firm conviction that, to win the war, the government must free the slaves
and use them against their former masters. As their strongest
argument, the Radicals cited the succession of Union defeats
on the Virginia front. The way the war was being fought, it
was not being won, and it therefore must be fought another
way. There was even the possibility that they might try to
stop the flow of money and supplies if Lincoln did not give
in. Only a conclusive victory, only a dramatic refutation of
the Radical argument, would restore his freedom of action.
He prayed for such a victory, and then came the disappointing news of Antietam.

To pursue this argument to its logical conclusion, Lincoln
then pulled out the proclamation as his trump. In issuing it he
did not really yield to the Radicals. Rather, he outfoxed them.
At first they hailed the document as a triumph for them and
their cause, but soon they were disillusioned, since the proclamation had as its purpose and effect the checking of the
Radical program. Having announced in September that he
would make a final proclamation the first of the following
year, Lincoln had an excuse for disregarding the laws about
confiscation and Negro troops throughout the intervening
months. He also had a policy with which to frustrate Stevens'
drive for legislation to make soldiers and freemen out of slaves
from the border states. During the months of delay he hoped
at last to gain approval for his own plan, the familiar plan of
gradual emancipation by the states themselves, with federal
funds to pay to slaveowners and to rid the country of the
freed slaves.

There is testimony, from some of the men who knew Lincoln, to give credence to this view. There is, for instance, the
testimony of Edward Stanly, a proslavery, states' rights, Unionist North Carolinian whom Lincoln had appointed as military governor of the occupied North Carolina coast. Stanly
had taken the job with the understanding that Lincoln would

not interfere with slavery in the states. Once the proclamation had been issued, Stanly went to Washington intending to resign. After several talks with Lincoln, however, Stanly was satisfied. He returned to his job, but first he called at the office of James C. Welling, editor of the *National Intelligencer*. Welling wrote in his diary: "Mr. Stanly said that the President had stated to him that the proclamation had become a civil necessity to prevent the Radicals from openly embarrassing the government in the conduct of the war."

Quite apart from testimony such as this, a fairly strong inference of Lincoln's delaying tactics can be drawn from the text of the proclamation. The preliminary announcement said that after January 1, 1863, the slaves in states then still in rebellion would be considered free. The final proclamation excluded from the area of freedom not only the loyal border states but all the Confederate states and parts of states that the Union forces had occupied. As cynics pointed out at the time, Lincoln was leaving the slaves untouched in places where he had the ability to free them, and he was offering liberty only to those he had no power to reach. Congress already had enabled him to do more than this. The second confiscation act provided for the liberation of all slaves belonging to disloyal masters, regardless of the masters' residence. Instead of issuing the kind of proclamation that he did, Lincoln needed only to proclaim that he was enforcing the second confiscation act, and then he could have proceeded to order the seizure of enemy-owned slaves in every place where the Union armies got control—if his object truly had been to weaken the enemy by making inroads into his Negro manpower.

Lincoln himself gave indisputable proof that, after the preliminary proclamation, he remained as passionately devoted as ever to his own gradual-emancipation scheme. In his message to Congress of December 1, 1862, just one month before the final proclamation, he had little to say about that forthcoming pronouncement and much to say about his favored plan. He proposed a constitutional amendment to put the plan into effect. On this subject he reached one of the peaks of his eloquence. "Fellow-citizens, *we* cannot escape history," he said. "We of this Congress and this administration, will be remembered in spite of ourselves. The fiery trial through which we pass, will light us down, in honor or dishonor, to the latest generation." These words are justly famous. What is often forgotten is the fact that they were conceived as part of a plea for deporting American-born Negroes from America. Lincoln in this message actually used the word *deportation*, as if he had in the back of his mind the thought of resorting, if necessary, to the compulsion which that word implies.

No inspired phrases were to be found in the paper that Lincoln signed with the gold pen, in the quavering hand, on January 1, 1863. In itself this proclamation was a dull and prosaic document—no ringing call to freedom. The proclamation had some effect in attracting slaves out of rebeldom and into the Union lines, where they were set free, but the existing laws of Congress provided for that much and more. After two years, when the war was ending, Lincoln estimated that some 200,000 slaves had gained their liberty under his edict. That was only about one in twenty of the total number of slaves, which amounted to nearly four million. And even that minority had no sure hold on freedom. Lincoln himself doubted the constitutionality of his step, except as a temporary war measure. After the war the freedmen would have risked re-enslavement, had nothing else been done to confirm their liberty.

All this does not necessarily disprove the commonly accepted story of what Lincoln did or tried to do in signing his famous proclamation. Maybe he meant to hasten freedom, maybe to delay it. Nobody knows.

Actual freedom for the Negroes—or at least the end of chattel slavery—came in consequence of the Thirteenth Amendment. President Lincoln played a part in bringing about this constitutional change, yet he was slow to take an out-and-out antislavery stand, and indeed he gave some indications that his conversion never was complete.

He did not claim to have originated the idea of such an amendment, though the abolitionists did. At Cleveland in May, 1864, a group of these extreme Republicans nominated John C. Frémont for the Presidency and adopted a platform with a Thirteenth Amendment as the key plank.

When the regular Republicans met in convention the following month, Lincoln was aware of the need for winning the dissidents back to the party fold. He called to the White House the chairman of the Republican National Committee, Senator E. D. Morgan, and gave him instructions for his speech opening the convention. "Senator Morgan," he is reported to have said, "I want you to mention in your speech when you call the convention to order, as its keynote, and to put into the platform as the keystone, the amendment of the Constitution abolishing and prohibiting slavery forever." Senator Morgan did as the President wished. That platform included a plank stating that slavery was the cause of the rebellion, that the President's proclamations had aimed "a death blow at this gigantic evil," and that a constitutional amendment was necessary to "terminate and forever prohibit" it. Undoubtedly the delegates would have adopted such a plank whether or not Lincoln, through Senator Morgan, had urged it.

When Lincoln was reelected on this platform, and the Republican majority in Congress was increased, he was justified in feeling, as he apparently did, that he had a mandate from the people for the Thirteenth Amendment. The newly chosen Congress, with its overwhelming Republican majority, would not meet until after the Lame Duck Session of the old Congress during the winter of 1864–65. But Lincoln did not wait. Using all his resources of patronage and persuasion on certain of the Democrats, he managed to get the necessary two-thirds vote before the session's end. He rejoiced as the amendment went out to the states for ratification, and he rejoiced again and again as his own Illinois led off and other states followed one by one in acting favorably upon it. He did not live to rejoice in its ultimate adoption.

Yet, for all he did to see that freedom finally was written into the fundamental law, Lincoln to the last seemed to have a lingering preference for another kind of plan. He still clung to his old ideas of postponing final emancipation, compensating slaveholders, and colonizing freedmen. Or so it would appear. As late as March of 1865, if the somewhat dubious Ben Butler is to be believed, Lincoln summoned him to the White House to discuss with him the feasibility of removing the colored population of the United States.

Lincoln is a paradoxical hero. His name has been lighted down from generation to generation as a synonym for liberty and equality. His name also has been made to symbolize the opposite doctrine of white supremacy and black oppression.

Lincoln the friend of freedom is well and widely known. For most liberals, he occupies a place beside that of Thomas Jefferson. For many Negroes, he long has held a lone position as a kind of folk god.

His exaltation dates back to January 1, 1863, when throughout the North and the conquered areas of the South the colored people held proclamation meetings to celebrate his deed in their behalf. At a Washington meeting, which began on New Year's Eve, a pastor told each member of his flock to "get down on *both knees* to thank Almighty God for his freedom and President Lincoln too." To people such as these, the proclamation, whatever its inward meaning, was the outward sign of an answer to their prayers.

Most of the abolitionists joined in honoring Lincoln at the time of his emancipation edict, but some of them qualified their praise, still doubting his sincerity. At last, when he had won congressional approval for the Thirteenth Amendment, almost all the lingering doubts were dispelled and almost all the doubters satisfied. Even William Lloyd Garrison no longer could contain himself. To a Boston meeting of celebrators Garrison said: "And to whom is the country more immediately indebted for this vital and saving amendment of the Constitution than perhaps, to any other man? I believe I may confidently answer—to the humble rail splitter of Illinois—to the Presidential chainbreaker for millions of the oppressed—to Abraham Lincoln!"

Less well known than Lincoln the slaves' chainbreaker is Lincoln the hero of Negro-baiters and white supremacists. Yet he has had that kind of image also. Few Negroes or friends of the Negro ever admired him more or praised him oftener than did a certain Mississippi advocate of white supremacy, James K. Vardaman.

In the early 1900's this long-haired, dramatic Great White Chief of Mississippi stood out as the most rabid racialist in the most racist-dominated southern state. When Theodore Roosevelt dined with Negro educator Booker T. Washington in the White House, Vardaman sneered at the President as a "wild broncho buster and coon-flavored miscegenationist." In his campaign for the governorship Vardaman said that if he were in office, he would do what he could to protect a captured Negro "fiend" from a lynching mob. "But if I were a private citizen I would head the mob to string the brute up, and I haven't much respect for a white man who wouldn't." As governor, he opposed what he called "this policy of spoiling young Negroes by educating them." In the United States Senate during the first World War, he took every opportunity to expound his belief in a white man's country. Do not draft Negroes into the Army, he advised his fellow senators, for it is dangerous to give them a sense of citizenship and a training in the use of guns. Repeal the Fifteenth Amendment so that Negroes cannot even pretend to have the right to vote.

Enforce segregation and do not let the races mix, for the Negro is by nature morally inferior and must never be allowed to corrupt the pure blood of the heaven-favored white. Such were the aims and the convictions to which Vardaman devoted his real eloquence.

This Mississippian once made a pilgrimage to his hero's home town, to Springfield, Illinois. The year was 1909, the centennial of Lincoln's birth. The previous year had been a disgraceful one for Springfield. Municipal leaders were looking ahead to anniversary celebrations when, on a summer night, thousands of the townspeople suddenly went wild with hate. They set out to lynch a Negro who (though innocent) was being held on the charge of raping a white woman, and when the sheriff frustrated them by spiriting the man away, they turned their vengeance upon the whole colored community. It took four thousand state troopers all of a week to quiet the city and end the so-called "race riot." (This incident, by the way, and not some crisis in the South, gave rise to the National Association for the Advancement of Colored People.) When Vardaman visited Springfield the feeling among local Negrophobes still ran high, and a huge crowd came out to applaud his lecture on the inherent virtue of the white race.

Vardaman never tired of praising "the immortal Lincoln," never tired of quoting "the wise words of this wondrous man." He insisted that he and Lincoln saw eye to eye. "I have made a very careful study of Mr. Lincoln's ideas on this question," he declared in a Senate speech, "and I have said often, and I repeat here, that my views and his on the race question are substantially identical." Next to Thomas Jefferson, he thought, Lincoln understood the Negro problem better than anyone else of former days. To prove his point, Vardaman cited Lincoln's advocacy of Negro colonization. He explained the Lincoln policy thus:

"Up to the very time of Mr. Lincoln's death he told the Negroes who came to see him here in Washington, 'You will not be permitted to share in the government of this country, and I am not prepared to say that you ought to be, if I had the power to give you that right.' He said further: 'The shackles of slavery will be stricken from your arms. You, the educated and more fortunate members of your race, take the others and go to some country'—his idea was the same that Jefferson's was—'and there work out your own salvation.' I do not pretend to quote Mr. Lincoln literally. The great desire of his patriotic heart was that the friction might be avoided by deportation."

The words of Lincoln that Vardaman repeated oftenest, the words he knew almost by heart, came from the debate with Douglas at Charleston, Illinois, on September 18, 1858. These words formed for Vardaman a sort of golden text. Here they are, exactly as Lincoln uttered them:

> I will say then that I am not, nor ever have been in favor of bringing about in any way the social and political equality of the white and black races, [applause]—that I am not nor ever have been in favor of making voters or jurors of Negroes, nor of qualifying them to hold office, nor to intermarry with white people; and I will say in addition to this that there is a physical difference between the white and black races which I believe will forever forbid the two races living together on terms of social and political equality. And inasmuch as they cannot so live, while they do remain together there must be the position of superior and inferior, and I as much as any other man am in favor of having the superior position assigned to the white race.

Yet, despite these contradictions, Lincoln does deserve his reputation as emancipator. True, his claim to the honor is supported very uncertainly, if at all, by the proclamation itself. The honor has a better basis in the support he gave to the Thirteenth Amendment. It is well founded also in his greatness as the war leader, who carried the nation safely through the four-year struggle that brought freedom in its train. But the best reason for his reputation is, perhaps, to be discovered in something else. Consider the example he set his fellow Americans by treating all men as human beings, regardless of the pigment of their skin.

The real and final emancipation of the Negro may depend more upon attitudes than upon laws. The laws, the constitutional amendments, are important, even indispensable. But, as the abolitionist Henry Wilson observed, many of those who voted for the Thirteenth Amendment and other antislavery measures did so without conversion or conviction. Many acted from a desire to hurt the slaveholder rather than to help the slave. Within their hearts still lurked the "foul spirit of caste," the spirit of race prejudice. Until this prejudice was overcome, the Negroes, though no longer the slaves of individual masters, would continue to be in a sense the slaves of the community as a whole.

Now, Lincoln himself was one of those who veered to an actively antislavery line for reasons of wartime expediency. He did not pretend to do otherwise. And he was well aware of race prejudice as an existing fact in the United States. Hence his pathetic eagerness to find new homes for freedmen in foreign lands. Yet he had the capacity to rise above prejudice, and he grandly rose above it. Again and again, during the last two years of his life, he made the White House a scene of practical demonstrations of respect for human worth and dignity. He proved that whites and Negroes, without the master-servant tie, could get along together happily in his own official home, no matter what the antagonisms that might trouble the nation at large. A kindly, unself-conscious host, he greeted Negro visitors as no President had done before.

The distinguished former slave Frederick Douglass called upon Lincoln several times at his summer cottage at the Soldiers' Home. Douglass made at least three visits to the White House. On the final occasion, when he tried to enter as an invited guest at the inaugural reception in 1865, policemen manhandled him and forced him out. Making his way in again, he managed to catch Lincoln's eye. "Here comes my friend Douglass," the President exclaimed, and, leaving the circle of guests he had been conversing with, he took Douglass by the hand and began to chat with him. Years later Douglass wrote: "In all my interviews with Mr. Lincoln I was impressed with his entire freedom from popular prejudice against the colored race. He was the first great man that I talked with in the United States freely, who in no single instance reminded me of the difference between himself and myself, of the difference of color, and I thought that all the more remarkable because he came from a state where there were black laws."

There were black laws in Illinois indeed—laws that denied the Negro the vote and deprived him of other rights. Illinois in those days was a Jim Crow state. That was where Lincoln had spent most of the years of his manhood, among people who had migrated from slave country farther south, as he himself had done. Naturally he had shared some of the Negrophobic feeling of his neighbors in Kentucky, in southern Indiana, in central Illinois. That was where, in geography and in sentiment, he came from.

But he did not stay there. The most remarkable thing about him was his tremendous power of growth. He grew in sympathy, in the breadth of his humaneness, as he grew in other aspects of the mind and spirit. In more ways than one he succeeded in breaking through the narrow bounds of his early environment.

This helps to explain and to reconcile those conflicting images of Lincoln—on the one hand, the racist; on the other, the champion of the common man, black as well as white. The one view reflects the position he started from, the other the position he was moving toward. There is confusion regarding particular phases of his presidential career because nobody knows for sure just what point he had reached at any given moment. But there should be little question as to which way he was going.

To see Lincoln in this light is to make him more than ever relevant, more than ever inspiring, for us in the stormy present, in the fiery trial through which we too must pass. Lincoln, as a symbol of man's ability to outgrow his prejudices, still serves the cause of human freedom. He will go on serving so long as boundaries of color hem in and hinder any man, any woman, any child.

2

ANDREW JOHNSON, OUTSIDER

Eric L. McKitrick

In the 1920's historians rehabilitated Andrew Johnson and portrayed him as a courageous President
who had stood for sectional reconciliation, constitutional rights, and popular democracy against
vindictive Radical Republicans and predatory
northern business interests bent on consolidating
their power and wartime gains. In 1960 Eric L.
McKitrick gave this view of Johnson its most serious challenge. McKitrick's new portrait of Johnson
is that of an obstinate, narrow-minded, politically
inept President who foolishly lost his bargaining
power with Congress, misread northern public
sentiment, drove the moderates into the opposition,
and misled the South as to northern expectations.
Much of the President's difficulty, McKitrick
argues, was that, unlike his predecessor, he operated
primarily as an "outsider."

The man who succeeded Lincoln, who thought of himself as
following in Lincoln's footsteps and carrying out Lincoln's
designs, was a lone wolf in almost every sense of the word. He
was a man of undoubted ability. Indeed, the order which he
brought to the administration of the Executive Office was in
sharp relief to the clutter of Lincoln's time. But the only
setting in which Andrew Johnson's powers could become
fully engaged was one in which the man would be battling
against great odds. The only role whose attributes he fully

understood was that of the maverick, operating out on the fringe of things. For the full nourishment and maximum functioning of his mind, matters had to be so arranged that all the organized forces of society could in some sense, real or symbolic, be leagued against him. In such array they could be overborne by the *un*organized forces of whom he always imagined himself the instrument—an assault whose only rhythm was measured out, as it were, by the great heartbeat of the people. These were the terms in which the battle of life had its fullest meaning for Andrew Johnson.

It is often said of Johnson, with much truth, that his plebeian origins bred in him a fierce and independent spirit. One does not, however, think of Lincoln in any such way. One does not say that *his* plebeian origins bred in him "a fierce and independent spirit." Why is this? Had Johnson come of poorer "poor white" stock than Lincoln—had his struggle been a harder one? It would certainly seem so; and yet these things are relative and not easy to measure. We know that Johnson eventually became a man of means and a slaveowner; it does not generally occur to us, on the other hand, to describe the Lincolns' circumstances as more than comfortable. We also know that for nearly thirty years prior to the Presidency, Johnson had enjoyed, to all intents and purposes, the highest honors in the public gift—legislator, governor, representative, and senator, whereas Lincoln had only served in the Illinois legislature and gone to Congress for a single term. The key to the contrast between the two men does not seem to be "success" in any objective measure; it lies rather in the way success was conceived. For Johnson, personal fulfillment had long since come to be defined as the fruit of struggle—real, full-bodied, and terrible—against forces specifically organized for thwarting him. Not so for Lincoln. Johnson, all his life, had operated as an outsider; Lincoln, in most of his worldly dealings, and temperamentally as well, was an insider.

The early life of Andrew Johnson was an incredible strug-

gle against grinding destitution that reads reads like a chapter
first of Dickens and then of Horatio Alger, with perhaps a
dash of Al Capp. His father, a good-natured porter at Casso's
tavern in Raleigh, North Carolina, had lost his life rescuing
two drunken gentlemen from an icy stream when Andrew
was only three. Andrew's mother, an amiable but rather inef-
fectual woman known as "Polly the Weaver," apprenticed
him to a tailor at fourteen when she could no longer support
him. He had no formal education. After a time the young man
ran away and hid out while his furious master advertised a
reward for his capture. Eventually Andrew, his mother, his
ne'er-do-well brother Bill (of "black hair, eyes, and habits"),
and his sometime-acquired impecunious stepfather, all headed
west over the mountains with their cart. They landed at
Greeneville, Tennessee. There Andrew set up a tailor shop,
practiced the rudiments of reading, and at nineteen married a
wife who taught him to write. Eliza McCardle had a little
education but no family connections whatever, being the or-
phaned daughter of a shoemaker. (Here one thinks, in contrast, of Lincoln's marriage to Mary Todd, the daughter of an
aristocratic family with excellent connections.) Through
scrimping and hard toil, Johnson bit by bit acquired a home, a
new tailor shop, a brick store in Greeneville, and a comfortable farm. He practiced debating with the young men of the
town, and in time held several local offices.

In spite of numerous signs that he was really getting on
quite decently in the world, the matter of class and social
acceptance churned sourly in Andrew Johnson's vitals. His
father, the happy menial, had never questioned his meager lot
in life; that poor soul had gone to his reward without ever
having thought much about the mysteries of "class" at all.
Andrew thought of nothing else; his own struggle to rise
consumed and obsessed him. Grimly ambitious, he brooded
over the wrongs, real and imaginary, which were thought-
lessly foisted upon him by his social betters, and out of his

inner world of suspicious fantasy he evolved an extravagant credo of plebeian democracy and honest toil. Once, after a snub from one of the Greeneville gentry, he raged: "Some day I will show the stuck-up aristocrats who is running the country. A cheap purse-proud set they are, not half as good as the man who earns his bread by the sweat of his brow." With a dogged masochism, he never ceased to harp publicly on his own humble origins; he was still doing it on the occasion of his inaugural as Vice-President. Even as governor of Tennessee, Johnson on one occasion insisted on cutting out a coat for a judge, a former blacksmith who had made a shovel for him; he accompanied the gift with an open letter proclaiming that "the main highway and surest passport to honesty and useful distinction will soon be through the harvest field and the workshop." Throughout it all, Johnson remained inordinately fastidious in matters of dress. One wonders what he must have thought, in later years, of the slovenly habits of the Great Emancipator.

Politically, Johnson's plebeianism served him wonderfully well in the fundamentalist atmosphere of the East Tennessee upcountry. Long hours of cultivating his voice in the solitude of his shop had made him a superb speaker. From the stump he would conjure up the spirit of Old Hickory; he would revive, in order that he might scourge, the ancient and terrible threats of tyranny and Federalism; he could call forth, as Mencken would later say of Bryan in that same country, all the dread "powers and principalities of the air." The simple mountaineers were deeply impressed by his philippics, and they would shiver in appreciation as his words rang through the valley in the gathering twilight. They said of him, as he thundered out his harsh paeans to equality, "Old Andy never went back on his raisin'." But there was no merriment in Johnson's performances. Unlike Lincoln, he had none of that humor which comes from an appreciation of the ever altering, shimmering complexity of things. "He was dead in earnest," says his biographer, "and he believed with his soul every doctrine he announced."

Johnson's conception of political life was one which had the merit of great simplicity, and in the loosely organized political setting of East Tennessee it was one which could be exploited with overwhelming personal success in the advancement of a career. Politics for Andrew Johnson was essentially a matter of principles that had to be defended rather than of a party organization that had to win elections. He was a Democrat but never really a party man.

Because of his unwillingness to cooperate with political parties or organizations, Johnson in Congress waged a guerilla warfare —a warfare sometimes inside the Democratic party and sometimes outside. Always, however, he stood upon the old platform, equal distribution of government favors, equal treatment of rich and poor, farmer, laborer, mechanic, manufacturer or what not. A strict interpretation of the Constitution and an observance of its letter had now become his guiding principle.

There was such a direct and immediate quality about Johnson's successes on the stump that he could hardly fail to construe re-election as a persuasive test of personal merit owing nothing to "the interests." His constituency sent him back year after year. In such circumstances it was perhaps only natural that he should never feel pressed to put a very high premium on party responsibilities. He was willing, time and again, to break with the organization on any pretext; indeed, much of his career was occupied in fighting it. It is hard to picture Lincoln, on the other hand, with either the taste or the talent for political operations conceived in such terms. Lincoln could not imagine working without his party connections.

It was perfectly in character for Johnson, at the drop of a hat, to "go to the people." Such was the nature of his constituency, combined with the simple values which he represented, that not only was the direct appeal successful time after time, but Johnson's own experience, in the process, could develop and sustain in him an almost religious sense of "the people." If the people did wrong, it was the fault of their conniving leaders. His inaugural as governor in 1853 saw him transfigured with the Democratic faith. On that occasion, he delivered an apocalyptic speech which was received with much amusement by the Whigs and anti-Johnson Democrats but which was greatly approved by the common folk. He dwelt upon the coming "divinity of man," likened the "voice of the people" to the "voice of God," and declared: "It will be readily perceived by all discerning young men, that Democracy is a ladder, corresponding in politics to the one spiritual which Jacob saw in his vision; one up which all, in proportion to their merit, may ascend. While it extends to the humblest of all created beings, here on earth below, it reaches to God on high . . . ."

The texture of Johnson's mind was essentially abstract. Concrete problems never had the power to engage his interest that "principles" had; the principles of equal rights, local self-rule, states' rights as well as Union, and strict constitutionalism had served him through all vicissitudes and had taken on mystic powers with the passage of the years. Faced with a crisis that had no parallels in his past experience, he would have found it next to impossible to imagine that the moral rules which had guided him in his youth should not suffice him then.

Despite Johnson's tendency to boast, he was not a person who had real confidence in his intellectual powers. For a public man, he was obsessed with himself to a degree that exceeded the normal, and most of his speeches, no matter what else they dealt with, may be read as demands for personal vindication and personal approval. Unlike Lincoln, whose "humility" was sustained by the odd arrogance of a superior man's self-knowledge, Johnson lacked assurance. He tended to hesitate in full realization of his own shortcomings. At bottom, general rules were an easy substitute for concrete thinking; confronted with a difficulty, Johnson's mind searched instinctively for such rules in order that it might once more close itself and be at rest. He was not really capable of intellectual courage until after he had made up his mind, and once he had, he would do anything rather than undergo the agony of further doubts. It was a peculiar kind of courage (if such it was): "He could bear insult, personal danger, obloquy; but he could not yield his point." In contrast, there is a downright blitheness about Lincoln's last speech, in which he said that bad promises were better broken than kept. Lincoln was never unprepared, should matters of great moment seem to make it necessary, to redefine something as a "bad promise."

The final stage of Johnson's career, culminating in his rise to the ultimate power, was launched with a characteristic act of dissociation. In 1860 and 1861, with superb disdain for his own personal safety, Johnson—then a senator—defied the secessionists of Tennessee. True to the principles of the sainted Jackson (for whom he had been named), he defended the Constitution and the Union with bitter devotion until no drop of hope for his state was left. He was loyal to the end, and when Tennessee went out, Andrew Johnson stayed on as the loyal senator from a disloyal state—he "could not yield his point." When the Union armies precariously occupied certain parts of the state in 1862, Lincoln asked Johnson to go to beleaguered Nashville as military governor; Johnson hesitated not an instant. For three years, amid unbelievable anxieties and dangers, through nightmares of uncertainty, Johnson stood at his post, playing the role of the outsider under the most heroic circumstances. It was his finest hour; and it was for this that Lincoln in 1864 picked him for his Vice-President.

Johnson had certainly earned his reward. But there was a difficulty which nobody thought much about at the time and the embarrassments of which would not really become apparent until well after Johnson's accession to the Presidency itself. The man had no real connections with the party organization which had placed him there, nor would he ever recognize any. There was little in his past that had given him any preparation for the role of party leader—a role whose essence Abraham Lincoln had understood in his bones.

Might any general predictions have been made as to the future course of the man who took the oath as President on April 15, 1865? What were the prospects for a man whose career had been successful on such a basis as Andrew Johnson's? He had never played his chances on the conservative side. He had played them on the margin—but he had always won. The role of the outsider had formed the political personality of this man; it was a role based on essentially non-political behavior, and it had been played through thirty years of politics—thirty years in the thick of things. It was a role to which he was now committed beyond choice, and it was not an asset to a man who had become President of the United States. The social outsider, the political outsider, and now the outsider who had power: such had been the stages of Johnson's rise, and it was not a background that augured well for political sensitivity or for "moderation," institutionally defined. Johnson was temperamentally and sociologically a "radical," whereas the insider, in our politics, has perennially found it very difficult to be that kind of "radical": he is weighted down by too many connections. To be a good freebooter, one must somehow—like Andrew Johnson—carry as few connections as possible.

Johnson's policy on Reconstruction, despite the hopes of the Republican Party, were, after all, fully consistent with all his past habits, and they should not have occasioned (and probably did not occasion) any surprise to men who really knew those habits.

In justice to Johnson, it would be well not to be misled by

"evidence" that the President, in the summer and fall of 1865, was somehow edging toward his ancient Democratic associations. He was temperamentally incapable of "selling out" in that sense. It was true that Democrats, emerging from interviews, found his conversation much more to their liking on matters of Reconstruction than did Republicans who discussed similar questions with him. But this satisfaction was based upon the President's principles, which the Democrats soon saw as those most conducive to their own political prospects. And yet for Johnson himself, those doctrines were not really conceived in party terms at all. To all such considerations he seemed oblivious.

Johnson's stand appears to have been settled in his own mind fairly early. Indeed, it was he who, with Representative Crittenden, had produced the resolutions of 1861 which declared that the war objectives should be restricted to defense of the Constitution and the Union and that "as soon as these objects were accomplished the war ought to cease." "I hope," he wrote to Montgomery Blair in 1863, "that the President will not be committed to the proposition of States relapsing into territories and held as such." When John A. Logan called upon Johnson to discuss Reconstruction on May 31, 1865, the President was said to have declared: "General, there's no such thing as reconstruction. These States have not gone out of the Union. Therefore reconstruction is unnecessary."

Flushed with passion, Johnson had exclaimed, in the celebrated audience with Wade and others on April 16, the day after Lincoln died, "Treason must be made infamous and traitors must be impoverished." Then, in view of a pardoning policy which became progressively milder as the months went on, many have supposed that a major shift of intention occurred in the President's mind sometime between his inauguration and the early summer. This softened attitude is attributed variously to the counsels of Secretary Seward, the intrigues of the Blairs, and the blandishments of southern ladies seeking pardons for their husbands. It is not unlikely that the President derived a certain pleasure from the position in which he found himself vis-à-vis these ladies; to be able to confer his boon upon them could hardly have failed to be a source of some satisfaction. In any case he could be, for all his obstinacy, a forgiving man. We can easily imagine, moreover, his constitutional convictions being fortified in lengthy talks with the Blairs at Silver Spring. But in the long run Johnson made his own decisions, and the really critical aspect of his Reconstruction policy—the constitutional relations of the states to the Union—had probably hardened for him, and thus ceased to vex his mind, early in the war.

The states, then, had never been out of the Union at all, and the constitutional right of the state to regulate its own internal concerns had never ceased to exist in all its vigor. The abstractness of such a dogma, in view of Johnson's willingness to use pressure (however erratically he may have exerted it) in getting the states to ratify the Thirteenth Amendment and repudiate their debt, never seemed to occur to him. He somehow had to convince himself—and apparently did—that these things were being done "voluntarily." Nor could his laissez-faire attitude on Negro suffrage fail to strike him as both fair and logical. It was true that, under such a policy, Negro suffrage would in all likelihood be ruled out, but there the inscrutable will of the Fathers (as he saw it) left him no choice. And so with the admission of the southern representatives, it was the *constitutional* thing to do, regardless of consequences.

Such were the President's views, doubtless fully articulated by the time he issued his May 29 proclamations. He still held them when Congress met in December, 1865, six months later. He would defend them, against merciless abuse, in his "swing around the circle" the following year. And in December, 1866, those principles would remain doggedly unaltered. In his message to Congress at that time he serenely announced:

"Upon this question, so vitally affecting the restoration of the Union and the permanency of our present form of government, my convictions, heretofore expressed, have undergone no change, but, on the contrary, their correctness has been confirmed by reflection and time."

3

JOHNSON AND THE NEGRO

LaWanda and John H. Cox

While revising previous judgments of Andrew
Johnson, Eric McKitrick still embraced to some
extent the traditional interpretation of Reconstruction. Between the Radical and presidential programs
for the South, he argued that Johnson's "contained
the greatest long-range wisdom and . . . best seemed
to serve the interests of the country at large." The
real tragedy, to McKitrick, was the failure of implementation, the breakdown of presidential leadership,
the way in which Johnson made it impossible for
the moderates—North and South—to work out an
enlightened solution. But to historians LaWanda
and John H. Cox, writing only three years later,
what was crucial in the failure of Andrew Johnson
was his refusal to demand even minimal civil rights
for Negroes and the crystallization of Republican
sentiment over this fundamental question. Unlike
McKitrick, they place considerable emphasis on the
President's attitude toward Negroes.

No uncertainty about the President caused more concern
among Republicans, particularly those of the eastern states,
than his attitude toward the freedmen. As a people, Americans
have always been alert to motives and intent behind matters
judged of moral consequence; and both Johnson's contemporaries and historians have passed judgment upon his attitude

toward the Negro. This raises a question which admits of no easy answer.

The December [1865] message . . . was generally received as reassuring. Sharp and bitter dissent, however, came from Wendell Phillips' *National Anti-Slavery Standard;* it found the tone of the President toward the freedmen "utterly repulsive." The *Liberator,* William Lloyd Garrison's venerable weekly, also challenged Johnson's sincerity. Fair words, according to the *Liberator,* must be interpreted by acts; and it saw the President as working to place the governments of the southern states in the hands of those already re-enacting Black Codes. A more moderate and friendly challenge to the President, but one that, for this very reason, must have been the more disconcerting to its readers, was voiced by the Brooklyn *Daily Union:*

> If the nation is bound to defend the rights of the blacks, why has not the President incorporated such a defence in the conditions of readmission? If justice only is the thing which can save us from suffering in the solution of the negro problem, why has the President quietly ignored justice just at the point where it becomes most absolutely essential that it should be observed? Just when the President proposes to establish each State securely and impregnably behind the banners of resumed Statehood, why does he leave the negro helpless?

President Johnson himself told a delegation of Negroes in February, 1866, that the "feelings of my own heart" had been "for the colored man"; that he had opposed slavery, first, because it had been a great monopoly that enabled an aristocracy to derive great profits and rule with an iron hand and, secondly, because of the abstract principle of slavery. But as a political leader in prewar Tennessee, Andrew Johnson, though an antagonist of the slaveholding aristocracy, had not been known as an opponent of slavery. A kindly master to the slaves of his household, he had on occasion spoken harsh words in respect to the Negro. It is clear that he regarded the whites as a race superior to the blacks, and that he harbored a deep antagonism to northern abolitionism. Shortly after Johnson took office as President, the antislavery New York *Tribune* pointed out that the new Chief Executive would not be open to charges of "nigger-worship" since he had "always till now voted and acted as though Blacks had no rights which Whites are bound to respect." Although the tone of the *Tribune*'s comment was friendly, its characterization may not have been altogether fair. During his wartime governorship of Tennessee, Johnson pledged to the Negro populace that he would be their "Moses"; he recognized that the war would kill slavery, welcomed its passing as the end of a disturbing element in the body politic, and loyally strove to implement Lincoln's desire that Tennessee should officially bury the institution. He did not, however, attempt to prevent the exclusion of Negroes "not only from the ballot box, but also from the witness-box," a fact that the Democratic press later delighted in citing.

In October, 1865, President Johnson went far toward repudiating the view associated with the Blairs and the Democracy, and the most obnoxious to Republican friends of the Negro, namely that "this is a white man's country." "This is your country as well as anybody else's country," he told a regiment of Negro soldiers who had gathered to pay him tribute. "This country is founded upon the principle of equality. . . . He that is meritorious and virtuous, intellectual and well informed, must stand highest, without regard to color." Private letters to the President, however, strongly suggest that Johnson's views were close to those of the Democracy. A Tennessee friend remembered well "your remark, and that was, Gorham, I am for a *White* Man's Government in America." Harvey Watterson, Johnson's trusted representative in the South, commended a general for command in North Carolina. "Like yourself, too, he is for a white man's government, and in favor of free white citizens controlling this country." There is grave doubt that Johnson's private views were ever completely emancipated from his heritage of southern racial attitudes. His private secretary, in 1868, noted in his shorthand diary that "the President has at times exhibited a morbid distress and feeling against the negroes." He made note of the President's querulous demand, on seeing a half-dozen Negroes at work about the White House grounds, whether "all the white men had been discharged." The secretary consoled the President with the comment that "the evident discrimination made here on behalf of the negroes, was sufficient to excite the disgust of all reflecting men."

Johnson's public statements, even that to the Negro soldiers quoted above, seemed to carry an implication that colonization or separate Negro communities might well prove the ultimate solution of the Negro problem. The great question, Johnson told the colored regiment, is whether "this race can be incorporated and mixed with the people of the United States—to make a harmonious and permanent ingredient in the population. . . . Let us make the experiment, and make it in good faith. . . . If we have to become a separate and distinct people (although I trust that the system can be made to work harmoniously) . . . Providence . . . will point out the way, and the mode, and the manner by which these people are to be separated." The December message also spoke of an "experiment in good faith" and cautioned against hasty assumptions that the two races could not live side by side. Some weeks later the President spoke with great emphasis to a Negro delegation of the mutual enmity between "the colored man and the non-slaveholders" and urged the Negro leaders, who had come with a plea for suffrage, to tell their people that they could "live and advance in civilization to better advantage elsewhere than crowded right down there in the South." Although the Thirty-eighth Congress had attempted to put an end to colonization schemes, James Mitchell, who had been appointed Commissioner of Emigration by Lincoln in 1862, clung to his office. In the fall of 1865, Mitchell was actively canvassing political centers from New York to Wisconsin for support of colonization. He reported to President Johnson that he had found many men "anxious to go with us on the question of the separation of the White and Black races." Men close to the President desired separation as the solution of the Negro problem, and Johnson himself may have viewed it with greater favor than his public comment indicated.

Even on the question of Negro suffrage, where Johnson's position seems clearer than on most questions relating to the freedmen, there was room for uncertainty and contradiction. Before his proclamation of May 29, 1865, establishing a provisional government for North Carolina, he considered the possibility of imposing Negro suffrage upon the rebellious states with enough sympathy to kindle the hopes of men committed to this end. Once this first step toward restoration was followed in mid-June by a similar government for Mississippi without extending the vote to any portion of the Negro people, Johnson's policy was generally recognized as based upon the position that the question of suffrage pertained exclusively to the states. There was a lively difference of opinion, however, as to whether or not the President approved and desired extension of the suffrage to Negroes by state action. In a June interview with a white delegation from South Carolina, Johnson indicated that he feared the late slaveholders would control the Negro vote, if suffrage were granted, and use it against the poorer white men of the South. A few days later Secretary Welles, while defending the administration's hands-off policy in respect to state suffrage, reassured Charles Sumner that there was not "on the part of the President or his advisers any opposition to most liberal extensions of the elective franchises."

In the battle over Negro suffrage waged in Connecticut during the fall of 1865, the Democracy . . . identified their opposition with the President's cause. Johnson's Connecticut Secretary of Navy, Gideon Welles, was reported in the local press as having expressed without hesitation "his opinion as decidedly opposed to negro suffrage," and this was used as evidence that "President Johnson is opposed to negro suffrage, as he is opposed to forcing negro voting upon the South." Connecticut Republicans, who were fighting hard for the liberalizing amendment to their state constitution, were alarmed at this damaging blow to the cause and appealed to Welles for a public contradiction. Welles declined to make a statement for publication but authorized a denial that he had "expressed any opinion on the subject of the constitutional amendment now pending."

Just as the voters of Connecticut were deciding the issue with the Democrats and against the Republicans, a dedicated but conciliatory antislavery man from neighboring Massachusetts, George L. Stearns, sought from the President a direct answer to this now politically freighted question. In an interview which he later obtained permission to make public, Stearns heard from the President that were he in Tennessee "I should try to introduce negro suffrage gradually; first those who had served in the army; those who could read and write; and perhaps a property qualification for the others, say $200 or $250. It would not do to let the negro have universal suffrage now; it would breed a war of races." This statement greatly pleased eastern Republicans. Greeley's *Tribune*, for example, commented that judicious men would "rejoice that Mr. Johnson is willing to use even his indirect and unofficial influence that justice may be done to the blacks of the South." The *World* was not unduly disturbed. If the *Tribune* or anyone else can find satisfaction in Johnson's "private views which he steadily refuses to embody in official action we do not object. Give us his official acts, and you are welcome to his private sentiments."

Much of Johnson's popularity among southerners rested upon the conviction that the President alone stood between them and the dire fate of Negro suffrage. They relied not only upon his official policy in restricting elections under the provisional governments to whites but also upon unofficial assurances. Watterson during his stay in North Carolina had let it be known "in the right quarter" that the President would never be driven by "the Chases and Sumners" from the position "that the suffrage question belongs to the States alone." Letters that reached the President made unmistakably clear the southern aversion to an extension of the suffrage and the gratitude for his stand. Like the *World*, southerners could pass over Johnson's remarks to Stearns, approving a limited state grant of voting privileges to Negroes, so long as he left the question in their hands. The prediction of an Alabama Unionist proved erroneous; the statement in favor of qualified Negro suffrage, he wrote the President, "is enough for these southern people not only to condemn you while liveing [*sic*] —but will try to blacken your future name and history." The Alabaman was not in error, however, in assuming an overwhelming opposition to Negro voting in the South. In view of this attitude, which was undoubtedly clear to Johnson, the following sentence in his December message appears evasive and misleading: "In my judgment, the freedmen, if they show patience and manly virtues, will sooner obtain a participation in the elective franchise through the States than through the General Government, even if it had power to intervene."

President Johnson's often cited recommendation to the provisional governor of Mississippi that the state grant limited suffrage to the Negro requires examination in a larger perspective than it has generally received. The Mississippi convention which met in Jackson on August 14, 1865, was the first such convention to assemble under Johnson's plan of restoration. On August 15, the President sent to Governor W. L. Sharkey a telegram urging abolition of slavery in the state constitution and the ratification of the pending Thirteenth Amendment. The telegram continued:

If you could extend the elective franchise to all persons of color who can read the constitution of the United States in English and write their names, and to all persons of color who own real estate valued at not less than two hundred and fifty dollars and pay taxes thereon, you would completely disarm the adversary and set an example the other states will follow.

This you can do with perfect safety. . . . I hope and trust your convention will do this, and as a consequence the Radicals, who are wild upon negro franchise, will be completely foiled in their attempts to keep the Southern States from renewing their relations to the Union by not accepting their Senators and Representatives.

On August 20, Sharkey wired back that the convention would amend the state constitution to abolish slavery, but that the right to testify in court and the right of suffrage would probably be left to the legislature. The President replied that he was "much gratified to hear of your proceedings being so favorable," and that "your convention can adopt the Amendment to the Constitution of the United States or recommend its adoption by the Legislature." He pointed out "the importance of being prompt and circumspect in all that is being done," since the Mississippi proceeding would "set an example that will be followed by all the other States." But not one word in the reply made reference to his previous recommendation for qualified Negro suffrage. Four days later the President sent another telegram of commendation, promising an early removal of federal troops and expressing his belief that if the other southern states followed Mississippi's example the day of restoration was not distant. Again he omitted any mention of the suffrage issue. Governor Sharkey read this telegram to the legislature, which heard it with satisfaction.

The convention soon adjourned, and Sharkey sent the President a report of its actions including its charge to the legislature to enact laws to protect the Negro in his rights of person and property. He continued: "How it will do this I cannot say, possibly it may allow the negro to testify. . . . The right of suffrage I do not think will be extended to them; indeed there is an inclination to limit the right of suffrage with the white man. In regard to the amendment of the Constitution of the United States prohibiting slavery I do not think the State ever will adopt the second article or provision of the amendment." He continued with complaints against the military and the Freedmen's Bureau and concluded by asserting that both he and the people of Mississippi thought they were entitled now to be relieved of martial law and "to be treated as though the rebellion had ended."

In the face of this recalcitrant reaction to his recommendations and the almost peremptory request for complete self-rule, Johnson permitted his congratulatory message to remain without qualification, public or private. He did not, however, completely remand Mississippi to the inclinations of its people. Two weeks after the assembling of the Mississippi legislature Johnson renewed his pressure for ratification of the antislavery amendment in a telegram to Governor Sharkey of November 1, 1865, holding out the inducement that its adoption would "make the way clear for the admission of Senators and Representatives to their seats in the present Congress." Once again he abandoned the recommendation for an extension of the vote to qualified Negroes. On the 16th, while a joint committee was considering the amendment, the elected governor, Benjamin Humphreys, sought additional reassurances. He reported that the legislators appeared willing to permit freedmen to testify in courts if assured the federal troops would be withdrawn, but they feared "that one concession will only lead to others. What assurances can I give on the subject?" In his reply the next day, the President stated:

There can be no other or greater assurance given than has heretofore been on the part of the President. There is no concession required on the part of the people of Mississippi or the Legislature, other than loyal compliance with the laws and constitution of the United States, and the adoption of such measures giving protection to all freedmen, or freemen, in person and property without regard to color, as will entitle them to resume all their constitutional relations in the Federal Union. . . .

There must be confidence between the Government and the

States—while the Government confides in the people—the people must have faith in the Government. This must be mutual and reciprocal, or all that has been done will be thrown away.

While refusing to make a definite commitment in respect to withdrawal of troops and while placing legislation to protect the freedmen under the designation of "concession required," in this same telegram Johnson gave the assurance, quoted earlier, that he was not dictating action but only offering kindly advice. Within ten days, the Mississippi legislature adopted a civil rights act for freedmen so inequitable that the administration had to set aside certain of its provisions. The legislature also accepted the recommendation of its joint committee *not* to ratify the antislavery amendment.

Thus, in the face of southern hostility and defiance, Johnson completely discarded his Negro suffrage recommendation. He had urged an extension of voting privileges, not as a matter of equity or of personal conviction, but as an expedient to outmaneuver the Radicals. Perhaps he felt confident of an early restoration without this concession. He did not repeat the advice of August 15, either to Mississippi or to any other of the southern states. Greeley's "judicious men" might rejoice at the Stearns interview of October 3 and hope that the President would use his "indirect and unofficial influence" for qualified Negro suffrage; but he had already tried and abandoned the effort. In his December message Johnson argued at length the case for state control of suffrage on the basis of history and the Constitution. He did not include the suggestion forwarded by his friend and political adviser, Lewis Campbell, that he recommend an end to suffrage restrictions which deprived of the vote men of any class—"white, black, or mixed"—who possessed virtue, intelligence, and patriotism. Most Republican advocates of Negro suffrage accepted Johnson's argument as sincere but took issue with his logic. It is not difficult to understand their view that Johnson had as much right under the Constitution to obtain an extension of suffrage

from the rebel states as he had to establish provisional governments, insist that they abolish slavery, ratify the Thirteenth
Amendment, and repudiate their acts of secession and war
debt. Even the *Herald* had stated that the President undoubtedly had the power in closing up the rebellion to insist upon
Negro suffrage but deemed it wiser to leave the matter to the
states. The correspondence between Johnson and the Mississippi governors illustrates the inconsistency and embarrassment in his "advice-not-dictation" posture, as well as the inef-
fectual character of his endorsement of limited suffrage for
the freedmen.

Two other incidents throw some additional light upon
Johnson's attitude toward Negro suffrage. On January 18,
1866, the House of Representatives passed by a large majority,
though no Democrat voted yea, a bill striking the word
"white" from the qualifications for voters in the District of
Columbia. A preceding motion would have recommitted the
bill with instructions to amend by extending the suffrage only
to those who could read the Constitution or had served in
the Union forces. These changes would have brought the
measure in line with Johnson's position. The Union-Republi-
cans split on this motion, but the Democrats to a man voted
against it, thereby defeating a qualified extension of the suffrage. The New York *Times* accused the Democrats of two
aims: to stir up trouble between the Union party and the
President, and to facilitate passage of a measure that could be
used to agitate the Negro question in their constituencies.

Johnson received word that there were enough votes in the
Senate to defeat the bill and was requested to send for the
senators who were "sound," tell them his views and unite with
them for action. His response is not a matter of record, but on
January 28, he had an interview with his loyal Republican
supporter, Senator Dixon of Connecticut, which was at once
made public. Here he "expressed the opinion that the agitation
of the negro franchise question in the District of Columbia at

this time was the mere entering-wedge to the agitation of the question throughout the States, and was ill-timed, uncalled for, and calculated to do great harm." The interview dealt principally with his position in respect to amending the Constitution, a matter then engaging the urgent attention of the Joint Committee on Reconstruction and of Congress. Johnson held that any amendment at the time was of dubious propriety, would tend to diminish respect for the Constitution, and was quite unnecessary. However, if any were to be made, he knew of none better than the simple proposition that direct taxation be based upon the value of property and representation be based upon the number of voters. Such an amendment, he thought, "would remove from Congress all issues in reference to the political equality of the races" and leave to the states the absolute determination of "qualifications of their own voters with regard to color." Johnson's reluctant approval for an amendment that would give to the South a choice between lessened representation and an extension of suffrage to Negroes represented the farthest limit of his support for a measure of Negro suffrage. In respect to the substance of the District of Columbia bill he avoided approval or disapproval, or any suggestion for its modification.

An amendment of the nature Johnson haltingly endorsed at the end of January, 1866, by then had no chance of obtaining congressional approval. The proposal that representation be based upon voters had been made by Robert Schenck, representative from Ohio, at the opening of Congress; it had been approved by Thaddeus Stevens and the Joint Committee on Reconstruction, but it had run into opposition from New Englanders. Their objection was that this formula would result in an inequitable decrease of representation for their section. Due to westward emigration New England's population, the current basis of apportionment, had a disproportionate number of women and children to men; also, the number of voters in the New England states was relatively less than in other states because of educational requirements for voting. New England objections had led to a revision of the proposed amendment retaining population as the basis of representation but providing a reduction wherever the franchise was denied on the basis of race. The President's endorsement of the original proposal could have no practical effect except to embarrass the New England Radicals. A Johnson political strategist was urging in March that a vote be pressed on the representation-based-on-voters amendment. New England would reject it, and thereby "show the country that New England selfishness is not willing to accept any basis of representation that diminishes her political power"—this would "shut their mouths."

Ten days after the interview with Senator Dixon, the President received a delegation of Negroes that included Frederick Douglass, who came to express the hope that their people would be fully enfranchised. In reply, Johnson spoke with emotion of the scorn which he insisted the slave had held for the poor white man and was the basis for a continuing enmity between Negro and nonslaveholder. The colored man had gained much as the result of the rebellion, he said, while the poor white had lost a great deal; on what principle of justice could they be "placed in a condition different from what they were before?" It would commence a war of races; to force universal suffrage without the consent of the community would deny the "first great principle of the right of the people to govern themselves." Without recognizing any inconsistency in his devotion to the principle of government by consent of the governed, Johnson claimed for white southerners the right to determine whether or not the Negro should vote. He made no allusion to the desirability of a beginning through a qualified franchise.

The interview buried the hopes of those who still looked to the President for unofficial support in breaching the race barrier against Negro suffrage. It delighted many a believer in white supremacy. "I cannot forbear to express to you the great pleasure I felt on reading your remarks to the colored man," wrote an old friend. He continued:

The principles you enunciated are the same expressed to me in a conversation I had with you last Autumn, and in which I fully agreed with you. You said to me then that every one would, and *must* admit that the white race was superior to the black, and that while we ought to do our best to bring them [the blacks] up to our present level, that in doing so we should, at the same time raise our own intellectual status so that the relative position of the two races would be the same. . . .

I am astonished, and more than astonished, at the persistency with which the radical idea of placing negroes on an equality with whites, *in every particular*, is pressed in Congress. . . . Until the tide of fanaticism, which is now in full flood, shall turn, as it must, unless sanity has departed from the people, we must place our trust in you to keep us safe "from the pestilence that walketh in darkness, and the destruction that wasteth at noon-day."

Men of like views might have looked with even greater confidence to the President as the bulwark against Negro "equality" had they been privy to Johnson's private reactions to the delegation headed by Douglass. According to one of the President's private secretaries who was present at the occasion, on the departure of the "darkey delegation" the President "uttered the following terse Saxon: 'Those d——d sons of b——s thought they had me in a trap! I know that d——d Douglass; he's just like any nigger, and he would sooner cut a white man's throat than not.' "

Republican opinion was far from united in respect to Negro suffrage, but it was substantially agreed that the freedmen should enjoy all other rights and privileges pertaining to free men and citizens. On the matter of these civil rights, Johnson's pre-veto record seemed to indicate that here he stood squarely with northern liberal opinion. There were grave apprehensions, however, that presidential authority might prove inadequate to obtain from the South that measure of justice which was considered the freedman's due, or at least, obtain it in time to effect speedy restoration. During the meeting of the Mississippi convention in August, 1865, the New York *Times*, which enjoyed an unofficial status as spokesman for the administration, gave warning in an editorial entitled "The Real Question as to the Future Political Status of the Negro." The "real question" was not whether the freedman should vote but whether he should be protected against injustice and oppression. The North would be watching to see that the convention did not proceed "upon the principle that the colored race are to be kept in a state of subordination, and made the subject of peculiar restraints and exactions." This would be "the great index" to whether or not restoration would soon be effected. "The government, anxious as it is to hasten this end, can make no concession here." The *Times* was not happy with the work of the convention though it acknowledged that northern doubts might be settled if the Mississippi legislature faithfully fulfilled the duties assigned it by the convention. But why, it asked, was so important a matter left to the faithfulness or unfaithfulness of legislators?

Ever loyal to the President, and adhering to his position as they saw it, the editorial staff of the *Times* succinctly posed the difference that divided the President and the Republican Radicals. "President Johnson founds all his practical policy upon the presumption that the South is fit to be trusted. His radical opponents found theirs upon the presumption that the South is unfit to be trusted." Though the *Times* agreed with the President, there was yet a doubt and a threat in its comment. "When the contrary is shown, then and not until then, will the time come for a different policy." The *Times* hoped for speedy reinstatement of the southern states, but recognized that in Congress various questions would first be considered, particularly whether more complete securities should not be required for the protection of the rights of the freedmen. As political activity accelerated under Johnson's plan of conventions, elections and legislative action, the *Times* hoped for a "clean sweep of the old black codes, and giving to the blacks substantially the same equality with the white men before the law, that prevails in the Northern states." No solid ground was left for opposition to admission of the formerly rebellious states, it asserted, save assurance that once reinstated in all their old municipal powers these would not be used to harm the freedmen; on this the government must find some kind of security in advance of readmission. The southern people would not be put in unlimited control of the freedman until they had given proof that they would befriend and not injure him. As of mid-November, "no such proof has yet been given."

The news from Mississippi in October and November was not reassuring. Where the question of Negro testimony had entered the local canvass for the legislature, the nonadmission candidates had won the elections. The defeat by a decided majority of a Negro testimony bill after the legislature convened was hailed by a local paper as a "Glorious Result," an honor to the legislators who had withstood "home threats" and "outside influences." "They have been importuned, threatened, reasoned with and implored to admit the negro to equality in our judicial tribunals, but the *representatives of the people* have frowned upon the proposition, and will never permit the slave of yesterday to confront his former master in the witness-box." Henry J. Raymond, the *Times* editor, was telling cheering Republicans in mid-October that the President's plan included such provision in southern constitutions and laws "as shall put all their citizens upon an equality before the law." Editorially, the *Times* reinforced the point by stating that President Johnson had given "the power and influence of his position without reserve" to securing for the freedmen "all the great civil safeguards of person and property. . . . They have made themselves felt in no small measure through his Provisional Governors and through the Freedmen's Bureau; and the effects will be made palpable to all in the favorable enactments for the freedmen, in the legislatures of the late rebel states, soon to assemble." To underscore the differences between the Democracy and the President, the *Times* pointed out that the former held that for restoration the southern states had only to reorganize "in accordance with their own will" while the President insisted that full rights were not restored until certain conditions had been met including "effective laws . . . for the protection of the natural rights of the freedmen." In a rejoinder to the Louisville *Journal*, which had criticized northerners for meddling with the status of the freedmen, the *Times* warned that the South could disarm the "fanatics" by taking measures to secure the Negroes in their civil rights, to educate them, and to prepare them for responsible duties. *"If the South will not do this, the nation* MUST. It cannot be left undone." The influential Louisville *Journal* would do better to stimulate the southern people to their duty rather than waste its energies in denouncing northerners.

The New York Democratic convention, while embracing the President and his policy, denounced any attempt by prolonging military rule or denying representation to coerce the southern states "to adopt negro equality or negro suffrage" as tending to subvert the principles of government and the liberties of the people. However, the Democracy's chief organ, the *World*, recognized as an integral part of Johnson's program "entire equality before the law" for the emancipated slaves. It even urged upon the South that it give Negroes the right to testify in court, and pointed with pleasure to favorable reaction to its suggestion in southern and northern Democratic newspapers. "In this fact is a conclusive refutation of the charge falsely made against the Democratic party that they are willing to exclude negro freedmen from that justice and *equality before the law* which is their right. . . . We believe that we express the views of President Johnson, as we know that we do the views of the great mass of the Democratic party of the North, in saying that this *equality before the law* ought not to be, and cannot prudently be, denied to negro freedmen." The *Herald* reinforced this view of the President's position. "It is the simple policy of recognizing the emancipated blacks as *citizens*, entitled without delay to all the rights and protection of other citizens in the civil courts." An editorial subtitled "What the Southern States Have to Do" listed civil rights for Negroes along with the requirements of abolishing slavery, ratifying the Thirteenth Amendment, repudiating ordinances of secession, and recognizing an obligation to share the national debt. The grant of limited suffrage was placed in a separate category, not a "must," but a "wise" concession.

Thus there was substantial evidence of Johnson's intentions: the agreement of the *Times*, the *World*, and the *Herald*; the President's public telegram to Governor Humphreys, quoted earlier, asserting that the Mississippi legislature must adopt measures to protect freedmen without regard to color; the enforcement of equal rights by the Freedmen's Bureau under the authority of the President. Republicans generally could, and did, credit him with the best intentions in respect to the freedman's civil status. Yet the situation in the South generally, not just in Mississippi, was disturbing. The southern states, under great pressure, were meeting the President's conditions reluctantly and partially. The President was quoted as saying that the "foolish Georgians were hindering him in the carrying out of his plans a good deal more than the worst of the northern radicals." The cruel part, continued the reporter, is that this occurs just when the President and his friends have been inculcating the idea of nonintervention in the South. Johnson's orders to provisional governors to retain their positions even after elected governors were ready to take over authority was interpreted as a stern presidential answer to southern obstinancy. Contrary to the President's known wishes, southern voters were choosing men to represent them at home and in Congress who had held leadership in the rebellion. Reports abounded that with the liberal grant of pardons and the apparently official standing of the theory that the states were entitled to full rights within the Union, the earlier submissive mood of southerners was turning to one of thinly disguised defiance. Private letters to the President, Secretary Seward, and Secretary Welles spoke with concern of this changing temper of "obstinacy and bitterness" in the South. The provisional governors for North Carolina and Georgia had in desperation appealed to the President for support in obtaining repudiation of the war debts and general acquiescence in the administration's program. Johnson had replied with strong telegrams that were used with effect upon lawmakers. Florida had ratified the amendment only after a pointed dispatch sent by Secretary Seward on behalf of the President. Even with open presidential pressure, South Carolina had refused to repudiate the debt and Mississippi to ratify the amendment. Florida and Georgia had balked at declaring the ordinances of secession "null and void," either "repealing" or "annulling" them instead.

Resistance to giving the freedmen equal treatment under state laws was even greater. Some states reluctantly allowed Negroes to testify in civil courts in order to be free of the jurisdiction of Freedmen's Bureau courts; but even where this was done under administrative agreement, lawmakers hesitated to act because of an overwhelmingly hostile public sentiment against receiving Negro testimony. In the face of this reaction, and despite the sharp pressure in the case of Mississippi and more discreet pressures upon other states, certain of Johnson's reactions to the issue of civil rights, though not publicized at the time, were ominous. In Alabama both Provisional Governor Lewis E. Parsons and the Freedmen's Bureau administrator, Wager Swayne, were laboring to obtain from the convention an organic law to permit Negro testimony.

Governor Parsons reported difficulty to the President in mid-September and asked to be informed "by telegraph immediately, if you regard it indispensible [*sic*] to the interests of the people of Alabama that such a clause should be inserted." No word came from the President. The convention merely enjoined the legislature to pass laws to protect the freedmen. Governor Parsons appealed again to the President. The important question "was and is whether it is necessary to declare in the Constitution that 'no distinction should be made on account of color, as to the competency of witnesses in this state.' There could be no room for cavil if that had been done. . . . But the individual members of Convention, some of them, were afraid of consequences to themselves if they put it in the constitution. If it had been done the fight [for restoration] would then have to be made on the precise line where I understand you to have placed it—viz—the right of the people of these states to declare who shall vote. . . . I beg to assure you that Alabama approves and will in good faith do all things necessary to sustain your policy with regard to her." The Alabama convention remained in session for another week, but no answer to Governor Parsons' appeal arrived from the President. After the convention's adjournment, Johnson sent a brief telegram commending its proceedings as having "met the highest expectations of all who desire the restoration of the Union. All seems now to be working well, and will result as I believe in a decided success."

From Tennessee also came requests, both unofficially in October and officially in November, that the President send a statement of his views on the subject of Negroes testifying in the courts. It "*would save infinite trouble*," so great is "the enthusiasm you have kindled among the people." Johnson finally replied on December 9. He would have answered sooner, he said, but thought his message which "would indicate my views, upon the subject of negro testimony, in all cases where they are parties, would be conclusive. It is to be regretted that our Legislature failed to make some advance at its present session upon this question." Two points in connection with this reply are of special interest: first, the December message made no specific mention of Negro testimony; secondly, Johnson's formula as to the right of Negroes to testify where "they are parties" was much less comprehensive than Governor Parsons' version that "no distinction shall be made on account of color."

Johnson had made specific reference to Negro testimony in an interview granted to a distinguished white delegation from South Carolina October 13, 1865. The statement was reported as follows:

The President thought many of the evils would disappear if they inaugurated the right system. Pass laws protecting the colored man in his person and property and he can collect his debts. He knew how it was in the South. The question when first presented of putting a colored man in the witness stand made them shrug their shoulders. But the colored man's testimony was to be taken for what it was worth by those who examined him and the jury who hear it. Those coming out of slavery cannot do without work. . . . They ought to understand that liberty means simply the right to work and enjoy the products of labor, and that the laws protect them. That being done, and when we come to the period to feel that men must work or starve the country will be prepared to receive a system applicable to both white and black. . . . But get the public mind right and you can treat both alike. Let us get the general principles and the details and collaterals will follow.

Johnson's advice is quoted above at some length, for this statement, like the December message, invited favorable reaction from men of fundamentally differing convictions. Republicans could seize with satisfaction upon the idea of "treating both alike"; southerners could read into the reference to taking testimony "for what it was worth" an invitation to concede the form without the substance of equality before the law. After bitter battles, southern legislators, during the period of Johnson's control over the reconstruction process, conceded to the Negro the right to testify. They limited this, however, to cases in which he was a party and denied to the freedmen—Tennessee made the denial a specific proviso of its testimony bill—the right to sit as jurors. Efforts made in the summer and fall of 1865 by Freedmen's Bureau officers to implement the President's desire to remand jurisdiction over Negroes to civil courts resulted, in a number of instances, in local courts permitting Negro testimony. The results of local justice, however, did not provide substantive protection for the freedmen.

Even more ominous for the future of the freedmen, and for future relations between Johnson and the Republican majority as well, was the concession made by Secretary Seward in the President's name in respect to the Thirteenth Amendment. Southern states were willing to recognize that slavery was dead, but they were not willing to ratify a constitutional provision that gave to Congress the power of enforcement. The fear was that under this authority Congress would pass legislation affecting the status of freedmen in the southern states. Considerable opinion in and out of Congress held that the amendment gave just such power to protect the rights of Negroes as free men. Even the *Herald* had stated editorially that the amendment "in giving to Congress the 'necessary legislation' to carry the abolition of slavery into effect, gives to Congress some discretionary power touching the late slave codes of the State concerned." Yet in a message to Provisional Governor B. J. Perry of South Carolina, November 6, 1865, Secretary Seward stated: "The objection you mention to the last clause of the constitutional amendment is regarded as querulous and unreasonable, because that clause is really restraining in its effect, instead of enlarging the powers of Congress." South Carolina then ratified the amendment with the following qualification:

That any attempt by Congress toward legislating upon the political status of former slaves, *or their civil relations*, would be contrary to the Constitution of the United States as it now is, or as it would be altered by the proposed amendment, in conflict with the policy of the President, declared in his amnesty proclamation and with the restoration of that harmony upon which depend the vital interests of the American Union.

Alabama and Florida subsequently accepted the amendment with the proviso that it did not confer upon Congress power "to legislate upon the political status of the freedmen in this State." Mississippi's consent was finally granted contingent upon qualifications even more extended than those of South Carolina. They included the explicit statement that the second section "shall not be construed as a grant of power to Congress to legislate in regard to the freedmen of this state."

Clearly the southern states were determined to obtain full control over the freedmen. In some instances there was open avowal of the intent, once restoration was complete, to repeal civil rights that had been granted under pressure and return the Negro to "his place." Various provisions of the legislation in respect to Negroes under consideration or recently enacted in Mississippi, South Carolina, and other southern states appeared to be flagrant attempts legally to remand the freedmen to an inferior status. Troubled Republicans found consolation in the President's reported characterization of his policy as an "experiment"; Democrats deprecated or denied the remark and insisted that the President would not be moved from his present policy. The administration gave assurances that it would stand by the freedmen, but it also had been thought to promise early withdrawal of military forces and Freedmen's Bureau jurisdiction in the South. To the confusion and concern that marked the fall and early winter of 1865 was added Seward's curious and limiting interpretation of the enforcement clause of the Thirteenth Amendment.

As Congress began its labors there was much evidence to arouse fears that southerners were not yet ready to meet the freedman in his new status with justice and without discrimination. The congressional majority approached the problem with confidence in the President's good intentions. But there were portents, not yet generally recognized, that Johnson's version of "the security of the freedmen in their liberty and in their property" might hold concessions to southern prejudice that could not be reconciled with the Republican view that Negroes were citizens entitled to equality before the law.

PART II

THE
RADICAL REPUBLICANS

Few periods of American history have lent themselves so readily to stereotyped portraits as that of Reconstruction. Not surprisingly, those historians who viewed Reconstruction as a "blackout of honest government" castigated the Radicals as the villains of the melodrama. If the Radicals were not simply misguided idealists, they were unscrupulous men who placed party, personal ambition, and the needs of northern business above considerations of national interest and sectional reconciliation. The portrayal of Thaddeus Stevens in the widely viewed motion picture *Birth of a Nation* was characteristic of the monolithic group portrait which historians helped to create. The recent historical re-evaluation of the Radical Republicans is not simply an attempt to rehabilitate certain individuals but to reveal the complexities of the movement, the sources and nature of its radicalism, the various considerations that influenced its actions, and the extent of its cohesiveness, support, and political effectiveness.

4

NORTHEASTERN BUSINESS AND RADICAL RECONSTRUCTION:
A Re-examination

Stanley Coben

Several historians—among them Robert P. Sharkey, Irwin Unger, and Stanley Coben—have re-examined the attempts to interpret Radical Reconstruction in strictly economic terms. What they have questioned is not the profound economic impact of the Civil War but the monolithic character of the capitalist class, the degree of unity which it achieved on economic issues and southern policy, and the extent to which the economic and social biases of a businessman or a Republican might have determined his view of Reconstruction.

Historians have generally accepted the view that Radical Reconstruction "was a successful attempt by northeastern business, acting through the Republican party, to control the national government for its own economic ends: notably, the protective tariff, the national banks, [and] a 'sound' currency." The Radical program is also said to have been "the method by which the 'Masters of Capital' . . . expected to exploit the resources of the southern states" behind federal protection. Western hostility to these eastern business designs was avoided by large appropriations for rivers, harbors, railroads, free land, and pensions, and by use of the ever-potent "bloody shirt." Thus is supposed to have been prevented a union of western and southern agrarian opposition to the industrial and financial masters of the East.

This thesis has met with little serious challenge and has been subjected to only occasional qualification. It continues to influence studies of the political and economic history of the post-Civil War era. Yet a closer examination of the important economic legislation and congressional battles of the period, and of the attitudes of businessmen and influential business groups, reveals serious divisions on economic issues among Radical legislators and northeastern businessmen alike. Certainly neither business leaders nor Radicals were united in support of any specific set of economic aims. Considerable evidence also suggests that the divisions among businessmen often cut across sectional as well as industrial lines. Furthermore, evidence indicates that few northeastern business groups were interested in southern investments in the early postwar years, and that these few were hostile to Radical Reconstruction.

The evident need for new interpretations of the motivation of northern Radicals and of the economic history of the entire period is demonstrated by a re-examination of the most important of the "economic ends" usually agreed upon as motives for Radical Reconstruction: the tariff and the currency issues, and the charge that northern business interests sought federal protection for the exploitation of the South.

The tariff split northeastern businessmen more than any other issue. So fierce was business competition in this era, and so eager were the antagonists to use every possible means of winning an advantage, that almost all important tariff schedules became battlegrounds between industries, as well as between firms within the same industry. The copper, iron, linseed, and woolen textile industries, for example, were bitterly divided on crucial tariff schedules. The most significant split, however, was between certain highly protectionist Pennsylvania interests on one side and influential low-tariff groups in New England and New York on the other. Pennsylvania coal mine operators feared the competition of rich Nova Scotia deposits, mined by low-wage labor, close to major American markets. Iron and steel manufacturers, the largest highly protected interest, were faced with the competition of long-established, technologically advanced English producers, whose wage scale was only a fraction of that of the Americans. Pennsylvania carpet, glass, and wool industries demanded protection for similar reasons. The Keystone State was the largest extractor of iron ore and coal, the largest manufacturer of every form of iron and steel, of carpets, glass, and chemicals. On the other hand, powerful opposition to the tariff objectives of the Pennsylvanians came from the cotton and many of the woolen textile manufacturers of New England, and from the intertwined importing, financial, and railroad interests of New York.

New Englanders had become strong advocates of lower tariffs in the 1850's. The sharp tariff reductions of 1857 were accomplished chiefly by southern and New England votes. New England manufacturers, especially textile producers, desired cheap imported raw materials in order to lower the price of their finished goods on the international market. Furthermore, they agreed to reduced rates on manufactured goods to discourage the growth of domestic competition. Among American manufacturers, New England producers as a group were farthest from domestic sources of raw materials, closest to sources of cheap foreign commodities. Cheap supplies of coal, lumber, flaxseed, building stone, fine wool, and other commodities were available in nearby Canada and Nova Scotia. Scottish and British iron, Indian linseed, and Russian and Philippine hemp were imported into Boston in large quantities for the benefit of manufacturers. Hardly any wool for the finer grades of cloth was produced in America, either before or after the war; nor were the rough, lowest grades, used in carpets and blankets, available at home. By the end of the war, northeastern cotton manufacturers were importing the cheap Indian Surat cotton already widely used in England.

English textile manufacturers, rivals of the New Englanders both in world markets and in America, obtained their raw materials free of duty. There were good reasons for northeastern producers to believe that only the American system of imposts kept them from equaling the British in world trade. By the 1850's, many American mills had been in operation for three generations. They had experienced managers and weavers, cheap and abundant credit, modern machinery and production methods. In cotton cloth manufacturing, for which machinery could be used most extensively, New England labor was the most productive in the world. By 1860, the average number of looms per weaver was four in America, two in Great Britain. French and German manufacturers lagged even farther behind in methods and machinery.

In addition to high productivity which made their goods competitive in the world markets, and the need to import cheap raw materials, many New England manufacturers preferred low tariffs from a fear that high textile duties would foster the growth of new competitors at home. New producers might bring cutthroat competition and periodic chaos to the industry by their poor judgment of market conditions. A special committee of the Boston Board of Trade acknowledged in 1858 that New England textile manufacturers had potentially dangerous rivals, especially in Pennsylvania; but the committee concluded that the tariff reduction of 1857 removed any immediate threat. "Under the impulse of a high protective tariff they accomplished so little, that now, under a change of policy, there seems no present cause of alarm." When the higher Morrill duties came before the House in 1860, Representative Alexander H. Rice of Massachusetts, speaking for the manufacturers of his state, declared that "excessive protection" would stimulate "ruinous and irresponsible competition at home." In the Senate, textile manufacturer Henry Wilson proclaimed: "A high protective policy . . . is calculated to raise up rivals at home, and is more injurious to us than foreign competition."

After the war, fear of the growth of protected competition continued to influence New England tariff sentiment. Edward Atkinson, president of the Cotton Spinners of New England, and a director of the Boston Board of Trade, wrote to Henry Wilson in 1866: "The strongest men in the trade are more afraid of the unskillful competition built up at home by high duties than they are of foreign competition." Enoch R. Mudge, one of the most influential New England textile men, told the organizing meeting of the National Association of Cotton Manufacturers and Planters in 1868: "When we speak of protection, I think it should be given only at the point where the cotton manufacturer requires it." For well-established, efficient New England producers, of course, there were comparatively few points at which protection was necessary. They had seen evidence of the success of their low tariff theories in the few years the 1857 schedules were in force. "The operation of the tariff of 1857 has contributed largely to the prosperity of our woolen manufactures," one of Boston's largest wool dealers reported in 1859. Exports of cotton cloth had risen steadily, from an average of $7,000,000 in the years 1851 through 1856, to almost $11,000,000 in 1860.

The government's need for revenue allowed protectionists an almost unchallenged ascendancy during the Civil War, but the battle between northeastern business groups over tariff schedules was resumed after Appomattox. For example, when a resolution for lower tariffs was placed before the National Board of Trade Convention in 1869, delegates from the Boston Board of Trade and Boston Corn Exchange voted 6 to 1 for the resolution; Philadelphia delegates voted 7 to 0 against it. The Boston Board of Trade also worked unsuccessfully to prevent abrogation of the reciprocity treaty with Canada; Philadelphia's Board joined western agricultural interests in demanding an end to reciprocity.

These divisions within the business community were likewise reflected in the congressional debates and voting on important tariff schedules. Cotton manufacturers resumed their prewar demands for lower schedules, even for cotton textiles. Senator William Sprague, whose sprawling Rhode Island mills were relatively inefficient, protested against the 25 percent cut in cotton textile duties proposed in 1867. He was answered by Senator William P. Fessenden of Maine, sponsor of the measure: "I am informed by the commissioner [Revenue Commissioner David A. Wells] that these duties were fixed at a rate perfectly satisfactory to those engaged in the manufacture of cottons, who appeared before him. . . . The cotton interest of this country has got so that it can stand of itself pretty much."

Schedules on coal similarly came under attack. As power looms replaced hand looms, and steam power replaced water power, New England manufacturers became increasingly interested in lower coal duties. Under reciprocity and the low tariff of 1857, imports of coal into Boston rose steadily from 88,531 tons in 1858, to 209,225 tons in 1865, most of this being cheap Nova Scotia fuel. Representative George S. Boutwell and Senator Charles Sumner of Massachusetts tried in vain to prevent higher coal schedules from being placed in the proposed tariffs of 1866 and 1867. Sumner acknowledged that there was a lot of coal in Pennsylvania, West Virginia, and the West. "But why," he asked, "should New England, which has a natural resource comparatively near at home, be compelled at a great sacrifice to drag her coal from these distant supplies?" Sumner's amendment was defeated 11 to 25, with eight New Englanders, both New Yorkers, and one senator from Oregon comprising those favoring lower duties on coal.

Many other schedules in the proposed bills of 1866 and 1867 were fought out by competing or conflicting business interests. Manufacturers, especially New Englanders, dependent upon cheap imported raw materials, were continually in opposition to the combined efforts of raw material producers and competing manufacturers closer to these native sources of supply. When Senator Benjamin F. Wade of Ohio moved to raise the duty on linseed, largely grown in the West, Fessenden of Maine accused him of asking the higher rate "for this simple, selfish reason: that the trade of crushing seed and manufacturing oil on the sea-coast may be utterly destroyed for the benefit of crushers of seed and the manufacturers of oil in the West."

Rolling mills, chiefly eastern, which controlled the American Iron and Steel Association, almost forced through an extremely low duty on scrap iron. Such a duty would allow the mills to import huge quantities of cheap European used rails, and to reroll them in lieu of using domestic pig iron for new rails. Senator Zachariah Chandler, from the iron producing state of Michigan, demanded that the proposed duty on wrought scrap iron be quadrupled, and the duty on cast scrap be almost tripled. Lower schedules, he declared, would close the iron mines, put out every blast furnace, and mean "total ruin to the iron interests of the United States. . . . It is a bill gotten up to suit the railroad rolling-mills, and to sacrifice every other iron interest in the United States." The rolling mills won one Senate vote, but Chandler forced another, which was won by those sympathetic with the mine operators and pig iron producers. Almost all the western senators and both Pennsylvanians voted for higher duties on scrap metal. All but one senator from New England and New York voted for the low schedule.

The only tariff adjustment besides the wool and woolens bill to become law in the early postwar years was a measure passed in 1869, greatly increasing the duties on copper. Eastern smelters, who used a combination of eastern and cheap South American ores, were forced out of business by this bill, passed for the benefit of Lake Superior mine operators, whose domestic ores did not require smelting. The Lake Superior mine owners, some of whom were eastern financiers, were thus given a monopoly of the American market. They were thereby enabled to charge much higher than world prices at home and to dump their surplus abroad at much lower prices. Similar conflicts among business interests developed on tariff schedules for salt (used for scouring wool), zinc, lead, nickel, and building stones.

The wool and woolens bill of 1867, which considerably raised most schedules, has been cited as a prime example of the cooperation of business interests, because it was devised in a conference between a committee of wool growers and representatives of the National Association of Wool Manufacturers. What has generally been overlooked is the fact that the manufacturers' association, like the American Iron and Steel Association, was dominated by a well-organized segment of the industry, in this case by worsted and carpet manufacturers, whose interests conflicted with those of other important groups within the woolen industry.

Most influential of the men who negotiated the agreement for the manufacturers were Erastus B. Bigelow, president and founder of the Association and America's leading carpet manufacturer; John L. Hayes, permanent secretary of the Association; and J. Wiley Edmonds, treasurer of the giant Pacific Mills, a leading worsted producer. Hayes reported to the membership that "for six months Mr. Bigelow gave himself unremittingly to the great work . . . [and to him they] must attribute the happy results of the conference." Before this 'happy" conclusion, Hayes conceded, most woolen manufacturers "were becoming more and more disposed to look abroad for the chief supply of raw material . . . and were inclined to advocate the British policy of free trade in raw materials, including wool." Certainly the results of the conference were not so happy for manufacturers of woolen cloth, the largest item of domestic woolen output. These producers would be forced to pay much higher rates for imported raw wool than the worsted manufacturers with whom they competed. Carpet and blanket manufacturers would pay by far the lowest rates.

The largest manufacturer of wool cloth taking part in the negotiations with the growers was Edward Harris of the Harris Manufacturing Company, Woonsocket, Rhode Island. Harris later declared that he had no part in deciding the schedules, and that his name had been appended to the agreement without his knowledge or consent. Senator Henry Wilson of Massachusetts, a manufacturer of fine woolen cloth, told the Senate Finance Committee that if the new schedules were put into effect, he would have to close his factory. He subsequently declared in the Senate: "Some of the very ablest men in Massachusetts and in New England earnestly believe that this bill, so far as it concerns two thirds of the woolen manufacturers of the country, is not so good as the present tariff. [Only] the carpet manufacturers are abundantly satisfied." Wilson's statement was reinforced by other New England senators. William Sprague of Rhode Island, William P. Fessenden of Maine, and Lot M. Morrill of Maine reported similar opinions of the wool and woolens bill among the cloth manufacturers in their constituencies. Nevertheless, there was no organized opposition in Washington to the energetic Hayes or to the large number of western congressmen who were anxious to honor an agreement which gave protection to wool growers. The wool and woolens bill passed easily despite adverse votes from men like Wilson, Sumner, and Sprague who had close associations with the New England woolen industry.

Northeastern opposition to the cloth schedules continued after the passage of the bill, and in the winter of 1869–70,

Edward Harris and forty-three other New England woolen manufacturers petitioned Congress to reduce the duties on wool for cloth as low as carpet wool duties, which were one-fifth as high. On reaching Washington with this petition, Harris was informed that the wool growers and John Hayes, who said he represented three hundred companies and individuals associated with the woolen industry, had first claim on congressmen's votes. In 1889, the woolen cloth manufacturers obtained 530 signatures from wool manufacturers and dealers asking for lower duties—and again failed. Finally, in 1909, the cloth manufacturers formed a separate organization to do permanent battle in Washington with the worsted and carpet interests.

For somewhat different reasons a low-tariff sentiment similar to that in New England was also strong in New York City, by far the largest importing and financial center in the country. New York merchants, shippers, and those who financed their activities opposed tariffs which might restrict imports, while the railroad financiers protested that under the proposed tariff of 1866 the Erie and the New York Central systems alone would have to pay out annually "about two million dollars by way of protection." The New York Chamber of Commerce had opposed the Morrill bill of 1861 as "a radical change in the tariff policy of the country," but had patriotically refrained from strenuous protests as tariff rates steadily rose during the war. In listing the organization's postwar objectives, however, Secretary John Austin Stevens declared: "The principles of free, unshackled trade, which it has ever upheld, must be reaffirmed." A few months after the war's end, the *Commercial and Financial Chronicle* observed: "Signs are not wanting that the subject of Free Trade will be made the text of the next political agitation in this country." The *Journal of Commerce* also began agitating for lower tariffs soon after the war; and the introduction of the first postwar tariff bill, providing for generally increased rates, naturally brought a strong protest from the New York Chamber of Commerce.

Clearly, then, New England cotton manufacturers and many wool and other manufacturers preferred and worked for lower tariff schedules—as did most of New York's financial and mercantile community. This fact was obvious to contemporary protectionists, especially the fervent Pennsylvanians. They recognized the role New Yorkers and New Englanders played in reducing many schedules, and in defeating, by obstructionist tactics, bills of which they disapproved. A delegate from Philadelphia's Board of Trade complained to the National Board of Trade in 1869 that New England's industries had been built up behind tariff walls. "Now they are marked disciples of free trade. . . . They overlook the interests yet in their infancy. . . . Is this right? Is this just?" Henry C. Carey, leading spokesman for Pennsylvania iron, coal, and other protected interests, charged in 1867 that for twenty years, on tariff questions, "It has pleased the representatives of Massachusetts to array themselves on the side of cotton planters, slave owners, railroad monopolists."

Northeastern businessmen were thus far from united in support of high tariffs after the Civil War. Leading business interests of New England and New York believed that they lost more than they gained from high postwar tariffs. Had Reconstruction politics allowed them a choice, it seems likely that these important groups would have preferred a return to the coalition which had produced the low tariff of 1857—a coalition which included the South. Certainly they would not have opposed the return of southern representatives in order to retain high imposts.

The business interests of the Northeast were divided into fiercely competing groups not only by the tariff issue, but by currency questions as well. These conflicts were brought into the open shortly after the Civil War by attempts to contract the swollen wartime currency. Secretary of the Treasury

Hugh McCulloch's proposals for contraction, designed for quick resumption of specie payments, won a cordial response from many importers and financiers, who would gain materially from the elimination of the premium on gold and a consequent rise in the market value of government bonds. Many businessmen longed for the currency stability they believed resumption would bring. But McCulloch met with warnings and protests from other important northeastern business groups. The Philadelphia Board of Trade immediately warned against hasty action, "lest by injudicious measures and rapid contraction" the people's interests should be sacrificed. A few weeks later, the *Commercial and Financial Chronicle*, a firm advocate of hard money, was forced to admit: "There is little doubt that the depression in public confidence, of which a proof will be found in our account of the week's fluctuation in the Stock Market, is closely connected with the anticipated effects of the contraction movement of the Secretary of the Treasury."

Although only a moderate amount of currency was taken out of circulation, businessmen continued to fear that goods bought at high prices with inflated greenbacks might have to be sold at much lower prices if McCulloch were allowed to proceed with contraction. Wholesale prices fell sharply after January, 1866, confirming their fears. As general price depreciation continued through 1866 and 1867, businessmen's objections to contraction became increasingly loud and widespread. The Commercial Exchange of Philadelphia adopted a resolution in January, 1867, "That premature resumption will prove a curse and not a blessing." A vice-president of the New York Chamber of Commerce, who approved contraction, recalled "living in the midst of the clamor against that process, where almost every man I met was denouncing the Secretary and predicting ruin upon all the interests of the country unless the policy was discontinued."

Opposition to McCulloch's policy spread to Congress,

where Representative William D. Kelley of Pennsylvania called it the "road to bankruptcy." Finally, in January, 1868, Senator John Sherman of Ohio introduced legislation to end contraction. "We hear the complaint from all parts of the country," he said, "from all branches of industry . . . that industry for some reason is paralyzed and that trade and enterprise are not so well rewarded as they were. Many, perhaps erroneously, attribute all this to the contraction of the currency."

Passage of Sherman's measure, however, did not end the conflict among northeastern businessmen over currency. Most seem to have favored a stable money supply, and to have opposed currency expansion and quick resumption alike. Many of the more conservative bankers, importers, and merchants, however, continued to support an early return to specie payments. There was also an influential and vocal group of businessmen which persistently called for currency inflation. This last group found adherents among those manufacturers and merchants who sought to take advantage of great postwar demand for their products, but who had difficulty obtaining capital for plant and inventory expansion, even at extremely high interest rates. Many of those who borrowed large sums for investments in factories, mines, and railroads, were apt to favor currency expansion, which they believed would lower interest rates, raise prices, and make debts easier to pay. Radical Senator Sprague, for example, in control of a Rhode Island empire of factories, real estate, utilities, and banks, complained to the Senate that "the interest paid by the borrower today is just double what it was at the close of the War." He placed the blame on "the power centralized in New York."

It is significant that Jay Cooke, once an ardent hard money man, became something of an inflationist after he borrowed millions to build the Northern Pacific, and saw his corporation become a huge land speculator through government grants. In a letter to his brother and partner, written in 1868, Cooke called for moderate currency expansion which would keep pace "with the new habits and enlarged area of Country." "Why," he asked, "should this Grand and Glorious Country be stunted and dwarfed—its activities chilled and its very life blood curdled by these miserable 'hard coin' theories —the musty theories of a by gone age?"

Pennsylvania iron and steel men, through their representatives and periodicals, led eastern demands for an increased supply of currency. Their industry was expanding rapidly behind high tariff walls, stimulated by the postwar spurt in railroad building. Iron manufacturer Thaddeus Stevens was a leader in congressional schemes to inflate the currency. Both Stevens and Kelley of Pennsylvania supported textile manufacturer Benjamin F. Butler's resolution to pay the wartime bonds in paper rather than gold. Representative Daniel J. Morrell, a bank president as well as former general manager of the giant Cambria Iron Works in Pennsylvania, called for more circulation, and contended that under a program of inflation "capital would be less valuable, and a larger share of the increase in wealth would go to the enterprise and labor which created it." Pennsylvania iron and steel periodicals took up the fight against the bankers. "In the seaboard cities," said *Iron Age* in 1867, "the money power seeks to attain a position of irresistible control, and to subdue and subordinate to itself all the interests of industry." The lines of battle were perhaps drawn most succinctly and cogently in a speech by Representative Kelley in January, 1867. "The contest," he said, "is between the creditor and the debtor class—the men of investments and the men of enterprise."

The issue, however, was not as simple as Kelley put it. Most foreign goods were paid for with gold, not greenbacks. Customs duties were also payable in gold. As long as specie payments could be postponed, the premium on gold would remain. In the early postwar years, the premium fluctuated between 30 and 40 percent. The effect was to raise the cost of foreign goods about one-third above what their cost would be if specie resumption should occur. Monetary inflation would tend to raise the premium and consequently the price of imports even higher. This fact was not lost on the Pennsylvanians. As early as 1863, the Philadelphia Board of Trade noted that the "premium on foreign exchange adds greatly to tariff and transportation costs." In 1864, Samuel J. Reeves, iron manufacturer and chairman of the executive committee of the American Iron and Steel Association, wrote the Commissioner of Internal Revenue: "The constant advance in the price of gold has acted as so much protection to the home manufacturer above the duty. . . . The iron manufacture now finds its safety only in the high cost of gold; what is to become of it when there will be no premium on gold?" The answer, so far as many iron manufacturers were concerned, was to retain the premium on gold.

The significance of the Pennsylvanians' currency policies was obvious to importers, financiers, and many manufacturers in New York and New England. Most of these favored hard money and low tariffs. The Boston Board of Trade's "Wool Report" for 1863 noted the effect of the gold premium on the price of wool. New York merchants protested that the high price of gold seriously discouraged imports, and the city's Chamber of Commerce adopted a resolution charging that "powerful interests are striving to perpetuate the existing depreciation of the currency."

When contraction was abruptly ended and tariff reform failed, in 1867–68, some businessmen in New York and New England felt that the government's policies were falling under the control of high tariff and paper money men. On the other hand, Henry C. Carey, spokesman for Pennsylvania protectionists, charged that New England, aided by New Yorkers, was attempting to create a monopoly in money and manufacturing. One instrument of the monopolists, said Carey, was a low tariff, which New England manufacturers could afford because of their low interest charges and modern machinery, and which they used to ruin domestic competition and to obtain cheap foreign raw materials to aid New England producers. A second instrument, he continued, was the banking system—"a great money monopoly for the especial benefit of the Trading States." Even with this monopoly, Carey complained, the traders wished to contract the currency, further reducing the pittance allowed Pennsylvania and further raising interest charges manufacturers would have to pay. Either the New Englanders would change their ways, he warned, or they would be compelled to do so by a combination of southern, western, and middle states, in which Pennsylvania would take the lead. In reply, cotton manufacturer Edward Atkinson "rejoiced" at this analysis of New England's advantage, and assured Carey that henceforth the New England representatives would support the low tariff and hard money policies even more strongly. Instead of fearing the threatened combination of sections under Pennsylvania's leadership against those policies, he prophesied that New England would join with the South and the West in promoting them.

Both Carey and Atkinson overstated the unity of New England manufacturers, oversimplified the varied and conflicting interests in the West, and conjectured about the probable political and economic alignments of the postwar South. Nevertheless, both were more realistic than historians who have explained northeastern leadership of Radical Reconstruction in terms of a unified northeastern business interest anxious to keep the South out of the Union in order to protect high tariffs and hard money.

Nor can the direction and support which northeastern representatives gave to Radical Reconstruction be accurately explained as an attempt to "make easy the road for northern economic penetration and exploitation of the South." Few important northeastern capitalists had any desire to place their money in a war-torn, unsettled region. Eventually, northerners invested huge sums in southern factories, mines, railroads, and real estate; but it is significant that only a small number did so as long as Radicals controlled southern state legislatures.

Many southern leaders and periodicals recognized the need for northern capital after the Civil War, and numerous cordial invitations were extended. That such invitations were futile was obvious to businessmen, North and South. "We want capital attracted to the South," said the *Commercial and Financial Chronicle* of New York City, "and this cannot be, so long as the States are under semi-military rule." And from the South *De Bow's Review* echoed, "It is idle to ask capital to venture until order is restored." South Carolina exempted manufacturers from all state and local taxation, but failed to attract northern capital partly because of the uncertainties of Reconstruction. Thomas W. Conway, a former Freedmen's Bureau official, who toured the North in 1866 trying to induce businessmen to make southern investments, reported to the New York Chamber of Commerce, which had encouraged his mission: "The substantial men met by me in all parts of the country are sick of the delay in regard to the settlement of our national political difficulties." Until such settlement occurred, he predicted, there would be continued uncertainty and violence in the South, and poor prospects for northern investment.

Even Pennsylvania's Representative William D. Kelley, who was both a Radical leader and an enthusiastic advocate of northern investments in the postwar South, soon found that Radical Reconstruction interfered with southern industrial growth. In March, 1868, Kelley demanded immediate readmission of Alabama—a potential economic paradise, he said, whose wealth was "paralyzed" while Reconstruction ran its violent course. Thaddeus Stevens, less interested in southern industrial development than was Kelley, fought against his colleague's haste, insisting that Alabama must first guarantee the suffrage rights of Negroes.

New England cotton manufacturers, dealers, and shippers

feared that northerners' refusal to send their capital south would result in an insufficient cotton crop. Edward S. Tobey, Boston cotton merchant and manufacturer, recommended that the Freedmen's Bureau be authorized to take over the role of private capital in organizing Negro labor for cotton cultivation. The South's deficiency of capital, Tobey told the Boston Board of Trade in a famous speech in November, 1865, was proved by "frequent applications from Southern men to Northern capitalists to invest in cotton lands at low prices." It would be ideal if private investors could supply this want; but capital, Tobey observed, "is seldom placed by its possessors where society is disorganized and life and property comparatively unprotected by a stable and efficient government." The Board approved Tobey's suggestion.

A few months after Tobey's speech, however, the New Englanders' plans were changed by a sudden shift in the cotton market. The southern cotton crop was larger than expected. Furthermore, the English, with new machinery and methods for manufacturing with cheap Indian Surat cotton, had become increasingly less dependent upon American producers. New England manufacturers and dealers were caught with large supplies of cotton as the price dropped almost 40 percent in the first four months of 1866. The momentary interest New England businessmen had shown in Reconstruction legislation dropped with the price of cotton. The Boston Board of Trade's "Review of the Boston Market for the Year 1867," declared: "Business men, generally, are loud in their complaints against the course of legislation for two years past. Important interests have been neglected by Congress, and too much time has been wasted on questions which only led to discord and bad feeling in the different branches of the Government."

Most large northern investors, instead of being concerned over the difficulties of investing in the South, turned their attention to the many lucrative opportunities elsewhere—in

Minnesota timberlands, Michigan iron and copper mines, Pennsylvania coal and oil, and railroads in almost every state. Significantly, the Pennsylvania Railroad, with abundant capital and great influence in Congress, did not attempt to create its "Southern empire" until Radical Reconstruction was nearing its conclusion. Until 1871, the Pennsylvania preferred to take advantage of investment opportunities in the Northwest. When Thomas A. Scott, who guided the railroad's expansion, decided to move South, he dealt with Conservative governors and legislators in the South as successfully as he had with Democrats and Republicans in the North and West.

Only one important northeastern business group was strongly attracted by investment opportunities in the South immediately after the war: New York financiers, the true "masters of capital," who had long-standing commercial ties with the South, and had sufficient funds to risk large amounts in a turbulent area. New York merchants, shippers, and financiers were as interested as Bostonians in large postwar cotton crops, but they emphatically disagreed with the Boston proposal to use the Freedmen's Bureau to grow cotton. When Tobey's plan was put before the executive committee of the New York Chamber of Commerce, the committee reported: "Our best reliance for attaining the desired end is to present to capitalists this most inviting field."

Insofar as northern capital was invested in southern railroads, both before and immediately after the war, most of it was provided by New Yorkers. A recent study shows, for example, that of some 280 directors of twenty-five major southern lines in 1867–68 only eleven were northerners, and ten of these were from New York. Two important New York investors in southern railroads were elected to Congress and were thus in a position to speak publicly about Reconstruction legislation. One of the two was William E. Dodge, metal importer, iron manufacturer, land speculator, railroad investor, and president of the New York Chamber of Commerce; the other was William W. Phelps, director of four large banks and eight railroads. The evidence suggests that the opinions these men expressed of Radical Reconstruction were typical of those held by New York's financial leaders.

When Thaddeus Stevens' bill for dividing the South into military districts reached the floor of the House in January, 1867, Dodge voted against it; and in explaining his vote he told his Republican colleagues: "I claim to be as loyal as any other man . . . [but] if these southern states are still to be kept year after year in this state of disquietude we at the North, sympathizing with them in our social and business relations, must to a certain extent suffer with them." Furthermore, said Dodge, businessmen believed that this bill would result in continued high taxation to support an army of occupation in ten states. And in the debate on Butler's civil rights bill in 1875, Phelps—one of three Republicans to vote against it in the House—expressed sentiments long held in the New York financial community. "You are trying to do," he said, "what it seems to me this House everlastingly tries in one form or another to do—to legislate against human nature. You are trying to legislate against human prejudice, and you cannot do it. . . . Let us end this cruel policy."

Many New York financiers made public their support of President Andrew Johnson in his battle against the Radicals. When Johnson vetoed the bill for the continuation of the Freedmen's Bureau, in February, 1866, a mass meeting to celebrate the veto was arranged by the city's business leaders, and a committee was sent to Washington to offer the President New York's aid. Among those on the committee were Moses Taylor, dean of New York bankers, and William B. Astor, known as the "landlord of New York." Six months later, when Johnson visited New York as part of his "swing around the circle," a grand dinner was given for him at Delmonico's. Chairman of arrangements was Alexander T. Stewart, the "dry goods king"; treasurer for the dinner was Henry

Clews, probably second only to Jay Cooke as a dealer in government bonds, and second to none as a dealer in southern railroad securities. A large number of New York's leading businessmen attended the dinner. This was followed on September 17, 1866, by a giant National Union celebration to demonstrate the city's support of the President at the height of his crucial campaign against the Radicals. The reception committee for this impressive meeting included Stewart, Taylor, Clews, Edwards Pierrepont, and August Belmont. Among those who gave public notice of their approval of Johnson's policies by allowing their names to be listed as vice-presidents of the meeting were such well-known financiers as William H. Aspinwall, Cornelius Vanderbilt, John J. Cisco, and Henry Grinnell, as well as numerous important merchants and manufacturers.

Similar indications of support or approval of the presidential reconstruction program rather than that of Congress also came from the New York Chamber of Commerce and from the financial press. In 1866 the Chamber of Commerce adopted a resolution, introduced by the banker brother of Radical leader Roscoe Conkling, which expressed the hope that Reconstruction "may be everywhere signalized by magnanimity and clemency and that it may nowhere be stained by a single act which will be condemned as needlessly harsh or revengeful." A copy of this resolution was sent to Washington as encouragement to the President. As early as July, 1865, *Hunt's Merchants Magazine* and the *Commercial and Financial Chronicle*—two of the leading business journals of the period—had applauded Johnson's program for the speedy restoration of the seceded states. As the Radicals gathered their forces in the fall of 1865, the *American Railroad Journal* announced that Reconstruction "is going on as well as could be hoped. The President . . . sets the example of kindness and benignity and a large majority of both parties . . . are evidently disposed to support his policy." And in January, 1866,

[105]

the *Journal of Commerce* proclaimed its support of Johnson.

From evidence such as this, the reconstruction program of the Radicals cannot be explained as an organized attempt by the business interests of the Northeast either to preserve and promote their own economic advantages or to obtain protection for economic exploitation of the South. Actually, northeastern businessmen had no unified economic program to promote. Important business groups within the region opposed each other on almost every significant economic question, and this lack of a common interest was likewise reflected in the economic views of Radical congressmen. Thaddeus Stevens, for example, dominant Radical leader in the House, was a fervent protectionist and a proponent of paper money inflation; Charles Sumner, Senate Radical leader, spoke and voted for lower tariff schedules and for resumption of specie payments. With both the businessmen and the legislators thus divided on economic issues, and with the New York merchants and financiers—who were in a position to gain most from economic exploitation of the South—definitely critical of the Radicals' program, it seems clear that factors other than the economic interests of the Northeast must be used to explain the motivation and aims of Radical Reconstruction.

5

THE "CONSPIRACY THEORY" OF THE FOURTEENTH AMENDMENT

Howard Jay Graham

"No state shall . . . deprive any person of life, liberty, or property without due process of law, nor deny to any person . . . the equal protection of the laws."
SECTION 1, FOURTEENTH AMENDMENT

Historians who emphasized economic motivation among the Radical Republicans placed considerable emphasis on the enactment of the Fourteenth Amendment to the Constitution. Although ostensibly designed to protect the civil rights of Negroes, this amendment was subsequently employed to afford legal protection to corporations. Some historians charged that this was precisely what its Radical authors had in mind. Howard Jay Graham examines the origins and validity of this "conspiracy" view.

In an argument before the Supreme Court of the United States in 1882 Roscoe Conkling, a former member of the Joint Congressional Committee which in 1866 drafted the Fourteenth Amendment, produced for the first time the manuscript journal of the committee, and by means of extensive quotations and pointed comment conveyed the impression that he and his colleagues in drafting the due process and equal protection clauses intentionally used the word "person" in order to include corporations. "At the time the Fourteenth Amendment was ratified," he declared, "individuals and joint stock companies were appealing for congressional and administrative protection against invidious and discriminating State and local taxes. One instance was that of an express company, whose stock was owned largely by citizens of the State of New York . . ." The unmistakable inference was that the Joint Committee had taken cognizance of these appeals and had drafted its text with particular regard for corporations.

Coming from a man who had twice declined a seat on the Supreme Bench, who spoke from firsthand knowledge, and who submitted a manuscript record in support of his stand, so dramatic an argument could not fail to make a profound impression. Within the next few years the Supreme Court began broadening its interpretation of the Fourteenth Amendment, and early in 1886 it unanimously affirmed Conkling's proposition, namely that corporations were "persons" within the meaning of the equal protection clause. It is literally true therefore that Roscoe Conkling's argument sounded the death knell of the narrow "Negro-race theory" of the Fourteenth Amendment expounded by Justice Miller in the *Slaughter House* cases. By doing this it cleared the way for the modern development of due process of law and the corresponding expansion of the Court's discretionary powers over social and economic legislation. Viewed in perspective, the argument is one of the landmarks in American constitutional history, an important turning point in our social and economic development.

Conkling's argument has figured prominently in historical writing since 1914 when B. B. Kendrick unearthed and edited the manuscript copy of the Journal which Conkling used in court. Checking the record in the light of his major propositions, historians became convinced of the fundamental truth of Conkling's story. Repeatedly, it appeared from the Journal, the Joint Committee had distinguished in its drafts in the use of the words "person" and "citizen." Under no circumstances could the terms have been confused. Moreover, as the committee had persistently used the term "person" in those clauses which applied to property rights and the term "citizen" in those clauses which applied to political rights, the force of this distinction seemed plain: corporations as artificial persons had indeed been among the intended beneficiaries of the Fourteenth Amendment. Convinced on this point, historians developed an interesting theory: the drafting of the Fourteenth Amendment had assumed something of the character of a conspiracy, with the due process and equal protection clauses inserted as *double entendres*. Laboring ostensibly in the interests of the freedmen and of the "loyal white citizens of the South," the astute Republican lawyers who made up the majority of the committee had intentionally used language which gave corporations and business interests generally increased judicial protection as against state legislatures.

What appeared to be corroboration for this viewpoint was presently found in the speeches of Representative John A. Bingham, the Ohio congressman and railroad lawyer who almost alone of the members of the Joint Committee had been responsible for the phraseology of Section One. Bingham, it appeared both from the Journal and the debates on the floor of the House, had at all times shown a zealous determination to secure to "all persons" everywhere "equal protection in the rights of property." Moreover, he had evinced an extraordinary preference for the due process clause and had developed and defended its phraseology in most vigorous fashion. As no other member of the Joint Committee, or of Congress, gave evidence of a similar desire to protect property rights, and none manifested his partiality for the due process clause, it seemed logical to conclude that Bingham's purposes had in fact been far more subtle and comprehensive than was ever appreciated at the time. Bingham had been the mastermind who "put over" this draft upon an unsuspecting country. The fact that he had tried and failed to secure the inclusion of a "just compensation" clause in Section One as still another restraint upon the states' powers over property, and the fact that in 1871, five years after the event, he declared he had framed the section "letter for letter and syllable for syllable" merely served to strengthen these suspicions.

Impressed by this cumulative evidence, and alive to its historical implications, Charles A. and Mary R. Beard, in 1927, developed in their *Rise of American Civilization* what is still, a decade later, the most precise statement of the conspiracy theory. Undocumented, and with conclusions implicit rather than explicit, the Beards' thesis was this: Bingham, "a shrewd . . . and successful railroad lawyer, . . . familiar with the possibilities of jurisprudence," had had much broader purposes than his colleagues. Whereas they were "bent on establishing the rights of Negroes," he was "determined to take in the whole range of national economy." Toward this end he had drafted the due process and equal protection clauses and forced them upon the committee by persistent efforts. Quoting Bingham's speeches and Conkling's argument in support of the view that corporations had been among the intended beneficiaries of the draft, the authors concluded:

> In this spirit, Republican lawmakers restored to the Constitution the protection for property which Jacksonian judges had whittled away and made it more sweeping in its scope by forbidding states, in blanket terms, to deprive any person of life, liberty, or property without due process of law. By a few words *skillfully chosen* every act of every state and local government which touched adversely the rights of persons and property was made subject to review and liable to annulment by the Supreme Court at Washington.*

Thus, while the Beards nowhere expressly state that Bingham was guilty of a form of conspiracy, this is nonetheless a fair

* Italics added.

inference from their account, and it is one which has repeatedly been drawn. Numerous writers, accepting the Beards' account and popularizing it, have supplied more explicit interpretations. Thus, E. S. Bates, in his *Story of Congress*, declares that Bingham and Conkling in inserting the due process phraseology, "smuggled" into the Fourteenth Amendment "a capitalist joker."

Despite widespread acceptance and a prestige which derives from the Beards' sponsorship, the conspiracy theory has not gone unchallenged. Numerous writers have expressed varying degrees of disapproval and skepticism. Constitutional historians in particular appear reluctant to accept its implications, although they, no more than the sponsoring school of social historians, have as yet presented their case in documented detail. One thus observes the curious paradox of a theory which cuts across the whole realm of American constitutional and economic history and which is itself a subject for increasing speculation and controversy, yet which has developed piecemeal, without systematic formulation or criticism.

How extraordinary certain aspects of this situation are may be judged from the fact that one is now left wholly in the dark as to the nature and degree of conspiratorial intent imputed to Bingham and his colleagues. Is one to believe, for example, that these men determined from the first to devise phraseology which included corporations? Or simply that they later perceived it possible, or advantageous, to do so? Again, what type of protection did the framers contemplate within the meanings of the due process phrase? Protection in the modern substantive sense? Or simply protection against arbitrary procedure? If simply the latter was intended, the "conspiracy" was scarcely worthy of the name, for to have used "person" and "due process" in this manner would have been natural for any well-informed lawyer of 1866, whatever may be said of the understanding of the layman. On the other hand, to have applied due process substantively with regard to corporations in 1866 would have been a thoroughly revolutionary step, even for a lawyer. For this reason it is a substantive usage that is most consistent with the theory. In both of these issues the implied difference in motive is great; and likewise the implied ambiguity in the theory. The matter of motive and intent would seem to be too fundamental an element of conspiracy to leave in so unsatisfactory a state.

It is the purpose of this chapter to re-examine the conspiracy theory and to determine, insofar as possible, the extent to which it meets certain essential conditions.

CONKLING'S ARGUMENT RE-EXAMINED

A priori, there are two major reasons for being skeptical of a declaration that the framers of the Fourteenth Amendment aimed to aid business interests when they devised the due process and equal protection clauses. First, as we have just seen, such a declaration virtually demands as its major condition that John A. Bingham and the other members of the Joint Committee regarded due process of law as a restraint upon the substance of legislation at the early date of 1866, whereas due process was at this time, with a few striking exceptions, merely a limitation upon procedure. The theory thus presupposes that the drafters assumed what was really an extraordinary viewpoint: it endows them with remarkable insight and perspicacity. The second objection is that, as an apparent explanation of the committee's choice of the word "person" in preference to "citizen," the theory ignores the fact that "person" was really the term employed in the Fifth Amendment, the phraseology of which Bingham simply copied. Further, in line with this last point is the fact that "persons," as a generic term and as a device employed in the original Constitution to refer to Negro slaves, clearly included "persons" of the Negro race and may logically have been preferred for this reason, since grave doubt existed as to whether Negroes were "citizens," and troublesome problems of definition arose if one tried to speak of them in still more precise terms.

The obstacles which these facts throw in the way of the conspiracy theory are at once apparent. Granted that Bingham's speeches reveal a solicitude for property rights not found in the speeches of his colleagues, granted that his drafts of the amendment were couched in much broader language than those of his associates—in language which today "takes in the whole range of national economy"—still, it hardly follows that Bingham in 1866 was thinking of corporations as the beneficiaries of his drafts, nor that he regarded due process in the modern substantive sense. He may, conceivably, have used the words "any person" merely as a sure means of including Negroes as well as whites; he may also have used "due process of law" as a sure means of guaranteeing fair trial and fair procedure to all natural persons. In fact, so long as these were the prevailing usages down to 1866 one is hardly warranted in attributing a more subtle or comprehensive purpose to Bingham without definite, positive evidence. To do otherwise is to risk interpreting Bingham's purposes in the light of subsequent events.

So long as these fundamental objections place serious obstacles in the path of the theory, the question at once arises whether the direct statements made by Conkling in 1882 are alone sufficient to sustain it. If they are not, search must be made for new evidence, and the whole problem of the circumstantial materials in Bingham's speeches must be thoroughly canvassed.

An examination of Conkling's argument properly becomes the starting point of our inquiry. To facilitate later discussion, an analytical abstract of his argument will be presented:

1. Conkling's basic proposition, inferred at the outset, was that the committee had had two distinct and clearly defined purposes. The first of these "related chiefly to the freedmen of the South" and dealt with the "subject of suffrage, the ballot,

and representation in Congress." The second was broader and far more important, namely, to frame an amendment which would secure universal protection in the rights of life, liberty, and property.

2. Having drawn this division in the agenda, he now declared, and offered extensive quotations from the Journal designed to show, that before the committee undertook the second of these tasks—i.e., the task of framing what later became the due process and equal protection clauses—it had in fact "completely disposed of" and "lost all jurisdiction and power over" the first, i.e., "the portion which did in truth chiefly relate to the freedmen of the South."

3. His quotations from the Journal were also designed to show that the committee had throughout its deliberations repeatedly distinguished between "citizens" and "persons," and that it had in general used "citizens" in the clauses designed to secure political rights and privileges (i.e., in what later became the privileges and immunities clause) and had used "persons" in the clause designed to secure "equal protection in the rights of life, liberty, and property."

4. He even quoted from the minutes to show that on one occasion he himself had moved to strike out of a draft "citizens" and substitute "persons."

5. Most important of all, he gave his listeners to understand —even emphasized the fact—that the draft of the equal protection clause as originally reported by a subcommittee had itself specified "citizens," and it is questionable, from a close reading of the argument, whether his listeners may not have gained the impression that it was he, Conkling, who had been responsible (by the previously mentioned motion) for the substitution of "persons" for "citizens" in this clause.

6. Without laboring his point, and relying on his listeners to recall that in the final draft of the amendment the privileges and immunities clause applied to "citizens" and the due proc-

ess and equal protection clauses to "persons," Conkling asked in conclusion if this record did not show that "the Committee understood what was meant" when it used these different terms.

7. Apparently to remove all doubt on this score, Conkling casually added, "at the time the Fourteenth Amendment was ratified . . . individuals and joint stock companies were appealing for congressional and administrative protection against invidious and discriminating State and local taxes"—inferring that the committee had taken cognizance of this situation and that a desire to protect corporations had been the real explanation for maintaining the distinction between "citizens" and "persons."

Two features of Conkling's argument, which in many respects is a masterpiece of inference and suggestion, are now to be stressed. First, nowhere does Conkling explicitly say that the committee regarded corporations as "persons"; nowhere does he say that the members framed the due process and equal protection clauses with corporations definitely in mind. These are simply the casual yet unmistakable impressions gained from dozens of hints, intimations, and distinctions made throughout his argument. The second feature, somewhat surprising in the light of the first, is that in his conclusion Conkling not only failed to press his points but, on the contrary, now substantially waived them. "I have sought to convince your honors," he said, "that the men who framed . . . the Fourteenth Amendment *must have known* the meaning and force of the term 'persons,'" and in the next sentence he spoke significantly of "this surmise." Later, in his peroration, he freely admitted the difficulties of the proposition he had maintained. "The statesman," he declared, "has no horoscope which maps the measureless spaces of a nation's life, and lays down in advance all the bearings of its career." Finally, he concluded in this vein, "Those who devised the Fourteenth

Amendment *may have builded better than they knew . . . To some of them, the sunset of life may have given mystical lore.*" *

These quotations reveal an equivocal and indecisive element in Conkling's argument, and they provoke various questions. Why, if he had definite knowledge that the Joint Committee really framed the amendment to include corporations, did he adopt this peculiar, tenuous, and indirect means of saying so? Why, after laboring to give the impression of intent, did he himself at times seem to belie that impression by use of such indecisive language? Was this simply a lawyer's caution, a desire for understatement? Was it because he felt that suggestion might here prove a stronger weapon than detail? Was it because he feared too concrete an account of unwritten history might harm his cause? Or was it because of some inherent weakness—even absence—of fact in his argument? A critical reader must puzzle over these questions and a cautious one will seek for tangible answers. In this connection several tests come to mind. Does Conkling's argument bear evidence of a scrupulous regard for facts, first in its major propositions, second in its essential details? Is it inherently consistent? Does it bear evidence of care and good faith in quotation from the Journal?

Application of these tests to the more than twenty pages of Conkling's argument leads to some startling discoveries. Not only does it appear as a result of such an inquiry that Conkling suppressed pertinent facts and misrepresented others, but it is hard to avoid the conclusion that he deliberately misquoted the Journal and even so arranged his excerpts as to give listeners a false impression of the record and of his own relation thereto. In framing a bill of particulars, the following may be set down in refutation of his major points:

1. With regard to his fundamental proposition that the Joint Committee had been charged with two distinct, clearly

* Italics added.

defined purposes and that these two purposes had at all times been kept separate and distinct, it is sufficient to say that Conkling himself quoted a resolution in the Journal which effectively disposed of his point. This resolution, introduced in the Joint Committee by Senator Fessenden on January 12, 1866, reads as follows: "Resolved that . . . the *insurgent States* cannot . . . be allowed to participate in the Government until the basis of representation shall have been modified, *and* the rights of all persons amply secured . . . ." * Obviously this resolution specified two tasks for the Joint Committee. But the important fact, not mentioned by Conkling and even disguised by him, was that it specified both tasks with regard to the "insurgent States." This being the case, it is hard to see how the two purposes could ever have been "separate and distinct" in the sense which Conkling contended, and harder still to believe that only those portions of the Fourteenth Amendment relating to "representation, the suffrage," etc., dealt exclusively with conditions in the South. The "insurgent States" reference practically destroys Conkling's case at the outset. His argument is rendered suspect by one of his own citations from the Journal. Only by laying emphasis upon Fessenden's use of the word "persons" in this resolution did Conkling steer listeners past this flaw in his case.

2. Auxiliary to his main proposition, Conkling was at great pains to show that the text of Bingham's amendment, which originally read "Congress shall have power . . . to secure to all persons equal protection in the enjoyment of life, liberty and property," had been dealt with by the committee as if members had at all times regarded it as distinct in both subject matter and purpose from the other amendments dealing with suffrage and representation. His particular point in this connection was that on January 24, 1866, the Bingham Amendment had been referred to a different subcommittee than the one that had considered the other drafts. What Conk-

* Italics added.

ling neglected to say was that when Bingham originally introduced this draft on January 12, 1866, it had been referred, at Bingham's own motion, to "the sub-committee on the basis of representation"—the same subcommittee, in short, which received the other drafts. This appears to be a damaging omission, for it suggests that Bingham himself may have regarded his draft merely as one which, applying to "the insurgent States," "amply secured the rights of all persons," thus, perhaps, effectuating the second purpose outlined in the Fessenden resolution.

Whether this last interpretation is warranted or not, failure to mention the fact that Bingham's draft had originally been referred to the "sub-committee on the basis of representation" led Conkling into embarrassing difficulties—difficulties from which he extricated himself only by strategem. We need here say no more than that at one point in his argument Conkling quoted this passage from the Journal: "The Committee proceeded to the consideration of the following [i.e., Bingham] amendment . . . *proposed by the sub-committee on the basis of representation.*" * Obviously, to have read the text in this form would have been to risk wiping out the very impression which he was laboring to establish, namely that the Bingham Amendment was a thing apart, and one dealt with by a separate subcommittee—the "sub-committee on the powers of Congress." If we judge by his printed argument, Conkling extricated himself from this hole by pausing after the word "sub-committee"—i.e., by inserting a comma in the written text—so that the reported passage reads as follows:

The Committee proceeded to the consideration of the following amendment . . . proposed by the sub-committee, on the basis of representation: "Congress shall have power to make all laws necessary and proper to secure to all citizens of the United States in each State the same political rights and privileges, and *to all persons in every State equal protection in the enjoyment of life, liberty, and property.*"

* Italics added.

[118]

By thus splitting off the final phrase, and relating it not to its proper antecedent "sub-committee" but to the text of the amendment which followed, Conkling salvaged his case. The fact that intrinsically the Bingham Amendment had nothing whatever to do with "the basis of representation," that it thus belied Conkling's motivating phrase, was probably not perceived by his listeners for the reason that this point was inconsequential to his main argument, and that in the reading of the text he laid great stress on Bingham's use of the word "persons," thus directing thought in other channels.

3. Turning now to Conkling's second proposition, one finds the evidence almost as damaging. Again and again Conkling intimated that the real reason Bingham and the Joint Committee used the term "persons" instead of "citizens" had been to include corporations. Close examination not only fails to substantiate this statement but even provides an alternative explanation. One discovers the word "persons" used in numerous contexts which suggest that the real reason for preferring the term to "citizens" was that the freedmen, as natural beings and former slaves, were unquestionably to be regarded as "persons," whereas numerous complications arose whenever one attempted to speak of them, or even to define them, as "citizens."

Nowhere is this shown to better advantage than in a draft of an amendment which Conkling himself sponsored, and from which, with rare audacity, he quoted in argument. "Whenever in any State," he read, making clear that the text was his own, "civil or political rights or privileges shall be denied or abridged on account of race or color, *all persons of such race or color shall be excluded from the basis of representation.*" One naturally wonders whether we do not have here a clue to the intended scope of the term "persons," and to the fundamental reason for choosing it. Surely the reference to "all persons of such race or color" suggests an explanation quite as plausible as Conkling's. It does not preclude the possibility of mixed or compound motives in determining the use of the term; it simply cautions against assuming that a single explanation is necessarily adequate and that other possibilities may be ignored.

4. Doubtless the most impressive point made by Conkling, so far as the Justices of the Supreme Court were concerned, was to the effect that Bingham's Amendment, as originally reported by the subcommittee, used the word "citizens" throughout; "persons," he emphasized by implication, appeared nowhere in the text. What gave real significance to this point was that Conkling had earlier emphasized that the text as originally introduced by Bingham, and ordered referred to the subcommittee, read, "Congress shall have power . . . to secure to all *persons* equal protection in the enjoyment of life, liberty and property." Recalling this emphasis, listeners could hardly have failed to have been impressed. For not only did it follow that the subcommittee had stricken out "persons" and substituted "citizens" in this early draft of what eventually developed into the equal protection and due process clauses, but it followed further, since in the ultimate form both clauses applied to "persons," that at some stage or other—Conkling did not say when, or touch directly upon this point—the broader of the two terms had been reinstated. Obviously the mere fact of these successive deletions and insertions justified a view that the committee had framed these clauses carefully, with utmost discrimination. And Conkling's statement regarding the joint stock companies provided a plausible reason.

To remove the underpinning from this part of the argument—and virtually from Conkling's entire case—one has to say merely that neither the subcommittee, nor anyone, at any time or under any circumstances, so far as the historical record indicates, ever used the word "citizen" in any draft of the equal protection or due process clauses. "Persons" was the term used by Bingham; "persons" was the term reported by the subcommittee; "persons" was the term discussed and approved by the Committee as a whole. Conkling misquoted the

Journal in his argument, and it is almost impossible to believe that he did not do this intentionally. The reason is that he paused, repeated, and rhetorically underscored the misquoted word "citizen" so that the passage, as it appears in the printed argument, reads as follows:

"Now come the independent article:
'Article—. Congress shall have power to make all laws necessary and proper to secure to all citizens of the United States, in every State, the same political rights and privileges; and to all citizens in every State.'
"I beg your Honors to remark that the term here employed was 'all citizens in every State' . . . 'equal protection in the enjoyment of life, liberty, and property.' "

So long as the presumption must be strongly against a mere lapse on Conkling's part, the question necessarily arises what he could obtain by so bold a move. The reader must remember in this connection that Conkling predicated his entire case on the distinction between the meaning of the terms "citizen" and "person," and that the effect therefore was immeasurably to strengthen his hand. Another aspect of the matter is that it is questionable from a reading of the argument, particularly from the standpoint of one hearing it delivered orally for the first time, whether, in the passage immediately following, listeners may not have received the impression that Conkling himself was responsible for the substitution of the word "persons" for "citizens" in this embryo equal protection-due process clause. The reason for this belief is that Conkling went on to quote excerpts from the Journal which showed that he had himself moved to substitute "persons" for "citizens" in one draft, and that he stated, but did not emphasize, that this motion to substitute was really with reference to one of the earlier quoted articles relating to representation and suffrage. The question, therefore, is whether his listeners—who must have been highly impressed by his dramatic underscoring of the misquoted word "citizens," and who were probably still wondering when the word "persons" had eventually been reinstated—did not jump to the conclusion, unwarranted by a close reading of the argument, that Conkling was himself the man responsible for this change. In view of these circumstances, it can be seen that Conkling undoubtedly gained a great deal from this part of his argument. Whether, and to what extent, his gains were the result of deliberate plan and artifice can never be known with certainty—and one must recognize some of the same pitfalls in imputing plot and design to Conkling as we have already mentioned in the case of Bingham *—but the present writer is convinced that the foregoing evidence is most reasonably explained as a deliberate misuse of facts. To say this is not to say that the Joint Committee may not have regarded corporations as "persons"; that, indeed, is a question which depends upon many things. It is simply to say that Conkling could not prove his proposition from the Journal itself. In making the attempt, therefore, he resorted to misquotation and unfair arrangement of facts. He made free use of inference and conjecture, and above all he imposed upon the good faith of listeners who undoubtedly had a high regard for his veracity.

In summing up, it appears that the portions of Conkling's argument which rest upon quotations from the Journal of the Joint Committee by no means sustain the impressions he drew. The whole argument, in fact, is found to be little better than a shell of inference built up in the course of attempted proof of inconsequential points. Not one but both of his major propositions collapse under weight of facts which he himself cited. Misquotation, equivocal statements, and specious distinctions suggest an inherently weak case—even point toward deliberate fabrication of arguments. All in all, the showing is so poor

---

* There is the important difference, however, that Conkling undoubtedly had a strong motive for misleading the Supreme Court, whereas the chief question must always be whether Bingham had any motive for desiring to aid corporations.

that one is forced to consider whether Conkling's personal reputation, and the advantage which he enjoyed as the first member of the Joint Committee to produce and make use of the Journal, did not account to large extent for his contemporary success, whereas the continued credence given his argument has been the result of these factors plus the natural tendency for us today to assume foresight in those matters which are reasonably clear to hindsight, it being forgotten that as applied to historical interpretation this is often an unwarranted—even dangerous—assumption.

Practically, the only point in Conkling's argument not so far discredited is his statement that "at the time the Fourteenth Amendment was ratified, joint stock companies were appealing for congressional and administrative protection against invidious and discriminating State and local taxes. One instance was that of an express company whose stock was owned largely by citizens of the State of New York. . . ." This is an explicit statement, and one which merits thorough investigation, but it must be stressed that by itself it is scarcely adequate proof of Conkling's point. Corporations may indeed have petitioned the Thirty-ninth Congress for relief, but alone this fact proves little. Without direct, contemporaneous evidence that the drafters of the Fourteenth Amendment devised its phraseology with corporations in mind, or at least without evidence that they regarded it as benefiting corporations, once drafted, the existence of these parallel occurrences may have been simply coincidence—a coincidence which Conkling, arguing long after the event and at a time when corporations were moving heaven and earth to broaden judicial interpretation of "persons" and "due process of law," may have shrewdly determined to capitalize. In view of the liberties he appears to have taken with other facts, in view of his temptations to stretch the record and of his unique opportunities for doing so, above all, in view of the dangers of relying upon purely circumstantial evidence to establish intent in cases

where intent presumes an exceptional viewpoint and perspicacity, one is warranted, at least until it is proved that
Bingham had a substantive conception of due process, in regarding this portion of Conkling's argument as essentially
immaterial.

THE EVIDENCE IN THE CONGRESSIONAL DEBATES

It becomes increasingly apparent that the conspiracy theory
can hardly attain satisfactory status until precise knowledge is
had of what the framers themselves conceived to be the meaning of the language they employed. Conkling's argument and
the circumstantial record of the Journal prove inconclusive
and therefore inadequate on this point. It remains to assay the
evidence which is found in the congressional debates of 1866.

The impressive thing here, of course, is the utter lack of
contemporaneous discussion of these clauses which are today
considered all-important. Hundreds of pages of speeches in
the *Congressional Globe* contain only the scantest reference
to due process and equal protection. Two opposing explanations will perhaps be offered in this connection. Critics of the
conspiracy theory will doubtless hold that dearth of discussion
indicates a universal understanding that these clauses were to
protect the freedmen in their civil rights. Sponsors, on the
other hand, may argue that silence indicates a universal misunderstanding of what were in fact the "real" purposes of the
framers.

It is desirable because of this double-edged character of the
argument from silence, and because of the peculiar dangers
inherent in its use as a proof of "conspiracy," that we digress a
moment at this point in order to avoid later confusion.

So long as intent or design is one major element in any
conspiracy, and so long as silence or secrecy is the other, it
readily follows that if the framers of the Fourteenth Amendment intended to benefit corporations, and yet failed to make

known their intentions—which otherwise were not suspected —then the framers were guilty of conspiracy. In short, intent plus silence in a situation of this kind equals conspiracy. When this formula is applied to the present case, it follows further, since the fact of silence is not questioned, that the actual intent of the drafters to afford corporations relief is the only point at issue. To prove intent is to prove the conspiracy theory. But it is precisely at this point that confusion arises. Since silence, along with intent, is one of the major elements of conspiracy, there is a natural tendency to use it not only to prove the theory, but also, by a confusion of purposes and ideas, to prove intent. This is done generally in the roundabout fashion of assuming that silence is evidence of secrecy, and that secrecy in turn is evidence of intent. It is hardly necessary to point out that this is a chronic form of circular reasoning which amounts practically to using the argument from silence as a screen to mask the assumption of what one is really trying to prove. Logically, it is a pitfall which one must take particular care to avoid. Intent to aid corporations must be proved by satisfactory evidence and not derived or assumed from the mere fact of silence.

Turning now to an examination of the evidence in the *Globe*, it can be said that the speeches of Bingham alone are really suggestive and worthy of analysis, although even they are found deficient in essential particulars. Stripping Bingham's arguments down to their vital points, one may list the following, particularly in their cumulative effect, as more or less favorable to the conspiracy theory:

1. Bingham deemed it to be a grave weakness that the entire Bill of Rights of the federal Constitution and more particularly the due process clause of the Fifth Amendment applied only as a restraint upon Congress. Holding citizenship to be national and denying, therefore, that the states had ever rightfully been able to interfere with the privileges of national citizenship—among which were the fundamental rights of

life, liberty and property—Bingham's first consideration was to devise an amendment which would remedy this defect. It can be said with assurance that to do this was the general purpose of all his various drafts, including the early forms which provided "Congress shall have power to . . . secure to all persons in every State equal protection in the rights of life, liberty and property." A desire to curb the states, to nationalize fundamental rights, and to do this using the phraseology of the Fifth Amendment, were the hubs around which Bingham's thinking revolved.

2. Bingham was emphatic at times in pointing out that the Fourteenth Amendment did not apply merely to the southern states and to the Negroes. "It is due to the Committee," he declared on one occasion when asked whether his draft "aimed simply and purely toward the protection of American citizens of African descent," "that I say it is proposed as well to protect the thousands and tens of thousands and hundreds of thousands of loyal white citizens of the United States whose property, by State legislation, has been wrested from them by confiscation, and to protect them also against banishment. . . . It is to apply to other States also that have in their constitutions and laws today provisions in direct violation of every principle of our Constitution." Asked at this point whether he referred to "the State of Indiana," Bingham replied, "I do not know; it may be so. It applies unquestionably to the State of Oregon." These allusions are obviously in harmony with some explicit and definite purpose.

3. Likewise suggestive of catholic motive, and of one somewhat in line with Conkling's claims, is the fact that Bingham on one occasion sounded out congressional sentiment in favor of an "added . . . provision that no State in this Union shall ever lay one cent of tax upon the property or head of any loyal man for the purpose of paying tribute and pensions to those who rendered service in the . . . atrocious rebellion . . . . I ask the gentlemen to consider that, as your

Constitution stands today, there is no power, express or implied, in this Government to limit or restrain the general power of taxation in the States."

4. At one point in his argument Bingham referred, though very casually, to the decision of the United States Supreme Court in "the great Mississippi case of Slaughter and another." Unquestionably this reference was to the slavery case of *Groves v. Slaughter*, decided by the Court in 1841. As such, it is a reference of great potential importance for the reason that Justice Baldwin, an ardent defender of slavery, anxious to place that institution beyond the control of both the states and the federal government, had here, for the first time, used the due process clause of the Fifth Amendment as a means of restraining Congress' power over slaves in interstate commerce. Baldwin's opinion thus applied due process in a definitely substantive sense, and it anticipated by fifteen years Chief Justice Taney's similar application in the case of Dred Scott.

A fact which seems to heighten the importance of Bingham's mention of *Groves v. Slaughter* is that in a later part of his dictum Justice Baldwin had used the comity clause (Article IV, Section 2) as the means of withdrawing the slave traffic from state control. In short, Baldwin used both of the identical clauses which Bingham and the Joint Committee eventually included in Section One. The question necessarily arises, therefore, whether Bingham may not have taken his cue from Baldwin—whether, as a means of protecting all property, including of course the property of (former) slaves, he did not deliberately build upon and strengthen the No Man's Land which Baldwin originally had created for the protection of property in slaves. For a Radical Republican to have done this would have constituted a great tactical triumph, in any event, and one can readily see how, if Bingham actually sought to protect foreign corporations in the manner Conkling intimated, the stroke would have amounted to positive genius. For, clearly, in addition to strengthening the barriers of that No Man's Land which—according to Justice Baldwin at least—existed in the original Constitution with regard to property per se, Bingham created still another No Man's Land which surrounded and protected the "persons" who owned property. He did this simply by making the due process clause—one half of Baldwin's original system of protection —itself a restraint upon both the federal government and the states. "Persons" in consequence were thus secured in their rights of property, against both Congress and local legislatures.

What is one to conclude from the discovery that John A. Bingham, author and sponsor of the equal protection-due process phraseology, (1) aimed to secure greater protection in the fundamental rights of property; (2) intended to curb all states, including Oregon; (3) desired an "added provision" limiting the taxing power; (4) cited a case wherein substantive use had been made of due process to protect property rights; (5) even used the identical clauses in Section One which Justice Baldwin had used in this early substantive opinion?

The first point to note in answering this question is that only when one places the most favorable interpretation upon each individual part of the evidence does the whole, taken collectively, suggest that Bingham may have had the purpose which Conkling intimated in his argument. A moment's examination, however, reveals numerous points at which the evidence is inadequate to support these separate conclusions. Three in particular may be cited:

1. Bingham simply declared himself in favor of an additional provision limiting the taxing power. One cannot determine from his speeches whether he regarded his own draft as having the effect of limitation or whether he simply meant to sound out sentiment in favor of a draft which would have this

effect. Obviously one must not infer the former motive from silence alone, without other evidence.

2. Bingham mentioned no particular opinion when referring to *Groves v. Slaughter;* he simply inferred that the case had decided that "under the Constitution the personal property of a citizen follows its owner, and is entitled to be protected in the State into which he goes." While these words might be construed as a reference to the comity clause portion of the Baldwin dictum, the conservative course is to draw no conclusion from such meager circumstances.

3. It will be noted that Bingham justified his draft on the grounds that it protected "loyal white citizens" and "any loyal man" as well as Negroes. In short, his references are all to natural "persons," never to artificial ones. Granted that a hidden motive would undoubtedly have impelled secrecy with reference to corporations, it is still true, as we have already pointed out, that secrecy is not here admissible as a proof of intent.

The chain of circumstances from which intent might be deduced thus being broken at several points, it is plain that the evidence in Bingham's speeches is not adequate proof of the conspiracy theory. It remains to linger a moment at this point, however, in order to note several features of his argument.

First of these features is a very important implication of his statement that his phraseology was designed to protect, not merely Negroes, but "the thousands . . . of loyal white citizens of the United States whose property, by State legislation, has been wrested from them by confiscation, and to protect them also against banishment. It is to apply to other States also that have in their constitutions and laws today provisions in direct violation of every principle of our Constitution."

The fact that intrinsically this statement suggests that natural persons were the only objects of Bingham's solicitude must not be permitted to obscure the significance of the type of legislation which had offended him. Laws enacted during and after the rebellion by the eleven "rebel" and apparently by a few "other States," laws which inflicted "banishment" and "confiscation" upon "loyal white citizens" were the particular objects of his ire. Such laws, in his judgment, violated "every principle of our Constitution" and in giving Congress power to "secure to all persons equal protection in the rights of life, liberty and property," he doubtless meant to extirpate these abuses.

The point which we here wish to stress is that this motivation practically assures—so long as Bingham appears to have associated "equal protection" with "due process of law"—that he had a substantive conception of due process. It is hardly conceivable, at any rate, that a Radical Republican, outraged by acts of rebel confiscation—which he regarded simultaneously as denials of equal protection and due process of law—objected to this confiscatory legislation simply because it denied such traditional requirements of due process as fair notice and hearing. Inherently the circumstances suggest that it was the substance of such legislation, not merely its effects upon the procedural rights of the accused, that one invoking the clause would have attacked. Stated otherwise, circumstances point to a "natural rights" usage, and a natural rights usage is here obviously a substantive one.

By a somewhat indirect and unexpected turn, one thus discovers evidence which indicates that Bingham in 1866 probably did have a substantive conception of due process of law, and did, therefore, regard the guarantee in a manner which was potentially of benefit to corporations. Paradoxically, however, the importance of this discovery is minimized, so far as its bearing on the conspiracy theory is concerned, by its own implications. Bingham used due process in a natural rights sense. He read into the clause his personal conceptions of right and justice. But the very circumstances under which he did this point to the existence of an intense and specific motivation which may very well have so absorbed his energies and interests that he gave little or no thought to the auxiliary uses of his phraseology. If one adopts this view, Bingham was a Radical Republican consumed by a determination to thwart those "rebels" and Democrats who were inclined to vent their animosity by discriminating against Negroes, loyalists, "carpetbaggers," etc. He was a crusading idealist, and it is an open question whether he was not, for this reason alone, one of the persons least likely to ponder the needs and constitutional status of corporations. A zealot is rarely so ambidextrous. . . .

6

THE BALLOT AND LAND
FOR THE FREEDMEN,
1861–1865

James M. McPherson

In their concern with economic and political self-
interest as prime motivating factors, historians tended
to ignore the abolitionist antecedents and commitments of many of the Radicals and chose to dismiss
Radical idealism as "claptrap." What James M. Mc-
Pherson makes clear, in his study of the antislavery
movement, is that abolitionists did not permit the
Emancipation Proclamation to obscure the struggle
for equal rights; instead, they confronted some of
the principal issues of Reconstruction and sought to
influence the content of the Republican program for
the South.

Reconstruction emerged as a burning issue even before the
war began. At first the word "reconstruction" was used by
Democrats and conservatives to designate a restoration of the
Union on the basis of compromise with the Confederacy. In
this form Radicals and abolitionists shunned the term. By the
second year of the war, however, "reconstruction" was beginning to acquire its later meaning of a genuine *reconstruction*
of southern society and politics. In January, 1862, George
Cheever published an article in the *Independent* outlining a
theory of reconstruction very similar to the later "conquered

provinces," "state suicide," and "forfeited rights" theories of
Thaddeus Stevens, Charles Sumner, and Samuel Shellabarger.
Cheever argued that by virtue of their rebellion the Confederate states had forfeited all rights and protection under the
United States Constitution. They were out of the Union *de
facto*. When finally conquered they should be administered as
territories until they could return to statehood under conditions imposed by Congress.

This was the essence of Reconstruction as conceived by
abolitionists and Radical Republicans throughout the war.
The theories of Stevens, Sumner, and Shellabarger varied
slightly in details, but at their core was the idea that conquered Confederate states had no rights under the Constitution. Their social and political systems lay prostrate and malle-
able. It was the job of Congress to remodel southern institutions into a form that would guarantee liberty and equal rights
to all men. In February, 1862, Sumner introduced a series of
Senate resolutions embodying these ideas in his "state suicide"
theory of reconstruction. Several abolitionists expressed support for Sumner's resolutions. John Jay succinctly summed up
the Radical theory of reconstruction as it emerged in 1862:
"The Southern states have ceased to be states of the Union—
their soil has become National territory."

This theory was certain to come into collision with the
presidential plan of reconstruction as developed tentatively
and experimentally by Lincoln and hardened into doctrinal
rigidity by Andrew Johnson. The presidential theory denied
that the Confederate states, *as states*, had ever really left the
Union. It was a rebellion of individuals, not states. Therefore
the function of reconstruction was to appoint loyal state
officials to breathe the spark of loyalty and life back into the
states. When certain minimum requirements were met these
states would again take their place in the Union, their institutions unimpaired and their rights unchanged except for slavery, which was a casualty of the war. In line with these ideas

Lincoln appointed a military governor for Tennessee early in 1862 and for several other Confederate states as they came under partial Union control in subsequent months. Some abolitionists expressed opposition to this policy of establishing provisional governments in rebel states. George Cheever protested that such a procedure usurped Congress' powers of reconstruction and defeated the very purpose of Sumner's "state suicide" resolutions, which had envisaged the administration of conquered states as territories under congressional control. In this argument can be found the germ of the later clash between Congress and the executive over the terms of Reconstruction.

From the start of the war abolitionists pondered the conditions of Reconstruction that would best secure the permanent freedom of emancipated slaves. As early as 1862 many abolitionists came to the conclusion that there could be no security for freedmen without Negro suffrage. But suffrage for the newly emancipated slaves seemed to be an impractical idea in 1862–63, and several abolitionists hesitated to demand it as a condition of Reconstruction. Samuel Sewall declared that he would be satisfied with a policy that granted equal civil rights and left the question of suffrage in abeyance. Not so Wendell Phillips and Frederick Douglass, who were in the vanguard of the movement to require Negro suffrage as a condition of Reconstruction. Phillips drew a parallel between the Irish immigrant and the emancipated Negro. When the number of Irishmen in the United States was small and politically insignificant, they were the butt of jokes and derision by politicians. But as soon as they became numerous and acquired political power, the attitude of politicians underwent a miraculous change. Phillips asked: "Do you know a politician who dares to make a speech to-day, without a compliment to green Erin? The moment a man becomes valuable or terrible to the politician, his rights will be respected. Give the negro a vote in his hand, and there is not a politician, from Abraham Lincoln down to the laziest loafer in the lowest ward in this city [New York] who would not do him honor. . . . From the possession of political rights, a man gets means to clutch equal opportunities of education, and a fair space of work. Give a man his vote, and you give him tools to work and arms to protect himself." In May, 1863, Douglass stated boldly that he would demand for the emancipated Negro "the most perfect civil and political equality." Negro suffrage was "the *only solid, and final solution* of the problem before us."

After the Union victories at Gettysburg and Vicksburg in July, 1863, there was a great increase in public discussion of reconstruction. The North believed that these victories heralded the collapse of the Confederacy, and the upsurge in reconstruction debate resulted from the assumption that peace was just around the corner. Northern opinion on the issue of reconstruction ranged from the Democratic demand that emancipation not be made a condition of peace to the call of Radical abolitionists for Negro suffrage. The whole country looked to Lincoln for a statement on reconstruction. As a supplement to his annual message on December 8, 1863, the President announced his long-awaited policy of restoration. He offered a full pardon to all Confederates (except a small class of prominent military and civilian leaders) who would take an oath of *future* loyalty to the Constitution and swear to uphold all acts of the executive and Congress relative to slavery. Furthermore, whenever a number of white voters equal to one-tenth of those who had voted in 1860 took the oath, they could proceed to reestablish a state government that would be recognized by the President. Lincoln declared that any provision adopted by reconstructed states with respect to the freedmen, "which shall recognize and declare their permanent freedom, provide for their education, and which may yet be consistent, as a temporary arrangement, with their present condition as a laboring, landless, and homeless class" would be acceptable to him. In other words, southern whites were to be allowed to handle the race problem in their own way, even if they adopted a temporary apprenticeship system and excluded Negroes from equal civil and political rights.

Recognizing that the President's plan was designed more as a measure to weaken the rebellion than as a permanent policy of reconstruction, the New York *Tribune* and several abolitionists approved the message. Even Theodore Tilton, who disliked parts of Lincoln's program, wrote that "the Message is only a suggestion, not a final plan—only a hint for the hour. It will create a good deal of wholesome discussion; and while this discussion goes on, the public sentiment marches steadily forward, & makes the politicians ready for a better plan."

But many abolitionists feared the consequences of Lincoln's conservative policy. Wendell Garrison, son of the pioneer abolitionist, denounced the President's exclusion of freedmen from the suffrage. "To free the slave, and then to abandon him in an anomalous position betwixt bondage and manhood, is not this as cruel as slavery?" asked young Garrison. He called for a total reorganization of southern society and politics. "There is no safety short of absolute justice. The reconstruction of Southern society must be thorough, and affect constitutions, statutes, and customs." The *Anti-Slavery Standard* thought that "the proposition to commit the care and education of the freedmen to those revived States is too much like giving the lambs to the nurture and admonition of wolves. That is a duty which belongs, by eminence, to the Nation, and should be entrusted to none but trustworthy hands."

The Boston *Commonwealth* published a blistering editorial denouncing the concept of states' rights which allowed the individual states to determine and regulate the rights of citizenship. "Are [we] going to slink any longer behind the sham, the miserable evasion, that the protection of personal rights and liberty for every citizen of the United States within the limits of any State belongs entirely to the State and in no case to the United States?" asked the *Commonwealth*. "This deplorable nonsense cost us the war, and the nation's life within an inch." Taking Tennessee as an example, the *Commonwealth* produced figures which showed that under Lincoln's 10 percent plan, fourteen thousand voters could establish the government of a state that contained more than one million inhabitants. These figures illustrated "the thoroughly anti-republican, undemocratic character of the President's proposition," asserted the *Commonwealth*. "This insignificant fraction determines who shall govern the State hereafter. They have the power to prevent every colored man from voting, and, in the present state of public opinion in all the slave States, *they will prevent it*. . . . Besides being such a burlesque upon popular sovereignty, the thing is impossible."

During the winter of 1863–64 more and more abolitionists began to condemn Lincoln's reconstruction policy. In January the *Principia* warned that "there is danger that some scheme of apprenticeship—such as that adopted but repudiated in Jamaica—may defeat, delay, or greatly impede and embarrass the progress of the country toward peace, unity, and freedom." The *Principia* joined the growing list of Radicals calling for Negro suffrage to avert this danger. Theodore Weld and Anna Dickinson lectured frequently during the winter, raising their eloquent voices in impassioned pleas for equal justice to the freedmen. The Massachusetts Anti-Slavery Society adopted a resolution written by Wendell Phillips demanding for the Negro "an equal share with the white race in the management of the political institutions for which he is required to fight and bleed, and to which he is clearly entitled by every consideration of justice and democratic equality."

Phillips was the most persistent, eloquent, and biting critic of the administration's reconstruction program. He traveled up and down the East Coast in the winter of 1863–64 giving his lecture on reconstruction to scores of audiences in crowded halls. Phillips called for a constitutional amendment to prohibit every state from passing laws "which make a

distinction among her citizens on account of race. (Cheers)"
Reconstruction was impossible on any other basis. Phillips
declared: "Never will this nation be a unit until every class
God has made, from the lakes to the Gulf, has its ballot to
protect itself. (Applause) . . . The negro has earned land,
education, rights. Before we leave him, we ought to leave him
on his own soil, in his own house, with the right to the ballot
and the school-house within reach. (Loud applause) Unless
we have done it, the North has let the cunning of politics filch
the fruits of this war."

Radical censure of Lincoln's reconstruction policy focused
on Louisiana in early 1864. The President had ordered General N. P. Banks, commander of the Department of the Gulf,
to proceed with the reconstruction of Louisiana under the
amnesty and reconstruction proclamation of December 8,
1863. The nucleus of a Unionist political force existed in New
Orleans in the form of a Free State General Committee, controlled by native Radicals. Many members of the Committee
supported a moderate degree of suffrage for the free Negroes
of the city. The committee favored the calling of a convention to write a new constitution prior to the election of state
officers. With the approval of Lincoln, however, Banks
scheduled elections for state officials on February 22, 1864,
under the old Louisiana Constitution. White men who took
the oath of allegiance would be eligible to vote. New Orleans
Radicals and Negroes were outraged by what they considered
Banks's high-handed proceedings. By scheduling state elections *before* the convening of a constitutional convention,
Banks had cut the ground from under the Radicals. New
Orleans' free Negroes sent a delegation to Washington armed
with a petition requesting the ballot. Abolitionists in the
North loosed a barrage of attacks on Banks for restricting the
suffrage to whites.

Three parties in Louisiana nominated candidates for governor in the February 22 election: Conservative, Moderate, and

Radical. Both the Moderate and Radical parties were pledged to end slavery, but the Moderate candidate, Michael Hahn, attacked the Radicals for their support of Negro equality. Banks threw his support to Hahn, and with the backing of the United States Army, Hahn won an easy victory. Abolitionists denounced the whole affair. The exclusion of Negroes from the polls, protested the *Commonwealth*, "has no parallel for meanness." Tilton asserted: "Prejudice, even with Gen. Banks to back it, and President Lincoln to confirm it, is a weak foundation for an enduring State. Official injustice is the very worst disturber of the public peace. . . . Let us establish no skin-deep discrimination among our citizens."

The representatives of New Orleans' free Negroes arrived in Washington in March, 1864, bearing their petition for suffrage. They cited the high rate of literacy and the large amount of property owned by free colored men in Louisiana. Their request, added to other Radical pressures, prompted Lincoln to write a private letter to Governor Hahn, who was preparing for the Louisiana constitutional convention scheduled for early April. "I barely suggest for your private consideration," wrote the President, "whether some of the colored people may not be let in [to the suffrage]—as, for instance, the very intelligent, and especially those who have fought gallantly in our ranks." This idea of a qualified Negro suffrage was gaining considerable support in the North. But most abolitionists wanted no qualifications which were not applied equally to both races. To give the ballot to only a limited number of Negroes would elevate them "into a caste which is dangerous to its members, humiliating to those of inferior grade, an anomaly in free republican society," argued Tilton. "One rule must be applied to all classes, or no rule must be made."

In Louisiana most of the Radicals boycotted the constitutional convention that opened in April, declaring angrily that the whole thing was a farce and that Banks had packed the convention with Moderates. Banks responded to northern Radical pressure to the extent of forcing the convention to empower the legislature to enfranchise Negroes. The provision was permissive, not mandatory, and the legislature elected under the new constitution did nothing whatever in the direction of Negro suffrage. Tennessee and Arkansas, the other states reconstructed under Lincoln's plan in 1864–65, also refused to enfranchise colored men. Frustrated radicals and abolitionists turned increasingly to Congress in their efforts to obtain equal civil and political rights for freedmen as a condition of Reconstruction.

Congress was in a mood to listen to Radical demands. Under the leadership of Henry Winter Davis and Benjamin Wade, congressional Republicans had been slowly maturing their reconstruction policy. On March 22, Davis finally got his bill before the House for its third reading. By implication the Wade-Davis bill endorsed the "state suicide" theory of reconstruction. It asserted that restoration of the Union was a congressional rather than executive function. Whereas Lincoln's policy envisaged the reestablishment of state governments by 10 percent of those voters who took an oath of future loyalty, the Davis bill stipulated that not until 50 percent of the white men of voting age took such an oath could a civil government be reestablished. Moreover, no one who had voluntarily particpated in or supported the rebellion could vote for delegates to the constitutional convention, and no rebel officeholder could vote or hold office under the new state constitution.

Abolitionists approved many features of this bill, but sharply disapproved of its limitation of the franchise to whites. "And this is called 'guaranteeing to the States a Republican form of Government,' is it?" asked William Goodell sarcastically. "What shall be said of the folly of excluding the votes of that part of the community that is most decidedly and unquestionably loyal [that is, the freedmen]?" Josiah Grinnell in the House and Charles Sumner in the Senate tried to amend the bill to include Negro suffrage, but their amendments were voted down by large majorities in both Houses. Wade explained that he favored the Negro suffrage amendment in principle, but "I would rather it should not be adopted, because, in my judgment, it will sacrifice the bill." Many proponents of the Wade-Davis bill probably considered it a stopgap measure to mark time until northern public opinion could be educated up to the point of accepting Negro suffrage as a basis of reconstruction.

The Wade-Davis bill was finally passed by Congress on July 2, but Lincoln slapped a pocket veto on the Radicals' handiwork. Incensed by the President's action, Davis and Wade issued a blistering manifesto denouncing Lincoln's usurpation of Congress' rightful function of controlling reconstruction. Wendell Garrison sympathized with their anger, but declared that he was just as glad to see the bill vetoed because it had left the Negro entirely out of the reconstruction process. The *Commonwealth* had "no tears to shed over the loss of this bill, which though in the main a good one, was . . . disfigured by a requisition that none but 'white' persons should take part in the work of reconstruction. Until Congress has sense enough and decency enough to pass bills without the color qualification, we care not how quickly they are killed."

Education and the ballot for the Negro were two of the most important abolitionist requirements for a sound reconstruction of the South. But many abolitionists realized that political equality and education would mean little to the freed slave without a solid foundation of economic independence. The freedmen must "be made proprietors of the soil in fee simple, as speedily as possible," wrote a correspondent of the *Liberator* in 1864. Otherwise the white planter would keep the Negro in a state of semi-serfdom by paying him low wages and making him economically dependent on the old master class. "It is going to make a mighty difference to the 'landless and homeless,' whether they are to get only the poor pittance of twenty-five or thirty cents per day, and be thus kept dependent, or whether they shall receive four or five times this amount by planting on their own land," asserted the *Liberator* correspondent. "The conflict between capital and labor is as old as the world; but in this case the contest could never be more unequal."

This was not a new idea to abolitionists. From the outset of the war many of them had desired the breakup of large southern plantations and their redistribution among landless farmers, black and white. Such action would accomplish two important objectives: it would promote democracy in the South by destroying the economic basis of the "landed aristocracy"; and it would promote the economic independence of the freedmen. Less than a month after the firing on Fort Sumter, William Goodell called for the confiscation of land belonging to rebels and its redistribution among freed slaves. In subsequent months many other abolitionists repeated and endorsed this proposal. When Congress opened its special session in July, 1861, several drastic confiscation bills were introduced. But the bill that finally passed was a very mild measure confiscating only property (including slaves) used in direct support of the Confederate military effort.

Abolitionists continued to press for full-scale expropriation. "By all the laws and usages of civilized nations," declared Charles K. Whipple in the *Liberator* in June, 1862, "rebels against a government forfeit their property, as well as their other rights and privileges, under it." He urged the administration to confiscate rebel lands and allot a portion of them to the landless laborers who had worked them under compulsion for generations and had thus earned a clear title to the land. This act of simple justice to the freedmen would build the new South on a foundation of small landowners thoroughly loyal to the government. It would expiate the sin incurred by the nation in allowing men to be kept in slavery for so many generations.

The Confiscation Act of July, 1862, as originally passed by Congress, met many of the abolitionists' demands. It provided for the permanent confiscation of all property belonging to traitors. Lincoln objected, however, that this provision violated the constitutional ban on bills of attainder that worked forfeiture of property beyond the life of offenders. Under presidential pressure Congress passed a joint resolution declaring that nothing in the act should be construed to work a forfeiture of real estate beyond the life of the offender. Abolitionists were dismayed. If such an interpretation of the Constitution were sustained, the possibility of confiscation and redistribution of southern lands would disappear. In the third edition of his *War Powers of the President,* William Whiting argued learnedly that the constitutional prohibition of bills of attainder did not debar Congress from confiscating property permanently by separate legislative act as a punishment for treason.

Whiting's legal erudition was widely respected, and his arguments were later utilized by Republican congressmen in their efforts to repeal the joint resolution of 1862. Meanwhile, some abolitionist spokesmen explored other means of accomplishing a revolution in southern land ownership. Even before passage of the 1862 Confiscation Act, Elizur Wright had published anonymously a pamphlet suggesting confiscatory taxation as a method of abolishing the southern landed aristocracy. Wright proposed that a tax of fifteen dollars per acre be levied on all Confederates who owned more than three hundred acres or who had owned slaves before the war. In nearly all cases this tax would not be paid and the government could seize the land and sell part of it to help defray the cost of war. The remainder could be sold or granted to the freedmen. "If the Federal Government, under its war power, has a right to charge batteries with projectiles that sweep down the active and [passive] rebels alike," declared Wright, "can it not charge a battery with an agrarian law which will only annihilate without killing the real rebels?" In a later article for the *Commonwealth* Wright asserted that "a free Republic is utterly impossible . . . where the soil chiefly belongs to a limited small number of princes, patroons, nabobs or ex-slave-holders." He realized that northern conservatives would throw up their hands in horror and conjure up visions of the Jacobins' excesses in the French Revolution. "But an agrarian law for the South is just the next inevitable question," Wright stated. "Let the programme be, not only liberty to the loyal, but the SOIL TO THE TILLER."

When emancipation became an official northern war aim in 1863, abolitionist demands for agrarian reform in the South became more insistent. In an oft-repeated address entitled "Amen to the Proclamation," Wendell Phillips declared that "the whole social system of the Gulf States is to be taken to pieces; every bit of it." All vestiges of slavery and the old aristocracy must be wiped out, said Phillips, and this could be done only by granting land to the freedman, for to him land was the symbol and substance of freedom. Senator Sumner introduced in February, 1863, a bill to grant ten acres of land to every Negro soldier. The bill did not pass, but it was a sign of the increasing congressional concern over the land question in the South. Early in 1863 Indiana Congressman George Julian, a veteran antislavery crusader and foe of land monopoly, urged Congress to adopt "an equitable homestead policy, parcelling out the plantations of rebels in small farms for . . . the freedmen . . . instead of selling it in large tracts to speculators, and thus laying the foundation for a system of land monopoly in the South scarcely less to be deplored than slavery itself."

Julian's remarks probably referred in part to the land sales about to take place on the South Carolina sea islands. In

August, 1861, Congress had levied a direct tax on every state to raise revenue for carrying on the war. Of course this tax could not be collected in most parts of the Confederacy, and the 1861 law made no provision for collection in the Union-occupied portions of rebel states. This was rectified by an act of June 7, 1862, authorizing the President to appoint tax commissioners to assess the proportion of taxes owed by occupied areas of the Confederacy and to offer the land of delinquent taxpayers for sale at public auction. In effect this was a confiscation act similar to Elizur Wright's proposal.

The tax commissioners arrived at Port Royal in October, 1862. They scheduled a public auction of lands for February 11, 1863. Many of the Gideonites * became alarmed, fearing that northern speculators would descend upon the islands and buy up most of the desirable land, leaving the Negro with little or nothing. Led by Mansfield French, some of the Gideonites began putting pressure on their friends in Washington to reserve part of the land for the freedmen. "I am greatly troubled in view of the land sales," wrote French to Secretary Chase. "The sharp-sighted speculators are on hand & with larger purses than those of the friends of humanity. If the plantations fall into their hands, *most* of the colored people will suffer greatly." French proposed that General Rufus Saxton, military governor of the islands, be allowed to purchase some of the land with the proceeds of the cotton fund and resell it in small lots to the freedmen. At the beginning of February, 1863, Laura Towne suggested to Saxton that he should request a postponement of the sales on grounds of "military necessity." Saxton, who sympathized entirely with the Gideonites, thought this a good idea and persuaded General Hunter to order a postponement of the auction until the whole question was clarified. News soon reached the Gideon-

---

* The so-called Gideonites were northern abolitionists who went to Port Royal early in 1862 to give aid to the slaves after their masters had fled.

ites that their efforts in Washington had paid off. On February 6, Congress amended the tax law to allow the tax commissioners to reserve a certain amount of land for educational and charitable purposes. There was "general jubilation" on the islands. The land sales were rescheduled for March 9, and the tax commission reserved most of the saleable property for the future benefit of the freedmen.

Many of the Gideonites believed with Mansfield French that the freedmen had earned a grant of land by long years of suffering and toil. Another group of northern plantation superintendents, led by Edward S. Philbrick of Boston, disagreed with them. Philbrick was a hard-headed practical businessman with years of experience as a successful civil engineer and entrepreneur. He was inclined at times to regard the philanthropic wing of the Gideonites as naïve do-gooders. Philbrick was alert to the danger of speculators grabbing all the good land. But instead of a direct grant of land to the freedmen or the sale of property to them on special terms, he wanted an opportunity for sympathetic northern capitalists to purchase plantations and continue the free-labor experiment on a private-enterprise basis. William Gannett agreed with Philbrick. He thought the freedmen would learn self-reliance best by being thrust into the labor market just like other men. Special grants of land would only reinforce their lack of initiative and self-reliance bequeathed by slavery. "To receive has been their natural condition," argued Gannett. "Give them land, and a house,—and the ease of gaining as good a livelihood as they have been accustomed to would keep many contented with the smallest exertion."

At the land sales of 1863 on the sea islands, 16,479 acres were put up for general sale (the rest of the land was reserved by the government). About 2,000 acres were purchased by freedmen who had pooled their savings. Most of the rest— nearly 8,000 acres—was bought by Edward Philbrick, representing a group of Boston capitalists, at an average price of less than $1 per acre. Philbrick hired several of the government's plantation superintendents, including Gannett and Charles Ware, to run his plantations in 1863 on the basis of private enterprise. The freedmen raised a large cotton crop on these plantations in 1863, and Philbrick cleared a huge profit. He publicized his successful crop and profits in the northern press as an unanswerable argument for emancipation and free labor. Many of the Gideonites, however, remained unconvinced that Philbrick's motives were entirely unselfish. During 1863 there was an undercurrent of belief among the more philanthropic-minded abolitionists that Philbrick's protestations of concern for the freedmen's welfare were mostly a cover for his own desire to make money.

Most northern abolitionists who gave serious thought to the land question agreed with the "do-gooder" wing of the Gideonites. "The confiscated lands of the Southern Rebels ought to be given in suitable portions to the colored people, who so long have tilled them without wages," wrote Samuel J. May in April, 1863. A month later the annual meeting of the American Anti-Slavery Society adopted a sweeping resolution calling for permanent confiscation of property owned by Confederates and the allotment of homesteads from these lands to freedmen, loyal southern whites, and Union soldiers. Wendell P. Garrison attacked Lincoln's pardon and amnesty proclamation because it provided for the restoration of confiscated property to southerners who took a loyalty oath. Wendell Phillips was angry because the President's reconstruction plan "leaves the large landed proprietors of the South still to domineer over its politics, and makes the negro's freedom a mere sham. Until a large share of those estates are divided, the aristocracy is not destroyed, neither is any *fair* chance given for the development of a system of free labor."

During the winter of 1863–64 the abolitionist-controlled Boston *Commonwealth* published a series of powerful editorials urging agrarian reform as a condition of Reconstruction. "What do we gain in point of peace, union, republican-ism, or genuine democracy by converting Jeff Davis and his patriarchs into Lord Palmerston and a fox-hunting, rent-roll gentry?" asked the *Commonwealth*. A landless peasant class in the South would be a constant source of social unrest. "To be safe, peaceable and permanent," reconstruction "must be pri-marily economical and industrial; it must commence by plant-ing a loyal population in the soil of the South, not only as its cultivators but its rightful and actual owners." The *Common-wealth* denounced Lincoln's pardon and amnesty program. "If the President can restore to these traitors all their rights to the land," wrote the editor, "then the Confiscation Act is a farce, and the war will have been a gigantic crime and fail-ure."

In February, 1864, a committee of prominent abolitionists and antislavery Republicans representing the secular freed-men's aid societies petitioned Congress "to give to the slaves made free by the power of the government, a legal and quiet possession of adequate land for their residence and support." On the South Carolina sea islands, plans were being carried out for precisely that purpose. In September, 1863, Lincoln had ordered the tax commissioners to put up for public sale at auction most of the lands reserved by the government at the previous auction in March, 1863. The President specified that certain tracts of this land were to be sold to freedmen in twenty-acre lots at the special price of $1.25 per acre. Gideon-ites and freedmen on the islands were overjoyed by Lincoln's order. General Saxton and the Reverend Mansfield French went even further than the order allowed in their zeal to obtain land for the freedmen. They encouraged the Negroes to preempt not only their allotted twenty acres each, but to build cabins on adjoining lots in the hope that bidders would respect their squatters' rights on these adjoining properties. Saxton and French defended their action on the ground that Lincoln's order reserved only 16,000 of 60,000 government-held acres for the freedmen. This, they argued, was hardly enough to support the 15,000 freedmen on the islands. Preemption would enable the Negroes to acquire much more property at the special price of $1.25 per acre than specified in Lincoln's orders.

Saxton actually issued instructions of his own on November 3 telling the freedmen to stake their claims wherever they wished. He was supported by most of the Gideonites, by Colonel Higginson, and by the *Free South*, a small Port Royal newspaper edited by Philadelphia abolitionist James Thompson. The tax commissioners, supported by Philbrick, were strongly opposed to the scheme, and put pressure on Washington to stop the activities of Saxton and French. But French went personally to Washington in December, 1863, to obtain a new set of instructions to ratify General Saxton's preemption orders. French returned triumphantly to Port Royal in January, bearing a new order dated December 31, 1863, allowing Negro heads of families to preempt any government-owned property on the islands up to forty acres apiece.

The Gideonites were elated. They immediately informed the freedmen of their rights. The tax commissioners' office was soon swamped with preemption claims. But the commissioners were adamantly opposed to preemption. They carried out passive resistance to the new instructions, ignoring some of the preemption claims, attacking the legality of the instructions, and complaining to Washington. Philbrick was outspoken in his opposition to special privileges for the freedmen. They had not earned the land, he argued, and special consideration would break down their moral fiber and vitiate their self-reliance. The Gideonites counterattacked. French and others denounced Philbrick as a selfish capitalist seeking to build a fortune on the sweat and toil of an "agricultural peasantry." In a milder tone Higginson remarked that few of the men in his regiment agreed with Philbrick's arguments. "Sergeant Rivers . . . summed it up in conversation the other day," Higginson reported. "Every colored man will be a slave, & feel himself a slave until he can raise him own *bale of cotton* & put him own mark upon it & say *dis is mine!*" Philbrick lost some of his allies; Gannett, for example, was converted to the proposition that the freedmen must have land and deserved special opportunities to acquire it because of their lifetime of unrequited toil. Nevertheless the tax commissioners persuaded Washington to reverse its policy and cancel the preemption privileges.

French was dismayed, but he was not through fighting. He asked Chase to allow those claims to stand that had been filed before the preemption instructions were rescinded. Since more than a thousand claims had been filed, this would have accomplished nearly everything French desired. Meanwhile in a series of incendiary speeches he urged the freedmen to take the land they needed and defend it with their hoes if necessary. French received no word from Chase, however, and when the sales took place on February 18 there was the utmost confusion over preemption rights, property claims, and so on. In most cases the tax commissioners ruled against the preemptors and sold large slices of preempted land to the highest bidders at an average price of $11 per acre. The freedmen purchased only 2,276 acres at the special rate of $1.25 per acre. In addition several groups of freedmen pooled their resources and purchased 470 acres at an average price of just over $7.00 per acre in the competitive bidding. The whole affair left a sour taste in everybody's mouth. French and the "do-gooder" Gideonites were furious with Philbrick, the tax commissioners, and the government for what they considered deliberate treachery to the freedmen. Philbrick was irritated by abolitionist attacks on him in the press. The freedmen themselves were angry, resentful, and distrustful toward the Yankees who first promised them land and then withdrew the promise.

Meanwhile there was increasing support in Congress for

some degree of confiscation. Early in 1864 George Julian introduced a bill to extend the Homestead Act of 1862 to cover the abandoned and confiscated estates of the South. Under Julian's bill these estates would be carved into forty- and eighty-acre tracts and made available to Union soldiers, southern freedmen, and loyal southern whites on the home-stead principle of full ownership after five years' residence and cultivation. Lydia Maria Child congratulated Julian for his speech in support of the bill, and proclaimed her opinion that land monopoly was "only another phase of Slavery; another form of the absorption of Labor by Capital, which has tormented and degraded the world from the beginning." The House passed Julian's bill on May 12, 1864, by a vote of 75–64; it was reported from Senate committee, but did not come up for discussion before the end of the session in July.

Julian realized that his confiscation-homestead measure would be of little value unless Congress repealed the joint resolution of 1862 (tacked on to the second Confiscation Act) limiting forfeiture of property to the life of the offender. In February, 1864, the House voted to amend the joint resolution to read no forfeiture "contrary to the Constitution," hoping that the Supreme Court would uphold permanent confiscation of rebel property. Julian confidently expected an endorsement of repeal by the Republican National Convention. The National Union League convention meeting the day before the Republican conclave approved repeal, but conservatives on the resolutions committee squelched a similar endorsement by the Republican convention. On June 28, however, the Senate passed an amendment to the Freedmen's Bureau bill repealing the 1862 joint resolution outright. Encouraged, Julian went to see Lincoln on July 2, hoping to convince the President of the constitutionality of permanent confiscation. Lincoln admitted that when he had forced Congress to adopt the joint resolution in 1862 he had not examined the question thoroughly. William Whiting's written and spoken arguments, the President said, had since convinced him of his error, and he was now ready to sign a bill repealing the joint resolution of 1862. The 1864 session of Congress ended, however, without House and Senate agreement on the precise form such a repeal should take. On February 24, 1865, the House repealed the joint resolution outright by the margin of one vote. But in the final conference committee report on the Freedmen's Bureau bill the repeal amendment was dropped in order to win conservative support for the bureau. Thus, although Congress had voted on three separate occasions to repeal the 1862 joint resolution, failure of both houses to get together on the exact form of repeal had defeated the measure. Nor was Julian's confiscation-homestead measure passed during the 1864–65 session. Abolitionists and Radical Republicans were disappointed, but they looked hopefully to the next session of Congress for favorable action on the land question.

One provision of the Freedmen's Bureau bill encouraged this hope. William Whiting had used his influence with members of Congress to get a land proviso inserted in the bill. As finally passed on March 3, 1865, the act contained a section stating that to every male refugee or freedman "shall be assigned not more than forty acres" of abandoned or confiscated land at rental for three years and an option to purchase at the end of that time with "such title thereto as the United States can convey." This was rather vague and indefinite, but it was the best Congress could do at the time. Friends of the freedmen hoped that subsequent legislation would provide the freedmen with clear and definite titles to land of their own in the reconstructed South.

As Sherman marched through Georgia in the last month of 1864, thousands of ragged and destitute freedmen straggled along behind his troops. When the army reached Savannah the problem of providing for the refugees became acute. General Sherman and Secretary of War Stanton, who was visiting Savannah, held a conference on January 12 with twenty Negro leaders of the city. Four days later Sherman issued Special Field Order no. 15, designating the coastline and riverbanks thirty miles inland from Charleston to Jacksonville as an area for exclusive Negro settlement. Freedmen settling in this area could take up not more than forty acres of land per family, to which they would be given "possessory titles" until Congress "shall regulate the title." No white persons except authorized military personnel were to be allowed in the area. Sherman's order gave General Saxton full power over freedmen's affairs from Charleston to Key West.

Abolitionist reaction to the order was mixed. Sydney Gay commended the provision granting land to the freedmen, but he disliked the feature setting the Negroes apart from the white race. This smacked too much of colonization. Sherman was known as a conservative on the Negro question, and Gay distrusted his motives. The *Commonwealth* also criticized the order and asserted that "all this effort at segregating the ne-groes will fail. If they were good enough to live in the pres-ence of white men as slaves, they are good enough to dwell in their presence as freemen."

On the other hand, Tilton wholeheartedly approved of the measure, considering it a long-overdue effort to settle a large number of freedmen on land of their own. He discounted the colonization fears of other abolitionists, and expressed the belief that white teachers and officials of freedmen's aid socie-ties would be allowed in the area. Secretary Stanton sent a private letter to Garrison seeking to allay the suspicions of abolitionists, pointing out that the Negro leaders themselves had expressed a desire to be set apart from whites. Stanton enclosed the minutes of the conference with Savannah Ne-groes, which Garrison published in the *Liberator* along with a defense of Sherman's order. Abolitionists received private as-surances from General Saxton that white teachers and mis-sionaries would be allowed in the area. In fact, said Saxton, the segregation aspect of the order had been designed to keep out speculators, slick traders, and other whites who might take advantage of the freedmen. Saxton had full power over admission or exclusion of whites, and any who had legitimate business in the area would be admitted.

These assurances mollified suspicious abolitionists and converted them to supporters of Sherman's order. Saxton, however, had been by no means as confident at first of the advantages of the plan as he appeared later in his assurances to abolitionists. He was reluctant to accept the duties of administering the order, fearing that it was just one more promise of land to the freedmen destined to be broken. Stanton, however, assured him that all would be well, and Saxton went vigorously to work to place thousands of Georgia and South Carolina freedmen on the land. He appointed Reuben Tomlinson inspector general of Freedmen's Affairs. French and Gannett also assisted Saxton in the massive project. By the end of June, 1865, they had settled more than forty thousand freedmen on the coastal lands. Many of the Negroes were growing good crops on their new land. The experiment seemed to be a success.

By 1865 abolitionists had achieved partial success in their drive to obtain land for the freedmen. Powerful congressional leaders such as Julian, Sumner, and Thaddeus Stevens were committed to the principle. Congress had gone on record in favor of repealing the joint resolution of 1862 forbidding permanent confiscation. The promise of land for the freedmen was embodied in legislation creating the Freedmen's Bureau. Freedmen on the South Carolina sea islands had purchased several thousand acres of land at tax sales. Freedmen from all over the southeastern United States were being settled with "possessory titles" on thousands of acres in South Carolina, Georgia, and Florida. Abolitionists looked ahead hopefully to action by future Congresses guaranteeing these titles and setting aside more land for the freedmen. During the war abolitionist spokesmen had called for a three-cornered policy to insure the safety and permanence of reconstruction: education, land, and the ballot for the freedmen. At the war's end there were encouraging signs in favor of the realization of all three objectives.

7

NEGRO SUFFRAGE AND REPUBLICAN POLITICS:
The Problem of Motivation in Reconstruction Historiography

LaWanda and John H. Cox

That historians should have viewed the enfranchisement of the Negro with some cynicism was consistent with their efforts to minimize or distort the
Radical commitment to equal rights. The generally
accepted interpretation was that the Radical demand
for Negro suffrage had been largely influenced by
political expediency (i.e., the need to perpetuate
Republican power), vindictiveness (i.e., the desire
to humiliate the white South), or "misguided humanitarianism." The tragic result, some argued, was
that illiterate ex-slaves were endowed with a political
responsibility for which they were entirely unprepared. Although many historians still explain the
Fifteenth Amendment in terms of political expediency, LaWanda and John H. Cox advance a
strikingly different interpretation.

In challenge to the dominant pattern of interpretation . . . we
should like to suggest that Republican party leadership played
a crucial role in committing this nation to equal suffrage for
the Negro not because of political expediency but *despite*
political risk. An incontestable fact of Reconstruction history
suggests this view. Race prejudice was so strong in the North

that the issue of equal Negro suffrage constituted a clear and present danger to Republicans. White backlash may be a recently coined phrase, but it was a virulent political phenomenon in the 1860's. The exploitation of prejudice by the Democratic opposition was blatant and unashamed.

The power base of the Republican party lay in the North. However much party leaders desired to break through sectional boundaries to create a national image or to gain some measure of security from southern votes, victory or defeat in the presidential elections of the nineteenth century lay in the northern states. With the exception of the contested election of 1876, electoral votes from the South were irrelevant—either nonexistent or unnecessary—to Republican victory. It was the loss of Connecticut, Indiana, and New York in 1876 and 1884, and of those states plus Illinois in 1892, which was critical; had they remained in the Republican column, Democrats would have waited until the twentieth century to claim residence for one of their own in the White House.*

What has been charged to timidity might better be credited to prudence. The caution with which Republicans handled the Negro suffrage issue in 1865, 1866, and again in 1868 made political sense. Had the elections of 1866 and 1868 been fought on a platform supporting equal suffrage, who could

* In 1872 Republicans had 286 electoral votes and would have held a substantial majority without the six southern states and the two border states which were included in the total. Republicans could have won in 1876 without the 19 contested votes of Florida, Louisiana, and South Carolina had they retained either New York (35 votes) or both Connecticut (6) and Indiana (15). In the elections of 1880, 1884, 1888, and 1892, the Republican candidate gained no electoral votes from any former slave state. In 1884, as in 1876, either the New York vote or a combination of those of Indiana and Connecticut would have won the election for the Republicans. In 1892 the electoral count was 277 Democratic, 145 Republican, and 22 Populist. Republicans needed an additional 78 votes for a majority, which could have come from New York (36), Illinois (24), Indiana (15), and Connecticut (6). The party kept Pennsylvania and Ohio (except for one vote); it had not held New Jersey (10 votes) since 1872.

say with certainty, then or now, that Republicans would have maintained their power?* In the state elections of 1867, when Negro suffrage was a major issue, the party took a beating in Connecticut, New York, Pennsylvania, and New Jersey, suffered losses in local elections in Indiana and Illinois, and came within 0.4 percent of losing the Ohio governorship despite the personal political strength of their candidate Rutherford B. Hayes. In Ohio the issue was clearly drawn, for, in addition to the nationwide commitment to Negro suffrage in the South made by the First Reconstruction Act of March, 1867, the Republican party bore responsibility for a statewide referendum on behalf of equal suffrage at home. The proposed suffrage amendment to the state constitution went down to defeat with less than 46 percent of the votes cast. Democrats gained control of both houses of the state legislature, turning a comfortable Republican margin of forty-six into a Democratic majority of eight. Even judged by the gubernatorial vote, Republicans suffered a serious loss of support, for the popular Hayes gained 50.3 percent of the vote as compared to 54.5 percent won by the Republican candidate for secretary of state in 1866.

There was nothing exceptional about Ohioans' hostility to Negro suffrage. In Republican Minnesota and Kansas equal-suffrage amendments also went down to defeat in the fall elections of 1867, with a respectable 48.8 percent of the vote in the former but with less than 35 percent in the latter despite the fact that Kansas Republicans in the 1860's constituted 70 percent of the electorate. From 1865 through 1869 eleven referendum votes were held in eight northern states on constitutional changes to provide Negroes with the ballot; only two were successful—those held during the fall of 1868 in Iowa

* More than a simple majority would have been necessary to retain control of Reconstruction in the face of President Johnson's vetoes and to pass the Fifteenth Amendment. Johnson supporters welcomed Negro suffrage as an issue on which they expected to redress their 1866 defeat.

and Minnesota. The Minnesota victory, gained after two previous defeats, has been attributed to trickery in labeling the amendment. The issue was never placed before the white voters of Illinois, Indiana, Pennsylvania, or New Jersey; and this fact probably indicated a higher intensity of race prejudice than in Connecticut, New York, and Ohio, where equal suffrage was defeated.* These seven were marginal states of critical importance to the Republicans in national elections. The tenacity of opposition to Negro enfranchisement is well illustrated in New York, where one might have expected to find it minimal since Negroes had always voted in the state although subjected to a discriminatory property qualification since 1821. After a Republican legislature ratified the Fifteenth Amendment in April, 1869, New Yorkers defeated a similar change in the state constitution, swept the Republicans out of control at Albany, and returned a Democratic majority of twenty, which promptly voted to rescind New York's ratification.

In short, Republican sponsorship of Negro suffrage meant flirtation with political disaster in the North, particularly in any one or all of the seven pivotal states where both the prejudice of race and the Democratic opposition were strong. Included among them were the four most populous states in the nation, with corresponding weight in the electoral college: New York, Pennsylvania, Ohio, and Illinois. Negroes were denied equal suffrage in every one of these critically important seven, and only in New York did they enjoy a partial enfranchisement. If Negroes were to be equally enfranchised, as the Fifteenth Amendment directed, it is true that Republicans could count upon support from an overwhelming majority of the new voters. It does not necessarily follow, however, that this prospect was enticing to "shrewd politicians." What simple political computation could add the number of poten-

* The other two states where equal suffrage was defeated were Wisconsin and Michigan.

[159]

tial Negro voters to be derived from a minority population that reached a high of 3.4 percent in New Jersey and 2.4 percent in Ohio, then diminished in the other five states from 1.9 to 1.1 percent, a population already partially enfranchised in New York and to be partially disenfranchised in Connecticut by the state's nondiscriminatory illiteracy tests; determine and subtract the probable number of white voters who would be alienated among the dominant 96.6 to 98.9 percent of the population; and predict a balance that would ensure Republican victory?

The impact of the Negro suffrage issue upon the white voter might be softened by moving just after a national election rather than just before one; and this was the strategy pursued in pushing through the Fifteenth Amendment. Yet risk remained, a risk which it is difficult to believe politicians would have willingly assumed had their course been set solely, or primarily, by political arithmetic. Let us, then, consider the nature of the evidence cited to show that Republican policy sprang from narrow party interests.

Since the days of Braxton, historians have used the public statements of public men, straight from the pages of the *Congressional Globe*, not only to document the charge of party expediency but also to prove it by the admission of intent. The frequency with which either Senator Charles Sumner or Thaddeus Stevens has been quoted on the arithmetic of Negro enfranchisement might well have suggested caution in using such oral evidence for establishing motivation. As craftsmen, historians have been alerted against a proclivity to seize upon the discovery of an economic motive as if, to quote Kenneth Stampp, they then were "dealing with reality—with something that reflects the true nature of man." Stampp cites Sumner as an example of the fallacy: ". . . when he argued that Negro suffrage was necessary to prevent a repudiation of the public debt, he may *then* have had a concealed motive—that is, he may have believed that this was the way to convert bondholders to his moral principles." An equal sophistication is overdue in the handling of political motivation. With reference to the Reconstruction legislation of 1867, Sumner did state—frankly, as the cynically inclined would add—that the Negro vote had been a necessity for the organization of "loyal governments" in the South. He continued with equal forthrightness: "It was on this ground, rather than principle, that I relied most. . . ." A man remarkably uncompromising in his own adherence to principle, Sumner obviously did not believe it wise to rely upon moral argument alone to move others. Thaddeus Stevens' belief in the justice of equal suffrage and his desire to see it realized were as consistent and genuine as Sumner's own, but Stevens was a much shrewder practitioner of the art of politics. It is worth noting, then, that Negro suffrage was not the solution to which he clung most tenaciously in order to guarantee "loyal governments" in the South; he looked more confidently to the army and to white disfranchisement. In the last critical stage of battle over Reconstruction policy, it was the moderate Republicans who championed an immediate mandate for Negro suffrage in the South, while Stevens led the fight to delay its advent in favor of an interlude of military rule.

All this suggests the need for a detailed analysis of who said what, when, in arguing that Negro suffrage, South or North, would bring Republican votes and Republican victories. Did the argument have its origin with the committed antislavery men or with the uncommitted politician? Was it used to whet an appetite for political gain or to counter fear of losses? Such a study might start by throwing out as evidence of motivation all appeals to political expediency made after the Fifteenth Amendment was sent to the states for ratification. By that time Republicans were tied to the policy and could not escape the opprobrium it carried; a leadership that used every possible stratagem and pressure to secure ratification in the face of widespread opposition could be expected to overlook no argument that might move hesitant state legislators, particularly one that appealed to party loyalty and interest.

It has been implied that election results in the 1870's and 1880's were evidence of political motivation behind the Fifteenth Amendment. The logic is faulty. Consequences are not linked causally to intentions. Favorable election returns would not constitute proof that decision making had been dependent upon calculation, nor would election losses preclude the existence of unrealistic expectations. Yet it would be of interest to know the effect of the enfranchisement of Negroes upon Republican fortunes, particularly in the marginal northern states. Election returns might serve to test the reasonableness of optimistic projections of gain by adding black voters, as against the undoubted risk of losing white voters. If the end result of Negro enfranchisement in the North was one of considerable advantage to Republicans, we may have overestimated the element of political risk. If enfranchisement brought the Republicans little benefit, the case for a careful re-examination of Republican motivation is strengthened. Inquiry can reasonably be restricted to the results of presidential and congressional contests, since these were of direct concern to the Republicans in Congress responsible for the Fifteenth Amendment.*

Negro votes in the critical northern states were not sufficient to ensure victory in three of the six presidential elections following ratification of the Fifteenth Amendment in 1870. For purposes of comparing the "before" and "after" vote, the election of 1872 is unfortunately of no utility. Horace Greeley proved so weak a Liberal Republican-Democratic candi-

---

* Local elections did, of course, have consequences for senators, who were elected by state legislatures; and a shift of political fortune in a critical state was always of national interest. However, the Fifteenth Amendment was not generated from local politics. The argument of political expediency implies political profit in national elections.

date that in every one of the critical seven states Grant would have won without a single Negro ballot.* In the 1876 contest, which affords the best comparison with 1868, the Republican percentage of the vote dropped in every one of the marginal states, four of which were lost to the Democrats. Comparison of the number of Republican losses in the seven states for the three elections before 1872 with those for the three elections after 1872, shows four losses in the earlier period as against nine losses after Negro enfranchisement.† Of course, it could be argued that Republicans would have done even worse without the Negro vote and the politicians in 1869 could not have anticipated the depression of 1873. Politicians would have known, however, that Negroes in the North, outside the border states, were too few to constitute a guarantee of victory in the face of any major adversity. In 1880 and 1888, years of success, Republicans might have lost Indiana without the Negro, but they would not have lost the Presidency. The only presidential contest in the nineteenth century in which Negro voters played a critical role was that of 1876, and the voters lived not in the North but in the South. Analysis of ballots in the 1870's and 1880's does not confirm the reasonableness of expectations for a succession of Republicans in the White House as the result of Negro enfranchisement.

As to Congress, Republicans could hope to gain very little more than they already held in 1869. Of thirty-six Democrats seated in the House of Representatives from the seven marginal states, only four came from districts with a potential Negro electorate large enough to turn the Republican margin

---

* The percentage of Negroes in the population as compared with the percentage margin of victory in 1872 follows: Connecticut, 1.8 percent with 2.4; New York, 1.2 percent with 3.1; Pennsylvania, 1.9 percent with 12.1; New Jersey, 3.4 percent with 4.4; Ohio, 2.4 percent with 3.2; Indiana, 1.5 percent with 3.2; Illinois, 1.1 percent with 6.2.

† Before 1872: New Jersey in 1860 (in part), 1864, and 1868, and New York in 1868. After 1872: Connecticut, New York, and Indiana in 1876 and 1884; New Jersey in 1876, 1880, and 1884.

of defeat in 1868 into a victory.* Of the four, Republicans gained just one in 1870, in Cincinnati, Ohio. Their failure to profit from the Negro vote in the Thirteenth District of Illinois, located at the southern tip of the state, is of particular interest. The district had gone Republican in 1866 and had a large concentration of Negro population. In 1868 the Republican share of the vote had been a close 49.1 percent; in 1870 it actually decreased with the Democratic margin of victory rising from 503 to 1,081. In the two counties with the highest proportion of Negroes to whites, over 20 percent, a jump in the Republican percentage plus an increase in the actual number of Republican votes cast—unusual in a nonpresidential year—indicate that Negroes exercised their new franchise. However, this apparently acted as a stimulus for whites to go to the polls and vote Democratic. In three of the five counties in the district where Negroes constituted over 5 percent of the population, more Democratic votes were recorded in 1870 than in 1868.†

The Republicans did better in holding seats won by slim margins in 1868 than in winning new ones. Eighteen congressional districts in the critical seven states had gone to Republicans by a margin of fewer than five hundred votes. Of these,

* The four were the Second District in New Jersey, the First in Ohio, the Sixth in Indiana, and the Thirteenth in Illinois. This conclusion is based upon an inspection of election returns as reported in the *Tribune Almanac*, comparing the margin of victory for Democratic winners in 1868 with an approximation of the number of potential Negro voters estimated as one-fifth of the Negro population in the counties comprising each district.

† That Negroes were responsible for the increase in the Republican vote cannot, of course, be proved but appears highly probable; similarly, the explanation for the larger Democratic vote is inference. The Republican vote in Alexander County with a Negro population of 21.73 percent rose from 656 to 804 (37.8 to 45.6 percent); in Pulaski with a Negro population of 27.4 percent from 543 to 844 (46 to 55.59 percent). The three counties showing an increase in the number of Democratic votes were Jackson (Republican votes increased there also), Massac, and Pulaski.

Republicans retained fourteen and lost four to the Democrats in 1870.* Three of the four districts lost had a potential Negro electorate large enough to have doubled the Republican margins of 1868. The record of voting in congressional elections from 1860 through 1868 in the fourteen districts retained suggests that half might have remained Republican without any benefit of the Fifteenth Amendment.† It is doubtful whether three of the other seven, all districts in Ohio, would have been placed in jeopardy had Negro suffrage not been raised as an issue in 1867 both at home and in Washington, for the margin of victory dropped sharply from 1866 to 1868.‡ One of the remaining four, the Second District in Connecticut, consisted of two counties, Middlesex with a Negro population of 372 and New Haven with 2,734, the largest concentration of Negroes in the state. New Haven had gone Demo-

---

* Districts lost were the Sixteenth Pennsylvania, the Third and Fourth Ohio, and the Seventh Indiana. Districts retained were the Second Connecticut, the Eleventh and Twelfth New York, the Third, Fifth, Tenth, and Thirteenth Pennsylvania, the Fourth New Jersey, the Second, Sixth, Seventh, Fourteenth, and Sixteenth Ohio, and the Fourth Indiana.

† This tentative conclusion is based upon Republican victories in at least four of the five congressional elections before 1870. In only one of the seven had the margin of Republican victory in 1866 been less than five hundred. This district, the Fifth in Philadelphia, may have needed Negro votes for victory in 1870 despite its Republican record. Together with it, the Thirteenth in Pennsylvania and the Fourth in Indiana had slim majorities in 1870. In the latter two, however, the margin decreased as compared with 1868, making it unlikely that Negro enfranchisement helped more than it hurt the Republican candidates.

‡ In every one of the seven close Ohio districts, the majority vote had been against the state's Negro suffrage amendment in 1867. Their congressmen, however, supported Negro suffrage, all having voted for the First Reconstruction Act of March, 1867, and also for Negro suffrage in the District of Columbia on January 18, 1866, and again on December 14, 1866. These men, each of whom served both in the Thirty-ninth and Fortieth Congresses (1865–1869) were Rutherford B. Hayes, Robert C. Schenck, William Lawrence, Reader W. Clarke, Samuel Shellabarger, Martin Welker, and John A. Bingham.

[165]

cratic in 1869 (Connecticut elected its congressmen in the spring) by 62 votes, though the Republican won the district; two years later, with Negroes enfranchised, the Democratic margin in New Haven actually increased to 270! Middlesex saved the day for the incumbent, who barely survived by 23 votes. This suggests that the district remained Republican not because of Negro enfranchisement, but despite it. Two seats, one in Pennsylvania and the other in New Jersey, were retained by an increase in the margin of victory larger than the number of potential Negro voters.* The last of the fourteen districts, the Eleventh of New York, consisting of Orange and Sullivan counties, may have been saved by Negro voters, although the election results there are particularly difficult to interpret.†

If we consider the total picture of the 1870 congressional races, we find that the Republican share of the vote decreased in five of the seven critical states, remained practically constant in Ohio, and increased in New Jersey. The party did best in the two states with the highest percentages of Negroes in their population, Ohio and New Jersey, netting one additional seat in each. However, in the seven states as a whole Republicans suffered a net loss of nine representatives. Democrats gained most in New York and Pennsylvania, almost doubling their congressional delegation in the latter from six to eleven out of a total of twenty-four. Republicans retained control in Congress but with a sharply reduced majority. In short, results of the northern congressional elections of 1870 suggest

---

* The Tenth District in Pennsylvania, made up of Lebanon and Schuylkill counties, had a Negro population of 458, or about 90 potential voters. The Republican margin increased by 404 votes. The Fourth District in New Jersey had a larger Negro population, but the incumbent's margin jumped from 79 to 2,753.

† The Republican incumbent lost in 1868 by 322 votes but contested the outcome and was seated. In 1870 another Republican won by 500 votes. There were 2,623 Negroes, somewhat more than 500 possible voters, of whom some would have qualified under the old freehold requirement.

that Negro voters may have offset to some extent the alienation of white voters by the suffrage issue, that they did little,
however, to turn Republican defeats into Republican victories, and that the impact of the Fifteenth Amendment was in
general disadvantageous to the Republican party.

Election returns blanket a multitude of issues, interests, and
personalities. In an effort to relate them more precisely to the
impact of Negro enfranchisement, we have identified all
counties in the seven marginal states in which Negroes constituted a higher-than-average percentage of the population.
Using 5 percent, we found thirty-four such counties.* An
analysis of the number of Republican voters in 1868 as compared with 1870 and of the changing percentage of the total
vote won by Republicans in 1866, 1868, 1870, and 1876
would indicate that Negroes did go to the polls and vote
Republican in numbers which more than offset adverse white
reaction, but this appears to have been the case in less than half
the counties.† The net effect upon Republican fortunes was

---

* One in New York (Queens); three in Pennsylvania (Chester,
Delaware, Franklin); eight in New Jersey (Cape May, Cumberland,
Salem, Camden, Mercer, Monmouth, Somerset, Bergen); ten in Ohio
(Meigs, Gallia, Pike, Ross, Brown, Clinton, Fayette, Clark, Greene,
Paulding); five in Indiana (Clark, Floyd, Spencer, Vanderburgh,
Marion); and seven in Illinois (Alexander, Jackson, Gallatin, Massac,
Pulaski, Randolph, Madison). The three urban centers with the
largest aggregate number of Negroes in 1870 did not meet the 5-per-
cent criterion and are not included.

† Twelve counties showed an increase in both the number and
percentage of Republican votes in 1870 as compared with 1868; in
nine of these, Republicans also made a better showing than in 1866.
In 1876 twelve counties had a higher percentage of Republican votes
than in 1868. Of these, eight were identical with counties showing
marked gains in 1870. The eight, with an indication of their pre-1870
party record, are: in New Jersey, Camden (R), Merger (D/R), and
Somerset (D); in Ohio, Pike (D) and Ross (D/R); in Indiana, Clark
(D); in Illinois, Alexander (D) and Pulaski (D/R). The two clear
instances of contested counties turning Republican in 1870 and remaining Republican were Mercer in New Jersey and Pulaski in
Illinois, the former with a Negro population of 5.1 percent and the
latter with 27.3 percent.

negligible, if not negative. Thus, in the first congressional election after Negroes were given the ballot, three of the thirty-four counties shifted from Democratic to Republican majorities, but another three went from the Republicans to the Democrats. The record was no happier for Republicans in the 1876 presidential election. Again, only six counties changed political alignment as compared with the 1868 balloting. Two were added to the Republican column, and four were lost!

From whatever angle of vision they are examined, election returns in the seven pivotal states give no support to the assumption that the enfranchisement of northern Negroes would help Republicans in their struggle to maintain control of Congress and the Presidency. This conclusion holds for all of the North. Any hope that may have been entertained of gaining substantial strength in the loyal border states was lacking in realism. It failed to take into account the most obvious of facts—the intensity of hostility to any form of racial equality in communities recently and reluctantly freed from the institution of Negro slavery. Only Missouri and West Virginia had shown Republican strength in 1868; of the ten congressional seats which Republicans then won, half were lost in the elections of 1870. Kentucky had the largest Negro population in the North, but in seven of its nine congressional districts the Democratic margin of victory was so overwhelming that the state could not possibly be won by the Republican opposition, and, in fact, all nine seats remained Democratic in 1870. Although no Republican had won a seat from Maryland in 1868, there the odds were better. The outcome, however, was only a little more favorable. In 1870 Republicans failed to make any gain; in 1872 they were victors in two of the six congressional districts; these they promptly lost in 1874. The pattern of politics in Delaware was similar, consistently Democratic except in the landslide of 1872.

The lack of political profit from the Negro vote in pivotal states of the North reinforces the contention that Republican sponsorship of Negro suffrage in the face of grave political risk warrants a re-examination of motive. There is additional evidence which points to this need. Circumstances leading to the imposition of unrestricted Negro suffrage upon the defeated South are not consistent with an explanation based upon party expediency. Two detailed accounts of the legislative history of the Reconstruction Act of March 2, 1867, have recently been written, one by Brock and the other by David Donald; in neither is there any suggestion that the men responsible for the Negro suffrage provision, Moderates led by John A. Bingham, James G. Blaine, and John Sherman, placed it there as an instrument of party advantage. They were seeking a way to obtain ratification of the Fourteenth Amendment, which the southern states had rejected, and to restore all states to the Union without an indefinite interval of military rule or the imposition of more severe requirements.

The nature of the Fifteenth Amendment also suggests the inadequacy of the view that its purpose was to make permanent Republican control of the South. The amendment did not constitute a guarantee for the continuance of Radical Republican regimes, and this fact was recognized at the time. What it did was to commit the nation, not to universal, but to *impartial* suffrage. Out of the tangle of legislative debate and compromise there had emerged a basic law affirming the principle of nondiscrimination. A number of Republican politicians, South and North, who measured it in terms of political arithmetic, were not happy with the formulation of the amendment. They recognized that under its provisions the southern Negro vote could be reduced to political impotence by literacy tests and other qualifications, ostensibly equal.

If evidence of Republican concern for the principle of equal suffrage irrespective of race is largely wanting in histories dealing with Negro enfranchisement, it may be absent because historians have seldom considered the possibility that such evidence exists. With the more friendly atmosphere in which recent scholarship has approached the Radicals of Reconstruction, it has become apparent that men formerly dismissed as mere opportunistic politicians—"Pig Iron" Kelley, Ben Wade, Henry Wilson—actually displayed in their public careers a genuine concern for the equal status of the Negro. It is time to take a fresh look at the Republican party record as a whole. For example, let us reconsider the charge that Republicans were hypocrites in forcing equal suffrage upon the South at a time when northern states outside New England did not grant a like privilege and were refusing to mend their ways. Aside from disregarding the sequence of events which led to the suffrage requirement in the legislation of 1867, this accusation confuses Republicans with northerners generally. In the postwar referendums on Negro sufrage, race prejudice predominated over the principle of equality but not with the consent of a majority of Republican voters. Thus the 45.9 percent of the Ohio vote for Negro suffrage in 1867 was equivalent to 84.6 percent of the Republican electorate of 1866 and to 89 percent of the Republicans who voted in 1867 for Rutherford B. Hayes as governor.* In truth, Republicans had fought many lost battles in state legislatures and in state referendums on behalf of Negro suffrage. What is surprising is not that they had sometimes evaded the issue but that on so many occasions they had been its champion. Even the most

* Republican support in Kansas was the weakest, with the 1867 referendum gaining only 54.3 percent of the vote for the party's candidate for governor the previous year. In the 1867 defeat for Negro suffrage in Minnesota, the proposal had the support equal to 78.7 percent of those voting for the Republican governor. The 1865 vote on the constitutional proposal in Connecticut amounted to 64 percent of the vote for the Republican candidate for governor; that in Wisconsin, to 79 percent of the Republican gubernatorial vote. New York rejected equal suffrage in 1869 with supporters equaling 60 percent of the 1868 Republican vote for governor and 80 percent of the party's 1869 vote for secretary of state.

cynical of observers would find it difficult to account for all such Republican effort in terms of political advantage. What need was there in Minnesota or Wisconsin or Iowa for a mere handful of potential Republican voters? In these states, as in others, the movement to secure the ballot for Negroes antedated the Civil War and cannot be discounted as a mere maneuver preliminary to imposing Negro suffrage upon a defeated South.

Historians have not asked whether Republicans who voted for the Fifteenth Amendment were acting in a manner consistent with their past public records. We do not know how many of these congressmen had earlier demonstrated, or failed to demonstrate, a concern for the well-being of free Negroes or a willingness publicly to support the unpopular cause of Negro suffrage. The vote in the House of Representatives in January, 1866, on the question of Negro suffrage in the District of Columbia offers an example of neglected evidence. The issue was raised before a break had developed between President Johnson and Congress; it came, in fact, at a time when an overwhelming majority of Republicans accepted the President's decision not to force Negro suffrage upon the South, even a suffrage limited to freedmen who might qualify by military service, education, or property holding. In other words, this vote reflected not the self-interest but the conscience of Republicans. They divided 116 for the measure, 15 against, and 10 recorded as not voting. In the next Congress, which passed upon the Fifteenth Amendment, support for that measure came from seventy-two representatives elected from northern states which had not extended equal suffrage to Negroes. Were these men acting under the compulsion of politics or of conscience? More than half, forty-four in all, had served in the House during the previous Congress. Every one of the forty-four had voted in favor of Negro suffrage for the District of Columbia. Why can they not be credited with an honest conviction, to use the words of a New York *Times* editorial, "that a particular color ought not of itself to exclude from the elective franchise . . . ?"

The motives of congressmen doubtless were mixed, but in a period of national crisis when the issue of equality was basic to political contention, it is just possible that party advantage was subordinated to principle. Should further study rehabilitate the reputation of the Republican party in respect to Negro suffrage, it would not follow that the 1860's were a golden age dedicated to the principle that all men were created equal. During the years of Civil War and Reconstruction, race prejudice was institutionalized in the Democratic party. Perhaps this very fact, plus the jibes of inconsistency and hypocrisy with which Democrats derided their opponents, helped to create the party unity that committed Republicans, and through them the nation, to equal suffrage irrespective of race.

PART III

THE FREEDMEN

In the aftermath of the Civil War, many white southerners gratefully recalled the loyalty of the black population, the faithful performance of plantation duties, and the absence of any significant slave insurrections. Crucial to this legend of the "faithful slave" was also the belief that emancipation was imposed upon an indifferent people who had exhibited no strong desire for freedom. But for a number of white southerners, the final days of slavery constituted a traumatic experience in which property suddenly and unpredictably assumed a personality and behaved in ways that were incomprehensible.

8

"THE OLD ALLEGIANCE"

Willie Lee Rose

In her description of the Port Royal experiment, Willie Lee Rose describes the legacy of slavery on the South Carolina Sea Islands and the ways in which the blacks demonstrated their newly won freedom; it was this initial experience with the ex-slaves, she argues, that helped to form the paternalistic and often ambivalent attitudes of "Gideon's Band"—that group of dedicated teachers and ministers who came to educate and proselytize the freedmen in the hope of remaking South Carolina in the image of Massachusetts.

Laura Towne stood on the veranda of Dr. Jenkins' plantation house on Station Creek and gazed across the salt flats to the distant point where the blue waters of Port Royal Sound narrow and flow past the straits of Bay Point and Hilton Head Island. It was here on this porch, the Negroes told her, that the St. Helena planters had converged on that Thursday back in November to watch the battle of Port Royal. They had hoped to see their sons and relatives in the Beaufort Volunteer Artillery drive off the invading fleet, but although they possibly had been too far away to hear the victorious strains of "Yankee Doodle," they had realized early in the afternoon that the forts were falling. Hastily mounting their horses, the planters had ridden away to spread the alarm.

For the few confused hours that followed, the missionaries soon learned that every plantation had its own special story. A few planters had succeeded in quickly driving their slaves and livestock to the Beaufort ferry, but for every one who had succeeded in this, there were a dozen who failed. The Negroes too had heard the guns, and some had hidden in the swamps and in the fields, crouched low between the corn rows. Others had sensed their power for the first time and had stubbornly stood their ground before their masters, impervious to cajolery and threats that the Yankees would sell them to Cuba. Master Daniel Pope's seamstress, Susannah, told Laura Towne that she had asked her master when he urged and threatened, "Why should they [the Yankees] kill poor black folks who did no harm and could only be guided by white folks?" The majority of the Negroes showed the shrewdness of a certain Dr. Sams's man Cupid, who recalled that his master had told his slaves to collect at a certain point so that "dey could jus' sweep us up in a heap, an' put us in de boat." The Negroes had taken to the woods instead. "Jus as if I was gwine to be sich a goat!" commented Cupid. Pompey of Coffin's Point informed Harriet Ware that some Negroes in his plantation would have been duped by the Cuba story but for the fact that the "poor whites" of Beaufort had made the slaves "sensible" to the fact that their own freedom was at stake in the conflict.

Not every planter had even tried to remove his slaves. There were perhaps a few others who followed the course of Captain John Fripp of St. Helena Island. This remarkable man, who was at once one of the richest landowners in the district and a Union sympathizer, called his slaves together and explained the situation. He warned that they would probably starve if they followed him to the interior and advised them to hide until the Confederate soldiers had passed through the island. They should then keep together, work their provision crops as usual, and forget about the cotton. It was late in the day when Henry, the cook at Coffin's Point, sounded the alarm on the northern end of St. Helena. He excitedly informed the overseer that he had better be off, for "all the Yankee ships were 'going in procession up to Beaufort, solemn as a funeral.'" The overseer left, but Henry did not.

Henry had been wrong in thinking the gunboats were occupying Beaufort so promptly. After effecting a lodgment at Hilton Head and making a few tentative explorations, the federal forces had waited patiently several days for some response to General T. W. Hunter's proclamation of assurance and protection to the citizens of the district. Had Du Pont's gunboats occupied Beaufort immediately, they would probably have intercepted almost the entire white population embarking for Charleston on a steamer that was docked conveniently at the town landing. Such action would also have frustrated the enactment of a most instructive morality play on the true character of slavery. In the few days that elapsed before federal authority was consolidated throughout the island region, the social and legal bindings of the peculiar institution unwound with the speed and ferocity of a coiled wire spring.

The sack of Beaufort was one event that the Negroes did not discuss with their new friends. The looting of the houses probably began with the motive of plunder, but in a short time crowds of field hands descended upon the town and took it apart, presumably for the satisfaction of doing it. Whatever manorial pride the field hands may have felt in the country estates of their late owners, it did not encompass the elegance of the family town houses. It is quite probable that most of these plantation Negroes had never been inside their masters' fine homes in Beaufort, but they were not intimidated. Over the protests of the house servants who had remained, they broke up furniture, loaded valuables onto boats to carry away, and helped themselves to the wine. Thomas Elliott, who returned to his Beaufort house the day following the November

7 attack on the forts, reported that he discovered "Chloe, Stephens' wife, seated at Phoebe's piano playing away like the very Devil and two damsels upstairs dancing away famously. . . ." They were all plantation Negroes who had come into town. The houses had little furniture left and had been "completely turned upside down and inside out. The organs in both churches were broken up," Elliott reported, "and the churches themselves robbed of many articles which were deposited there for safe keeping."

The correspondent of the New York *Tribune* described the destruction that Du Pont and his landing party found when they went up to Beaufort on November 12. "We went through spacious houses where only a week ago families were living in luxury, and saw their costly furniture despoiled; books and papers smashed; pianos on the sidewalk, feather beds ripped open, and even the filth of the Negroes left lying in parlors and bedchambers." The destruction had been "wanton," and much of it could have served "no purposes of plunder" but only a "malicious love of mischief gratified." Nothing that happened illustrated better the frustrated hostilities of generations than the desecration of the stylish houses in the east end of town.

Commodore Du Pont was saddened by what he saw but at the same time remembered with contempt how South Carolina fire-eaters had said their own slaves "would drive out the Yankees." They had known very little, reflected the Commodore, "of the relations existing between master and servant. Oh my! It was with difficulty they could get away [with] a household domestic—the field hands remained to a man . . . and immediately commenced plundering until we stopped them."

Du Pont heard other, darker things as well. The planters and overseers were in some cases shooting down rebellious slaves who would not leave the plantations with them. In a panic to retrieve the most portable part of his evaporating fortunes, each planter had, in his own way, borne witness by action to his private conception of chattel slavery. For every man like Captain John Fripp, who thought first of his slaves as people, there was another who thought of them first as property. During the revolutionary days before the federal pickets were posted over the islands, numerous planters concluded that there was yet time to evacuate Negroes and burn their cotton. When Thomas R. S. Elliott returned to his plantation and found the Negroes idle, he attempted to force them away with him. He was unsuccessful and commented grimly, "I think we will have to make a terrible example of many of them." Although Elliott's meaning is not precise, it is clear that many "terrible examples" were made.

William Elliott had once written, in a candid defense of slavery, that masters were usually kind and that slavery served the interests of civilization. "Against *insubordination alone*, we are severe." That was precisely what the masters had been obliged to deal with when the islands were invaded. The only eyewitnesses of these atrocities were the Negroes themselves, but their accounts were complete in many cases with names and places and were sufficient to convince the naval officers who questioned them. Commodore Du Pont was horrified to hear from an army officer, whose information had come "from reliable testimony," of recalcitrant slaves being burned to death in their cotton-houses. George W. Smalley, the correspondent of the New York *Tribune*, concluded that "the horrible fact stands out with appalling clearness and certainty that the murder of slaves who cannot be compelled to follow their masters is a deliberate and relentless purpose." His informants too gave names and places. A responsible Negro named Will Capers told Laura Towne that he had known of thirty Negroes who were shot for resistance.

In the early days at Port Royal the missionaries heard many

such stories. When all possible allowance is made for exaggeration, understandable mistakes, and even for the possibility that Negroes met death by accident while hiding in burning cotton-houses, the sheer weight of the evidence leads to the belief that many white men were willing to go to extreme lengths to retrieve their human property. James Petigru, following the Port Royal story from Charleston, heard of a planter who had burned all the buildings on his plantation, including all stores of corn and cotton, "and by so doing compelled his negroes to follow him, as they were on an island without food and shelter."

The masters' problems were by no means over if they succeeded in recovering their slave property. Petigru wrote, "They have to find new homes, and provide for their people for a whole year, while the abandonment of their crops just harvested leaves them penniless." For men in the Confederate army, obliged to conduct these affairs through their wives and overseers, the problem was acute. Sometimes, when hiring out failed and there were no funds to meet financial pressures, the sale of slaves was the only answer.

Masters who owned slaves on the periphery of the territory held by the Union forces were faced with the possible loss of all their slaves through running away. John Berkeley Grimball, who owned slaves and plantations in Beaufort and Colleton Districts, recorded in his diary for the early days of March in 1862 the gradual depopulation of his estates. The forty-eight slaves who stayed, including the old and sick, had their reward at the end of the season in being sold for the round figure of $820 each. Some masters relied upon severe punishment to discourage running away. When Ralph Elliott frustrated the escape of his father's slaves from Oak Lawn, he had two of the leaders sold in Charleston, and "the others were punished by whips and hand-cuffing." Every night they were chained and watched while Elliott waited for the danger to pass.

But the danger did not pass. To William Elliott the Negroes seemed "utterly demoralized" by Yankee propaganda. The missionaries saw it differently. The streams of Negroes were coming out of the interior as a result of their total dissatisfaction with the "patriarchal institution." Generations of servitude had not stamped out of these people the desire to do as they pleased, although any real understanding of the responsibilities of freedom must have been, for most of them, very remote. E. L. Pierce wrote, in a moment of insight, that "the slave is unknown to all, even to himself, while the bondage lasts." Not even the keenest outside observer, "much less the master can measure the capacities and possibilities of the slave, until the slave himself is transmuted to a man."

He might have added that the moment of freedom revealed the essence of ownership as well. The barbaric behavior of certain of the masters was probably no surprise to the Negroes who had been their slaves. A slave's life was one long lesson in accommodation to his master, and the slaves *did* recognize their own economic value. The missionaries, on the other hand, demonstrated occasionally a real sense of shock at the more severe aspects of the slave system as it was exercised in the old Sea Island region. There were plantations where nearly every Negro's back showed the marks of whipping, and the testimony of the Negroes against certain of the old owners was remarkably consistent. Occasionally, the discovery of a revealing letter in the correspondence of the vanished white people bolstered the verdict of the Negroes. The missionaries heard again and again the same condemnation of certain cruel men and virtually unanimous praise of others. . . .

The Negroes of the islands, wrote Edward Pierce, "had become an abject race, more docile and submissive than those of any other locality." Nowhere else had "the deterioration from their native manhood been carried so far. . . ." Pierce was by no means alone in this conclusion, for all the missionaries were struck with certain childish qualities manifested by many of the Negroes. Elizabeth Botume described a class of young adults:

They rolled up their eyes and scratched their heads when puzzled, and every line in their faces was in motion. If any one missed a word, or gave a wrong answer, he looked very grave. But whenever a correct answer was given, especially if it seemed difficult, they laughed aloud, and reeled about, hitting each other with their elbows. Such "guffaws" could not be tolerated in regular school hours. They joked each other like children; but, unlike them, they took all good-naturedly.

A superintendent concluded that the Negroes were entirely dependent, lacking in initiative, and that they needed "the positive ordering that a child of five or ten years of age requires." The sum of these observations added up to a picture of the personality known in American literature as "Sambo," the plantation slave, "docile but irresponsible, loyal but lazy, humble but chronically given to lying and stealing."

But it is well to remember that although "Sambo" finds many illustrations in the observations of the teachers on the islands, he remains a *statistical* concept, and the record contains as many stories of protest, disloyalty to the late masters, and manly independence as of servile acquiescence. The extent to which the personality of the common field hand had been fundamentally altered by the experience of slavery finds a good test in his response to the opportunities offered by the new order inaugurated in the wake of the northern occupation. The first reaction can be found in the large numbers of slaves willing to risk severe punishment and even death by running away from their masters. The wild sacking of Beaufort and the plantation houses and the complete destruction of the cotton gins show a bitter and long dammed-up hostility that, if perhaps childish in its discharge, is yet remarkably similar to the venting of spleen demonstrable among more "civilized" peoples. Other and more positive tests as to the fundamental damage to the slaves' personality would be provided as time went on in the success, or lack thereof, of the missionaries' labors to make the people self-reliant.

A more probable and immediate explanation of the obsequious and infantile behavior of the majority of slaves who demonstrated childish traits is that playing "Sambo" had its rewards and that failing to play him incurred many risks. That the role could be one of conscious hypocrisy is illustrated by the case of Elijah Green. This ancient veteran of slavery remembered with rancor, many long years after his freedom came, having been obliged to give an affectionate endorsement of the new brides and grooms who joined his master's family, whether he liked them or not.

The main effect of slavery was a thick residue of accumulated habits and responses that a slave child learned early in life. It was a culture, in short, that invested its members with a number of character traits useful in slavery but unbecoming in free men. The extent to which these traits developed in an individual slave depended in part upon the class to which he belonged. It has been a general assumption that more enlightenment and self-respect were to be found among house servants and the Negroes of the towns than among field slaves. The common corollary, however, that these "Swonga" people, as they were denominated by the field hands, also possessed a greater spirit of *independence* is, at the very least, a debatable point. They had merely absorbed more of the white man's culture, and they paid for it in daily contacts with the "superior" beings whose very presence was a reminder of their own inferior status. Sometimes the loyalty of a well-treated house servant could make war on the very notion of independence. There is considerable evidence to support the idea that, while the Swonga people had perhaps more self-esteem and were better dressed, the field hands had more self-reliance. It would be hard to conceive of a more independent spirit than that shown by the six strapping sons of "Mom Peg." They had all been field slaves, and they defied an overseer to whip them. When one brother was threatened, all took to the woods in a body and had to be guaranteed immunity before returning. Described as "tall and handsome," the brothers held "high rank in church and council" and were to enjoy a bright future in freedom. On the other hand, Laura Towne met two women in Beaufort, formerly house servants, who assured her that they would not have run away from their masters except for their desire not to be separated from their kin. But they were already feeling nostalgic for the old ways, with the coming of April, for in the spring they had always come to Beaufort with their masters' families and had had "such gay times." They hoped the teachers would not go away, for it "seemed like they couldn't be happy widout white ladies 'roun.'"

The story of Lydia Smalls is most instructive. When she was a girl, her mistress had taken her away from field work on the Ashdale plantation on Ladies Island and had brought her to Beaufort, where she became a trusted house servant. When Lydia's own son was growing up as a pampered pet in the Prince Street house of their master, Henry McKee, Lydia was afraid he did not realize the meaning of slavery or the full indignity of his position. Ever a rebel in her heart, Lydia forced her son to watch a slave being whipped in the yard of the Beaufort jail. Then young Robert went himself to stay for a time at the Ashdale plantation. He had seen the seemingly dull and cringing plantation people every week when he had come with his master to bring their rations. He never understood much about them, however, until the day he stayed and his master rode away. The apathetic people suddenly found the spirit to grumble and complain heartily about their diet. It was on the plantation that Robert Smalls first heard about Frederick Douglass and decided that he too would become a free man.

For many a servant, a close personal tie with a good master or mistress could go a long way toward reconciliation to a dependent condition. Henry, formerly cook for Mrs. Thomas Aston Coffin, spoke affectionately of his former mistress to Harriet Ware and readily seized upon Miss Ware's offer to write to Mrs. Coffin for him. He had hesitated to make the request himself for fear "they wouldn't think it right to have anything to do with the old people—'but she's a Nort' lady, you know, Ma'am,'" he said to Miss Ware, "'a beautiful lady, I would serve her all my life.'" When Thomas Chaplin's slave Anthony died, Chaplin wrote, perhaps a little self-consciously, "he is regretted by many—white and black—I miss him more than I would any other negro that I own," and added, "Peace be to his *soul*."

Anthony had belonged, as a "driver," to the uppermost rank of plantation life. These foremen and the skilled laborers enjoyed an even more exalted position than the house servants. The driver held the most responsible position a slave could occupy. His job included maintaining order in the quarters as well as calling the Negroes to work, assigning the daily tasks, and seeing that the work was well done. That the driver was sometimes a cruel despot, as he was frequently portrayed in abolition literature, is undeniable; but there is little evidence in the Sea Island story to indicate that he was commonly such. If the driver developed a fine knowledge of farming and enjoyed his master's confidence over a period of years, their relationship could become one of mutual esteem and friendly respect, contrasting most favorably with the often unstable and transient connections between plantation owners and their overseers.

Isaac Stephens, "master servant" to William Elliott, was able to keep his master informed of the condition of the crops on Elliott's numerous estates while the latter was on extended trips from home. He had been certain enough of his own standing to pass judgment on the relative qualities of the white overseers at the several plantations and to exchange social information with his master about the family at home:

Old Mistress and Miss Mary are quite well. I was quite sorry that some of my young mistress and masters wear [*sic*] not in Beaufort to enjoy some of the fine dinners and Tea partys [*sic*] old Mistress has been giving for her grandchildren. . . .

Master will be so kind as to give my love to my wife—all her friends are well—and say howdey to her and myself just like an old Buck—hearty and prime. . . .

There must have been few Negroes on the islands who had enjoyed so relaxed a relationship with their masters, or who had had such opportunities to develop judgment and leadership. The evangels could count on these few, however, to provide an example for the rest in making an adaptation to freedom.

There had even been a few opportunities for slaves to develop special talents outside the economic hierarchy of the plantation. Religious leaders enjoyed special standing with their fellows, and women sometimes achieved status as midwives. For all the slaves there was a small economic venture open in the raising of poultry and a little garden crop, or perhaps a pig. The surplus was sold to the master for cash; occasionally, it was sold outside the plantation by the slave himself. Although a statute against trading with slaves existed, it was usually ignored. Outside these limited interests, there was nothing for most slaves but the dull routine of the cotton field. The real trouble with slavery as a "school" for anything was that the institution provided so few directions in which to grow and so much necessity to conform.

The Negro child on a large Sea Island plantation began learning how to be a slave almost from the moment of birth. In view of the generally acknowledged impact of early childhood experiences upon personality, the restrictions of a slave's childhood may go further than institutions or laws to explain certain of "Sambo's" failings. When the slave mother emerged from her confinement and returned to the field at the end of the third or fourth week, she saw her baby in the day only long enough for feeding and had very little time for the affectionate caressing so important for the development of the child's personality and security. On the other hand, the mother herself could not experience the happiest aspects of motherhood when the child was merely an additional drain upon a tired body. The missionaries frequently observed that numbers of mothers on the great plantations appeared to demonstrate very little affection for their offspring. Arthur Sumner complained that the children "are invariably spoken to in harsh and peremptory tones" by adult Negroes and were "whipped unmercifully for the least offence." A stern system called for stern discipline, and an old Negro woman asked Elizabeth Botume: "What the Lord Almighty make trees for if they ain't fur lick boy chillen?" Toys were little known, and games usually took the form of fighting and wrestling in lieu of more constructive play. But the numbers of tender stories of maternal love show that, even among the victims of such a severe regimen, the human instincts served to soften the general harshness of the lives of children.

When the mother returned to the field the child usually went, on the large Sea Island plantations, to a nursery, where he joined numbers of other children under the supervision of superannuated "Maumas" or grannies. Frederika Bremer pronounced this system "repulsive." She had seen "sometimes as many as sixty or seventy or even more [small children] together, and their guardians were a couple of old Negro witches who with a rod of reeds kept rule over these poor little black lambs, who with an unmistakable expression of fear and horror shrunk back whenever the threatening witches came forth, flourishing their rods." Aunt Jane Grant recalled in her old age some vivid details of her childhood in Beaufort. The little children of her establishment were cared for by an old mauma who fed them thus: "Dey'd clean off a place on de ground near de washpot where dey cooked de peas, clean it off real clean, den pile de peas out dere on de ground for us to eat."

For fortunate slave children there came a time when they might, as the chosen playmates of the master's children, be able to take a part in the free country life about them. Sometimes the white parents objected that "the little negroes are ruining the children," but sooner or later the democracy of childhood broke down parental resolutions. Mrs. Thomas Chaplin might complain of the "badness" little Jack was teaching her son Ernest, but shortly she would see the two riding off on the same horse to gather wild plums or mulberries. The slave child's formal education would consist of learning the catechism, on plantations where that was deemed important, and he was instructed that his duty to his master was faithful work and that he was responsible to God for a good performance. An important lesson most small slaves learned early was their relation to the white race in general and to the master in particular. Little Jane, of the Robert Oswald household, learned it the day she objected to calling her mistress' small son "Marse" and was sent around to Wilcox's store for a cowhide switch.

The plantation child quickly grasped other things also. He learned how the slave enjoys life a little more at his master's expense. Thomas Chaplin wrote with some sense of resignation:

More robery [sic].—discovered that my little rascal William, who I had minding the crows off the watermellons [sic] had been the worst crow himself, and does the thing quite sistematically [sic]. He turns over a mellon, cuts a hole on the under side large enough to admit his hand, eats out the inside, when he finds a ripe one, then turns the mellon back again, not breaking it off the vine, there it lays, looking as sound as ever. No one would suppose it hollow. In picking some—we found no less than 23 or 4 in this fix. Cunning, very.

It is not surprising that the missionaries should have found the former slaves irresponsible. At no point in his passage to adulthood did the slave youth have the experience of learning to accept responsibility. The peculiar circumstances of his life became most apparent at the time of marriage. Nehemiah Adams was usually blind to the worst aspects of slave life, but even he saw clearly that slavery was inimical to the family as an institution, and he wrote particularly of "the annihilation . . . of the father in the domestic relations of the slaves. . . ." The master supplied the necessaries of life, and what else there was to receive was far more likely to be in the power of the wife to dispense than in that of her husband. The cabin was regarded as hers, and the small poultry and garden operations were usually her primary responsibility. She converted the yard goods into clothing for herself and her family and did the cooking. Even the children were acknowledged to be the mother's and were usually known by her name, as in the case of "Binah's Toby" or "Moll's Judy." Unless he had a friendly alliance with some good-natured woman, the male slave did without many conveniences. Laura Towne commented drily that the liberated Negro men were better satisfied about being released from domestic tyranny than about any other aspect of their freedom. It is worth mentioning that the family picture under slavery was actually a reinforcement of the West African family pattern, arising, as it had there, from the polygynous household. The individual wives in the African community no doubt had to bow to the will of the husband; but within her own hut, and to her own children, the mother had been the omnipotent reality. Rivalry for preferences and honors to her children had provided the African woman with political outlets not unknown in the courts of Europe.

Despite the legal and social obstacles, marriage had a reasonable chance of lasting if it was honored and respected by the owners of the principals. Thomas B. Chaplin complained of the "tomfoolery" of his wife, who took care to make a special occasion of the double wedding of her two maids, Eliza and Nelly. The girls were married by Robert, the spiritual leader of the plantation, and the party was provided with "a grand supper." "They had out," Chaplin complained, "my crockery—Tables, chairs, candle-sticks, and I suppose everything else they wanted." Then there was some of Chaplin's "good liquor made into a bowl of punch" for the guests. Twenty-seven years later, Chaplin penciled into the margin of his diary that the two girls were still alive, well, and still married to "the very same husbands." Many owners did not devote this interest to their slave marriages, but some element of formality was usually present. Without legal protection, however, marriages suffered real stress under the conditions of slavery, which often promoted transient unions and easy partings. The religious leaders among the slaves complained often of unchastity and tried, sometimes without good effect, to bring moral suasion to the aid of family stability. An understanding of this situation requires only the remembrance that the social and legal forces at work to bind together unhappy nineteenth-century white couples were largely inoperative with the slaves. One major problem for the evangels would clearly be to strengthen the Negro family, encouraging the fathers to assume hitherto unknown responsibilities.

So many of the faults of the slave had been perversions of laudable impulses, impulses of protest; those who learned them best frequently comprised the most spirited people on a plantation. Even Master Chaplin had a species of respect for his small slave who had thought of a smart way to steal watermelons. Grown slaves learned how to gain a little time for themselves by idling or pretending illness, and as often as not the matter simply had to be faced with resignation. "Jim and Judge both lying up today," complained their master, "they will have their time out."

When a man carried protest to the passionate length of running away, he had to be prepared for extreme punishment.

Sweet must have been the knowledge to a "prime" runaway, even while reflecting on the bitter cost, that he was depriving his master of a week's hard work in the cotton field. Overt rebellion indeed existed, but it was for the few. Most slaves had learned to accept their condition, as one evangel said, just as "sand receives the cannon-ball, neither casting it off nor being shattered by it." For the majority, the humdrum and safe satisfactions of a well-timed lie, petty theft, or feigned illness had seemed the appropriate defenses of reasonable beings. This mood permeates a folk story that was long told on St. Helena, of an old slave who had never worked in his life because his master was convinced he was a cripple. His master caught him one day, however, strumming his banjo to the words:

> I was fooling my master seventy-two years,
> And I'm fooling him now.

The enraged master prepared to whip the old man, but the timely magic of a "Negro doctor" intervened. "When his master started to whip him, none of the licks touch: And he had freedom."

Frederika Bremer wrote after her visit to the Sea Islands just before the war that she had not found a single plantation where the master was able to advance the social well-being of the slaves. Even the efforts of progressive men who tried to institute some means of self-regulation among the slaves had merely achieved a superior form of discipline. She concluded somberly, "In the darkness of slavery I have sought for the moment of freedom with faith and hope in the genius of America. It is no fault of mine that I have found the darkness so great and the work of light as yet so feeble in the slave states."

There was hardly a plantation that had not a harsh old tale of abuse, and on many the abject fear the slaves had of all white men said all that needed to be told. In the final analysis, however, it was the institution in all its aspects, knowing and foolish, kind and cruel, that had created the prevailing problems confronting Gideon's Band: an exaggerated attitude of dependency; a weak sense of family; an inevitable tendency toward the classic faults of the slave—lying, theft, and irresponsibility. As one Gideonite clearly saw, the barbarism of exceptional slave masters did not really signify much in the total picture. "The real wrong in slavery did not affect the body; but it was a curse to the soul and mind of the slave. The aim of the master was to keep down every principle of manhood and growth, and this held for good and bad planters alike, and was the natural growth of slavery itself." And that was why, despite the moving and testimonial exceptions of strength and character found among the slaves, the larger number of the liberated Negroes of the islands constituted, according to Gannett, "a race of stunted, misshapen children, writhing from the grasp of that people, which, in so many respects, is foremost of the age."

9

THE MEANING OF FREEDOM

Joel Williamson

Among the most neglected stories of the Civil War
and its aftermath is the way in which liberated slaves
tested their freedom. Joel Williamson, who has approached South Carolina Reconstruction in terms of
what Negroes did and thought, relates the transition
from slavery to freedom.

Freedom was a nominal legacy of the war, yet telling the slave
that he was free did not make him so. Ultimately, the Negro
had to establish his freedom by some deliberate, conscious act
entirely his own, or he would remain a slave in fact, if not in
name. Emancipation simply gave him that choice. With near
unanimity, Negroes in South Carolina chose liberty.

In the spring of 1865, the news of emancipation and the
close of the war filtered slowly into the hinterland of South
Carolina. In mid-May, the commanding general of the Department of the South, Q. A. Gillmore, issued a proclamation
declaring that governmental policy would soon be made
known. "It is deemed sufficient, meanwhile," he said, "to
announce that the people of the black race are free citizens of
the United States, that it is the fixed intention of a wise and
beneficent government to protect them in the enjoyment of
their freedom and the fruits of their industry. . . ." Upon
hearing of the order, a few masters formally released their

slaves. Francis W. Pickens, for instance, the secession governor of the state and an extensive planter on the Savannah River in Edgefield District, heard of the order on May 23, and on the same day he called his slaves together, acknowledged their emancipation, and contracted to pay them for their labor during the remainder of the year. Most slaveholders were not so forehanded, releasing their slaves only after occupation forces arrived from the coastal area late in May and subsequently. Even after the occupation was completed, a few masters, particularly among those living in the uplands in the extreme western portion of the state, stubbornly refused to recognize the new status of their Negro laborers. Under these circumstances, many Negroes became certain of their emancipation only by traveling to the lower districts with the men who still acted as their masters. A resident of Pendleton, visiting Columbia late in June with a neighbor and the neighbor's slave, noted with alarm that Toney, the slave, had "shown symptoms of demoralization since his arrival here." Apparently observing the presence of Union troops in the city and the formal recognition of emancipation generally accorded to the Negroes there, Toney "got somewhat excited and talked of making a 'bargin' when he returned to Pendleton." "No Negro is improved by a visit to Columbia," the Carolinian concluded, "& a visit to Charleston is his certain destruction."

By whatever means the Negro learned of emancipation, the most obvious method of affirming his freedom was simply to desert the site of his slavery and the presence of his master. Patience Johnson, an ex-slave on a Laurens District plantation, must have expressed the sentiment of many freedmen when she answered a request by her mistress that she remain in her usual place and work for wages. "No, Miss," she declined, "I must go, if I stay here I'll never know I am free."

Contrary to tradition, however, the typical slave upon hearing of emancipation did not shout with delight, throw his hat into the air, gather the few possessions he claimed, and run pellmell for Charleston. The great majority received the news quietly and began to make deliberate preparations to terminate their slavery definitely by some overt act. Representative of the reaction of the freedmen in the lower and middle districts was that of the Negroes on the Elmore plantation near Columbia. On May 24, as the secret channels of slave communication crackled with rumors of emancipation, an impatient field hand named Caleb ran away. On May 27, Union forces occupied Columbia. "We told the negroes they were free on the 30th"; noted young Grace Elmore, "they waited patiently and respectably." Nevertheless, the freedmen initiated arrangements for separation. "Philis, Jane and Nelly volunteered to finish Albert's shirts before they left and to give good warning before they left," Grace reported, while Jack, the driver, "will stay till the crops are done." Not all of the freedmen were as explicit in stating their plans. "Old Mary, the nurse, took the news quietly on Sat evening; said that none could be happy without prayer, and Monday by day light she took herself off, leaving the poor baby without a nurse."

In the upcountry, the same pattern prevailed. In Spartanburg District, David Golightly Harris first heard of Gillmore's emancipation order on June 5, but made no mention of the news to his slaves. On the same day, however, and apparently before Harris himself had heard of the order, York, one of his field hands, "disappeared." The remainder said "nothing on the subject" and continued to "work as usual." Desertion on neighboring plantations became increasingly frequent, and, in early July, another of Harris' slaves, Old Will, disappeared, "to try to enjoy the freedom the Yankey's have promised the negroes." By late July, it was rumored that some masters in the neighborhood were recognizing formally the freedom of their laborers. Finally, in mid-August, occupation forces stationed in Spartanburg ordered masters to explicitly inform the Negroes of their freedom. On August 15, most did so. When

Harris made the announcement to his slaves, only one, Ann, left immediately, while "the others wisely concluded they would remain until New Years day."

Desertion was a common means by which the ex-slave asserted his freedom; yet variations in the time and spirit of the desertion yield interesting insights into the Negro's attitudes toward his new status. Generally, freedmen who as slaves had labored as domestics, mechanics, and in the extractive industries departed at the first reasonably convenient opportunity. In doing so, they typically exhibited some degree of malice toward their recent owners. On the other hand, those who had labored in the fields generally finished the year in their accustomed places, and when they left seldom departed with expressions of ill will toward their late masters.

It is astonishing that among the servant or domestic class (where slave labor was reputedly least arduous and relations with the master most intimate and satisfactory), defection was almost complete. Correspondence and diaries of the period are replete with instances in which the master or mistress declared "all of our servants have departed." The disintegration of the household staff of the Holmes residence in Camden was typical of the process in the larger houses. None of the dozen adult slaves on the staff departed with General Sherman, but two were lost to Potter's raiders in April. Early in May, two maids were discharged for insubordination, even though the mistress of the household persisted in her refusal to recognize the freedom of those who remained. Later in the same month, an occupation force arrived in the village, and the mistress told the servants of the emancipation order but refused to release them "because it was not at all certain that they would be freed." By mid-June, Isaac, Marcus, Mary (with her two children), and Catherine had, nevertheless, deserted the household without warning. The mistress became fearful that Chloe, eminently necessary to the house as cook and queenpin of the serving staff, might go the same way. After a conversation in which the mistress presumed to explain President Johnson's position as implying that the slaves were not really free, she implored the cook "not to sneak away at night as the others had done, disgracing themselves by running away, as she had never done." Chloe agreed to stay, "but if she could she would like to go to Charleston in the autumn when the railroad was finished." Having won one battle, however, another was immediately lost. On the same day, Ann, the laundress, "poor deluded fool, informed mother she could not wash any longer, nor would she remain to finish the ironing . . . and off she went." By late August, even the "faithful" Chloe had left "after two days notice," and without waiting for the repair of the railroad. Thereafter, hired servants came and went at a rapid rate, and when they departed they usually did so in a cloud of irritation. "We have had a constant ebb and flow of servants," wrote Emma Holmes on October 1, "some staying only a few days, others a few hours, some thoroughly incompetent, others though satisfactory to us preferring plantation life." What was true in the Holmes household was true of their neighbors. "In every direction we hear of families being left without a single servant, or, those who stay doing almost nothing," reported Emma. "All have turned fool together."

In the face of wholesale desertions the more pretentious white families were forced to resort to extremes. Many came to rely entirely upon the service of Negro children. "Our servants here behaved very badly & have all left us, with little exception," quipped one Camden resident in August. "Two of Patty's children are now waiting upon us, little William & Veny." The vacuum in domestic labor, however, was most generally filled by the white ladies of the household. A gentleman refugee in the upcountry, noting the widespread desertion by domestics, was "struck by the cheerful & smiling manner" in which the ladies assured him that "it's a great relief to get rid of the horrid negroes." In May, Emma Holmes had expressed the same spirit of independence. ". . . the servants find we are by no means entirely dependent on them," she wrote with a literary toss of her head. Yet, by mid-August, cheerful independence had soured into galling resentment. After a long day of arduous household labor, Emma complained, "but I dont like cooking or washing, even the doing up of muslins is great annoyance to me and I do miss the having all ready prepared to my hand." In late August, there was only fatigue. "I am very weary," she confessed, "standing up washing all the breakfast and dinner china, bowls, kettles, pans, silver, etc.—a most miscellaneous list of duties, leaving no time for reading or exercise."

The frequency with which domestics deserted their masters discredits the myth of the "faithful old family servant" (the ex-slave) loyally cleaving to his master through the pinching years of Reconstruction. Most of the "faithful few" were literally old, or else very young, or infirm, or encumbered by family arrangements which made desertion impossible. James Hemphill, a wealthy lawyer and politician residing in Chester, indicated that faithfulness among this class of freedmen could be something less than a blessing—a feeling many of his contemporaries shared. "My crowd of darkies is rapidly decreasing," he reported to his brother in September, 1865. "Almost two weeks ago, my cook departed with her child. Last week, our house girl left, and this morning, another girl, lately employed in the culinary department, vacated. We still have six big and little—one old, three children, one man sick, so that you may perceive there are mouths and backs enough, but the labor is very deficient." Three days previously, a former slaveholder in Abbeville District verbalized the same complaint. Of his fifteen slaves, only three remained, "one woman and her two children," who, he lamented, were "in place of a benefit . . . a heavy expense to me for their bread and clothing."

Doubtless, some servants did remain with their late masters

from motives of genuine loyalty and contentment. A Charlestonian wrote in September, 1866, that his "old" coachman and the coachman's wife held steadfast in their devotion to him all during the war and afterward. Such instances were rare, however, and became increasingly so as Reconstruction progressed. An instance of real, but not unlimited, faithfulness was provided by Patty, a Negro woman who had served the John Berkeley Grimball family for thirty-six years before emancipation, fleeing with them during the war from the coast to Greenville and remaining with them after emancipation. In the first disordered months of peace, she had taken out articles to sell and brought back food for the family, stubbornly refusing to take anything for herself. In January, 1866, when finally she did leave to join her son and husband in the lowcountry, she washed all the clothes, gave the young ladies of the house presents, and left two of her younger children to wait on the family.

In spite of obvious and often painful realities, the myth of the "faithful old family servant" persisted both North and South and even grew in the years following Reconstruction. In 1881, John W. De Forest, a Connecticut Yankee who had been a Freedmen's Bureau officer in South Carolina and who certainly knew better, published a remarkably successful novel set in postwar Charleston. Among the host of noble stereotypes who crowded its pages were the "high bred," proud, but impoverished young "Miss Virginia Beaufort" of the Carolina aristocracy and her old crone of a servant, Maume Chloe, "the last faithful remnant of the feminine property of the Beauforts," who, of course, played her role to perfection and lived happily ever after. Most northerners were probably relieved to find that they had left their erstwhile charges in such good hands; but in the South the myth had a rather more tragic aspect. Living in a world they never made, life for southerners was somehow eased by this small fiction which evoked a pleasurable image of the better world they had aspired to build. This was possibly what a lady of Charleston was saying in 1873 when she wrote to a friend upon the death of an elderly woman servant who had been her slave. "I feel a link has been broken, an occasion lamented," she sadly declared, "a really burial of what can never take place again." And it could not, if, indeed, it ever had.

Mechanics and laborers outside of agriculture (in lumbering, mining, turpentine, and other industries) were as quick as domestics to leave their masters. Even where they did not desert their late owners, there was often a disposition to do so. In July, 1865, E. J. Parker, engaged in the turpentine business in the deep piney woods of Williamsburg District, despaired of inducing his former slaves to continue laboring for him even for wages. "I do not believe we shall hire our own negroes to work," he wrote to his partner; "it would be much better if we could hire other negroes. They would work much better." By late September, he had persuaded most of his late bondsmen to contract; but the conflict in their minds between economic necessity and their desire to be free of their recent master was evident. "They signed it with grate reluctance," Parker reported. "And Isaac Reid would not do it and had to take him to Kingstree. He cut up all sorts of Shines. Said he would suffer to be Shot down before he would sign it. That he did not intend to do anything for any man he had been under all his life."

The liberty of freedmen engaged in agriculture to leave their former masters was restricted by the insistence of the occupation forces and the Freedmen's Bureau that plantation owners and laborers contract to harvest and divide the 1865 crop before parting. Many who did not contract found it convenient, nevertheless, to complete the agricultural season. But even as they worked they eagerly anticipated the New Year and the Christmas holidays that preceded it as a kind of second emancipation. Augustine Smythe, managing his mother-in-law's plantation, Lang Syne, near Fort Motte in Or-

angeburg District, described the expectancy among his laborers early in December. "The poor negro," he wrote to his
mother, "besotted with ignorance, & so full of freedom, looking forward to January as to some day of Jubilee approaching,
with all the difficulties & dangers of a free man's life to encounter, & none of the experience or sense necessary to enable
him successfully to battle with them, thinking only that freedom confers the privilege of going where & doing as they
please, work when they wish, or stop if they feel disposed, &
yet be fed, supported & cared for by his Master, lazy, trifling,
impertinent! Mother, they are awful!"

Christmas Day, 1865, saw many South Carolina plantations
entirely deserted by their Negro populations. Smythe's plantation was thus abandoned, and, in Spartanburg District,
David Golightly Harris recorded in his journal that all of his
"negroes leave to day, to hunt themselves a new home, while
we will be left to wait upon ourselves." After visiting the
plantation of a relative on February 9, 1866, the Reverend
John Hamilton Cornish reported that, "not one of their Negroes is with them, all have left." Like many domestics, most
of those field hands who remained on the plantations were
very old, very young, ill, or encumbered. The mistress of the
Ball plantation in Laurens District recalled at the turn of the
century that at the end of 1865 "many of the negroes sought
employment on other places, but the least desirable stayed
with us, for they could not easily find new homes and we
could not deny them shelter."

This pattern was broken only on the very large plantations.
Here, apparently, many freedmen deliberately chose to remain on the "home place."

The inclination of domestics, mechanics, and laborers in the
extractive industries and on relatively small plantations to
leave their masters at the first reasonable opportunity while
agriculturalists on the larger plantations remained suggests
that desertion correlated very closely with the degree of prox-

imity that had existed between the slave and his owner and, further, that the freedman was much more interested in leaving behind the personal remainders of slavery than he was the physical.

In South Carolina, the mass movement among the Negro population was not the "aimless," endless, far-flung wandering so often described. Freedmen most often left their homes to separate themselves distinctly from slavery, but their destination was nearly always fixed by economic design or necessity. Most migrants resettled themselves within a matter of days or weeks and within a few miles of the place which, as slaves, they had called home. "In almost every yard," wrote Emma Holmes in June, 1865, "servants are leaving but going to wait on other people for food merely, sometimes with the promise of clothing." Many former domestics went into the fields to labor, and, conversely, a few agricultural laborers entered household service. For instance, in February, 1866, the Grimballs hired Josey, one of their ex-field hands, and Amy his wife and their daughter Delia to replace the "faithful" Patty. Also, northerners on the Sea Islands, during and after the war, frequently drew their servants from among the plantation hands.

Large numbers of agricultural laborers left their native plantations during the Christmas season to camp in a neighboring village while they searched for an employer. Employment, however, was not always easily found. David Golightly Harris, visiting Spartanburg on New Year's Day, 1866, "saw many negroes *enjoying* their *freedom* by walking about the streets & looking much out of sorts. . . . Ask who you may 'What are you going to do,' & their universal answer is 'I dont know.'" Augustine Smythe found much the same conditions prevailing in the vicinity of Fort Motte in Orangeburg District. "There is considerable trouble & moving among the negroes," he reported. "They are just like a swarm of bees all buzzing about & not knowing where to settle."

Having proved their freedom by leaving their former masters, many Negroes, apparently, were soon willing to return to them. By late September, two out of the three servants who had deserted James Hemphill's Chester household had returned; and Cuffee, a domestic in the residence of John Richardson Cheeves (a son of Langdon Cheeves) in Abbeville, returned to his usual labors in October, 1865, after having savored both freedom and hunger downriver in Savannah. A large number of agricultural laborers also returned to their native plantations after a short stay abroad. In mid-January, the wife of the manager of Lang Syne in Orangeburg District jested that "fifteen turkeys 'nebber come home,' " indirectly indicating that more than half of the laboring force had again settled in their places on the home plantation. Frequently, agricultural laborers returned to remain against the wishes of the owners. The manager of Lang Syne reported that one Negro woman had returned and asked to be hired. He refused but she declined to leave and secreted herself in one of the outbuildings. Several days later, she appealed over the manager's head to the owner of the plantation to order her acceptance and was again refused. Finally, the manager "walked her off," but later suspected that she was still hiding in one of the Negro houses. A small planter in Union District cried out in anguish early in 1866 when some of his late slaves, being discharged, returned against his wishes and persisted in going into the fields and laboring alongside those he had agreed to employ.

Apparently, many freedmen were driven to return to their old places by economic necessity. Isabella A. Soustan, a Negro woman who had somehow found freedom in a place called Liberty, North Carolina, in July, 1865, expressed her thoughts on the dilemma that many ex-slaves faced in their first year of emancipation. "I have the honor to appeal to you one more for assistance, Master," she petitioned her recent owner. "I am cramped hear nearly to death and no one ceares for me heare, and I want you if you pleas Sir, to send for me." Some few freedmen were willing to exchange liberty for security. "I don care if I am free," concluded Isabella, "I had rather live with you, I was as free while with you as I wanted to be." Yet, even those who did return soon found that freedom bore no necessary relationship to geography.

While migrants were motivated by combinations of many desires, much of their behavior is explained by their love of the homeplace—the "old range" as they themselves rather warmly termed it. White contemporaries, perhaps obsessed with the idea that theirs was a white man's land, never fully appreciated the fact that Negroes, too, were strongly devoted to the soil upon which they had been born and labored. "The aged freedwomen, and many also of the aged freedmen," reported a Bureau officer, "had the bump of locality like old cats." Similarly, a local official of the state, frustrated in his attempts to resettle Negroes on public lands in Georgetown County, found this sentiment a serious deterrent. "Local attachment, you know, has always been a ruling passion with the agricultural classes of our people," he explained to his superior. Thus, ironically, the Negro frequently moved to get away from his late master, but he almost always moved to settle in the very locale where he had served in bondage.

The desire to return to the "old range" was particularly evident in the coastal areas in the year following the war. On the one hand, very nearly all the Negroes who had fled to the islands during the conflict returned to the mainland within the first two or three years of peace. On the other hand, thousands of Negroes who had been taken inland by their masters during the war returned to the coast. In the months following emancipation, the stream of coastward migration was continuous, but as the upland farming season closed in October and November, 1865, the flow swelled into a flood. By December, it was estimated that Negroes were passing through Columbia at the rate of a thousand a month. In January, the migration reached its crest and declined to a trickle by late February when the new planting season was underway. Doubtless, it was the return of these freedmen to their coastal haunts that led northern observers, virtually all of whom felt compelled to make the pilgrimage from Charleston to Columbia to see the ruins, to exaggerate the volume of Negro movement throughout the state and to conclude that the migrants were bound for Charleston simply because there "freedom was free-er." Later writers accepted and perpetuated these erroneous impressions.

Many of the coastward migrants moved with assurance of employment upon arriving at their destinations. Many also returned without such guarantees, but with the aid of the bureau and promises that work could be found in their native communities. Whatever their prospects, the road of the migrant freedman was never easy, and the obstacles they overcame to return home suggest the great strength of the pull of place upon them. From deep in the interior, many of them trudged along the ribbons of mud called roads to the fire-gutted city of Columbia. Riding with the driver in the "boot" of a westbound stagecoach one clear, cold December morning in 1865, one northern traveler counted within a distance of eight miles thirty-nine Negroes walking toward Columbia. All were underclothed, miserable, and tired in appearance, carrying their possessions in bundles on their backs. One middle-aged Negro woman, he noted, was carrying a bundle on her head and a baby on her back. At the same time she was leading a little girl by the hand, while a small boy followed behind. As they passed, the driver shouted down to her, "Goin' down to Columby after you 'free, be ye? Well, go on." From Columbia, they plodded some 100 miles along the line of the railroad to Charleston. There, while awaiting transportation to the homeplace by bureau steamer, they took refuge in the deserted houses of their masters or in the burned-out buildings of the lower district. In January, 1866, a northern correspond-

ent saw fifteen hundred of them camped on the waterfront,
wretched and pitiable, some living in the open coal sheds
along the wharves. As he walked among them, they cooked
and ate their breakfasts around smoky fires, amidst "tubs,
pails, pots and kettles, sacks, beds, barrels tied up in blankets,
boxes, baskets, [and] bundles," while "hens were scratching,
pigs squealing, cocks crowing, and starved puppies whining."
An old woman belonging to a group bound for Colleton
District catalogued their miseries. "De jew and de air hackles
we more'n anyting," she declared. "De rain beats on we, and
de sun shines we out. My chil'n so hungry dey can't hole up.
De Guv'ment, he han't gib we nottin'. Said dey would put we
on Board Saturday. Some libs and some dies. If dey libs dey
libs, and if dey dies dey dies." After such Odysseys, one can
readily believe those early returnees who told a northern
teacher on Edisto Island in June, 1865, that they were "glad to
get back to their old homes."

Some freedmen, cut loose from their moorings by war and
emancipation, continued to drift wherever the winds and cur-
rents of chance carried them; yet, by the spring of 1866, the
great mass of Negroes in South Carolina had come again to
settle upon the "old range."

In the first weeks of emancipation, many (perhaps most)
freedmen interpreted their liberty as a temporary release from
labor. "Already in the neighborhood they have refused to
work & c," wrote Augustine Smythe in June, 1865, speaking
of the vicinity of Fort Motte. The difficulty, he thought, lay
in the presence of northerners in the state. "Here we are
having Yankee, Yankee, Yankee, White Yankee and nigger
Yankee, till we are more disgusted with them than ever."
Early in July, an elderly planter living near Walterboro noted
the prevalence of much the same sentiment. ". . . negroes
generally very idle," he observed, "wandering about the
country enjoying their freedom, tho to my mind wonderfully
civil, under the circumstances."

Yet, the mass of Negroes did not equate freedom with permanent idleness. In fact, they wanted to work, but only for themselves and at their own discretion. Almost universally, they showed an aversion to cultivating the great staple —cotton, and a willingness to grow food crops sufficient for themselves and their families. In March, 1865, for instance, the mistress of a Christ Church plantation, along with one of her neighbors, gave her slaves freedom to work or not as they pleased. "In every place they have gone to work planting for themselves on their usual places," she reported, meaning that the Negroes were cultivating the garden plots allowed them as slaves. The average freedman expected to work for his own subsistence, but he wanted to choose the time and place of that labor. Late in May, 1865, Grace B. Elmore, living in her mother's house near Columbia, interviewed Philis, her maid, on the subject. Asked if she liked the idea of freedom, Philis answered "yes, tho she had always been treated with perfect kindness and could complain of nothing in her lot, but she had heard a woman who had bought her freedom from kind indulgent owners, say it was a very sweet thing to be able to do as she chose, to sit and do nothing, to work if she desired, or to go out as she liked and ask nobody's permission, and that was just her feeling." Even so, Grace was assured, "Philis says she expects to work."

When arrangements were satisfactory, the great mass of Negroes exhibited an eagerness to labor. Indeed, enforced idleness made the Negro agrarian uneasy. "We wants to git away to work on our own hook," explained a migrant waiting on a Charleston wharf for a steamer to return him to his home plantation. "It's not a good time at all here. We does nothing but suffer from smoke and ketch cold. We want to begin de planting business." By the early spring of 1866, most Negro farmers had done precisely that.

Apparently, Negroes labored less arduously in freedom than they had in slavery. To many whites, the slowdown seemed a stoppage. During the hot, dry summer of 1865, when the woods were in danger of bursting into flames, a planter near Grahamville complained to the bureau officer that "my negroes in the fairest weather refuse to go out to work at all, to save my place from danger of fire." A flagrant show of ingratitude, he thought, "as this was their old home, to which they said they were anxious to move, it seems now to avoid work altogether." However, he admitted, "they did do some work." Similarly, the lessee of a lowcountry tract declared in early August that his plantation was "litterly taurn up" since "under the present labour system but little is done & what is done is badly done, it being impossible to get work done as it aught to be." Planters above the fall line were also distressed. In Chester, James Hemphill lamented in September, "there is a general indisposition to labor, both among whites and blacks, and nothing is more needed than steady hard labor at present"; and an Abbeville resident declared, "the negro is so indolent and lazy that he is incapable of any exertion to better his circumstances." A freedman's version was expressed on August 13, 1865, at Lewisfield, a small station on the North Eastern Railroad some forty miles from Charleston. There a Negro "asked the Yankee officer if they would be expected to do as *much* work as formerly. He replied certainly. Upon which the freedman said they did not intend to do any such thing."

Of course, there were freedmen who lost the habit of labor during the transition from slavery to freedom. These tended to collect in the larger cities, on abandoned plantations, and, occasionally, on the farm of some larcenous poor white. Finding his former slaves encamped in his Charleston house late in the summer of 1865, one island planter "made arrangements to take his people back to Hilton Head and provision them, but only Anthony would then agree to go." In time, however, the military and the bureau were successful in clearing idlers from the population centers. More frightening to the whites than urban idlers were those in the country. Early in September, 1865, a planter near Georgetown complained to the absentee owner of a neighboring plantation that it was "being rapidly filled up by vagabond negroes from all parts of the country who go there when they please and are fast destroying what you left of a settlement. They are thus become a perfect nuisance to the neighbourhood and harbor for all the thieves and scamps who wont work."

Idleness of this hardened sort soon dwindled to negligible proportions. Much of the continued malingering was apparently a manifestation of the Negro's dissatisfaction with his rewards under the new system, a sort of unorganized slow-down by which he fought his employer or prospective employer. Idleness, of course, had been a normal part of slavery, and it was no less evident among the whites than Negroes. Sundays, Christmas, and New Year's Day were customarily holidays from labor for both races and remained so. Further, agrarian communities normally recognized the laying-by season in the early summer and the end of the harvest season in the fall and winter as periods of reduced labor, celebrations, and idleness. It is not surprising that the Negro in freedom continued to recognize them as such, and to relish them all the more.

Desertion, migration, and idleness were temporary as mass phenomena among the Negro population in postwar South Carolina. Much more lasting was the universal tendency among freedmen to identify their freedom with liberty to ignore the infinite minor regulations that had been imposed upon them as slaves. They assumed new forms of dress, kept dogs and guns, hunted, and they traveled about without passes. Many refused to yield the sidewalks to the white gentry, omitted the slave-period obeisances, and rode horses or mules or in carriages in the presence of white pedestrians. They conversed in public and in secret with any number of other Negroes and entered into associations for a variety of purposes.

The master class, exasperated and outraged by the assertiveness of the freedmen, was particularly alert in noting and meticulously recording this metamorphosis of their erstwhile bondsmen. In Camden, early in April, 1865, Emma Holmes, attending services in the Methodist Church where the Negroes sat in the galleries, was incensed at the Negro women who wore "round hats, gloves and even lace veils, the men alone looking respectable." A white resident returning to Charleston in June of the same year was appalled by "Negroes shoving white person[s] . . . [off] the walk. Negro women dressed in the most outré style, all with veils and parasols for which they have an especial fancy. Riding on horseback with negro soldiers and in carriages." At the same time, a planter on the lower Cooper River complained that the Negroes would not stay out of Charleston, where they "claim they are free," and the women are frequently seen "with blue & pink veils, etc." The same planter was mortified while hunting in the swamps with a group of white gentlemen to encounter suddenly a number of Negro men engaged in the same entertainment, armed with shotguns and following the hounds like ebony images of their white superiors.

To the freedman, his new liberty conveyed the right to assemble in public, to speak, and to celebrate—the cause most often and extravagantly celebrated being freedom itself. Celebrations occurred frequently, on plantations, in villages and towns, and pre-eminently in Charleston. The Negro community in Charleston was large, wealthy, well informed, and organized. Zion Church, having been established by the Presbyterians before the war primarily for the accommodation of their Negro members and having a seating capacity of two thousand, logically became the focal point of organized activity among the Negroes and their northern friends.

Perhaps one of the most impressive parades ever seen in Charleston was staged by the Negro community on March 29, 1865, scarcely a month after the occupation of the city. The marchers began assembling at noon and a procession of about four thousand was soon formed. It was led by two Negro marshals on horseback. Among the marchers were fifty butchers carrying knives and preceded by a display of a large porker. Then followed a band and the Twenty-first United States Colored Troops (the Third South Carolina Volunteers), a company of school boys, and a car of Liberty carrying thirteen young girls representing the original thirteen states (which were cheered enthusiastically). The main body of the parade consisted of eighteen hundred school children with their teachers. The trades were represented by tailors carrying shears, coopers with hoops, blacksmiths, painters, carpenters, wheelwrights, barbers, and others. Eight companies of firemen wearing red shirts paraded with their equipment. Also in the procession was a cart bearing a mock auction block. While a boy rang a bell, an auctioneer extolled the salability of two Negro women seated on the block with their children standing around them. The cart carried a sign: "A number of Negroes for sale." A long rope was tied to the cart and a number of men were tied to the rope. Another cart bore a coffin displaying the signs: "Slavery is dead," "Who owns him, No one," and "Sumter dug his grave on the 13th of April 1861." The cart was followed by mourners in black. Then came fifty sailors, a company of wood sawyers, the newspaper carriers, and several clubs and associations. The procession was three miles long and wound through the streets below the Citadel. The Negroes, both participants and spectators, were "wild with enthusiasm," reported one observer. "Good order and appreciation of freedom were evident."

As the war drew to a close other mass meetings of Negroes followed in rapid succession. On April 5, while Potter was making a sortie from Georgetown, the Negroes of Charleston met in Zion Church and passed resolutions thanking the army for their liberation. Fort Sumter, already reduced to rubble by artillery fire, might well have sunk beneath the waters under the sheer weight of victorious abolitionists who flocked from the North to stand upon its ruins. On April 14, Robert Anderson himself returned to raise the flag over the ruins. Before the ceremonies began, Robert Smalls brought the *Planter* alongside and set ashore more than three thousand Negroes from the city. Remaining aboard to watch the proceedings from the quarterdeck was the son of Denmark Vesey, the man who thirty-three years before had shocked the state—and, indeed, the South—with the threat of mass insurrection. "As the old silken bunting winged itself to its long-deserted staff, thousands of shouts, and prayers fervent and deep, accompanying, greeted its reappearance." And then the speeches began. "I have been a friend of the South," declared William Lloyd Garrison, and Henry Ward Beecher, Theodore Tilton, Henry Wilson, Joshua Leavitt, William D. Kelley, Joseph Holt, and George Thompson applauded.

Other Negro communities were not long in following the example of Charleston. The editor of the New York *Times* praised the stand of the Negroes of Columbia in refusing to abandon plans to celebrate Independence Day in 1865 despite the protests of the whites. "They may not get the vote or court rights in this way," asserted the editor, "but there are a hundred petty regulations of the slave period which they can break to exert their influence. It is good that the white become accustomed to negro meetings." In the village of Aiken on the Fourth, the Reverend Cornish observed that "the Negroes had a Pic Nic—somewhere, & a prayer meeting & a dance at the Hotel Headquarters." Even in the remote hamlet of Spartanburg, scarcely a month after most of the slaves had been formally released by their masters, David Golightly Harris noted that "the negroes had a jubilee . . . at the village, the yankeys and the negroes going hand in hand." Throughout

Reconstruction, the Negroes made New Year's Day and Independence Day their special holidays and devoted them to the celebration of emancipation and union, concepts which were inseparably intertwined in their minds. On these days, even in the smallest villages, the Negro community usually staged some sort of jubilee.

These celebrations were significant as assertions of freedom, but they were also important in other ways. They obviously gave the Negro population a feeling of unity and an awareness of the power that unity bestowed. Further, they pushed forth leaders from among their own numbers who, in time, would translate that power into political realities.

Freedmen often interpreted their liberty as a license to express candidly, either by words or deeds, their true feelings toward the whites in general and their late masters in particular.

Many Negroes continued to show the same respect and cordiality toward individual whites which they had exhibited in slavery. "I have been very agreeably disappointed in the behavior of the negroes," wrote a young planter visiting Charleston in August, 1865. "They are as civil & humble as ever. All I met greeted me enthusiastically as 'Mass Gus.'" In September, another visiting native white concurred. "The negroes behave admirably," he reported to his wife, "when you consider the ordeal of temptation & teaching they have passed through." And an elderly Charlestonian observed, "The negroes about town behave as far as I see extremely well. I have met with nothing but respect and good-will from them . . . ." On the plantations, returning masters sometimes encountered the same response. "I met with universal politeness from our former slaves," wrote a Beaufort District planter after a visit to the family plantations in December, 1865. "They were glad to see me & inquired after all the family."

Yet, while many Negroes manifested cordial feelings toward the whites, others exhibited insolence and insubordination. As the war drew to a close, and before emancipation became a certainty, such displays often served as a device by which Negroes tested their freedom. "There is quite a difference of manner among the Negroes," Grace B. Elmore noted in Richland shortly after Sherman's passage, "but I think it proceeds from an uncertainty as to what their condition will be. They do not know if they are free or not and their manner is a sort of feeler by which they will find out how far they can go." Grace's brother, fresh from a visit to slave-rich lower Richland District, "found quite a spirit of insubordination among the negroes who supposed they were free, but they are gradually discovering a Yankee army passing through the county and telling them they are free is not sufficient to make it a fact." As emancipation became assured many ex-slaves took obvious pleasure in expressing heretofore concealed feelings of animosity toward their recent owners. In June, 1865, Edward, personal servant to Henry W. Ravenel, accompanied his master from their refuge in Greenville to Columbia. There Edward obtained permission from Ravenel to find his wife, and was given five of the master's last nine dollars to enable him to follow Ravenel to Charleston. Ravenel proceeded to Charleston where Edward subsequently appeared, but "was excessively insolent—told the Servant in the yard that he had no further use for me and that he had been left in Columbia to starve." The indignant Ravenel concluded: "So much for the fidelity of indulged servants." Even more blatant was the insubordination of a "so-called" servant who, when ordered by her Charleston mistress to scour some pots and kettles, replied: "You betta do it yourself, Ain't you smarter an me? You think you is—Wy you no scour fo you-self." Not all freedmen were so vociferous; many were content simply to ignore their late masters. "Rosetta, Lizze's maid, passed me today when I was coming from Church without speaking to me," wrote one aristocrat to his wife. "She was really elegantly dressed, in King Street style."

A very few Negroes believed that freedom warranted the exercise of vengeance upon the whites—that theft, arson, and violence even to the extremity of homicide were justifiable retributions for their bondage. This sentiment was particularly apparent in areas subjected to Union raids and it persisted through the summer and fall of 1865. After Sherman had passed through Camden, a serious case of arson was narrowly averted, and "many other attempts at setting fire were discovered either just in time, or after some damage had been done—both in Camden and the surrounding country—keeping everyone in a constant state of anxiety and alarm." In several communities, disturbances reached the proportions of insurrections. In March, in the vicinity of Christ Church on the lower Cooper River, an area which lay between the Union lines and Confederate pickets, the mistress of a plantation reported: "A band of armed negro men, principally from one of the neighboring plantations, until put to flight by Confederate Scouts, did without any authority for what they did, arming & marching about the country, stopping people on the highway with guns pointed at their heads, suddenly surrounding a man on his own plantation attending to his own affairs, going to peoples homes at night threatening them & in one instance I hear firing on the man who came out to see what the noise was about. . . ." Another planter "was threatened with having his house burned and himself shot if he tried to save a single piece of furniture." The relief afforded by Confederate cavalry in this area was only temporary. In mid-July, a Cooper River planter complained that in Christ Church and St. Thomas Parishes and on the river in general, the Negroes claimed everything and, in some cases, had driven away the owners. Five or six Negroes had come to three plantations— Richmond, Basis, and Kensington—and encouraged the freedmen to seize everything for themselves. "Insubordination & insolence," he concluded, were frequently observed. Other lowcountry communities witnessed similar scenes. Near Plantersville in Georgetown District, a Union raid in March, 1865, released a large number of Negro slaves who were "indulging in the free use of wine & liquors obtained from the houses of former masters," and "preparing themselves for the commission of crime," or worse, who "might break into open insurrection at any time." "During the stay and after the departure of Genl Potters army," a group of Pineville planters complained in September, 1865, "the negroes evinced treachery and vindictiveness—illustrated by robbery, plundering, false accusation and insolence, in the three weeks after the departure of said army, by an open outbreak in arms—taking possession [sic] of and patroling this village night and day, threatening the lives of men and the chastity of women, & finally firing upon Confederate Scouts by whom they were dispersed." During the same period on the mainland in the vicinity of Beaufort, a planter complained that robbery and theft were committed wholesale by the Negroes "& no redress given"; while "Mr. Chavis & others, as you are aware has been compelled with his Family to fly his home, from vagrant negroes, returned from the Islands, chiefly." Such was the case, he averred, "every where where officers of Colored troops have had jurisdiction any length of time."

Notwithstanding the charges of the whites that Negro soldiers often instigated such disorders, the occupation rapidly established comparative peace. It is true, nevertheless, that the Negro population was most restless in those areas occupied by Negro troops—an area which included the lowcountry from Georgetown to Savannah and, roughly, the southern half of the state from the sea to the mountains. The effect of the Negro military on the population of Aiken, as seen through the diary of the Reverend Cornish, presents a good case study. In June, 1865, the village was occupied by a detachment of the Thirty-third United States Colored Troops (the First South). On Sunday, June 18, about twenty Negro soldiers entered the Baptist Church with the apparent intention of attending services. They were ordered by the white ushers to find places in the galleries. As some of the soldiers began to ascend the stairs, one of their number ordered them to halt, and the whole group attempted to take seats on the main floor. When some of the white men rose and blocked their way, the soldiers flourished their bayonets and began to curse. Finally, they were allowed to seat themselves below, but the church closed that evening. Monday morning, Cornish's serving woman, Phobe, used "intemperate" language in addressing the Reverend, and, upon being reproved, continued the abuse. When asked whose servant she was, Phobe answered, "My own servant." She was then told to recant or leave. She left. On the same morning, a Mr. Wood "was badly beaten by the 'Black and Blues,'" as the Negro soldiers were called. The beating brought the inspector general from Augusta, but on Saturday, August 5, there was another such "disturbance."

It is difficult to distinguish fact from fiction in the disordered first weeks that followed the war; but the rumor circuit buzzed with tales of whites murdered by Negroes, usually their ex-slaves. Emma E. Holmes reported that William Prioleau returned to his lowcountry plantation after the Union forces had passed and spent the night, "but never woke again. His throat was cut from ear to ear." Another planter reported killed was William Allen, "who was chopped to pieces in his barn," as Emma graphically related. A less impressionable recorder wrote from Walterboro early in July that "several citizens about Ashepoo & Combahee, eight or nine, have been murdered by negroes." Much of this lawlessness he blamed on the presence of Negro troops. "We have had them here and tho the officers & men behave as well as I had expected the soldiers (black) made great mischief among servants generally and plantation negroes particularly," he declared. "Things were bad before, but their influence made them infinitely worse."

The great mass of Negroes in South Carolina at the end of

the Civil War hoped and expected that freedom meant that each would soon be settled upon his own plot of earth. Indeed, to the Negro agrarian freedom without land was incomprehensible. "Gib us our own land and we take care ourselves," a Union officer quoted as the sentiment of the mass of country Negroes in the spring of 1865, "but widout land, de ole massas can hire us or starve us, as dey please." The desire for land touched all classes of former slaves. "She also said," wrote a young mistress late in May, paraphrasing the words of her maid, that "the commonest and most universal view was that each man would have his farm and stock and plenty to eat & drink and so pass through life." The prevalence of this roseate view of the future among freedmen was confirmed by Mary Boykin Chesnut of Kershaw District, wife of a Confederate senator and general, and herself heiress to three generations of cotton culture, who reported that the Negroes "declare that they are to be given lands and mules by those blessed Yankees." Similarly, a northern correspondent, arriving in Orangeburg after a trip through the lowcountry, declared that the desire for land was active and widespread among the Negroes. "Some of the best regiments have white soldiers who tell the negroes they are the rightful owners of the land, that they should refuse to work or go to the islands to get lands."

"Forty acres and a mule," that delightful bit of myopic mythology so often ascribed to the newly freed in the Reconstruction period, at least in South Carolina during the spring and summer of 1865, represented far more than the chimerical rantings of ignorant darkies, irresponsible soldiers, and radical politicians. On the contrary, it symbolized rather precisely the policy to which the government had already given and was giving mass application in the Sea Islands. Hardly had the troops landed, in November, 1861, before liberal northerners arrived to begin a series of ambitious experiments in the reconstruction of southern society. One of these experiments included the redistribution of large landed estates to the Negroes. By the spring of 1865, this program was well under-way, and after August any well-informed, intelligent observer in South Carolina would have concluded, as did the Negroes, that some considerable degree of permanent land division was highly probable. . . .

Thus, even in the early days of freedom, former slaves with amazing unanimity revealed—by mass desertion, migration, idleness, by the breaching of the infinite minor regulations of slavery, by a new candor in relationships with whites, and by their ambition to acquire land—a determination to put an end to their slavery. It is true that the Negro's freedom was still severely circumscribed a year after emancipation, and his ex-perience during the whole term of Reconstruction could hardly be described as a success story. Yet, the Negro did not, upon emancipation, immediately jump a quick half-step for-ward and halt. In the favorable atmosphere generated by his political ascendency during Reconstruction, freedom for the Negro in South Carolina was a growing thing, flowering in areas political historians have often neglected. The growth was, in part, the result of cultivation by alien hands; but it was also the result of forces operating within the organism itself. The gains won during these early years enabled the Negro community to continue to move forward in vital areas of human endeavor in the post-Reconstruction period while, ironically, its political freedom was rapidly dwindling to vir-tual extinction. In this sense, far from being the disaster so often described, Reconstruction was for the Negroes of South Carolina a period of unequaled progress.

PART IV

RADICAL RECONSTRUCTION IN THE SOUTH

In December, 1909, Negro scholar W. E. B. DuBois warned the annual meeting of the American Historical Association that "the intense feeling of the South and the conciliatory spirit of the North" could easily distort the role of the Negro in Reconstruction history. Reviewing the constructive achievements of the much-maligned Radical governments in the South, DuBois suggested that the increased tax burden had been necessary to correct neglected social problems (such as illiteracy), that the amount of corruption had been exaggerated, and that historians had virtually ignored the biracial, bipartisan, and bisectional nature of such corruption. This was an extraordinary thesis to advance at a time when the Dunning School dominated the writing of Reconstruction history. But DuBois' call for a new look at Reconstruction went unheeded. Some twenty-six years later, when he published *Black Reconstruction in America*, the *American Historical Review* and most of the profession chose to ignore it altogether. Much the same indifference greeted the pioneering state studies of Negro scholars Alrutheus A. Taylor and Horace Mann Bond.

In 1939 and 1940, two white historians, Francis B. Simkins and Howard K. Beale, called for a more "critical, creative and tolerant attitude" toward Reconstruction. But it was not until after World War II, and with young scholars leading the way, that the once cherished myths of Reconstruction were effectively challenged and the complexities of the period made much clearer. It was now possible to grapple with the implications of DuBois' assertion that "the attempt to make black men American citizens was in a certain sense all a failure, but a splendid failure. It did not fail where it was expected to fail."

10

CARPETBAGGERS RECONSIDERED

Richard N. Current

Few characters in American history have excited more condemnation or achieved greater notoriety than the carpetbaggers. Richard N. Current examines the validity of the "carpetbagger" stereotype.

The story of the postbellum South is often told as if it were a morality play or a television melodrama. The characters personify Good or Evil, and they are so clearly identified that there is no mistaking the "good guys" and the "bad guys." One of the villains, who deserves the boos and hisses he is sure to get, is the carpetbagger. As usually portrayed, this contemptible Yankee possesses as little honor or intelligence as he does property, and he possesses so little property that he can, quite literally, carry all of it with him in a carpetbag. He is attracted southward by the chance for power and plunder that he sees when the vote is given to southern Negroes and taken from some of the southern whites by the Reconstruction Acts of 1867. Going south in 1867 or after, he meddles in the politics of places where, as a mere roving adventurer, he has no true interest. For a time he and his kind run the southern states. At last, when the drama ends, Good has triumphed over Evil, and the carpetbagger has got his comeuppance. But he leaves behind him a trail of corruption, misgovernment, and lastingly disturbed race relations.

That picture may seem an exaggeration, a caricature. If so, it nevertheless has passed for a long time as a true, historical likeness, and it continues to pass as such. A standard dictionary defines *carpetbagger* as a term of contempt for northern men who went south "to seek private gain under the often corrupt reconstruction governments." Another dictionary, based on "historical principles," contains this definition: "One of the poor northern adventurers who, carrying all their belongings in carpetbags, went south to profit from the social and political upheaval after the Civil War." A recent textbook refers to "the Radical carpetbaggers who had poured into the defeated section after the passage of the First Reconstruction Act of March, 1867." The prevailing conception, then, is that these men were late arrivals who waited till the Negro was given the suffrage and who then went off with their carpetbags, cynically, to take advantage of the colored vote.

Even those who hold that view concede that "a few were men of substance, bent on settling in the South," and that some of them took up residence there before the passage of the Reconstruction Acts. With respect to men of this kind, however, the question has been raised whether they should be considered carpetbaggers at all. Many of the northerners active in Mississippi politics after 1867, the historian of Reconstruction in that state observes, had arrived as would-be planters before 1867. "It is incorrect, therefore, to call them 'carpet baggers,'" this historian remarks. "They did not go South to get offices, for there were no offices for them to fill. The causes which led them to settle there were purely economic, and not political." Thus the brothers Albert T. and Charles Morgan, when they moved from Wisconsin to Mississippi, "came not as carpetbaggers," for they brought with them some $50,000, which they invested in planting and lumbering enterprises (and lost). And the much better-known figure Albion W. Tourgée, who moved from Ohio to North Carolina, was perhaps no carpetbagger, either, for he took with him $5,000 which he put into a nursery business (and also lost).

Now, suppose it could be demonstrated that, among the northern politicians in the South during Reconstruction, men essentially like the Morgans and Tourgée were not the few but the many, not exceptional but fairly typical. Suppose that the majority moved to the South before 1867, before the establishment of the "corrupt reconstruction governments," and hence for reasons other than to seek private gain or political power under such governments. One of two conclusions must follow. Either we must say that true carpetbaggers were much fewer and less significant than has been commonly supposed, or we must seek a new definition of the word.

In redefining it, we should consider the actual usage on the part of southerners during the Reconstruction period. We may learn something of its denotation as well as its connotation if we look at the way they applied it to a specific person: the one-time Union army officer Willard Warner, of Ohio and Alabama.

Warner might seem, at first glance, to exemplify the latecomer rising immediately in southern politics, for he completed his term in the Ohio legislature and was elected to the United States Senate from Alabama in the same year, 1868. But he was not really a new arrival. He had visited Alabama and, with a partner, had leased a plantation there in the fall of 1865. He bought land in the state the next year, and he spent most of the spring and summer of 1866 and most of the autumn and winter of 1867–68 on his Alabama land. He intended to make an economic career in the South (and indeed he was eventually to do so).

At first, Warner had no trouble with his Alabama neighbors. "A Northern man, who is not a fool, or foolish fanatic," he wrote from his plantation in the spring of 1866, "may live pleasantly in Alabama, without abating one jot of his self-respect, or independence." At one time or another, as he was to testify later, the leading Democrats of the state, among them the ex-Confederate General James H. Clanton, came to him and said: "General, when we talk about carpetbaggers we want you to understand that we don't mean you; you have come here and invested what means you had in property here, and you have the same interest there that we have."

The Alabamans changed their attitude toward Warner when he was elected to office with Negro support. Afterwards (1871) General Clanton himself explained:

If a man should come here and invest $100,000, and in the next year should seek the highest offices, by appealing to the basest prejudices of an ignorant race, we would call him a political carpet-bagger. But if he followed his legitimate business, took his chances with the rest, behaved himself, and did not stir up strife, we would call him a gentleman. General Warner bought land; I fixed some titles for him, and I assured him that when men came there to take their chances with us for life, we would take them by the hand. But we found out his designs. Before his seat in Ohio got cold, he was running the negro machine among us to put himself in office.

Another Alabama Democrat, from Huntsville, in the area where Warner had bought land, elaborated further upon the same theme in testifying before a congressional committee, as follows:

Question: You have used the epithets "carpet-bagger" and "scalawag" repeatedly . . . give us an accurate definition.

Answer: Well, sir, the term carpet-bagger is not applied to northern men who come here to settle in the South, but a carpet-bagger is generally understood to be a man who comes here for office sake, of an ignorant or bad character, and who seeks to array the negroes against the whites; who is a kind of political dry-nurse for the negro population, in order to get office through them.

Question: Then it does not necessarily suppose that he should be a northern man?

Answer: Yes, sir; it does suppose that he is to be a northern man, but it does not apply to all northern men that come here.

Question: If he is an intelligent, educated man, and comes here for office, then he is not a carpet-bagger, I understand?

Answer: No, sir; we do not generally call them carpet-baggers.

Question: If he is a northern man possessed of good character and seeks office he is not a carpet-bagger?

Answer: Mr. Chairman, there are so few northern men who come here of intelligence and character, that join the republican party and look for office alone to the negroes, that we have never made a class for them. . . . They stand *sui generis*. . . . But the term "carpet-bagger" was applied to the office-seeker from the North who comes here seeking office by the negroes, by arraying their political passions and prejudices against the white people of the community.

Question: The man in addition to that, under your definition, must be an ignorant man and of bad character?

Answer: Yes, sir; he is generally of that description. We regard any man as a man of bad character who seeks to create hostility between the races. . . .

Question: Having given a definition of the carpet-bagger, you may now define scalawag.

Answer: A scalawag is his subservient tool and accomplice, who is a native of the country.

So far as these two Alabamans were concerned, it obviously made no difference whether a northerner came before 1867 or after, whether he brought with him and invested thousands of dollars or was penniless, whether he was well educated or illiterate, or whether he was of good or bad character in the ordinary sense. He was, by definition, a carpetbagger and a man of ignorant and bad character if he, at any time, encouraged political activity on the part of the Negroes and thus arrayed the blacks against the whites, that is, the Republicans against the Democrats. He was not a carpetbagger if he steered entirely clear of politics or if he consistently talked and voted as a Democrat or Conservative.

This usage was not confined to Alabama; it prevailed throughout the South. To speak of "economic carpetbaggers," as historians sometimes do, is therefore rather hard to justify on a historical basis. Politics—Republican politics—

was the distinguishing mark of the man whom the Democrats and Conservatives after 1867 dubbed a carpetbagger, and they called him by that name whether or not he had gone South originally for economic rather than political reasons. To speak of "Negro carpetbaggers" is also something of an anachronism. Colored men from the North did go south and enter politics, of course, but in the Reconstruction lexicon (with its distinction among carpetbaggers, scalawags, and Negroes) they were put in a category of their own. Northern-born or southern-born, the Negro was a Negro to the southern Conservatives, and they did not ordinarily refer to him as a carpetbagger. From contemporary usage, then, we derive the following as a non-valuational definition: the men called carpetbaggers were *white northerners who went south after the beginning of the Civil War and, sooner or later, became active in politics as Republicans.*

With this definition at hand, we can proceed to make at least a rudimentary survey of the so-called carpetbaggers as a group, in order to find out how well they fit the traditional concept with respect to their background. Let us consider first the state and local officeholders. There were hundreds of these people, and many of them left too few traces for us now to track them down. Studies have touched upon the subject in some of the states, and though fragmentary, these studies at least suggest that most of the men under consideration do not conform to the stereotype.

In Arkansas the carpetbag governor (1868–72) Powell Clayton had owned and lived on a plantation since 1865. Many years later he was to gather data showing that the overwhelming majority of the so-called carpetbaggers, who were in office when he was, had arrived in Arkansas before 1867, and that the small minority who came as late as 1867 "did so when the Democrats were in full power, and before the officers to be elected or appointed, together with their salaries and emoluments, had been fixed by the [reconstructed] State Constitution." Clayton adds:

With a very few exceptions, the Northern men who settled in Arkansas came there with the Federal Army, and . . . were so much impressed with its genial climate and great natural resources as to cause them . . . to make it their future home. A number, like myself and my brother William, had contracted matrimonial ties. Many of them had been away from home so long as practically to have lost their identity in the States [from which they had come]. . . . These were the reasons that influenced their settlement in Arkansas rather than the existence of any political expectations.

That, of course, is *ex parte* testimony, from one of the carpetbaggers himself. Still, he supports his conclusion with ample and specific evidence.

And, with respect to some of the other states, southern historians have tended toward similar conclusions. In Alabama, says one of these historians, "many of the carpet-bag politicians were northern men who had failed at cotton planting." In Florida, says another, about a third of the forty-six delegates elected in 1867 to the state constitutional convention were white Republicans from the North. "Most of the Northerners had been in the state for a year or more and were *bona fide* citizens of the commonwealth." "As a class," they were "intellectually the best men among the delegates." In Mississippi, says a third, "the genuine 'carpet baggers' who came after the adoption of the reconstruction policy were comparatively few in number." The vast majority of the so-called carpetbaggers in Mississippi were men who had arrived earlier as planters.

Information is not available regarding all the carpetbag officeholders in all the reconstructed states. What is needed, then, is information about a representative sample of such officeholders. A sample could be made of the carpetbag governors, of whom the total was nine. Eight of the nine arrived in the South before 1867. Two were officers of the Freedmen's Bureau, two were civilian officials of the federal government, and four were private enterprisers—two of them planters, one a lawyer, and the other a minister of the gospel. The single late-comer, Adelbert Ames of Massachusetts and Mississippi, first appeared in Mississippi as a regular army officer and as a military governor, not as an adventurer in search of a political job.

A larger sample consists of the entire body of white northerners who during the Reconstruction period were elected as Republicans to represent southern constituencies in either branch of Congress. Altogether, there were about sixty-two of these men, seventeen in the Senate and forty-five in the House of Representatives. It is impossible to be absolutely precise in listing these congressional carpetbaggers. There were a few borderline cases where, for example, a man was born in the South but raised or educated in the North, and it is hard to know whether he should be classified as a northerner or not.

Of the sixty-two senators and congressmen, practically all were veterans of the Union army. That is not surprising, and it does not alter the accepted stereotype. More surprising, in view of the carpetbagger's reputation for "ignorant or bad character," is the fact that a large proportion were well educated. About two-thirds of the group (forty-three of the sixty-two) had studied law, medicine, or engineering enough to practice the profession, or had attended one or more years of college, or had been school teachers. Of the senators alone, approximately half were college graduates. Seemingly the academic and intellectual attainments of the carpetbaggers in Congress were, on the whole, at least as high as those of the other members of Congress, whether from the North or from the South.

Still more significant is the fact that nearly five-sixths of the entire carpetbag group—fifty of the sixty-two—had arrived in the South before 1867, before the passage of the Reconstruction Acts, before the granting of political rights to the Negro. Of the fifty early arrivals, only fifteen appeared on the southern scene as Treasury Department employees, Freedmen's Bureau officials, or members of the postwar occupation forces (and at least a few of these fifteen soon left the government service and went into private enterprise). Thirty-five of the fifty were engaged in farming or business or the professions from the time of their arrival or soon after.

As for those other twelve of the sixty-two—the twelve who did not begin to live in the South until 1867 or later—more than half (at least seven) took up some private occupation before getting public office. Their comparatively late arrival does not, in itself, signify that they moved south merely for "office sake."

If, then, the sixty-two carpetbag congressmen and senators make up a representative sample, we must conclude that a majority of the carpetbaggers, taken as a whole, do not conform to the traditional view, at least so far as their backgrounds are concerned. With comparatively few exceptions, the so-called carpetbaggers had moved South for reasons other than a lust for offices newly made available by the passage of the Reconstruction Acts. These men were, in fact, a part of the multitude of Union officers and soldiers who, during or soon after the war, chose to remain in or return to the land they had helped to conquer.

To thousands of the young men in blue, at and after the war's end, the South beckoned as a land of wondrous charm, a place of almost magical opportunity. "Northern men are going to do well in every part of the South. The Southern men are too indolent to work and the Yankees are bound to win." So, for example, a cavalry sergeant wrote from Texas to his sister back home in Ohio in 1866. "I have some idea that I will not remain in Ohio long, and maybe I will locate in the sunny South," he continued. "What think you of roses blooming in open air in November, and the gardens glorious with flowers."

Here, in the South, was a new frontier, another and a better West. Some men compared the two frontiers before choosing the southern one, as did the Morgan brothers, who first looked over Kansas and then decided upon Mississippi. Albert T. Morgan afterwards wrote that the former cry, "Go West, young man," had been changed to "Go South, young man," and in 1865 the change was "already quite apparent, in the purpose of those of the North who were seeking new homes." Many years later Albion W. Tourgée recalled the hopes and dreams with which, in the fall of 1865, he had settled as a badly wounded veteran in Greensboro, North Carolina:

He expected the future to be as bright and busy within the conquered territory as it had been along the ever-advancing frontier of the West. . . . He expected the whole region to be transformed by the power of commerce, manufactures, and the incursion of Northern life, thought, capital, industry, and enterprise. . . . Because he thought he bore a shattered life he sought a milder clime. He took his young wife with him, and they builded their first home-nest almost before the smoke of battle disappeared. . . . His first object was restored health; his next desire, to share the general prosperity.

Once they had been released from the army, thousands of other Union soldiers and officers returned to the South with similar dreams of prosperity and a pleasant life. For the moment, land was cheap and cotton dear. Labor was abundant, and the Negroes were expected to work more willingly for their liberators than for their late masters. So the veterans turned South. At the end of 1865 a newsman from the North learned that, in Alabama alone, there were already five thousand of them "engaged in planting and trading." Even more than the uplands of Alabama, Tennessee, and Georgia, the Mississippi Valley was proving an "attraction to adventurous capital," this traveling reporter found. "Men from the Middle

States and the great West were everywhere, buying and leasing plantations, hiring freedmen, and setting thousands of ploughs in motion." No impecunious wanderers were these, but bringers of "adventurous capital." They paid cash for lands or leases, for wages, for supplies. At a time when the South was languishing for money, these newcomers provided it, put it into circulation, and thus gave the economy a lift.

Most of those who thus adventured with their capital were to lose it. They failed for several reasons. At cotton planting the Yankees were novices, unused to local conditions and deluded in their expectations of the Negro as a free worker, or so the southerners said. Actually the southerners as well as the Yankees ran into economic difficulties during the first few years after the war. "Various causes have arisen to prostrate the people, leaving them nearly ruined," a contemporary observed early in 1867, "among which I may more especially mention the following, which could not have been foreseen or provided against: The too great drouth at one season, which destroyed and blasted their corn; too much rain at another season, which injured their cotton; and then the army worm, which came out of the ground in vast numbers, destroyed what was left." There was, besides, the federal cotton tax, which both northern and southern planters denounced as ruinous.

Often, whether as planters or as businessmen, the northerners faced a special disadvantage—the hostility of the people around them. "The rebels will not buy from a Galvanized Yankee, or Loyal Unionist, nor from a Yankee either," a Unionist Virginian complained late in 1865, "the result being that loyal or Northern merchants are failing all over the South." In many places the Yankees were boycotted if they sympathized with or voted for Republicans. "Only one hundred and one men were found base enough to vote for the Radical ticket," a Memphis newspaper reported in April, 1866. "We have held up the names of a portion of these men and written small pox over their doors in order that our people might shun them."

Discouraged and disillusioned after a year or two in their new homes, large numbers of the Yankees abandoned them and returned to the North. Others, of whom some were successful and some were not, remained in the South. Of those who remained, many turned to state and local politics as Republicans in 1867 or after. These comprised the majority of that class of men who eventually came to be known as carpetbaggers.

Before 1867 the northerners in the South possessed only limited opportunities in politics. As Republicans, they could not hope to be elected to office. As newcomers, they often found it difficult even to vote, because of the residence requirements. The Georgia constitution, as remade after the war, extended the residence requirement in that state from six months to two years. "Now it is generally admitted," a northern settler in Georgia protested, "that this change . . . has been effected to prevent loyal men who were obliged to leave here during the war and those who have come here since the war from having any voice in choosing the officers of the State and representatives to Congress." Of course, the newcomers could seek federal jobs, and many of them did so, but again they faced something of a handicap, for they understood that President Johnson preferred "Southern citizens" when "suitable persons" among them could be found.

To the northern settlers remaining in the South the congressional acts of 1867 suddenly brought political opportunity and also, as some of them saw it, political responsibility. Tourgée, for one, sought election to the new constitutional convention in North Carolina because, having failed in business and lost the savings he had brought, he needed the money he would be paid as a delegate. But he sought election also because he was concerned about Negro rights and wished to do what he could to protect them. A more prosperous settler, a planter of Carroll Parish, Louisiana, who once had been an Ohio school superintendent, took an active interest in southern politics for reasons that he explained, in April, 1867, to Senator John Sherman:

On the closing of my services as a Soldier, I became a member of the firm of Lynch, Ruggles & Co., which was organized in Circleville, Ohio, for the purpose of buying lands in the South and planting. We have located at this point, which is 40 miles above Vicksburg, have purchased lands, have organized most efficient labor forces, & our investment now is on a scale which makes us on *that* account deeply interested in every effort made to bring peace to the South. . . .

I . . . respectfully ask your advice as to the proper course to be pursued by Northern men in the South who sympathize with Congress in the present crisis. . . . I have never held a civil office and never intended to, if I can avoid it; but we have a large force at work, have their confidence, and now as they are voters, they look to our advice, and I want to give it as wisely as possible. Other Northern men are similarly situated. . . .

The position of some of these other northern men was later recalled by C. M. Hamilton, a Pennsylvanian who had gone to Florida in 1864, as a Freedmen's Bureau agent, and had become after 1867 one of the most prominent carpetbaggers of that state. In 1871 he told a congressional committee investigating the Ku Klux Klan:

. . . when the reconstruction acts first passed Congress, the Yankees, as we are called, most of us soldiers who were in the South, rather stood back, did not really feel at that time that they [we] had any particular right to interfere in politics, or to take part in them. But the reconstruction laws were passed; reconstruction was necessary; . . . the democratic party of the South adopted the policy of masterly inactivity . . . ; there was a new element here that had been enfranchised who were without leaders. The northern men in the South, and there were but a handful of them in this State, who had been in the Army, took hold of this matter of reconstruction, and they have perfected it so far as it has been accomplished.

These northerners, already in the South in 1867, felt they had a right and a duty to be where they were and to do what they did. They were Americans. They had fought a war to keep the nation one. South as well as North, it was *their* country. They had chosen to live in the southern part of it. This was now their home, and they had a stake in its future as well as the future of the country as a whole. Their attitude should be quite understandable—as understandable as the feeling of the majority of southern whites.

Naturally, the native Conservatives and Democrats resented the northern Republicans and reviled them with such epithets as "aliens," "birds of passage," and "carpetbaggers." As applied to most of the men, however, these were not objective and descriptive terms. The Union veterans who settled in the South were impelled by a variety and a mixture of motives: restlessness, patriotic idealism, the desire to get ahead, and what not. But so were the pioneers at other times and places in the United States. So were the southerners themselves who moved westward or northward during the Reconstruction period. At that time the newer states of the Southwest (such as Alabama, Mississippi, and especially Arkansas) were filled with fairly recent arrivals from the older states of the Southeast. And at that time there were more southerners residing in the North than northerners in the South. The latter were no more "birds of passage" than the former. Perhaps the frontiersman has been too much idealized for his propensity to rove. Certainly the carpetbagger has been too much condemned for the mere act of moving from one part of the country to another.

Even if all this be conceded, there remain of course the other elements of the carpetbagger stereotype—the charges of misgovernment, corruption, and racial disturbance.

With regard to the charge of misgovernment and corruption, it is hard to generalize about the carpetbaggers as a class. Nevertheless, a few tentative observations may be made. First, the extent and duration of "carpetbag rule" has been exaggerated. In six of the eleven ex-Confederate states (Texas, Tennessee, Alabama, Georgia, Virginia, North Carolina) there was never a carpetbag governor; there was never a majority of carpetbaggers among the Republicans in or out of office; certainly there was never anything approaching carpetbagger domination of state politics. In all those states the Republicans held power only briefly if at all, and they held it, to the extent that they did so, by means of their strength among Negroes and scalawags. In the other five states (Arkansas, Mississippi, Louisiana, Florida, South Carolina) there were carpetbag governors part of the time, but even in these states the carpetbaggers could maintain themselves only with Negro and native white support. Second, the extent of illegal and illegitimate spending by the carpetbag governments has been exaggerated—if spending for schools, transportation, and other social and economic services be considered legitimate. Third, the improper spending, the private use of public funds, was by no means the work of carpetbaggers alone, nor were they the only beneficiaries: heavily involved also were native whites, including Conservatives and Democrats as well as scalawags. Fourth, probably the great majority of the carpetbaggers were no more corrupt than the great majority of contemporary officeholders throughout the United States.

Consider the carpetbag governors, who are generally mentioned as the most conspicuous examples of dishonesty. One of them, Joseph Brooks of Arkansas, did not succeed in exercising uncontested power, for either good or evil, and was soon ousted. Two of the governors, R. K. Scott of South Carolina and W. P. Kellogg of Louisiana, are rather difficult to defend. Four others—Powell Clayton of Arkansas, Harrison Reed and M. L. Stearns of Florida, and H. C. Warmoth of Louisiana —were loudly accused but never really proved guilty of misusing their offices for private profit. Only one of the four, Warmoth, seems actually to have made much money while in

Reconstruction politics, and he made a fortune. While governor, he admitted that there was "a frightful amount of corruption" in Louisiana. He explained, however, that the temptation came from the business interests who offered bribes, and he insisted that the Republicans, black as well as white, had resisted bribery as well as had the Democrats. It might be more true to say that Louisiana corrupted Warmoth (if indeed he was corrupted) than to say that Warmoth corrupted Louisiana. The other two carpetbag governors, Adelbert Ames of Mississippi and D. H. Chamberlain of South Carolina, were economy-minded and strictly honest.

There remains the charge that the carpetbaggers disturbed the relations between the races in the South. Of course, the carpetbaggers did so. Their doing so was the basic cause of the animus against them. This is the reason why the honest ones among them, the men like Ames and Chamberlain and Warner, were as thoroughly hated and as strongly opposed as were any of the Yankee scoundrels. Most of the southern whites opposed the granting of political rights to the former slaves. The carpetbaggers encouraged the Negroes to exercise such rights. Thus the carpetbaggers upset the pattern of race relationships, the pattern of Negro passivity, which most white southerners considered ideal.

The party struggle in the postwar South amounted to something more than ordinary politics. In some of its aspects it was equivalent to a continuation, or a renewal, of the Civil War.

On the one hand, southern Conservatives thought of themselves as still fighting for home rule and white supremacy—in essence much the same war aims as the Confederacy had pursued. Carpetbaggers, on the other hand, saw their own basic objective as the reunification of the country, which had been incompletely won at Appomattox, and as the emancipation of the Negroes, who had been but partially freed by the adoption of the Thirteenth Amendment.

On both sides the methods frequently were those of actual,

though irregular, warfare. The Ku Klux Klan, the White League, the Red Shirts, and the various kinds of rifle companies were military or semi-military organizations. So, too, were the state militias, the Union Leagues and Loyal Leagues, and the other partisan institutions of the carpetbaggers and their Negro allies. The carpetbaggers served, so to speak, as officers of frontline troops, deep in enemy territory, "on the picket line of freedom in the South." The embattled Republicans undoubtedly suffered much heavier casualties than did their foes.

True, the Republicans had the advantage of support by the regular United States Army, but often that support was more a potentiality than a fact, and at critical moments it failed to materialize. As for the warriors of white supremacy, they had the backing of northern sympathizers in strength and numbers that would have gladdened the heart of Jefferson Davis in that earlier war time when he was angling for the aid of the Knights of the Golden Circle. The carpetbaggers were divided and weakened by the Republican party schism of 1872, by personal rivalries among themselves, and by jealousies between them and their Negro and scalawag associates. Finally, as some of the carpetbaggers saw it, they were stabbed in the back—abandoned by the government and the people at the North.

The history of this losing campaign has been written almost exclusively from the southern, or Democratic, or disillusioned Republican point of view: the story of the carpetbaggers has been told mainly by their enemies. Historical scholarship has given its sanction to the propaganda of the victorious side in the Reconstruction War. That propaganda, like most, has its elements of truth, and like most, its elements of distortion and downright falsehood. Not that the carpetbaggers were invariably the apostles of righteousness and truth. We would make little progress toward historical understanding if we merely took the same old morality play and switched the labels of

Evil and Good. But surely the time has long since passed when we can, uncritically, accept the "carpetbagger" stereotype.

No doubt men can be found who fit it. No doubt there were political tramps who went South to make cynical use of the Negro vote and who contrived to win both office and illicit gain. But such men were few and comparatively unimportant. Far more numerous and more significant were those energetic and ambitious men who, with or without carpetbags, brought their savings or their borrowings to invest, who eventually got into politics for idealistic as well as selfish reasons, and who in office behaved no better and no worse than most of their contemporaries. Some of these men, like some others of their time, proved corrupt. It would be interesting to know whether, as peculators, the carpetbaggers took out more than a small fraction of the money that, as speculators, they had brought in.

11

THE CARPETBAGGER
AS CORRUPTIONIST:
Henry Clay Warmoth

Richard N. Current

The difficulty in generalizing about the motives and behavior of the carpetbaggers was made clear in two biographical studies: Jonathan Daniels' *Prince of Carpetbaggers* and Otto H. Olsen's *Carpetbagger's Crusade: The Life of Albion Winegar Tourgée*, and even more recently in Richard N. Current's examination of the careers of three carpetbag governors, including the "notorious" Henry Clay Warmoth.

After the end of Reconstruction, conservative white Louisianians looked back upon eight years of what they called "Warmothism," which to them was synonymous with "political gypsyism." Warmothism, they said, had operated for eight long years. The man for whom they named it, Henry Clay Warmoth, was governor for only half of that time (from 1868 to 1872), but his carpetbag successor, William Pitt Kellogg, only carried on the system that Warmoth already had set going. Or so they said.

According to the conservatives' account, this "political gypsy" Warmoth had made himself the "idol and hero of the negro race" and, thereby, governor. He then proceeded to set up a dictatorship. With the aid of a compliant legislature, he concentrated all the registration and election machinery in his own hands. His most ingenious creation was the Returning Board, which could sift the election returns from every parish and throw out those that, in its judgment, had been invalidated because of bribery or intimidation at the polls. Governor Warmoth also secured the passage of police and constabulary laws which created, both in New Orleans and in the parishes, what amounted to a standing army under his personal command. He further reinforced his position by seeing to the establishment of Republican newspapers throughout the state and giving them a monopoly on printing the laws and public advertisements.

While concentrating all power in himself, Warmoth, according to the conservatives' indictment, organized a system of spoliation which "raised the taxation to the highest limits ever known in America, swelled the state debt to many times what it had been before, and reduced the proud commonwealth to unexampled poverty." Among the Republicans in the Reconstruction legislature, only ten were taxpayers. "Corruption and bribery reigned supreme, and the knaves, to avoid any possible danger, refused to pass any bribery law, so that it was no crime to bribe a public official." Expenditures that caused taxation and the debt to increase—expenditures on railroads, levees, and other public works—also provided excellent opportunities for graft. The full extent of the peculation came to light only when the vulturous Republicans quarreled over their prey and turned their talons on one another. One of these men, testifying about the bribes his fellows had received, said it had cost more to get Governor Warmoth to sign a certain railroad subsidy bill than it had cost to get the legislature to pass it. The governor's share of all the plunder, it was widely believed, had made him a rich man within a year of his taking office.

Thus Warmoth has been pictured as a demagogue, a dictator, and a corruptionist. From some of the things that were said about him, he appears to have been a monster of wickedness, a kind of carrier of moral contagion, who brought with him to Louisiana the germs of a political plague which spread through that otherwise healthy and happy land. Before taking a closer look at this man and his role in Louisiana politics, let us glance briefly at the main facts of his career as a whole.

Henry Clay Warmoth was born on May 9, 1842, the son of a saddle and harness maker, in the village of McLeansboro, Illinois. His mother died when he was a small boy. He got what education he could from the village school, from his experience as a typesetter in the local printing office, and from the miscellaneous law books of his father, who for many years was a justice of the peace. A few days before the firing on Fort Sumter, Warmoth left for Missouri and hung out his lawyer's shingle in the Ozark Mountain town of Lebanon.

Shortly after the first battle of Bull Run, when he was barely eighteen years old, Warmoth obtained an appointment as colonel of a pro-Union militia outfit. Later, as the lieutenant-colonel of a Missouri regiment and then as an officer on General John A. McClernand's staff, he took an active part in U. S. Grant's Vicksburg campaign. When Grant quarreled with McClernand and removed him from command, he also dismissed Warmoth from the Army. Warmoth went to Washington, talked with President Lincoln, and was restored to the command of his original regiment, which he led in the battle of Chattanooga. Then, as a staff officer of McClernand's again, he served in the Red River campaign in Louisiana and Texas. Late in the war, the general commanding the Department of the Gulf, N. P. Banks, detailed him as a judge of the provost court in New Orleans. By the end of 1864, Warmoth was out of the Army and was practicing law at the New Orleans bar. He was in Washington for Lincoln's second inauguration and the inaugural ball, and he was in Richmond, as a tourist, only a few days after Lee's evacuation of it.

[243]

From the spring of 1865 to the spring of 1867, while President Johnson and the congressional Republicans took their separate courses toward Reconstruction, Warmoth busied himself with politics in and out of Louisiana. In November, 1865, he helped to sponsor an extralegal election in which Negroes voted; he was thus chosen as Louisiana's "territorial delegate" to Congress. He was given a seat on the floor of the House, while the regularly elected representatives from the state of Louisiana had to watch the proceedings from the gallery, but he failed to gain official recognition as a territorial delegate. In September, 1866, he attended the convention of Southern Loyalists in Philadelphia, and during the fall of that year he campaigned in Connecticut, New York, Ohio, Indiana, Illinois, and Missouri to help elect anti-Johnson representatives to Congress. At the beginning of 1867, in New Orleans once again, he was enrolling Union veterans, Negro and white, in the Grand Army of the Republic, of which he was provisional commander for Louisiana.

By the time the Reconstruction Acts of 1867 were passed, giving the vote to southern Negroes, Warmoth had made himself the most prominent of Louisiana Republicans. In the new state constitution of 1868, they removed the minimum-age requirement so that he would be eligible for governor, though only twenty-six years old. After taking office, he lost the support of many of those who had helped elect him, and before long he began to cooperate with the Democrats. In the election of 1872 he supported the Democrat John McEnery against Kellogg for governor and the Liberal Republican and Democratic candidate, Horace Greeley, against Grant for President. Warmoth and his allies claimed a victory for their state ticket, but their opponents, with federal backing, took and held the offices. Confusion and disorder, with frequent bloodshed, prevailed in Louisiana politics until 1877, when incoming President Rutherford B. Hayes removed the last of the troops and abandoned the Reconstruction effort.

Meanwhile, Warmoth had taken up the life of a sugar planter, having purchased an interest in a Louisiana plantation. In 1877 he married the daughter of a New Jersey jewelry manufacturer and went to Europe on a wedding trip. After one year as a member of the Louisiana Legislature (1876–77), he held no state office but became and remained the Republican boss of the state. In 1888 he ran a hopeless race as a gubernatorial candidate and from 1890 to 1893 was collector of customs at New Orleans. He stayed in Louisiana and lived on and on, long enough to observe the rise of another Louisiana figure who also was called a demagogue, a dictator, and a corruptionist—Huey P. Long. In 1930, Warmoth published a volume of memoirs titled *War, Politics and Reconstruction: Stormy Days in Louisiana*. He died in the course of his ninetieth year, on September 30, 1931.

What kind of person had Warmoth been as a young man? Was he the hideous monster, corrupt at heart, that his later reputation would seem to imply?

Certainly the young Warmoth was far from hideous in appearance; rather, he was a man of striking presence and arresting good looks. He was very tall and very slender, standing well over six feet and weighing no more than 140 pounds. He had appealing brown eyes and a dark mustache (a rather full one in the style of the time), and his skin was said to be "as fair and smooth as a woman's." Wherever he went, he attracted attention, and he was quite aware of it. At one of the many Washington social affairs he attended in 1865–66, a stranger wanted to know who "this fellow Warmoth" was. "He walks with such a lordly air!" When this remark was reported to Warmoth, he put it in his diary, with obvious satisfaction. Not bad, for a small-town boy from Illinois.

The handsome Warmoth was a fun-loving, hell-raising sort, who attracted a great many like-minded friends. He had a number of enthusiasms, among them theater-going, steamboat-racing, cigar-smoking, and poker-playing. His mission to

Washington as a would-be territorial delegate he viewed at times as something of a lark. On a side trip to New York he attended a reception where Horace Greeley and others of the city's notables were among the guests. "Had a jolly time and came home tight," he noted in his diary. He was staying at the New York Hotel, which catered to southerners. "It is certainly a very sassy thing for a man with my political views to stop at a hotel . . . where all the rebels stop," he wrote. "But anything for fun." On his electioneering tour through the North in the fall of 1866, he found convivial companions among Republican politicians in various places where he spoke. "Jolly bunch," he commented on one occasion. "Had a good time with the Boys of Cleveland." His former comrades in arms remembered him well. One of them, referring to the "historic fields of Dixie," recalled how he had "so often listened with unfeigned pleasure to jokes and narratives" that Warmoth told. "The echo of your clarion voice . . . has not died away. . . . Everybody says bully for Warmoth and more especially your many lady admirers whose names are legion."

Warmoth was indeed attractive to women, old and young, married and unmarried, northern and southern. At a wartime ball in New Orleans, when he was just twenty, he met General Banks's wife. "Mrs. Banks complimented me," he confided to his diary, "by saying that when she saw me she was taken back to old times—that I looked talked & acted like Genl Banks when he was young. I blushed. Thanked her and felt better—danced with her." (Less than a week after that, the General asked him to remain in New Orleans as judge of the provost court. Apparently Mrs. Banks had spoken to her husband about him.) In Washington, Warmoth met Mary Harlan, daughter of an Iowa senator and wife-to-be of Lincoln's son Robert. Miss Harlan took the initiative by inviting Warmoth to accompany her to a reception, and thereafter he squired her about a good deal. After his return to New Orleans, he received a letter from a friend in Washington who reminded him of "that little affair of yours with the young creole lady on Canal St," which he said was a "difficult problem. . . . It can't be solved satisfactorily both to Miss Harlan and her." From a former comrade, living in Salt Lake City, Warmoth heard about the insatiable desires of Mormon women; he was warned: "You would kill yourself here in about one year." An admiring Louisiana lady, when he was governor, referred in an unsigned letter to his "grand physical beauty." And so it went.

When, at thirty-five, Warmoth finally chose to end his bachelorhood, the lucky girl was a nineteen-year-old brunette named Sally Durand. "She has very pretty eyes, a clear, fresh complexion, a neat figure, a graceful carriage, and dresses modestly and tastefully," according to a news report of the wedding. "She possesses many accomplishments, and has but recently completed a very finished education." She also had a very wealthy father.

Not all had been brashness and merriment, however, with the youthful Warmoth in his bachelor days. He also had his sensitive, impressionable, idealistic side, and he could be serious enough when the occasion demanded. A New York *Tribune* reporter, after an interview in 1872, described him as having "a quiet air of clear-headed determination, and a straightforward but temperate manner of expressing himself."

Warmoth was deeply impressed by some of his Washington experiences in 1865. At Lincoln's second inauguration, when the sun, the moon, and a bright star were all at once visible, after days of rain and clouds, he was moved to exclaim: "Oh! the spectacle! Oh! the omen! May God grant that it is the omen of peace and reunion." At the news of Robert E. Lee's surrender, he told himself: "God bless the country & its people. May peace & good will be speedily restored & swords be beaten into plough shares, & we learn to fight no more. The rebellion is over. God Almighty be praised." On April 15 he wrote: "Yesterday so beautiful & the air so dry & clear with a happy President & a happy people. Today a dead President murdered by a citizen of the United States, a mourning people, & the city, the country & the Heavens mourning & weeping at his loss." That night, Warmoth slept fitfully. "When I would wake up from my troubled sleep, the first thing that would enter my mind would be Sic Semper Tyrannis, the South is avenged, & the description I have of Booth's walking across the stage after the murder of the President." Warmoth's reaction to Lincoln's death may have had something to do with the development of his Radical feelings toward the South.

Again, the following winter, Warmoth had his thoughtful moments in Washington. After hearing a lecture by the famous Henry Ward Beecher, he jotted down the following note: "Beecher's theme was Man's Want of Confidence in Man. He had every confidence in Man. Labor was respectable, and so are laborers. Suffrage for all men, the right to vote a natural right. Radicalism. Discussion interesting." One Sunday, Warmoth occupied himself with the Bible, reading the entire book of Matthew. On another occasion he observed to himself: "Men are foolish things—afraid of God, but will not acknowledge His power."

Warmoth made a fine impression on many of the prominent men he met in the North in 1865 and 1866. These men certainly did not look upon him, when he became Louisiana's governor, as bringing an evil influence into southern politics. Just the opposite. As Lincoln's former secretary John Hay wrote, congratulating him on his "well earned success" in the election of 1868, "It is a most cheering indication for the South that the fresh young energy of the West is taking so large a share in the management of civil affairs."

Once he had taken office as governor, did this brash, energetic, and on the whole attractive young Illinoian proceed to make himself "dictator" of Louisiana? True, he attempted to supervise elections by means of the Returning Board, and he tried to enforce the state's authority through the metropolitan police, the parish constabulary, and the state militia as well. It does not necessarily follow, however, that either the purpose or the result of these undertakings was dictatorship.

The original purpose was defensive. Ever since the end of the war, the Republican party in Louisiana had faced the hostility of armed gangs of irreconcilable white men. Republicans, especially Negroes, were at the mercy of such terrorists. "You will see in the [New Orleans] Tribune of this morning," the party leader Thomas J. Durant informed Warmoth, January 13, 1866, "another account of a typical outrage committed on a poor negro in Terrebonne by the patrol, which is the name given to the organization of returned Confederate soldiers established by Governor Wells and the Louisiana Legislature [which then, of course, was Conservative, or Democratic]." In April of the same year another Republican wrote to Warmoth from Donaldsonville: "It is impossible to convey even a slight suspicion of the dread which prevails among our little party. Persecutions the most unjust and diabolical are of every day occurrence. The object seems to be to drive out of the parish and state every loyal man. . . ." Warmoth himself witnessed the New Orleans riot of July, 1866, in which dozens of Negroes were killed and wounded.

This terrorism did not diminish but increased after Warmoth and the Republicans had taken office. He himself promptly received a death threat from the Ku Klux Klan. During the fall campaign of 1868, the wartime loyalist governor, Michael Hahn, reported from New Orleans: "Murder and intimidation are the order of the day in this State. There is now more cruelty practised towards Republicans than there was against Unionists during the rebellion. Every night democratic clubs parade the streets of this city, and violence & bloodshed almost invariably follow. During the past two or three weeks Republicans were leaving the country parishes & were seeking protection in this city, but now the prominent men of the party are daily leaving the city for protection elsewhere." The presidential and congressional elections of that year went against the Republicans in Louisiana. "The pistol and the knife are more potent than the ballot," a defeated Republican candidate for Congress explained. "Less than three hundred republicans voted in this city [New Orleans] where we can poll eighteen thousand votes. Men were not only intimidated from voting but were intimidated into voting the democratic ticket."

Given these circumstances, Warmoth and his fellow Republicans certainly had good reason for resorting to some device, such as the Returning Board, to offset intimidation at the polls and for adopting police measures to protect the voters and provide some semblance of law and order. Even if it be granted that the aim was legitimate, however, there still remains the question of the consequences, the question whether Warmoth used the new measures to set up a dictatorship. The plain fact, as will be seen, is that these did not really give him absolute control of the state. They did not even enable him to control his own party, and soon he was fighting for his political life. Among his Republican foes were many of the white southerners (scalawags), many of the Negroes, and eventually many of the carpetbaggers as well.

Warmoth and his northern friends antagonized the southern white Republicans by taking too many offices for themselves. As Michael Hahn, who was one of the disgruntled southerners, complained in 1868: "Instead of [the northerners] extending the Republican fold, old citizens of Union and Republican proclivities were ostracized & only new comers were placed in positions of honor & emolument. They were not satisfied with filling the positions of Governor and other State officers and U.S. Senators with 'Carpet-baggers,' but went further: in the present campaign every white man on the electoral ticket [for presidential electors] & every one of the five nominations for Congress is a 'Carpet-bagger.' This

greediness naturally excites & inflames the old rebel population, & disgusts the tried old Union citizens."

The same greediness eventually offended many of the Negroes too. "It seems that the negroes have had enough of the
'carpet-baggers,'" the New Orleans *Bee* reported late in 1870.
"They say the latter have been profuse in promises to them
but sparing in performance—that the 'carpet-baggers' told
them their turn would come 'to-morrow' but 'to-morrow'
never came. The negroes therefore say they are going in for
'to-day' and are determined to secure their share of the spoils."
Some Negroes were displeased also because Warmoth, as governor, had failed to press as hard as they thought he ought to
have done for their civil rights.

Far more disastrous to Warmoth than the loss of part of his
scalawag and Negro support was the alienation of many of his
carpetbag associates and, along with them, President Grant.
Warmoth's fellow Illinoian and for a time close personal and
political friend, the United States Senator William Pitt Kellogg, turned into a dangerous and implacable enemy. The
break between these two resulted mainly from further disa-
greements over the division of the spoils and, more particularly, over the role of James F. Casey in the spoils system.
Casey, the husband of Mrs. Grant's favorite sister, had received from the nepotic President an appointment as collector
of customs in New Orleans. Senator Kellogg and other members of the Louisiana delegation in Congress at first opposed
Casey's appointment and tried to bring about his removal, but
Warmoth, in response to an appeal from Casey, sent a letter to
Grant in his behalf. When Grant showed this letter to Kellogg and the others, "they left the President without Collector
Casey's scalp," as Warmoth tells the story in his memoirs, "but
with 'red blood in their eyes for Governor Warmoth.'" The
stands of Governor Warmoth and Senator Kellogg were re-
versed, however, when, in 1871, the word got out that the
President "would like to have Collector Casey sent to the

Senate so that he might be near Mrs. Grant." Kellogg now was ready to welcome Casey as a Senate colleague, but Warmoth threw his influence in the legislature against Casey and secured the election of his own candidate. Thereafter Warmoth had to contend against a powerful Kellogg faction, which included the "custom house ring" and had the full backing of the Grant administration.

During the last two years of his four-year term, Warmoth found himself constantly on the defensive against his factional foes. In 1871, with the aid of United States soldiers, they attempted a coup by which to oust him as governor and purge the party of his followers. The Democratic allies whom he began to cultivate were powerless to save either him or themselves in the 1872 election. After the election the Warmoth Returning Board counted in the candidates of the new coalition, but the Kellogg men produced a returning board of their own, and they claimed a majority for their ticket, including Kellogg himself as their candidate for governor. With federal assistance—a court order, a marshal, and troops—the Kellogg Republicans took possession of the state house. They started impeachment proceedings against Warmoth, to hurry him out before his term was up, and in the confusion at the end it was hard to know just who really was governor.

All this hardly adds up to a Warmoth dictatorship. His patronage powers, even if he had used them more effectively, were unequal to those of Kellogg and the custom house ring; his state militia and metropolitan police were no match for the United States Army; and his Returning Board, lacking as it did the united support of the Republicans in Congress, failed its final test. By 1872 the domination of Louisiana by outside forces was practically complete, but Warmoth had ceased to be the dominating figure.

If not a dictator, was Warmoth a demagogue? Did he seek power—before, during, or after his governorship—by trying to rouse the rabble, either black or white? Many of his critics

in Louisiana thought so. When he first made himself conspicuous as a politician, in 1865, the New Orleans *Times* described him as follows: "The Judge [Warmoth had been
judge of the provost court in Banks's army] is an ambitious
young gentleman of great volubility of tongue—one of that
dangerous class that think it 'better to reign in hell than serve
in heaven.' Having a strong dash of the demagogue in his
composition, he coquetted for a while after his arrival here
with the white element of our population, but finding that
darkness to him was more promising than light, he joined
himself to the ebony idol, and now claims to be the mouth-
piece of the blackest sort of republicanism."

At that time, Warmoth's Republicanism was indeed black,
from the southern Conservative point of view. As a public
speaker, he had a way of winning the good will of Negroes,
though his racial humor would hardly strike them as funny
today. He told them, at a New Orleans mass meeting just
before his departure for Washington in 1865, that the Yankees
were remarkably ingenious. They were "inventing new machines every day, and when he went North, it was his intention to try to get a Yankee to invent a machine to pump out
their black blood and pump in white." This brought laughter
and applause. "There would be no trouble then about their
voting," he went on, "for all they would have to do would be
to wash their faces and go to the ballot box." Renewed laughter. Continuing, he promised to tell the people in the North
how the Louisiana Negroes had been misrepresented as ignorant, lazy, and degraded. "I will tell them of your loyalty and
enthusiasm for the Government; that you are the only people
who love the Republic; and sing the songs of the Union and
wave the flag; that the rebels hate the flag, and do not love the
Republic, and sing only one song, and that is Dixie."

In other speeches during 1865 and 1866, Warmoth denounced the ex-Confederates and demanded that the South be
reduced to a territorial condition. "He contended that the

[federal] Government had the power and right to hang every rebel in the South." While campaigning for governor in 1868, he continued to talk in the same spirit. "I think that you feel with me that our object is to persecute nobody, punish nobody, confiscate nobody's property, but to make a government under which all may live upon terms of perfect equality before the law," he said, innocuously enough. Then he declaimed: "What has Congress done that merits the condemnation of rebels? It was well enough to curse their luck when they got whipped, but after that they had no right to say anything. They are prisoners, enemies captured in war, with no rights, no privileges, no anything but what the government in its magnanimity sees proper to give them. This I say with no feeling of revenge, or anger, but for the purpose of placing this question fairly before you."

Warmoth began to change his tune, however, after he had assumed the responsibilities of the governorship. He now felt some concern—or so he afterwards said—about the schemes of the Pure Radicals, the extreme Negro faction which, according to him, was led by three Santo Domingo Negroes "who owned and published the New Orleans *Tribune*, and who urged the negroes of Louisiana to assert themselves and follow Hayti, San Domingo, and Liberia, and to make Louisiana an African State." The Pure Radicals blamed him, he said, for failing to enforce an unenforceable state law which provided for equal rights on steamboats and railroad cars and in hotels and places of amusement. He had signed that law in 1869, but when another law was passed, making it a criminal offense for any person to refuse accommodation to Negroes, he vetoed this one, in 1871. His veto gave Negroes another grievance against him, in addition to their complaint that he was not awarding them a fair share of the patronage.

While disappointing many of his Negro followers, Governor Warmoth was making overtures to the rebels he once had so bitterly denounced. He supported a constitutional amendment to restore political rights to those former Confederate leaders who had been disfranchised by the reconstructed state constitution. He appointed James Longstreet and other one-time Confederate officers to command his state militia. These things he emphasized in a political speech he delivered before a predominantly white audience near Shreveport in 1870, and he reminded his hearers that he "had not forced the race issue upon them." As he recalled afterwards: "I told them that my great-grandfather was born in Virginia, and that my father was born in Tennessee, that I commanded a Missouri regiment in the Civil War, and that every drop of my blood was Southern." After concluding his speech, he had the band play "Dixie"—which no longer seemed to him such a wicked song as it had seemed five years earlier.

Still, Warmoth never quite forgot the Negro voters, and the more trouble he had with the Kellogg faction, the more attention he paid to them. When he and his Liberal Republican followers fused with the Democrats in 1872, delegates representing the coalition unanimously resolved: "That we recognize the political and civil rights of all men, and pledge ourselves to maintain them." The next year, when General P. G. T. Beauregard and other business leaders of New Orleans tried to start a broad and inclusive conservative movement, they dedicated themselves to the "unification of the people" and made specific pledges against discrimination in politics, business, education, or public facilities of any kind. This "unification" movement made little headway, as white supremacists preferred to join the White League, arm themselves, and prepare for violence against Negroes and against the Kellogg regime. Before the end of 1874 the white supremacists of New Orleans had succeeded, as one of them put it, in "obtaining the purification of the public schools" (some of which had been integrated for a time) and in restoring the "inviolability of the places of public amusement and resort." The white supremacists next undertook to bring segregation back to the mule-drawn street railways, with Negro passengers confined to special cars, each marked with a star.

In 1874, Warmoth boldly spoke out on the question of Negro rights and, in doing so, revived old enmities. He wrote a letter to the New Orleans *Bulletin* to protest that paper's advocacy of "star" cars. He reminded the editor of the solemn commitments that the Conservatives had made in recent years. "Are we now, in the very dawn of our success," he asked, "to allow ourselves to violate our pledges, and pursue a course which will for all time consolidate the colored vote against the Conservative organizations in this country?" The *Bulletin* answered Warmoth with columns of abuse. "He despairs of being taken up by the white people, and in his desperation resolves to return to his first love," the paper said. "He hopes . . . to humbug the colored people, secure their confidence and esteem, and unite them once more in his behalf." And then a concluding slur: "Like the 'dog returning to his vomit again and the sow to her wallowing in the mire,' so does the ex-Governor return to the fond and loving embrace of his former disreputable associates." Warmoth came back with a letter accusing the *Bulletin* of "lying—unmitigated lying."

Thereupon the editor issued a challenge, and on the day before the duel was to take place, his partner, drunk and armed with a heavy cane, attacked Warmoth on the street. Warmoth, pulling out the contemporary version of a switch-blade knife, stabbed his assailant to death. "This encounter pointedly illustrates two things . . . ," the Chicago *Tribune* commented. "In the first place, it shows the utter and uncompromising ultraism of the Southern Democrats, which is worse, if possible, than the opposing ultraism of the carpetbaggers. The trouble is, there is nothing like Conservatism in Louisiana. Warmoth has been acting with the so-called Conservatives ever since 1872, but this could not save him from brutal assault simply because he refused to join in a general war against 'the niggers.' "

In after years, Warmoth continued his efforts to secure what he called "a fair show for everybody black & white." As late as 1900, opposing the "lily white" faction of the Louisiana Republicans, he insisted that there were more than 15,000 Negroes in the state who were "as much entitled to vote as any white man." Still later, however, when he prepared a typescript of his 1864–67 diary, he made subtle revisions in it so as to tone down its implications of Radicalism. And when he wrote his memoirs, he emphasized his efforts, as governor, to prevent the extreme Radical Negroes from "Africanizing" the state.

How much truth there was in the charge of "demagogue" depends largely on the definition of the term. No doubt Warmoth appealed to Negroes for their votes, but, after all, it is the function of a politician to solicit the votes of the electorate. It hardly seems that Warmoth went to those extremes of inciting the masses—and doing it on specious grounds—which set the demagogue apart from the mere politician. Certainly, in cultivating Negro support, he never went to anything like the extremes to which later southern demagogues went in courting the anti-Negro vote. Warmoth does, of course, appear to have been more the politician than the idealist in his record on racial issues. Obviously, he trimmed and turned in accordance with the needs of Louisiana politics in his time.

If Warmoth was neither quite a demagogue nor quite a dictator, was he nevertheless a corruptionist? Did he corrupt the politics of Louisiana even though he did not completely dominate them?

According to his critics, he was an old hand at turning a dishonest dollar; it was said that even before he became governor, while he was on legal business for the federal government in Texas, he had embezzled a sum of $30,000 or $40,000. The main charges against him as governor were the following: 1) He assigned the public printing to the New Orleans *Republican*, which his henchmen in the legislature owned, and within two years they received more than $1,000,000 for work that might have been done profitably for $50,000; 2) He sold state-owned stock in the New Orleans and Jackson Railroad to one of his cronies and made $100,000 on the deal; 3) He issued $3,000,000 in bonds for levee construction, but less than $1,000,000 worth of work was actually done; the rest of the money went to him and his followers; 4) He "got up a project for monopolizing the profits of all the butchering done in New Orleans"; he induced the legislature to pass an act creating the Crescent City Slaughter House Company and requiring all butchers to use its facilities; 5) He was willing to accept bribes, and he used his veto power as a means of extortion. Thus he vetoed the Nicholson pavement bill—for paving New Orleans streets with wooden blocks by a patented process—because the proffered bribe of $50,000 was not enough; he demanded $75,000 plus a percentage of the paving company's profits.

Warmoth repeatedly and specifically denied every one of these (and other) accusations. He defended all the improvements projects he had authorized, and particularly the slaughter-house monopoly, which he described as a sound and necessary measure of public hygiene. He conceded that there was "a frightful amount of corruption" in Louisiana, but pointed out that the blame for this lay at least as much with the bribe-givers as the bribe-takers.

When, in 1870, a delegation of prominent New Orleans citizens called on him with a petition for good government, he replied to them: "You charge the Legislature with passing, corruptly, many bills looking to the personal aggrandizement of individuals and corporations. Let me suggest to you that these individuals and corporations are your very best people. For instance, this bank bill that is being lobbied through the

Legislature now by the hardest kind of work. We have been able to defeat this bill twice in the House, and now it is up again. Who are doing it? Your bank presidents. The best people of the City of New Orleans are crowding the lobby of the Legislature continually, whispering bribes into these men's ears to pass this measure. How are we to defend the State against the interposition of these people who are potent in their influence in this community?" Warmoth reminded his callers that he had vetoed many subsidy bills, but the influence of the lobby was so strong that some were repassed over his veto. He told how "one of these same good citizens" had offered him $50,000 to sign the Nicholson pavement bill. Finally, he "invited the assistance and co-operation of all good citizens" in restoring purity to Louisiana government.

When, in a political speech the next year, Warmoth named the "good citizen" who had offered him a bribe, this man— John A. Walsh—admitted having offered it and said Warmoth had declined it only because it was not enough. When Warmoth called him a liar, Walsh asked him to designate two friends to meet and make arrangements with two of Walsh's friends. Walsh was, of course, challenging Warmoth to a duel, but Warmoth cleverly turned the challenge aside by pretending that Walsh was inviting him to submit the "question of veracity" to arbitration. Warmoth readily agreed to send two men to meet with the other two, the four of them to choose a fifth if necessary. "This," said Warmoth, "on condition that if I can establish to the satisfaction of the gentlemen named, by statements of yours . . . that you approached me with an offer of fifty thousand dollars . . . that I refused it and told you no consideration, pecuniary or otherwise, could induce me to sign it, then you are to admit that the statement, as above given, is false and that the breach of veracity was committed by you." Walsh, however, insisted on "an apology or retraction . . . or, in the absence thereof, such an adjustment as usually obtains among gentlemen." Warmoth persisted in refusing to fight, explaining that a duel, no matter who killed whom, would not determine which of the two had been lying. Walsh, in demanding a trial of honor according to the southern code, had a very weak case, since he had already confessed to violating his own honor when he admitted that he had offered a bribe.

In an 1872 interview with a New York *Tribune* reporter, Warmoth elaborated upon his views of Louisiana corruption in general. He said: "The negro legislators have held out against bribery quite as well as the white Republicans, and at least as well as the Democrats. We have no law in our State against bribery. . . . I proposed a law against it . . . and it passed the Senate unanimously, but in the House it mysteriously disappeared. . . . All the bills with money in them were voted for by a very large majority, and sometimes by all of the Democratic members of both houses. There is no doubt that reform is greatly needed in our State among all classes of society."

Obviously, during Warmoth's governorship, there was something rotten in the state of Louisiana. There remains the question, however, of the extent to which he participated in and was responsible for the rottenness. The bandying of corruption charges was a common practice in Reconstruction politics. When Congress made its repeated investigations of Louisiana affairs, the charges and counter-charges were so conflicting and confusing that the investigators could scarcely reach any conclusion except on the basis of political prejudices. One of the investigators remarked to Warmoth: "We cannot determine whether you are an angel from Heaven, or a devil from Hell." Viewing the question now, from the perspective of nearly a century, it seems that, in his confrontations with his accusers, especially the egregious Mr. Walsh, Warmoth came out somewhat better than they did. Though he undoubtedly profited from some dubious deals, he apparently was guiltless of the grosser forms of corruption, such as the taking of bribes. On the other hand, many of the so-called "good citizens," who came from old and respected Louisiana families, were guilty of offering them. In short, if Warmoth was corrupt, it would be nearer the truth to say that Louisiana corrupted *him* than to say that *he* corrupted Louisiana.

Nevertheless, there is no doubt that Warmoth did make a good deal of money while he was governor. According to a friend, "He made his money in the depreciated State bonds, by an investment based upon his knowledge of the time fixed to resume paying interest upon them." He "bought Louisiana bonds standing at thirty-five; by funding the coupons and resuming interest they rose more than one hundred per cent." The friend insisted that this was a perfectly legitimate speculation—which is questionable—but did not explain where Warmoth had got the money to buy the bonds in the first place. Warmoth himself said in his memoirs: "I had plenty of money with which to begin my life after I left the army; and I at once entered upon a lucrative practice of law in the United States Courts, before courts martial, military commissions, and governmental departments, which paid me large fees and a handsome income." Here he may have exaggerated a bit, but surely his critics have exaggerated both his impecuniosity at the beginning of his governorship and his riches at the end of it. By 1872 he was indeed "well-to-do," as even his friends conceded. There is no reason to believe, however, that he was literally a millionaire.

At least he was wealthy enough, by 1874, to invest more than $100,000 in a 2,700-acre sugar and orange plantation, "the finest plantation of its kind in the world," situated on the west bank of the Mississippi about forty-five miles below New Orleans. This was Magnolia Plantation, and with his investment Warmoth acquired a one-third interest in it from his southern friend, Colonel Effingham Lawrence. During the 1874 season the plantation produced 750,000 pounds of sugar, which sold for $75,000, and more than 1,000,000 oranges, which sold for more than $10,000. Through the profits from this enterprise, Warmoth added to his fortune, and eventually he became sole owner of the property.

There, in their old-fashioned southern mansion, the master of Magnolia and his charming wife lived out their years in antebellum style. When, in 1897, a group of congressmen visited Magnolia, the host and hostess entertained them with what a newspaper called "true Southern hospitality." The visitors were shown the cane fields, the sugar mills, and the "whitewashed quarters" where, the reporter said, an ancient Negro named "Uncle Tom" took them in tow, while other old men and women "who had grown gray in the service of Magnolia" smiled happily, and "long rows of pickaninnies looked on in open-mouthed wonderment."

Henry Clay Warmoth had come a long way since his arrival in Louisiana as a youthful soldier in 1864. His term as a carpetbag governor was but a brief interlude in his long life, though that interlude made possible his remarkable material success. By the time he reached old age, his success had gained him a certain measure of respect in Louisiana society, yet nothing like full acceptance in it. That he was eager for such acceptance is suggested by a passage in his memoirs: ". . . having not a drop of any other than Southern blood in my veins, I think I may say, at eighty-seven years of age, that I was never a 'Louisiana Carpet-bagger,' though I might, in common parlance, be termed a 'scallawag.'"

The fact is that Warmoth was never a scalawag at all, and he was unquestionably a carpetbagger. According to the usage of the Reconstruction period itself, the term *carpetbagger* included all men who had come from the North during or after the war and had entered southern politics as Republicans —regardless of their ancestry. The term *scalawag* was applied only to those Republicans who had supported the Confederacy or who, if wartime Unionists, had been born in the South or had established residence there before the war. From the white supremacist point of view, a scalawag was every bit as contemptible as a carpetbagger, but Warmoth in his old age seems to have forgotten that.

Few Louisianians of the best old families could ever quite forgive him for the methods he used—or was supposed to have used—back in the Reconstruction days. There was, however, one man in Louisiana who admired him for his techniques and consciously set out to imitate and adapt some of them. That man, as T. Harry Williams has discovered, was Huey P. Long.

12

THE SCALAWAG IN
MISSISSIPPI RECONSTRUCTION

David Donald

The historical portrait of the scalawags has varied
from DuBois' sympathetic assessment of them as
men "who saw a vision of democracy across racial
lines" to the more popular view that they were
traitors to their own race and representative of the
lowest orders of southern society. But in 1944 David
Donald studied the origins and political behavior
of native white Republicans in Mississippi and revised some of the simplistic notions about the
scalawags.

The scalawag is the forgotten man of Reconstruction history.
In spite of the excellent work of recent revisionists, the old
stereotypes as to the political course of Reconstruction in the
South have remained largely undisturbed. On the one hand, it
is said, were the Democrats, the vast majority of the white
population, battling valiantly for the creed of the Old South,
and on the other the Republicans, black in morals as in skin.
The Republican party, so the story goes, consisted of the great
body of uneducated Negroes, dominated by carpetbaggers
from the North or—worst of all—by a few renegade southerners opprobriously termed scalawags. These were, it is
usually considered, the very lowest dregs of mankind; they
were "southern white men . . . [who] sold themselves for

office"; they were the veritable Esaus of the Caucasian race.

A fresh study of the Reconstruction era in Mississippi, however, casts some doubt on the conventional interpretation of the scalawag's role in that troubled time. Republicans ruled Mississippi for five years after its readmission in 1870, and during this period one-third of the congressmen, one of the governors, two of the three supreme court justices, and about one-third of both houses of the state legislature were southern-born white Republicians. Further analysis shows that almost every one of these officeholders had before the war been an old-line Whig and a bitter opponent of the Democrats.

Surprisingly little attention has been paid to the postwar attitudes of southern Whig leaders. That party, after all, had been numerous. In 1852 its candidate in Mississippi had defeated no less a person than Jefferson Davis for the United States Senate. As Unionists the Whigs had cast a respectable vote for John Bell in 1860. And, as late as 1863, they had secured a majority in the Mississippi Legislature, selected a Whig for Confederate senator, and elected a former Whig as governor. They were the wealthiest and best educated element in the state.

It has generally been assumed that after the war southern Whigs immediately joined with the Democrats to combat carpetbag and Negro rule. Actually this was far from the case. Some few Whig leaders did from the beginning urge the disbanding of the old party in favor of such an alignment, but their efforts came at a time when the Democratic party itself was virtually defunct, and when influential southern newspapers were urging a dissolution of that party. But Whigs were not attracted by the Democratic policies or leadership anyway. "[W]ould it not be absurd," questioned one, "for Whigs to abandon their high conservative position, and aid in the reorganization of the Democratic party?" Much of the prewar bitterness between parties still remained, and the editor of one of the best papers in the state asserted: "Men who think that 'the war' knocked all of the old Whig spirit out of the Whigs are just . . . fatally mistaken."

Throughout the Reconstruction period, therefore, there were efforts to reorganize the party. Again and again Whig leaders called on the Democrats to abandon their party and join other moderates in battling both Radical Republicans and radical secessionists. A general "Consultation" was held in 1870 so that Whig leaders over the state could agree on policies. The action of this group, termed by hostile Democrats "the grandest fizzle of the age," reflects the difficulties in the way of a third party in the South. Finding too much resentment connected with all the old party names, these men decided that a union of conservatives should be formed, "composed of Whigs, Democrats [and] Republicans," but as a commentator noted, the new party was to be "upon a Whig basis." No very tangible results were to come from such efforts to revive the Whig party. The appeal was, after all, to a limited class of conservative planters and businessmen, and popular feeling was too strong for most southerners to repudiate Democracy.

Many Whigs had realized these difficulties from the beginning and had joined the Republicans. Within two years after readmission to the Union they were joined by most of their party. Although any statistics for this difficult period must be regarded skeptically, it has been estimated that from twenty-five to thirty percent of the Mississippi white voters had by 1873 joined the Republican party, and nearly all of these were former Whigs. Such action is not hard to understand. The Whigs were wealthy men—the large planters and the railroad and industrial promoters—who naturally turned to the party which in the state as in the nation was dominated by business interests.

A glance at the leadership of the scalawag element in Mississippi confirms these generalizations. Most important of all was James Lusk Alcorn, elected first governor of the reconstructed state in 1869 and later chosen United States Senator. One of the wealthiest plantation owners in the rich Mississippi delta, a large slaveholder, and a Whig opposed to secession, he had reluctantly gone with his state in 1861 and had served briefly in the Confederate army. After the war he was one of the first to admit that secession had been wrong, indeed, treasonable. Now a Republican leader, his program was basically a simple one: "I propose," he declared, "to vote with . . . [the Negro]; to discuss political affairs with him; to sit, if necessary, in political counsel with him." By recognizing the legal equality of the Negroes, Alcorn hoped to gain their political support for his own policies.

Alcorn's legislative program shows plainly the direction in which the Whig element hoped to lead the Republican party. First of all, the Negroes had to be conciliated by the adoption of civil rights measures. On economic questions the governor naturally favored the planter class, urging the rebuilding of levees, reduction of land taxes, leasing of convicts to secure a steady labor supply, and state aid in the reconstruction of railroads. The powers of the state government were to be expanded in order to exercise close control over county finances. It was, of course, a program of class legislation, but it was not corrupt. The administration was both intelligent and honest, and it has not been found that any of Alcorn's followers misused their state offices for personal profit. There is much to be said for their program of guaranteeing civil rights, improving schools, and expanding the judiciary.

The Alcorn-Whig program was not to be carried through to completion. It met with difficulties on all sides. The Democrats, of course, objected violently, partly from politics, partly from principle. It was believed that the economic policies of the Alcorn administration tended to discriminate against the predominantly Democratic hill regions in favor of the Whiggish delta bottoms. The rallying point of the Democrats was opposition to Alcorn's plan of granting the Negro legal equality. A prominent Mississippi newspaper, doubtless voicing the sentiments of its readers, felt that "Nigger voting, holding office and sitting in the jury box are all wrong, and against the sentiment of the country." For recognizing Negro rights Alcorn became known as "an open and avowed enemy of his race." It was asserted that "the name of Benedict Arnold ought to occupy a more exalted and honorable . . . position in the annals of american history than that of J. L. Alcorn." A Democrat had rather be called a horse thief than a scalawag.

Carpetbaggers were also bitter against Alcorn and the southern Republicans. One northerner declared that the governor was "an old whig and in some of his appointment he has put in his style of whig d—m rebels . . . and . . . he is fixing up a party of his own (whig) and using the negro for a blind." The basic trouble was that, though he might advocate legal equality and civil rights as a measure of expediency, the southern planter could not bring himself to accede to the Negro's demand for social equality. Many of the carpetbaggers had come to the South with preconceived and doctrinaire ideas concerning race relations in their adopted section and felt that the Negro's rights were not secure. More, perhaps, were disgruntled when well paid offices were filled by men of southern birth. These factors, intensified by Alcorn's known dislike of northerners [though Alcorn himself was born in the North], caused an early break between the Whig and the carpetbag factions of the Republican party. When the governor failed to call in federal troops after a minor disturbance in 1871, a Radical Republican charged that he was trying to gain "power and favor from the democracy at the price of . . . the blood of his friends." After two years of rule by Alcorn, another was convinced that "old line whigs are worse men to-day than any whipped (in the war) Democrats."

The Negroes, too, were dissatisfied with the Alcorn regime. Increasingly conscious of the importance of their votes, they demanded a share of the offices proportional to their numerical strength. The freedmen cared little about the Whigs' economic policies, but they distrusted their former owners and, prompted by the carpetbag leaders, were inclined to demand social and civil equality.

The opposition of any one of these elements would have been formidable, and the chances for men of Alcorn's views to succeed were from the start very slight. But—contrary to the version of the Democratic state historians—these three groups worked closely together to bring about Alcorn's defeat. As early as 1871 the Democrats approached the carpetbag group for a political alliance. This alignment was strikingly revealed the following year when Democrats and Radical Republicans joined forces to prevent a Whig paper from securing the lucrative state printing contract. Hoping to break the governor's control of the colored vote, the Democrats encouraged the political aspirations of the Negroes, while carpetbaggers were more successful in organizing the blacks into Union Leagues.

The real test of the Whig program occurred in 1873, when Alcorn—who had resigned to take a seat in the United States Senate, leaving a faithful disciple in his place at Jackson—decided to run again for governor. His opponent for the Republican nomination was Adelbert Ames, a carpetbagger born in Maine and a son-in-law of Benjamin F. Butler of Massachusetts. Ames—variously characterized by the Democrats as "Addle-pate" Ames or "onion headed" Ames—was a man of real ability and had a sincere belief in his duty to protect Negro rights, which he felt Alcorn was neglecting. When the carpetbagger secured the Republican nomination, Alcorn bolted and formed a new party of his own, composed almost entirely of former Whigs. Though this group had the nominal endorsement of the Democrats, many Democratic leaders voted for the carpetbagger rather than for the delta planter. Ames was elected by a huge majority. While conservative papers blamed Alcorn's defeat on the indifference of the

Democrats, it might also be attributed to the growing realization by the Negro of his political power.

This election of 1873 marked the end of a period. Former Whigs had joined and then dominated the Republican party in Mississippi. They had sponsored a legislative program that would attract to their party sound and conservative men regardless of former political affiliation. Now, repudiated by the Negro and carpetbag sections of the Republican party and rejected by the more fanatical element of the Democrats, they were thoroughly defeated. They had no choice but to make their way slowly and reluctantly over to the Democratic camp.

The exciting next two years are the best known portion of the state's Reconstruction story. The account of the final restoration of "home rule" in Mississippi has been told many times by historians attracted by the drama of the carpetbag debacle. It was a time when party feelings ran high and when race relations were at a critical point. Old residents of the state still recall vividly the tension and excitement of these years. Mississippi was torn between two hostile political camps, and there was no longer a place for middle-of-the-road, Whig policies.

Beginning in 1874 the Democrats made definite plans to carry the elections of the following year, by persuasion if possible, by force if necessary. This is the entire content of the Mississippi Plan of 1875. Objecting on many grounds to the corruption and excesses of the Radicals, they made the drawing of a color-line the central theme of their campaign—the universal opposition of all white men to any Negro participation in politics. In order to secure the goal of white supremacy—meaning, of course, a Democratic victory—it was necessary first to rally all Democrats to the party standard, then to persuade the scalawags to vote on the color-line, to harry carpetbaggers out of the state, and to frighten the Negroes from the polls.

At the same time the Republican party was becoming a well-oiled political machine. Under the shrewd carpetbag leadership the Negroes were herded into the notorious Union Leagues and voted in droves as their leaders dictated. Both state and federal patronage were used to bolster a weakening regime. To an increasing extent the Republican party stressed the necessity for social and civil equality for its black members. And to an increasing extent southern-born white leaders were discarded for carpetbaggers or Negroes.

In this crisis Mississippi Whigs had to choose between open support of color-line policies and a program which they firmly believed would lead to racial amalgamation. While to some it was Hobson's choice, there could never have been any doubt as to the course the majority would eventually take. As men of wealth and property they were indignant over extravagances of the carpetbag government, which were reflected in high taxes; they disliked the northerners as aliens and resented their control over the Negroes; they were alarmed by the facility with which federal troops could be called in whenever the Republicans seemed about to lose an election. But it was the Negro that was the deciding factor. For the southern planter who had never been able to accept ideas of racial equality, the present political power and organization of the colored vote, accompanied by Radical proscription of conservative white leaders, made opposition to the Republicans inescapable.

Under these pressures the former Whigs gradually drifted into an alliance with their Democratic foes of previous years. Even former Governor Alcorn participated in color-line meetings in his county, and he publicly declared that he was not and really never had been a "negro Republican." On the few recalcitrants tremendous social and economic pressure was exerted. Democratic papers carried conspicuously the names of white Republicans who must no longer be spoken to on the street and whose attentions must be scorned by "every true woman." The scalawag who persisted in his obduracy was publicly labeled "a beast in man's clothing" or "a traitor to his country." Those who failed to renounce their Republican affiliations faced ostracism. "No white man," a former Republican wrote, "can live in the South in the future and act with any other than the Democratic party."

Heartened by Whig support, the Democrats waged a lively campaign. There were political demonstrations in every town: parades two miles long, fireworks and Confederate cannon, floats and transparencies of spectacular size, barbecues, picnics, and interminable speeches. Half the villages in the state claimed the local rally as "The Grandest Affair of the Campaign." The more martial elements, donning the red-shirt badge of southern manhood, formed armed rifle companies and drilled and marched in public. These were no secret Ku Kluxers; they wanted the Negro and his friends to know that the entire white population of Mississippi was against continuance of Republican rule.

Most of the color-liners were convinced that efforts to win the colored votes would fail, and it was felt that the best policy was to keep the Negroes from the polls. Republican meetings were disturbed by red-shirt horsemen who remarked loudly that "maybe they might kill a buck that day." When Confederate cannon were fired in the immediate vicinity of Negro rallies, the terrified freedmen believed the war had begun again. There were countless tales of torchlight processions, of disrupted Republican rallies, of nocturnal raids, of whippings, and worse. Whenever the Negroes tried to retaliate, there occurred a race riot. At least a dozen of these conflicts happened during the campaign, and in every case the result was the same. Trained bands of white men were able to defeat the badly led Negroes; dozens of blacks were killed, few if any whites injured.

Every race riot brought two results. The whites were more solidly united than ever. Whig and Democrat, secessionist and unionist, and even Confederate and Federal joined hands against what they regarded as aggression from the carpetbag-Negro combination. And on the other hand, the Republican party was completely demoralized. The Negroes were terrified; President Grant refused to send additional troops; and Governor Ames, to prevent a race war, virtually surrendered to the Democratic leaders. The Republican regime in Mississippi was doomed.

The important elections of 1875 were ominously quiet. As one observer put it, the Negroes were afraid to make any trouble and the whites did not need to. Election frauds, in spite of a number of hair-raising tales, seem not to have been unusually large. The result was a sweeping Democratic success. Virtually all the counties now passed under the control of color-line administrations. The whites gained heavy majorities in both houses of the legislature and elected all but one of the congressmen, while in the only general race the Democratic candidate for state treasurer had a lead of over thirty thousand votes.

The sequel of the election may be noted very briefly. The Republican governor, Ames, and the lieutenant governor were impeached when the new legislature met. The former, although there was no real case against him, resigned, and the latter was convicted. By 1876 "home rule" was officially restored, and Mississippi has ever since been a Democratic state.

The combination of force and intimidation known as the Mississippi Plan received much attention in other southern states, where Democratic leaders imitated the Mississippi tactics. Much of the political history of the South in the decades after 1875 was centered about the idea that white supremacy could be maintained only by preventing the Negro from voting. This point of view is closely connected with the customary explanation of the success of the Mississippi Plan. It has been held by every student of Reconstruction since William A. Dunning that white supremacy in the South was secured through the intimidation of the Negro. "The real Mississippi plan," it is contended, "was to play upon the easy credulity of the negroes and inspire them with terror so that they would . . . stay away from the polls."

This explanation seems to be an oversimplification of the problem. The difficulties of making an adequate study of a Reconstruction election in the South have seldom been realized. First of all, it is impossible to secure accurate statistics of population, since the 1870 census is almost worthless, even as an estimate. In most cases the number of potential and registered voters cannot be discovered. The disfranchised Confederate element is another unknown. It cannot be determined with any degree of accuracy what proportion of the vote each race cast, and it is even more impossible to ascertain how many Negroes were herded to the polls by Democratic landlords or by Republican politicians. Finally, the amount of actual election fraud, always considerable during the period, adds another indeterminable variable. The whole situation is one of the utmost complexity, and any sweeping generalizations must be received with caution.

But even in the face of these difficulties it can be determined that the conventional explanation of the success of the Mississippi Plan is not satisfactory. If the Negroes were kept from voting, there should have been fewer Republican ballots cast than in former years. This is not the case. Actually the Republicans were nearly as strong as in previous elections, and if it is admitted that most whites had by 1875 left the Republican fold, the election returns show that in reality *more* Negroes voted than ever before.

It seems safe to conclude that in the Mississippi election of 1875 the Negroes as a general rule voted the Republican ticket. But there are exceptions even to this assertion. In certain counties anti-Ames Negro Republicans joined the Democrats to fight the administration's candidates, and "fusion" tickets were elected. In some five delta counties, moreover, the

Democratic vote was so large as to justify the belief that wealthy landowners "voted" their colored tenants for the Democratic party.

With the white population, the picture is somewhat clearer. To the old Democratic nucleus there were now added many recruits. Southern white men who since the war had felt that the political situation was hopeless now saw a chance for their principles to triumph and returned to support their party. But the greatest accession of Democratic strength came from the thousands of so-called scalawags—mostly former Whigs—who now denounced the Republican party and voted on the color-line.

It appears, therefore, that a number of misconceptions concerning the course of Reconstruction need revision. The southern political scene in this postwar period was never simple. In Mississippi the importance of the former Whigs has generally been neglected. Toward the beginning of Reconstruction most of these joined the Republican party. Their moderate program of gradual adjustment to the realities of Reconstruction was defeated by a combination of extremists from all parties. By 1875 these Whigs, disgusted by Radical excesses and attracted by color-line principles, had gradually changed political allegiance and joined the Democratic party. Not until this shift was completed did the Democrats win an election. The triumph of the Democratic color-line policies, known as the Mississippi Plan of 1875, would seem to be due to the successful union of all southern whites into one party rather than to the intimidation of the Negro.

13

PERSISTENT WHIGGERY
IN THE CONFEDERATE SOUTH
1860-1877

Thomas B. Alexander

The importance which David Donald assigned to
the role of old-line Whigs in Mississippi Reconstruction was given added impetus with the publication of several articles by Thomas B. Alexander on
the nature and persistence of Whiggery in the post-
Civil War South.

It is often stated that the Whig party in the United States
disintegrated during the 1850's in all parts of the country,
including the eleven states that were to comprise the Confederacy. Students of the South's political history are not una-
ware that the Constitutional Union party of 1860 was substantially a continuation of the Whig party of the South; but the
rare mention of the term "Whig" in studies of the section
after 1860 would seem to imply that the party disappeared
with the firing of the first gun at Fort Sumter, and that its
leaders promptly forgot that they had ever venerated Henry
Clay or vilified their Democratic opponents.

On the contrary, Whig influence continued to exist within
the Confederacy and to oppose Democrats behind a facade of
wartime solidarity. Furthermore, after the war many southern

Whig leaders remained keenly conscious of their former party affiliation, partial to fellow Whigs in political contests, and hostile to the Democratic party. Indications abound that this persistence of Whig loyalty was an important influence in the South and must be properly assessed before an adequate understanding can be gained of Civil War and Reconstruction politics.

In the five presidential elections from 1840 through 1856, except in the contest of 1852, the popular vote cast by Whigs increased in the eleven southern states which later joined the Confederacy. In 1860 John Bell, the Constitutional Union candidate, received a larger popular vote in these states than had ever been cast there for a Whig presidential candidate—approximately 40 percent of the total. Bell's vote was not the full measure of southern Whig strength, however, because part of the vote for the northern Democrat, Stephen A. Douglas, was cast by men who had been Whigs until 1856 or 1857. Some former Whigs were even Douglas candidates for presidential elector. It would thus appear that the shift in party nomenclature from Whig to American in 1856 and to Constitutional Union in 1860 had but little impact on Whig voting strength or party organization in the South.

During the secession crisis not all southern Whigs adopted the same attitudes, but before Lincoln's call for troops they were so preponderantly Unionist in sentiment that southern Whiggery and Unionism became almost synonymous in many of the states that seceded. Alabama and Georgia counties where Negroes constituted a large majority of the population seem to have presented exceptions to this Whig-Unionist pattern, but it is by no means certain even there that the rank and file of the Whig voters followed their local leaders into secession sentiment. In the Black Belt counties of Alabama, for example, popular voting for delegates to the secession convention was so light that it is possible that few Whigs voted. Certainly Alabama Whigs outside the Black Belt followed the

South-wide Whig pattern of Unionism. It is true that some Democratic areas, chiefly in the Appalachian Highlands and the adjacent Piedmont, were Unionist in sentiment, but the great bulk of southern Democracy was found in the secession camp at some stage before Lincoln's call for troops. There seems little reason, therefore, to question a general association of Whiggery with Unionism and Democracy with secession. When the Civil War began, the Confederacy had a voting population of which 49 percent had cast ballots for John Bell or Stephen A. Douglas, indicating at least something less than ardent southern nationalism, if not an unconditional aversion to secession.

In making the cabinet appointments President Jefferson Davis followed the traditional United States pattern of one-party responsibility and named a straight Democratic cabinet, although two members had been State Rights Whigs before becoming Democrats. In later cabinet shifts another State Rights Whig and two Union Whigs of 1860 were appointed. Of the fourteen men who held cabinet posts in the Confederacy, none of the nine regular Democrats became open opponents of Davis, while three of the five former Whigs resigned to become bitter critics of the administration. Vice-President Alexander H. Stephens, formerly a Whig and in 1860 a Douglas Democrat, also became openly hostile to the Davis administration.

The members of the Provisional Congress were not elected by the voters, but in the summer and fall of 1861 Confederate general elections were held. In six states—Virginia, North Carolina, Tennessee, Georgia, Florida, and Louisiana—there seems to have been a general agreement in the legislatures to divide the Senate positions between parties. In South Carolina and Texas, where the Whig party was not an organized force, and in Alabama and Arkansas only Democrats were selected. Mississippi sent to the Confederate Senate one Democrat and one whose party affiliation is not established. The House membership in the First Congress was divided between parties in approximately the voting pattern of the late antebellum period (assuming certain representatives of unidentified party affiliations fall into the same proportions as the 87 percent whose political loyalties are known), that is, about 66 percent Democrats.

The Democratic party as chief sponsor of the attempt at southern independence rapidly lost popularity as the war became more burdensome. In the mid-war elections, held in 1863 in most of the states, considerable discontent was shown by the voters through the election of Whigs to replace Democrats. The party affiliations of 73 percent of the members of the second Confederate House of Representatives have been determined, and it would appear that the Whigs may have become the majority. In North Carolina a Whig sweep which had carried Zebulon B. Vance into the governorship in 1862 was repeated in 1863 when the voters replaced a Confederate House delegation of six Democrats and four Whigs with one of nine Whigs and one Democrat. In Alabama all the Whig congressmen were re-elected, a Whig defeated the most important Democrat in the Alabama delegation, and Whigs replaced the two Democrats in the Confederate Senate. In at least two Georgia districts and two Virginia districts Whigs replaced Democrats. Alabama and Mississippi, for the first time in their histories, elected Whigs to their governorships. Tennessee and Louisiana Confederates, handicapped in holding a valid election by Federal occupation of portions of their territory, nonetheless held such elections as they could and elected Whigs as Confederate governors in both states.

It is not to be assumed that all these Whig victories represented peace movements in the South. Most of the elected Whigs posed at least nominally as advocates of southern independence, although some insisted that independence could be obtained by a compromise peace. On the other hand, there is evidence that in the 1863 election the Whig Unionists of 1860 and even those who had reputations as compromisers from the 1850's were the beneficiaries of a general revulsion against the Davis administration. Considerably more than party politics was involved, but politics was both an important ingredient and a vehicle for registering discontent. In some cases, however, the Whig victories were a direct result of advocacy of a compromise peace that would restore the Union. Jonathan Worth, a North Carolina Whig, commented that those in his state who had been the most determined in their opposition to secession and the Democratic party were by 1863 the most popular. This trend was probably general throughout the Confederacy.

Petitions for pardon, directed to President Andrew Johnson in 1865 and 1866 from the numerous group of southern Whigs excluded from the benefits of the general amnesty proclamations, suggest a considerable lack of loyalty to the ideal of southern independence. William C. Rives of Virginia, who was elected to the Confederate Congress but soon resigned his seat, wrote that he had positively refused to be a candidate but when elected without his consent could not decline the call made upon him "in the spirit and intention . . . that my influence should be used, as it was, to promote a termination of the war, as soon as practicable, by mutual agreement & negotiation." This could mean, under the circumstances, nothing but arrangements for restoration of the Union. William Russell Smith of Alabama, who later became president of the University of Alabama, wrote Johnson in 1865 that he would have left the South had he been financially able to move his large family, and that both of his elections to the Confederate Congress had been by the Union party of his district against secession candidates. He further explained that he had tried to bring about an early peace on the basis of restoration of the Union and had retired from Congress because his peace plan was considered treasonable. William H. Felton of Georgia, a successful Independent Democratic politician after the war, wrote Johnson that he had done as little as possible to aid the Confederacy and had sought election to the Georgia Confederate legislature solely to keep from being drafted into the army. So common was this type of statement to President Johnson in 1865 that Zebulon B. Vance, Confederate governor of North Carolina, wrote in his petition with evident disgust: "The undersigned does not desire . . . to mitigate the offense of abandoning one government, by showing that he was likewise false to another."

Since party politics remained alive in the South during the war, it comes as no surprise that the Democratic party was shattered by the debacle for which it bore chief responsibility. Most of the Whigs had advised against secession in the first place and could now pose as having been vindicated in their earlier judgment. A prominent Union Whig of Georgia, Benjamin H. Hill, recalled Whig attitudes in 1865 as follows:

Well, you see all the evils of secession that we prophesied have become true; now we suppose the people will believe us, and not believe the old secession democrats, who wanted to drink all the blood that would be shed by the war; we suppose now that the old whig party will arise from its ashes in some form, at least what we call the anti-democratic element.

The elections held in 1865 under the presidential plan of Reconstruction, with substantially the antebellum electorate eligible to vote, reflected the political climate among the whites of the South before congressional Reconstruction obscured the white voting pattern. Five years earlier in the eleven states soon to form the Confederacy there had been no Whig governors, only two Whig senators, and but fourteen Whig representatives in Congress, as compared with fifty-three Democrats. In the 1865 elections Whigs won at least eight governorships, eleven United States senatorships as compared with five won by known Democrats (plus two by ultra-conservative South Carolina Union Democrats who represented the Whiggish element in that state), and thirty-six

House seats as compared with thirteen won by known Democrats. Lack of information about the party affiliation of twelve members-elect of Congress prevents definitive statement, although some of these clearly had not been in active politics. As nearly as can be estimated, Whigs elected to Congress from these states held a ratio to Democrats before the war of less than 1 to 4, as contrasted with more than 2 to 1 after the war. But the full impact of the Whig victory can better be observed by omitting Texas and South Carolina, where Whig party organization had not existed for years. In the remaining nine states, among candidates who have been identified, Whigs were elected in 1865 to almost nine-tenths of the congressional seats.

In the 1865 elections for state constitutional conventions the Whig landslide was also cataclysmic. In the Tennessee constitutional convention, among the ninety-five members whose antebellum party affiliations have been discovered, Whigs outnumbered Democrats 8 to 1. In Florida, Whigs had an understanding that they would not vote for Democrats, whom they charged with bringing on the war. The Mississippi constitutional convention had seventy Whigs in a membership of ninety-seven. The Alabama constitutional convention contained forty-five who had voted for Bell, thirty who had voted for Douglas, and twenty-four who had voted for Breckinridge; but so many of the Douglas supporters had formerly been Whigs that this convention was said to have a Whig majority. The New York *Times* reported that the Alabama convention, "like that of Mississippi [was] generally composed of old Whigs, who originally were utterly opposed to the secession movement." In the conventions of North Carolina and Georgia, Whigs and Douglas Democrats together reportedly comprised a majority.

The Tennessee Legislature elected in 1865 had nearly 100 Whigs in a total membership of 109. All but one member of the Virginia House of Delegates were Whigs, and the Virginia Senate was described as "pretty much the same." Whigs dominated the North Carolina legislature entirely, and Whigs probably controlled the Alabama Legislature, which elected Whigs to be presiding officers in both houses and gave the long-term United States senatorship to a Whig.

Whig triumph throughout much of the South was accompanied by a minimum of open comment on Whig versus Democratic loyalties, because in most of the South the Whigs had been in the minority during the 1850's and would naturally not wish to drive away from their voting columns all former Democrats. Wherever it was practicable, a coalition of Whigs and Douglas Democrats quite openly seized the reins of state power. In other areas, where the Democrats had been very strong, it was more politic to talk of wise advice in the past and of the propriety of asking those who had misled the people to take back seats. And everywhere in the South the term "Conservative" was substituted for "Whig" with little question.

No such reticence was shown by the southern Whigs in private letters or conversation. In the fall of 1865 one North Carolinian urged another to run for the governorship for "the benefit that will be derived to our party, the Whig party." When a Whig, Jonathan Worth, did win the North Carolina governorship, he was fully aware of Whig patronage matters, writing several letters in which he boasted of appointing Whigs to the great majority of positions and defended in detail his few appointments of former Democrats. Writing to William H. Seward in July of 1866 to ask for a pardon for another Whig, Josiah Turner, Governor Worth commented that such firm Whigs as Turner and himself had been popular favorites in North Carolina since the waning of the secessionist excitement of 1861. Worth divulged that Turner, in filing his petition for pardon in 1865, had gone out of his way to assail the Democratic party and had therefore failed to receive approval for pardon from the provisional governor, William W. Holden, who happened to be an ardent Democrat who had turned strongly Unionist during the war. Many North Carolina Whigs believed that Holden had deliberately prevented former Governor Zebulon B. Vance from being pardoned in order to keep Whig strength from concentrating on him in the gubernatorial contest in which Holden was seeking election.

A traveler in North Carolina in the fall of 1865 wrote:

. . . here, in North Carolina, I discover, with proper amazement, that the old parties are both alive, and neither of them a whit older or less pugilistic than it was twenty years ago. . . .

This old party spirit is . . . the foundation-stone of this North Carolina Constitutional Convention . . . . It is the Democratic party, one class affirms, that made secession a possible thing, and brought the State to the verge of ruin. It is the Whig party, the other class retorts, that was half disloyal to the State, and caused disaster by its supineness and coldness in behalf of the war.

. . . in private conversation half the delegates had no measuring-rule for a man but the fact that he is either a Whig or a Democrat, and no judgment for a measure but that it originates with one of these parties.

Benjamin H. Hill, a Georgia Union Whig, commented: "I tell you frankly that after the war ended, we, the old whigs and the Union men, expected to take control of affairs down here . . . ." From Tennessee a disgruntled Democrat wrote to President Johnson, himself a Democrat, that "The *old line* Whigs, or the leaders, are your bitter enemies . . . . Most palpable preferences over true & capable *Union*-Democrats have told too plainly of this thing. There is hatred of everything that is Democracy . . . ." An East Tennessee Democrat seeking patronage for Democrats wrote the President that Whigs planned to rid his area of Democrats by persecution, and claimed that even the violence directed toward former Confederate conscription officers by irate Union men was politically selective. A Mississippi Whig editor urged that the friends of President Johnson's Reconstruction policy not adopt a distinctive party name because it would be quite as hard for the old Democrats to become latter-day Whigs as it would for "us old Whigs to become Democrats in 1866." A Mobile, Alabama, editor noticed the Whig aversion to being classified as Democrats and wrote: "We have heard some men say that under no circumstances would they act with a Democratic party. They would prefer to stand still and see the country 'go to the bad,' and the Radicals triumph, than to save it under a Democratic banner."

This editor was reflecting one of the accidental difficulties of the Reconstruction period: President Andrew Johnson was a Democrat. By any reasonable canon except that of political availability, a southern Unionist chosen to be Lincoln's running mate in 1864 should have been a Union Whig, but appealing to northern War Democrats had been the paramount consideration in 1864. As a consequence, in 1865 and 1866 both southern Whigs and northern former Whigs in the Republican party feared that success in presidential Reconstruction policies would aid Johnson in reviving the Democratic party. One North Carolina Whig probably expressed the attitude of southern Whigs in general when he wrote that he "abominated" Johnson's "antecedents" as much as anyone, but that Whigs must of necessity play along with the President for the time being.

When the National Union Convention was called for Philadelphia in the summer of 1866, on the eve of the congressional election campaign in the North, southern Whigs responded to the bipartisan nature of the call and participated fully. Union Whigs and Douglas Democrats seem to have dominated the various state and district conventions which selected the delegations to the national convention. On the basis of identification of a majority of the delegates-at-large and a considerable portion of the district delegates from Virginia, North Carolina, Georgia, Tennessee, Alabama, Mississippi, and Louisiana, it would seem reasonably safe to state that the

Whigs greatly outnumbered the Democrats, or possibly in some instances excluded the Democrats entirely from participation.

The purpose or purposes of the National Union Convention were at the time not universally agreed upon and still remain in some degree an interesting question. Many southern Whigs undoubtedly considered this the opportunity to revive the Whig party by reunion with northern conservative Republicans of Whig extraction. This would necessarily involve swallowing up in the new organization a number of Democrats, but it was assumed that these would be followers and not leaders. Southern Democrats, however, looked at the matter from the other end of the horn; and one of the Douglas Democrats in the Alabama delegation, who edited the Mobile *Advertiser and Register*, claimed that there were but two parties in the country, Black Republicans and Conservative Democrats. "So the Conservative party," he wrote, "which will rally under the old Democratic banner, will embrace all the moderate, peace-loving and constitutional men of the country . . . ." A prominent Tennessee Whig who was selected as a delegate to this Philadelphia convention wrote afterward that there had been an effort to form a true Conservative party, but that the Democrats present sabotaged the plan by refusing to give up their party organization.

The Philadelphia National Union Convention failed in its immediate objective of assisting President Johnson to win a friendly majority in the congressional elections of November, 1866. The result was replacement of the presidential plan by the congressional plan for reconstruction, which involved disfranchisement of certain classes of former Confederate leaders and enfranchisement of Negro men. Now southern Whigs were confronted with a new set of alternatives. Some of the unconditional Union Whigs who had developed a hatred for all former Confederates welcomed the congressional plan as a chance to dominate the politics of the states. The great majority of southern Whigs had not been unconditional Unionists, however, and had given aid and comfort to the Confederacy after secession was an accomplished fact. These latter Whigs were not favorable to the congressional plan but could not agree what course was wisest. They could refuse to vote and thus leave the Radical Republicans in control of the state governments, trusting that the plan would either be declared unconstitutional by the courts or repealed by the Democrats if they could win the election of 1868. Or they could assume that these were the best terms the South could expect and advocate full participation, in the hope that whites could control state governments and might ultimately obtain a relaxation of the plan's partial disfranchisement feature.

In Alabama, for example, Whig leaders such as Alexander White, Lewis E. Parsons (who had been made provisional governor by President Johnson in 1865), and James H. Clanton organized a state convention in the interests of nonparticipation. But other Alabama Whigs, such as Governor Robert M. Patton and Robert Jemison, Jr., advised strict obedience to federal laws and full cooperation under the congressional plan unless the United States Supreme Court declared it unconstitutional. Although the self-styled stanchest Whig editor in Mississippi vigorously advocated full participation and advised that this was the best set of terms the South would get, the Whig "Bible," the Washington *National Intelligencer*, gave aid and comfort to the nonparticipation Whigs by advising them to boycott the elections and await relief from northern Democrats.

Never after the spring and summer of 1867 were the southern Whigs to know the degree of unity they had achieved in 1865. Division concerning the proper course to follow in the election of constitutional conventions under the congressional plan was followed by further dissension about the constitutional amendments proposed by these conventions. At the time of the federal elections of 1868, conservative southern

Whigs were uncertain whether their most discreet course was to enter the Republican party and cooperate with its conservative faction or to work with the Democrats nationally in the hope that the Democrats could win control of Congress and repeal the congressional plan. Republican nomination of General U.S. Grant as a moderate clouded the issue for many southern Whigs, and a minority of them supported Grant. The majority of the southern Whigs entered the Democratic ranks but did not accept the Democratic label.

Attitudes of southern Whigs supporting the Democratic presidential nominee, Horatio Seymour, were probably well expressed by Jonathan Worth of North Carolina when he wrote:

The democrats of the North now wear the livery of the old Whig party. Their watch-words are the Constitution and the Union. . . . the old Whig party . . . abhorred Democracy and Abolition as disunion elements. We now find the only consistent advocates of the Constitution and the Union act under the name of Democrats.

Or, as Thomas A. R. Nelson, a Whig who went to the Democratic National Convention as chairman of the Tennessee delegation, said:

As it seemed impossible to get the [northern] democratic party to give up its organization and as there was no other organization opposed to Radicalism, it became necessary for those who were opposed to the Radical party to act, if they acted at all, with the democracy.

Southern Whigs did not regard themselves as converted Democrats because of their support of Seymour. William A. Graham of North Carolina described himself at this time as "a Whig from principle, never having had any other party connection. . . ." Another North Carolinian wrote that since the old Whig party had gone under there had been "no party to which an honest, good man could cordially attach himself." In Virginia, Governor Francis H. Pierpont was prevented by his Whiggery from any thought of alignment with Democrats, and his hope was "to get the conservative white men in the state to form a party against the radical rebels."

When a Tennessee lifelong Democrat published a letter shrewdly calculated to furnish southern Whigs with a rationalization for abandoning the Whig party to become Democrats, a Mississippi Whig editor demurred strongly. Whigs of the country, he retorted, had great cause to question the sincerity of the Democratic party, and Whigs who had participated in the campaigns of 1844 through 1852 had had enough of "Democracy" to last a lifetime. Southern Whigs who had remained faithful to the bitter end against Democratic ascendancy, he continued, "never can, never will, acknowledge that they are 'Democrats.'" The editor of the Richmond *Whig* added that Radical was simply Democrat "writ large" and that where Democrats stopped, the Radicals began and pushed all the worst Democratic doctrines to the extreme of oppression and meanness.

After the Democratic defeat in the national elections of 1868, some of the southern Whigs who had cooperated with the Democrats, more than ever convinced that the Democratic party's support was the kiss of death, cast their lot with the Republican party. Thus by 1869 southern Whigs who had not abjured politics entirely were divided into four camps. Some of the unconditional Union Whigs were frankly allied with the Radical Republican leadership of the nation. A larger group of southern Whig leaders were in the Republican party, striving to bring about universal suffrage and universal amnesty and to end military occupation in the South. This latter group were confronted by a peculiarly difficult dilemma: to hold the support of white Republicans required a conservative stand on race questions, but to alienate the Negro voters left the door wide open for northern men who had migrated southward to seize control of the Negro vote and with it the state Republican party organizations. James L.

Alcorn of Mississippi was typical of the Whig leaders who sought to control the southern state Republican party organizations for conservative policies. He was successfully outbidden for Negro support and defeated by a northern man, General Adelbert Ames.

The third group of southern Whigs were in the Democratic and Conservative parties of the various states. They sought alleviation of Reconstruction conditions, particularly relegation of the Negroes to passive participation, and occasionally managed with considerable success to retain leadership and to be available for desirable offices whenever election victories crowned their efforts. It is probable that these comprised the largest single group of southern Whigs as early as 1869 or 1870; it is certain that they were the most numerous after 1872.

The fourth group, ever shrinking in numbers, were the die-hard rejuvenation-of-Whiggery group. They advocated refraining from binding alliances with either Democrats or Republicans and awaiting that "shining hour" when, as one put it, the passions of the moment would have passed away and "the fundamental principles ever boldly avowed by Mr. Clay [would] become the settled policy of the country, and . . . the grand old Whig banner again be thrown to the breeze, and around it . . . gather all friends of good government." Meanwhile, advised another Whig, southern Whigs should steer clear of Democrats because "no good Whig [could] be permanently incorporated with them. Oil and water [would] not mingle although put in the same vessel."

In 1869 and 1870 the collapse or fatal weakening of Radical Republican party control occurred in Tennessee, Virginia, North Carolina, and Georgia. This was followed by a wave of editorials in the northern Democratic press crediting the Democrats with victory over the Republicans in those states. Coming so soon after the Democratic defeats of 1868, these claims were resented strongly by the southern Whigs, who were

insulted by being classified as Democrats and fearful of renewed military reconstruction if the northern Democrats
should again seek to undo the permanent parts of the congressional plan. The Richmond *Enquirer and Examiner* maintained that northern Democratic papers were making a great
error in ascribing the Conservative victory in Virginia to
the Democratic party, adding: "There has been no such party
in this state for eight years, and its very bones have rotted and
now crumble at the very touch." The Richmond *Whig* said
of the Conservative party of Virginia: "A majority of them
are Whigs, were Bell and Everett Union men, were never
Democrats, and are never likely to be, unless driven to it as the
only defense from persecution by the party in power." The
Appeal-Avalanche noted that the opponents to Radicalism
had rallied in not one single former Confederate state under
the name "Democrat." The editor of the Mississippi *Hinds
County Gazette* wrote that there was no feeling in common
between the Whigs and Democrats of Mississippi.

It is true that old-line Democrats bestirred themselves in
states escaping from Radical sway and tried to restore the use
of the Democratic label as well as to rectify what they considered the outrageous preponderance of Whigs in the state
offices. But concerted efforts to reorganize the Democratic
party as such were scotched by the Whigs in Virginia and
Tennessee. One Whig interpretation of the current revival of
Democratic aspirations was that antebellum Democratic policy had brought on the war and had ruined the South, as every
Whig had predicted:

What followed? Why the Democrats, who destroyed everything,
looked very sorry for a time. . . . They took back seats, mutter-
ing, in broken accents ". . . What a pity it is that we did not see
and act as you Whigs did. . . ." Now, that the great National
Democracy is on its legs once more, engaged in a wild hunt for
loaves and fishes, the weeping Democracy of the South have
wiped their eyes. They have blown their noses. Scenting a chance
for another career of plunder . . . and monopoly of ten thousand

fat offices, they are crawling out of their holes. They are beginning to look fierce and talk big like they did before. . . .

The 1872 Liberal Republican movement produced a momentary wave of joy among those southern Whigs who
thought this was the opportunity for northern conservative
Republicans of Whig extraction to shuck their Radical colleagues and form the long-awaited new Conservative party of
the country by union with southern Whigs. Exultation was
short-lived, however, for the nomination of the Liberal Republican candidate, Horace Greeley, by the Democratic National Convention excised from the movement the essential
elements of new party organization. The Greeley campaign in
the South was run by the same coalitions of Whigs and Democrats that had already been cooperating in the Democratic and
Conservative state parties. It did furnish a bridge by which
some Whig leaders who had been disappointed in their efforts
to control the state Republican organizations could return to
the Democratic and Conservative party camps without loss of
face.

Between the 1872 and 1876 presidential elections Alabama,
Arkansas, Mississippi, and Texas were captured by the Democratic and Conservative state organizations. In these elections,
as in the Democratic and Conservative victories before 1872,
southern Whigs were prominent in elective offices in areas
where they had been strong before the Civil War. By this late
period, however, so many southern Democrats and former
secessionists had regained voting privileges that Whig preponderance was severely reduced everywhere and in some areas
eliminated. Such a large proportion of the southern Whigs
was now within the Democratic and Conservative parties of
the southern states that the chief issue seems to have been
division of the spoils between Whigs and Democrats, or even
between factions of each party group.

As evidence became conclusive that alignment with the
national Democratic party was to be permanent, most south-

ern Whigs gradually surrendered their prejudice against the name "Democrat." Meanwhile, old-line Democrats, recognizing the unstable nature of the political combinations which were overthrowing Republican organizations and observing the uncomfortable rash of Independent Democratic candidates of Whig background, sought to assure the loyalty of former Whigs to the party of redemption. For example, the Columbus, Mississippi, *Democrat*, a strictly Democratic party organ, courted the Whigs with extravagant praise: "There is something touching and beautiful in the devotion of the 'old line Whigs' to the memory of the grand old party . . . . It reminds us of the sacred love which we sometimes find a husband cherishing for the wife he loved and lost in early manhood." Asserting that nine-tenths of the southern Whigs now acted with Democrats, the editor continued: "As the Hebrews scattered abroad become active, useful citizens, and yet forget not their citizenship of the Land of Promise, so the Whigs, though found in all parties, retain their attachment to the memory, if not the distinctive principles, of the old Party."

Reciprocally, the Jackson, Tennessee, *Whig* advised that it was time that all who had cherished a traditional hatred for the word "Democrat" should cease to do so because the Democratic party was composed of all that was best in material and principle in the two old parties. The Nashville *Banner* agreed, adding that if their ancient rivals had lately been getting the better of the name on the battle flag of the common cause, the Whigs had been getting the best of the offices.

A delay in this blending of southern Whigs and Democrats was occasioned in 1876 and 1877 by the internal change in the national Republican party which set aside the Radical leaders and brought the old-line northern Whig element into power. It is highly significant that Rutherford B. Hayes, himself a former Whig, was the first Republican President to appoint a cabinet without a single northern Republican of Democratic extraction. Hayes's name wrought some enthusiasm among southern Whigs, and although few of them would desert their Democratic alliances to vote for him, many looked upon his inauguration calmly.

Professor C. Vann Woodward, stressing the influence of lobbyists for the Texas & Pacific Railroad, has indicated the role of southern Whigs nominally in the Democratic party in checkmating the northern Democrats who would have resorted to radical measures or even violence to prevent the installation of Hayes. As early as January 1, 1877, Augustus H. Garland of Arkansas was writing that he and his successor as governor were carefully arranging to avoid any hostile attitude or even to give the people an occasion to become aroused. And on January 5, 1877, A. H. Markland wrote to Hayes that there were twenty-six southern members of Congress of old-line Whig extraction who were secretly pledged to resist all extreme measures and who were desirous that Hayes be inaugurated. Considering the fact that many southern Whig leaders had all through the Reconstruction years denounced the northern Democratic leadership, a more detailed study of the individual old-line Whigs in Congress might well establish the conclusion that the southern bloc would have acted as it did in 1877 had there been no railroad lobby involved. One prominent Hayes manager on the scene could not decide as late as February 22 whether the Texas & Pacific lobby or the "purely political" part of the plan had been more potent.

Whatever the circumstances surrounding Hayes's inauguration, it is undeniable that there followed a ninety-day sensation over his presumed intent to build a new southern Republican party on the basis of old-line Whigs and Douglas Democrats. Letters offering evidence of Whig discontent at being in the Democratic party, always accompanied by suggestions as to patronage, flooded the President's mail until federal appointments were almost completed. In April the

Washington *Nation* added lightwood to the fire by announcing that it was offering itself as a central organ for a new Whig-Republican party, and the same paper published an interview with Hayes's Secretary of the Navy, Richard W. Thompson, to the general effect that southern Whigs were to be fused with the conservative element of the northern Republican party to create what would amount to a new party, purified of Radicalism. This provoked editorial comment pro and con throughout the nation and resulted in another deluge of letters on Hayes and his administration leaders—with the usual patronage recommendations.

This flurry was soon over, however, and after the 1878 Democratic sweeps in the South whatever notions Hayes had had on this subject were considerably cooled. Part of the explanation for the rejection of this bid to southern Whigs may be the success these Whigs were having in the Democratic and Conservative state organizations in the South. One measure of Whig success in the New South may be found by a comparison of the division of the choicest political plums, the United States senatorships, for twenty years before and twenty years after the war. If one considers the twenty-two Senate seats through ten Congresses to be 220 units, the Democrats overwhelmed the Whigs in the 1841–60 period by 72 percent to 28 percent of the units. Among the two-thirds whose antebellum party affiliations have been discovered (considering only the southern whites who were old enough to have been active in politics before the war), almost the exact reverse is true of the years from 1867 through 1886: former Whigs outnumbered the antebellum Democrats in a ratio of 71 percent to 29 percent.

For many years the idea of drawing southern Whigs to Republicanism continued to crop out sporadically, especially when patronage was involved. And expressions of Whiggery continued to make isolated appearances, as when the Republican editor of a North Carolina paper wrote in 1884 that ". . .

many Whigs in the South have co-operated with the Democratic party, for several years; but no man who ever was a Whig or whose father was a Whig ever has been or ever will be a Democrat." Some Whigs, such as this editor, found comfortable political homes in the Republican party in the South; but this was the case chiefly in the Appalachian Highlands, where the Negro was a small factor in politics. A few Whigs were perennial bolters from party discipline and self-styled Independent Democrats who quietly sought and often obtained Republican support. But the bulk of the southern Whigs were firmly lodged in the Democratic party after 1877, making their conservatism and even some of their antebellum policies the dominant themes of the southern Democratic party.

Continuing awareness of a common political past, adoration of Henry Clay as the almost legendary hero-symbol of that past, and the persistence of a sense of separateness from antebellum Democrats characterized so many southern Whig leaders during the years of the Civil War and Reconstruction that a number of significant topics for further investigation are suggested. If the Whigs of the Confederacy were, generally speaking, Unionists on party principle, can it not be assumed that this 40 percent of the Confederate population would count the cost of southern independence more carefully and sooner reach the conclusion that it was not worth the price it was exacting? Defeatism in the Confederacy may have been in large measure merely the revival of never-surrendered Unionism on the part of many Whigs.

During presidential Reconstruction the South, except for South Carolina and Texas, was in the hands of Whigs and Douglas Democrats, with the latter as junior partners. The Black Codes of the South were enacted not by secessionists and Democrats but by Unionists and Whigs; rejection of the Fourteenth Amendment was by these same groups. How much responsibility must these southern conservatives bear for the failure of the presidential plan? And why were the self-appointed conservatives of both sections unable to communicate more effectively to avoid the disastrously mistaken evaluation of northern sentiment so obviously made by southern Whigs? An exhaustive analysis is needed on the subject of the Philadelphia National Union Convention and other abortive efforts to create a national conservative party.

As a contribution to the extensive economic revisionism in Reconstruction historiography it would be valuable to learn how much the antebellum Whig doctrines concerning the role of government in fostering transportation influenced Whig-dominated Republican regimes in several southern states. Extension of state credit to railroads accounted for the larger part of the debt left by Republican administrations in the South, and government aid to railroads was evidently Whig doctrine. The Whigs in control of Alabama during presidential Reconstruction inaugurated the program there before the Radicals gained power. Another important question is whether southern Whig leaders were themselves deeply biased against the Democratic party or merely using Whig loyalties to direct voters in support of certain economic interests.

How much of the national Democratic party conservatism in the generation after Reconstruction may be attributed to southern Whigs in Congress under the Democratic party label? And did the Democratic party organization in many southern states become so nearly the reincarnation of Whiggery that the agrarian revolt may be seen largely as the attempt of those with more traditional Democratic party attitudes to recapture the houses of their fathers? Republican support of agrarian revolt organizations in the South, merely to weaken the Democratic party, obscures the picture at times; but political geography of the 1890's shows enough similarity to that of the 1840's to justify more investigation of Whig leaders in regular Democratic party organizations.

A better understanding of the effects of persistent Whiggery, and of the purposes to which it was directed, should illuminate some of the murky aspects of southern history since 1860.

14

WHO WERE THE
SCALAWAGS?

Allen W. Trelease

Employing various statistical methods, Allen W.
Trelease tested the sources of white Republican
strength in the South and arrived at some different
conclusions.

In the demonology of Reconstruction no reputation is blacker than that of the native white Republican. The illiterate and poverty-stricken Negro was often an object of compassion, and the carpetbagger could be partially excused as an outlander with no ties of kinship or sentiment in the land he plundered. But native white Republicans were traitors to race and section alike, and thus deserving of the deepest contempt. The term "scalawag," by which they were designated, is said to have come from Scalloway, "a district in the Shetland Islands where small, runty cattle and horses were bred." Later it became a synonym for scamp, loafer, or rascal, whence it found its way into the lexicon of Reconstruction politics. In this context some people would confine the term in all its impurity to actual officeholders or office seekers. The *Dictionary of Americanisms*, however, defines scalawag more broadly as "a Southerner who supported the Congressional plan of reconstruction." It includes, therefore, white Republican voters, who are the real subject of this article.

Like so much of the conventional view of Reconstruction, the caricature of the scalawag as a traitor to race and section gained more and more currency with the lapse of time, as the original receded from sight. What began as a political canard was carried over into canon within a generation by historians and the general public North and South, who came to accept the Democratic opposition's view of Reconstruction as historical truth. Many historians, like the southern Conservatives of the period, made little or no effort to explain the alleged treason of the scalawags beyond assigning them such character deficiencies as disloyalty, cowardice, greed, or lust for power. Others identified them with wartime Unionists who had opposed secession and cooperated unwillingly if at all with the southern war effort. Seldom until recently were the white Republicans credited with worthy motives, and then it was usually in the course of impugning their judgment. Rare indeed was the scholar who would agree with W. E. B. Du-Bois' characterization of them as "that part of the white South who saw a vision of democracy across racial lines." Commonly the only good word to be said of the whole lot was that a better element existed among them which went over to the Conservative camp at an early date.

Until the 1940's, white Republicans were usually identified with the lower or poorer elements of southern society, if they were identified at all. An exception was Walter Lynwood Fleming, who referred to them in one of his later writings as possessing "whatever claims the [southern Republican] party had to respectability, education, political experience, and property." By the same token, Fleming was one of the few until recently who paid any attention to their political antecedents, listing them as "former Whigs" as well as "former Unionists . . . Confederate deserters, and a few unscrupulous politicians."

Reconstruction historiography has itself been reconstructed since 1940. In the process the scalawag has been reclassified to

a degree, if not fully rehabilitated. Much credit for this belongs to David Donald, whose 1944 article in this book,
"The Scalawag in Mississippi Reconstruction," represented
one of the freshest breezes to sweep this landscape in many
years. In Donald's view the Mississippi scalawags were predominantly "old-line" Whigs who had opposed the Democrats before the war, opposed secession at its commencement,
and, whatever their attitude in wartime, were now eager to
resume battle with the states' rights and (supposedly) egalitarian Democracy. As the cream of the old planter-business
aristocracy, they accepted Negro suffrage in the hope of
controlling the votes of their former slaves for their own
purposes. More recently, in his revision of James G. Randall's
book, *The Civil War and Reconstruction*, Donald extends this
interpretation to most of the South. The major exceptions, he
says, were North Carolina and Alabama, where the scalawags
were chiefly hill-country farmers who had opposed both the
prewar plantation system and the war itself.

By implication at least, Donald's interpretation gains support from the recent investigations by Thomas B. Alexander
of "persistent Whiggery" in the postwar South. In the elections of 1865, held under presidential auspices, former Whigs
very nearly swept the field according to Alexander's findings.
By 1869, he believes, the southern Whigs fell into four
groups. A small number of old "unconditional Unionists"
were wholeheartedly in the Radical camp from the beginning
of congressional Reconstruction. A larger number, answering
Donald's description, were also in the Republican party, advocating universal suffrage and universal amnesty in the hope of
leading the movement into more conservative channels. A
third group, which Alexander believes to be the largest by
1869 or 1870 and destined to grow larger still after 1872, had
affiliated with the Democrats or Conservatives in opposition to
Radical Reconstruction. The fourth group, ever shrinking in
size, consisted of die-hard Whigs who refused to join either

existing party and worked for a rebirth of the old party of Henry Clay.

Despite the appeal of Donald's ex-Whig interpretation, it has gained only partial acceptance. Speaking also of Mississippi, Vernon L. Wharton asserts that the white Republicans at first "were largely a poverty-stricken element who had been Unionists during the war." Then, more in keeping with Donald, he continues: "There was also an element of planters and businessmen which increased rapidly in numbers until 1874. Many of these men had been Whigs before the war . . . ." John Hope Franklin says in his recent survey of the period that the white Republicans were basically Unionists who had opposed secession and the war. Most of these people, he implies, were distinctly not of the planter class and had long resented its domination. He says nothing of prewar political affiliation.

There is no agreement on the point of wartime Unionism either. Many of Donald's ex-Whig Republicans had been officers in the Confederate army, and E. Merton Coulter goes further yet in declaring that many prominent southern Radicals had been outstanding secessionists. Coulter is more loath than the others to abandon the old Conservative fortifications; to him the scalawags were "those who had a grievance against the ante-bellum ruling class; who felt social inferiority; who disliked the rigors of war; who opposed conscription, impressment, and the suspension of the writ of habeas corpus during the war; in fact, almost 'every one that was in distress, and every one that was in debt, and every one that was discontented'. . . ."

Until recently the only common ground among treatments of the scalawag was a common aversion to him, and now we have lost even that. Moreover, such characterizations as have been made were frequently given in the process of moving on to other, more congenial topics. Apart from a few leaders like James L. Alcorn in Mississippi and Parson Brownlow in Tennessee, the native Republicans have received next to no attention. Thus despite their acknowledged importance in the Radical movement, they remain an unknown quantity.

A wider acquaintance can be gotten by several means. That which follows is primarily statistical. It attempts in the first place to isolate the bulk of the native white Republicans geographically through a comparison of election returns and census data for each southern county for which election returns were available. Using this information, it tries next to supply a basis for closer study and surer generalization than has been possible heretofore concerning their economic and social conditions, their prior political affiliations, and their reasons for supporting the Radical party.

Several assumptions are made at the outset which, in the nature of things, will be more controversial than the arithmetic proceeding from them. The first is that Negroes during the period of Radical ascendancy cast their votes overwhelmingly for Republican candidates. Although there are exceptions, the assumption is borne out by an examination of election returns from the Black Belt counties and by a comparison of the Republican percentage of the vote with the percentage of Negroes in the population. (See Tables 1 and 2.) There are very few counties in which the proportion of Republican votes to the total number cast was significantly lower than the proportion of Negroes to the total population, and in some of these cases the result clearly was produced by Negro abstention, voluntary or enforced, rather than by their voting the Democratic ticket.

A second assumption hardly requires verification: despite the influential role of the northern carpetbag element in shaping the course of southern Reconstruction, the northerners were so few in number in any locality that they cannot materially affect a statistical computation based on population and election totals.

The third assumption—the working principle on which this

analysis mainly rests—follows from the first two: wherever the percentage of Republican votes significantly exceeds the percentage of Negro population, and where the total voter turnout in a fair election is near normal, we may expect to find native white Republicans.

Students of the period will recognize several methodological hurdles to be cleared in making a study of this nature. Many Reconstruction elections were carried or miscarried by fraud, violence, or intimidation; disfranchisement of ex-Confederates was a factor in some elections; and the census of 1870, which would normally be used in figuring the proportion of Negroes, was notoriously inaccurate in that respect. None of these obstacles can be evaded or explained away altogether; yet they are less critical on closer inspection than they at first appear.

It is true that most election returns of the time are not ideal bases for statistical analysis. In this study the presidential election of 1872 was singled out for special attention, other contests being used only to ascertain the political complexion of each county during the period as a whole. For this latter purpose, from four to six (normally, five) elections were chosen in each of the ex-Confederates states, nearly all of them involving statewide contests for either the Presidency or high state office. They include the presidential elections of 1868, 1872, and 1876, as well as intervening state contests, chiefly in 1870 and 1874. (For the states of Mississippi, Virginia, Texas, and Tennessee, the election of 1868 was not used; the first three had not yet been readmitted, and in Tennessee there was such wholesale proscription of ex-Confederates as to render the returns nearly valueless in determining actual opinion.)

Of them all, the election of 1872 was the natural choice for a closer analysis in determining the location of white Republican voters. By comparison with the other presidential elections of 1868 and 1876, it was conducted with relative fairness in nearly every state. Disfranchisement of ex-Confederates was largely over by that time and the wholesale proscription of Negroes was still in the future, except in Georgia. In this election President Grant won a second term by defeating the Democratic-Liberal Republican coalition headed by Horace Greeley. Although Greeley, the old abolitionist crusader, failed perceptibly to warm the hearts of southern Conservatives, this contest had the advantage of presenting to all southern voters the Reconstruction policies of the Grant administration in about as clear-cut a fashion as any policy is apt to be presented in an American election. It fell during the period of Radical ascendancy in most states and found two-party politics in as active and healthy a condition as the South has known them since before the Civil War. The Liberal Republican movement had comparatively little impact in the South, where 1872 constituted the high watermark of postwar Republicanism.

Population figures for 1872 normally would have been drawn from the preceding census, then only two years old. But in view of the inadequacy of the 1870 census, especially in its underenumeration of southern Negroes, that of 1880 was chosen as being more accurate on the whole. The difference in time was not so critical as it might appear on the surface, since census data were used primarily to determine the proportion of Negroes rather than total population. There is no evidence to suggest that this ratio changed significantly in many places between 1872 and 1880.

Changes in county boundaries occurring between 1872 and 1880 create another complication, but only in Texas was the number of changes significant. In most cases they had little effect on the proportion of Negro population in the counties so altered, if we are to judge by similar changes between 1880 and 1890. Such counties, therefore, were not omitted from the computation.

The natural first step in determining political patterns and isolating the white Republicans is to look at the electoral majority of each county in the light of its racial composition. When all southern counties making returns in 1872 are arranged according to their proportion of Negro population, with Black Belt counties like Issaquena in Mississippi and Beaufort in South Carolina at the top and white counties like those of the Appalachian highlands at the bottom, several predictable but nonetheless striking facts emerge. The predominantly Negro counties were overwhelmingly Republican in 1872 and most of them remained in that column through 1876. By the same token, the white counties tended to vote Democratic during these same years, although there were frequent exceptions. In 1872 all the twenty-seven counties where Negroes constituted 80 percent or more of the population were Republican; those 70–79 percent Negro were Republican by 44 to 4; the proportion falls gradually through those counties having 20–29 percent of their population Negro, only 17 percent of which voted Republican; then the proportion voting Republican rises to 26 percent in each of the last two classes. This last phenomenon, in counties where less than a fifth of the population was Negro, can be explained only by the presence of substantial numbers of white Republicans.

The same pattern holds true of these counties in a majority of the elections chosen between 1868 and 1876. In these elections the number of counties in the Republican column is somewhat less in each Negro population class, but the two sets of figures, if reduced to lines on a graph, run nearly parallel. The greatest spread—that is, the greatest Republican attrition for the period as a whole, compared with the high of 1872—appears in those counties having between 30 percent and 59 percent Negroes. Here, presumably, Negro disfranchisement was most feasible and most effective by 1876 in creating Democratic majorities, and here, too, a relatively slight shift in white sentiment could more easily transform Democratic minorities into majorities. Although these figures, for both 1872 and the other election years, do not indicate the numbers of individual voters involved, they suggest that the freedmen were overwhelmingly Republican in sentiment, that most whites voted Democratic, and that the white Republican minority was largely concentrated in counties with the smallest Negro populations. Further evidence on these points can be gotten by comparing the Republican and Negro percentages in 1872 in each county.

A standard criticism of the American electoral process is that so few eligible voters bother to participate. The situation was generally worse a century ago. Across the country only half of the adult males (according to the 1880 census) cast votes for President in 1872, but unlike today the South exactly equaled the national average. Alabama led the former Confederacy with a turnout of 65 percent, while Arkansas and Georgia brought up the rear with 43 percent. The South's relatively favorable position was owing in large measure to an active two-party system and Negro suffrage.

Insofar as white Democrats failed to vote, their action would raise artificially the percentage of Republican voters in a given county. And since the computations which follow are based on a comparison of the Republican percentages with Negro population ratios, it could lead to an exaggeration of white Republican strength. Non-voting among Negroes would of course create the opposite effect. For this reason abstention involving one race more than the other is a matter of some concern. The available figures on turnout of eligible voters between 1868 and 1880 would indicate that abstention was a recognizable factor in 1872 in South Carolina, North Carolina, and Georgia. In all three states fewer persons voted than in 1868, and the number of voters rose sharply again in 1876. White persons were primarily involved in the Carolinas; only in Georgia is there evidence of non-voting on a large scale among Negroes.

With so many pitfalls and incalculables, it is wise to concede a wide margin for error and look for white Republicans in quantity only in those counties where the Republican percentage exceeded the percentage of Negroes by at least twenty. (Tables 1 and 2 both show horizontally the relationship between these two proportions, giving the number of counties in each category. Table 1 is arranged vertically by states, and Table 2 according to density of Negro population.) In about half of the southern counties for which we have 1872 election results (411 out of 843), these two percentages were within ten points of one another. Probably these figures are more than coincidental, and represent a substantial division between white Democrats and Negro Republicans. These counties were to be found in every region of the South, in areas that were preponderantly white as well as in the Black Belts. As a matter of fact, about two-thirds of the Black Belt counties fell in this category, as did a majority of all counties, which were more than 40 percent Negro in composition. Below that point, the smaller the proportion of Negroes, the more likelihood there was of finding white Republicans.

In less than 10 percent of the counties (78, of which two-thirds were in Georgia) the Republican percentage was materially below that of Negroes, indicating that substantial numbers of freedmen either voted Democratic or did not vote at all. That the latter was common is shown by a relatively low voter turnout in these counties, especially in those where the Republican and Negro proportional differences were greatest. Columbia County, Georgia, for example, with a population 71 percent Negro, cast but 6 percent of its vote for Grant and only 14 percent of its adult males voted at all. Counties with a similar population distribution in other states commonly showed a voter turnout of 65 percent and a Republican majority of about 70 percent.

In the remaining counties (354 out of 843, or 42 percent of the whole) the Republican percentage exceeded that of Ne-

TABLE I

Republican percentage of vote in southern counties in 1872 compared with
percentage of Negroes in the population—by states
(figures in line with states represent number of counties)

	Exceeds Negro percentage by:						Diff. less than 5%	Less than Negro percentage by:						Totals
	50 or more	40–49	30–39	20–29	10–19	5–9		5–9	10–19	20–29	30–39	40–49	50 or more	
Ala.	1	3	3	6	7	7	22	6	6	3	1			65
Ark.	9	4	4	9	11	8	9	4	1	1				60
Fla.			2	2	7	5	13	6	2		1			38
Ga.	4	4	4	5	12	12	35	9	16	19	6	5	5	136
La.*					4	4	7	1	1	1				14
Miss.				1	13	12	38	3	4					71
N.C.	5	11	10	20	19	14	12	1						92
S.C.			3	6	16	4	2	1						32
Tenn.	20	12	7	8	12	9	16	5	2					91
Tex.	6	3	6	7	34	25	46	5	2			1		135
Va.**		2	2	9	25	17	45	8		1				109
Totals:	45	39	41	73	156	117	245	49	34	25	8	6	5	843

| 354 | | 411 | | 78 |

* Incomplete
** Includes independent cities which voted separately

TABLE 2

Republican percentage of vote in southern counties in 1872 compared with percentage of Negroes in the population—by density of Negro population

(figures in line with percentages represent number of counties)

% Negro 1880	Exceeds Negro percentage by:						Diff. less than 5%	Less than Negro percentage by:						Totals
	50 or more	40–49	30–39	20–29	10–19	5–9		5–9	10–19	20–29	30–39	40–49	50 or more	
90+							2							2
80–89						8	8	1	1	2	1			21
70–79					1	7	26	2	4	5			2	47
60–69			1	2	14	12	32	8	7	4	1	3	3	87
50–59			1	3	12	14	54	12	6	5	3	3		110
40–49			1	4	18	20	36	5	3	2	1	3		93
30–39	2		2	14	31	20	25	9	4	3				111
20–29	12	3	7	13	31	13	20	9	6	4				108
10–19		15	11	13	21	16	16	1	3	3				108
5–9	16	9	9	16	16	4	7	2						79
0–4	15	12	9	8	12	3	19							78
Totals:	45	39	41	73	156	117	245	49	34	25	8	6	5	843

354 · · 117 · · 411 · · 78

groes by at least ten. It is here that we must look for the great majority of white Republicans. In almost half (156) of these counties the Republican percentage was larger by only 10 to 19 points; in the rest it ranged up to a differential of more than 50. The presence of white Republicans by no means insured Republican victories in these counties; in fact a slight majority (179 to 173) went Democratic in 1872 and even more voted that way in a majority of other elections of the time. (See Table 3.) In most of those which went Republican, Negro voters contributed significantly to the victory and often the Negro Republicans outnumbered the white. As a general rule, however, most of the white Republican votes were cast in counties where the Negro population was slight. More than nine-tenths of the counties in which white Republicanism is identifiable had white majorities, and over half were at least 80 percent white in composition. (See the left-hand columns of Table 2.) In only forty-five, or about 5 percent of all southern counties, did the Republican percentage outweigh the proportion of Negroes by fifty or more, indicating an absolute majority of white Republicans among the electorate.

Geographically, the counties containing the largest proportions of white Republicans are chiefly concentrated in the mountain regions of East Tennessee, western North Carolina, and northwest Arkansas. Those with smaller proportions are scattered more widely, with every state except Louisiana represented by at least nine counties in which the Republican percentage outweighed that of Negroes by 10–29 points. Texas and, deceptively, South Carolina are the only states besides the three mentioned above in which the state-wide differential was more than ten. In Texas the greatest number of white Republicans was found along the Rio Grande River and in the central part of the state. Both areas were more or less frontier regions, the former containing a large Mexican and the latter a large German element in its population. Elsewhere hilly, remote, and less prosperous areas

TABLE 3

Political Behavior, 1836–76, of Counties Containing White Republicans

Rep. vote % in 1872 exceeds Negro pop. % by:	Total Counties	1836–52 * (Majority of Pres. elections)		1860				1872		1868–76 (Majority of Pres. elections)	
		Whig	Dem.	Democrat (Breckinridge)	(Douglas)	Const. Union (Bell)	Union Majority**	Rep.	Dem.	Rep.	Dem.
50 or more	45	15	16	20	0	16	18	45	0	33	10
40–49	39	12	16	21	0	14	18	28	10	12	27
30–39	41	10	16	22	0	10	14	15	26	3	37
20–29	73	18	33	35	1	22	24	29	44	10	61
10–19	156	22	85	98	2	26	35	56	99	33	120
Totals:	354	77	166	196	3	88	109	173	179	91	255

* Omits South Carolina
** Combined popular majority for Bell and Douglas

were most prominent, such as the northern parts of Alabama and Georgia. Fully half of Arkansas is represented, nearly all of it lying above a diagonal line drawn between the northeast and southwest corners of the state. By contrast, the areas most noticeable by their lack of white Republicans are east Texas, Louisiana (insofar as we have reliable election records), the bulk of Mississippi, Florida, Georgia, and Virginia, and the southern half of Alabama.

In no state, taken as a whole, were white Republicans even close to a majority of all white voters in 1872. Any estimate of their total numbers is hazardous in the extreme because it must rest on so many variables. In terms of votes cast, however, a figure in the neighborhood of 150,000 might be near the mark. Almost half of this number were found in the two states of Tennessee and North Carolina, where they may have constituted a third of all white voters. Arkansas, Texas, and Virginia, in that order, accounted for most of the remainder. Throughout the South, white Republicans cast perhaps 10 percent of all the votes recorded in 1872, about 20 percent of those cast by white men, and about 20 percent of those cast by Republicans.

Few as they were, these voters provided the margin of victory in many counties. The election of 1872 found 384 southern counties in the Republican column, compared with only 248 during a majority of the elections sampled from 1868 through 1876. Most of the Republican attrition in these other contests occurred in predominantly white counties or those of nearly equal racial distribution, rather than in the Black Belts. While 173 counties with appreciable numbers of white Republicans cast Republican majorities in 1872, only 71 did so in 1876 and only 91 in a majority of the sampled elections. (See Table 3.) On the other hand, counties in which Negroes formed 70 percent or more of the population (and in which, accordingly, there were few white Republicans) showed little change in voting behavior: these counties went Republican in

1872 by a margin of 71 to 4 and remained in that column during most of the sampled elections by a margin of 66 to 7. Although Negro disfranchisement was a factor by 1876 in creating some of these shifts, the white Republican minority of 1872 contained most of the independent voters who to a significant degree held the balance of power during Reconstruction.

Through its figures on assessed valuation, the census of 1880 provides a further means of examining the white Republicans. In the 125 counties in which the Republican percentage of the vote exceeded the percentage of Negroes by 30 or more, the per capita wealth was only $106, compared with $145 for the South as a whole. The larger the proportion of white Republicans, in fact, the lower was the per capita wealth. It amounted to only $90 in those counties where white Republicans were presumably in a majority, $104 where the Republican percentage exceeded that of Negroes by 40–49 points, and $122 where the difference was 30–39. Nine states (all but Louisiana and Mississippi) possessed counties in at least one of these three categories, and in all but Texas the per capita wealth of the counties involved was significantly less than that of the state at large. With some exceptions, the chief of them being in Texas, these were regions of comparatively low soil fertility where the plantation system and Negro slavery had not penetrated extensively. The evidence suggests, therefore, that most white Republican voters of 1872 were small farmers, noticeably poorer than the southern average, and having little in common with the ex-slaveholders who had frequently dominated affairs in their respective states.

Having located these people with at least rough precision, we can go further and test the theory that most of them were former Whigs. In the first place, the counties in which the Republican percentage exceeded that of Negroes by 40 or more (that is, where white Republicans were a majority or large minority of all voters) were divided almost evenly between those which had voted Whig in a majority of the five presidential elections between 1836 and 1852, and those which had voted Democratic. (See Table 3.) Significantly, all but one of the 27 ex-Whig counties were found in Tennessee and North Carolina. The 32 ex-Democratic counties, on the other hand, were scattered in seven states. Where the Republican percentage exceeded that of Negroes by only 10 to 39, the proportion of ex-Democratic counties is much larger (134 to 50); again, most (35) of the ex-Whig counties were in Tennessee and North Carolina, with Virginia contributing 11 of the remaining 15.

If we reverse our viewpoint and examine the postwar affiliation of all antebellum Whig counties, we must note first that about half of these had Negro majorities. The Black Belt counties were largely Whig in their prewar affiliation and, as we have seen, the white minority which cast these votes before 1861 was almost solidly Democratic during Reconstruction. That these counties voted Republican overwhelmingly after the war was owing almost exclusively to the newly enfranchised black majority. In the ex-Whig counties where whites predominated slightly less than half (53 out of 117) voted Republican in 1872 and less than a quarter (26) did so in most of the sampled Reconstruction elections. Again Tennessee, North Carolina, and, to a lesser extent, Virginia, were conspicuous variants. They accounted for 50 of the 53 white ex-Whig counties voting Republican in 1872, and 24 of the 26 voting that way in a majority of the sampled contests between 1868 and 1876. (Even in these three states almost as many of the white ex-Whig counties voted Democratic as Republican in 1872, and a large majority did so in most of the sampled elections.) Only in these three states, apparently, was there much ground for identifying postwar Republicans with prewar Whigs, and even there the correspondence was by no means complete.

One may still object, perhaps, that elsewhere white Republicans constituted a Whig minority before the war, too few in number to carry their counties in most of the elections between 1836 and 1852, and thus not shown in the preceding calculations. This objection is not sustained by an examination of the formerly Democratic counties outside of these three states, where white Republicans in 1872 were a majority or near-majority of all voters. There were 29 such counties, located in Alabama, Arkansas, Georgia, and Texas, nearly all of them less than 10 percent Negro in composition. In these counties the Republican voters of 1872 so far outnumbered the highest total of prewar non-Democratic voters—those who cast Constitutional Union party ballots in 1860—that almost half of them had to have switched from the Democratic party. This proportion may well have been much greater. Moreover the Republican gain was not owing significantly to population growth, for except in Texas the total vote in these counties was smaller in 1872 than in 1860.

In general, therefore, a sound basis for identifying prewar Whigs with postwar Republicans exists only in Tennessee, North Carolina, and to some extent in Virginia. Elsewhere the converse was often true: most of the white Republicans of 1872 seem to have been Jacksonian Democrats before the war. Furthermore, the Whig areas of white population which went Republican during Reconstruction were the habitat of the Appalachian highlander. The planter-businessman aristocracy to which Professor Donald and others have referred seems in general to have found the postwar Democratic or Conservative camp more congenial. Doubtless the minority of this group who did join the Radicals carried more weight in terms of leadership and prestige than their numbers alone would indicate, but they were hardly more typical of the white Republicans as a whole than of their own class.

Unionism before and during the war is more difficult to trace through election returns. To a degree, support of John C. Breckinridge in 1860 implied sympathy for a stronger assertion of southern claims against the North, while Stephen A. Douglas and John Bell were more definitely Unionist candidates. Lincoln of course drew almost no votes from the states that were shortly to form the Confederacy. Of the counties with a significant number of white Republicans in 1872, 196 had cast a plurality of their votes for Breckinridge, 88 voted for Bell and the Constitutional Union ticket, and only 3 went for Douglas. (See Table 3.) Bell and Douglas together received a majority of the votes cast in 109 of these counties, slightly more than a third of the total. Even among the top few counties where white Republicans were most numerous in 1872, less than half had cast "Unionist" (Bell plus Douglas) majorities in 1860. The states of North Carolina and Tennessee again contribute—as they did in the analysis of formerly Whig areas—a large percentage of the "Unionist" counties where white Republicans were later prominent. As a matter of fact, support for the Whig party between 1836 and 1852 so nearly coincided with support for Bell in 1860 that (even after Douglas' votes were added to Bell's) both of these bear the same relationship to postwar Republicanism. Support for Bell and Breckinridge, at least, seems to have reflected political habit as much as Unionist or secessionist feeling in 1860. A majority of Whig voters probably supported Bell in 1860 and became Democrats or Conservatives during Radical Reconstruction.

A better index to Unionist sentiment lies in the attitudes reflected during the secession movement in the several states, and in evidences of wartime disaffection. Here the correlation with postwar Republicanism seems a good deal clearer. It is well established that, while Unionism was to be found in all parts of the South in 1860 and afterward, the areas of greatest concentration were the mountain regions of East Tennessee, western North Carolina and Virginia, and adjacent portions of other states, as well as northern Alabama, northwest Arkansas, and parts of west and north Texas. These, as we have seen, are almost precisely the areas where white Republican votes were most numerous in 1872. A great many Unionists (including many in the regions mentioned) never affiliated with the Republican party and some Republicans had been Confederate sympathizers, active as well as passive, during the war. But the correspondence between the two is closer than that between Whiggery and Republicanism—so close as to be more than coincidental.

It is worthwhile, therefore, to attempt a reconstruction of the relationships which existed between these three elements of Whiggery, Unionism, and Republicanism. The southern Whigs were not a class party, associated everywhere and exclusively with a single economic interest. In most states, however, they appear to have been strongest among the large planters and among those professional and mercantile groups closely allied with or dependent upon the planters. Except for East Tennessee and adjacent parts of North Carolina and Virginia, they were weaker in the "white belts" of small farms and few slaves.

Unionists in 1860–61 fell into two main categories. The first of these was composed of large planters and their allies, though by no means all or even necessarily a majority of them, and the second consisted of persons near the opposite end of the spectrum—yeoman farmers in the more isolated parts of the South where slavery had penetrated comparatively little. Of the two groups, the former had been primarily Whig in politics and was decidedly the more lukewarm in opposing the tide of secession. True conservatives, they abhorred disunionist extremism; but they also had a vested interest in the status quo and the South's peculiar institution. Their Unionism was often conditional, therefore, taking the form of cooperationism in preference to immediate and separate state action in withdrawing from the Union. But once the die was cast, they either threw in their lot with the Confederacy (frequently rising to positions of military or political prominence), or retired to the sidelines for the duration.

The second group, more often Democrats than Whigs except in parts of the Appalachian highlands, was more uncompromising. Its members were either openly or covertly disloyal to the Confederacy, and some even served in the Union army; among these people especially the wartime peace societies flourished. Their militant hostility to the dominant order in the South was born of economic and social conditions, which in turn sprang from their geographic environment. Lacking slaves, they had no vested interest in protecting or perpetuating that institution, and in fact were often hostile to it. The threats to white supremacy or the "Southern way of life" posed by abolitionists and free soilers were often no more immediate to them than to farmers of Pennsylvania or Illinois. Their opposition to the dominant planter class in their respective states was of long standing; by 1860 it was a customary and primary political motivation, regardless of the local vagaries of party affiliation. Occasionally ethnic factors entered the picture too, as among the Texas Germans, who tended to be antislavery in outlook.

Under presidential Reconstruction, as Professor Alexander has shown, the first group of Unionists came fully into its own. Political leaders who had been least conspicuous in the secession movement—and most of these were ex-Whigs—tended to dominate the scene in most states in 1865 and 1866. Only in Tennessee did the mountain Unionists (also Whigs primarily) sufficiently coincide with this group, or were they sufficiently numerous, to take over themselves the process of reconstruction. Elsewhere they were a relatively small minority which supported the Johnson governments without exercising much control over them.

With the passage of the Reconstruction acts in 1867 and 1868, the political scene changed abruptly in every state but

Tennessee. The old Whig planters, lawyers, and merchants presently in control were as shocked at the implications of Radical Republicanism as most Democrats and secessionists. Although some of them, like Alcorn in Mississippi and Lewis E. Parsons in Alabama, decided to go along with the new dispensation in the hope of controlling or at least tempering it, a larger number were actively or passively hostile from the outset. Those who joined the Republican party were disillusioned on discovering that they could not control the movement in the interests of conservatism; moreover they were reviled by their fellows as traitors to their caste and class, and they soon began dropping out. Such men certainly fall in the category of native white Republicans—or scalawags, if we must use the term—but they provided only part of the leadership before 1872 or thereabouts and almost none of the votes.

The great majority of native white Republicans, as the statistical analysis above shows, came within the second category, the hill-country farmers. Merely to establish their identity as a group and point out their dissimilarities from the surrounding white majority is to leave a great deal unsaid. It must suffice as a basis of generalization, however, until fuller studies are made, indicating in some detail where they stood on the issues of the day, both local and general, and why. For many of these people, though by no means all, affiliation with the Radicals was a natural resumption of their earlier political outlook.

While opposing many interests of the planter class, the Republican party was identified with policies which had been almost uniquely popular in the mountain areas before the war. These included political and social reform of an egalitarian cast, together with such governmental aids to economic development as the protective tariff and subsidies for railway construction. They held a natural appeal for people living in areas of relatively unprofitable agriculture but blessed with abundant supplies of power, labor, and mineral resources. In some mountain districts the local Whig party was most closely identified with these demands before the war, and in other areas it had been the Democrats. But probably no party in the nineteenth century, locally as well as nationally, was as closely associated with all of them as the Republican party in the years immediately following the Civil War. Many of the mountaineers therefore gravitated to the Republican party during Reconstruction, where they remain in large measure today. Their radicalism was a factor in temporary fusions with the Populist party and other insurgent groups after Reconstruction, and is still recognizable in recent years.

The spectacular events taking place between 1860 and 1877 make it easy to overlook the substantial element of continuity which underlay them. Even during Radical Reconstruction, party allegiance was in some measure dependent upon local issues, habits, and loyalties as opposed to the greater questions of state and national concern. This was especially true, in all likelihood, of the more remote districts where the Negro and slavery were less critical issues. Thus despite the overall appeal of the Radical program in these regions, there is no more reason to believe that all mountain Republicans consistently favored all Republican policies (where these were consistent) than that all white Democrats consistently opposed them.

The question of racial equality is a case in point. Anti-Negro prejudice had infected nearly all southern whites (and most northerners, too) regardless of party, class, or geographic location. In most areas there were enough freedmen to constitute at least the illusion of a threat to white supremacy; thus few whites joined the Republican party to begin with and many of those who did dropped out early. Personal conviction united with social pressure—often expressed physically—to keep a large majority in the party of conservatism and white supremacy. But if this preoccupation was indeed the "central theme of Southern history," it confirms once more the highlanders' isolation from the main stream of southern life. For they almost alone enjoyed the luxury of ignoring it without undue pain. Among them as among northerners, traditional loyalties and antipathies within the white community, as well as issues normally unrelated to the race question, had freer rein. There was comparatively little distinction locally between the top and bottom rails of society, and Radical policies did little or nothing to disturb unpleasantly the customary ways of life. These small farmers were free, therefore, to join (or not to join) the anti-planter, Radical, Union party with less reference either to the albatross of Negro equality or to other major issues of Reconstruction policy.

If secession and the "solid South" of later days were sectional responses to purely sectional conditions, it may be said that southern white Republicanism (like mountain Unionism) was in part an even more provincial response to yet more local issues. Although a working political democracy may have come closer to realization in parts of the hill country than elsewhere in the South, DuBois' "vision of democracy across racial lines" was—alas—too utopian.

15

DESEGREGATION IN NEW ORLEANS PUBLIC SCHOOLS DURING RECONSTRUCTION

Louis R. Harlan

> Some historians have sought to explain the imperma-
> nence of Radical Reconstruction partly in terms of
> the conservative nature of the Radical state govern-
> ments and their failure to engage in significant social
> and economic experimentation. It remains a valid
> generalization. That there were some exceptional
> cases is made clear in Louis R. Harlan's description
> of the desegregation of public schools in New Or-
> leans.

It is a fact not generally known even to historians that the
New Orleans public schools during the Reconstruction period
underwent substantial racial desegregation over a period of six
and a half years, an experience shared by no other southern
community until after 1954 and by few northern communities
at the time. This essay is limited to a summary of the evidence
that there was indeed desegregation in New Orleans in the
1870's and to an effort to explain it chiefly in terms of circumstances in New Orleans at the time. It is obvious that
New Orleans, as the only real urban center in the overwhelmingly rural South, could not be an example from which
any general conclusions can be drawn about Reconstruction

in the region or even in Louisiana as a whole. The experience of one southern urban community during Reconstruction, however, may hold interest for students of the rapidly urbanizing contemporary South.

For a generation of historians rather suddenly concerned with past struggles over civil rights, the interest of this study lies partly in the new crop that it makes in the much-plowed field of Reconstruction history. The historians both of Louisiana Reconstruction and of southern education have pronounced the desegregation experiment of New Orleans an almost total failure. The conclusions of historians of the Dunning school may be explained by their preoccupation with political themes or their racialistic and sectional blind spots, but perhaps a better explanation is that they read in the partisan press the headlined stories of white walkouts and Negro evictions, but failed to note the undramatic evidence of the return of most of these pupils in the following days and months. Historians of southern education seem to have relied too heavily on a secondary source by the Louisiana educational historian Thomas H. Harris, who in turn depended vaguely on the "testimony of men who lived through the period." Harris declared in 1924: "The schools were never mixed. The law was evaded from the first, and the negroes were about as active in evading it as the whites."

It is with some surprise, therefore, that we read the testimony in 1874 of Thomas W. Conway, the Radical state superintendent and prime mover of New Orleans desegregation:

I had fully concluded to put the system of mixed schools to a thorough, practical test, and I did. The white pupils all left . . . and the school-house was virtually in the hands of the colored pupils. This was the picture one day. What will you think when I tell you that before I reached my office that day, the children of both races who, on the school question, seemed like deadly enemies, were, many of them, joined in a circle, playing on the green, under the shade of the wide-spreading live oak. In a few days I went back to see how the school was progressing, and, to my surprise, found nearly all the former pupils returned to their places; and that the school, like all the schools in the city, reported at the close of the year a larger attendance than at any time since the close of the war. The children were simply kind to each other in the school-room as in the streets and elsewhere! A year ago I visited the same school and saw therein about as many colored children as whites, with not a single indication of any ill-feeling whatever.

All that is wanted in this matter of civil rights is to let the foes of the measure simply understand that we mean it. Do this, and as in the case of the enemies of free schools in Louisiana, they will be quiet.

The whole truth, of course, embraces both the historians' evidence of evasion and strident resistance and Conway's idyl of dancing on the green. Evasion lasted for three years, until the last legal recourse was exhausted, and then desegregation began. As desegregation spread slowly into more and more schools, as Conway said, there was indeed resistance, but it was fruitless, sporadic, separated by long periods of tacit acceptance, and successful in the end only because Reconstruction itself failed.

The forces of evasion were in effect even before the state constitution in 1867 prohibited the establishment of separate schools and required that no public school should deny admission on account of race or color. On the eve of the constitutional convention the city hastily established its first Negro schools to give credibility to its stand for "separate but equal" rather than desegregated schools, and Freedmen's Bureau officials opposed to mixed schools hastily transferred their local schools to the city board. State Superintendent Robert M. Lusher resigned before the end of his term to become the state agent of the Peabody Education Fund, which spent more money in Louisiana than in any other state to aid a system of private white schools.

In New Orleans, where whites outnumbered Negroes nearly 3 to 1, white Republicans in the city government cooperated with the city school board in efforts to thwart Superintendent Conway in his equally determined effort to give desegregation a thorough trial in that city. The city's newspapers meanwhile undertook to create an atmosphere of resistance and fear, advocating desertion of the schools en masse by the whites, establishment of private schools, and refusal to pay school taxes, and predicting the destruction of the public schools and race war. The city school board resorted to a pupil placement system and all of the legal stratagems so familiar today. The loopholes of every school law were sought out, and a bewildering succession of suits and injunctions cluttered the courts. At one time five school cases were simultaneously on the dockets. Finally the sands of delay ran out; a court decision of December, 1870, was acknowledged by all parties to be decisive, and desegregation began within a month.

To overcome the forces of delay and evasion, the Radicals found it necessary to centralize and strengthen the school system. The city school board was replaced by another appointed by the state board of education, which in turn was appointed by the governor. The city board was allowed by state law to estimate its annual needs and require the city government to levy and collect a local tax sufficient to supply the amount. The high salaries that this arrangement made possible, though often tardily paid, attracted good local teachers and created a reasonably good *esprit de corps*.

The extent of desegregation cannot be measured precisely because the official reports made no separate accounting of the races and because the population of New Orleans was so peculiarly mixed, with so many very light colored persons and swarthy white ones, that observers often found it impossible to distinguish between them. Nevertheless, there is considerable evidence of desegregation in official records and in newspapers, particularly in the reports of the annual examinations or closing exercises of the schools. From such sources it is possible to identify by name twenty-one desegregated schools and some others that may have been desegregated, about one-third of the city's public schools. The school authorities at no time initiated desegregation, but simply required the admission of Negro children to white or mixed schools whenever they applied. Thus by choice or social pressure a majority of the city's school children attended either the separate Negro schools or white schools. A surprising number of colored children, nevertheless, entered mixed schools under this arrangement. In 1877 the number was estimated at three hundred, but that was some six months after the end of Reconstruction. Other evidence indicates that between five hundred and one thousand Negroes and several thousand whites attended mixed schools at the height of desegregation. Light colored children, who could move about more easily in the white world, were usually the first to enter mixed schools and the last to leave them after Reconstruction, but children "as black as ebony" were reported "side by side with the fairest Caucasians" in the same classrooms.

All of the five mixed schools with seventy-five or more Negroes enrolled were in the Second and Third Districts, below Canal Street, where descendants of the original French and Spanish inhabitants and the Irish, German, and Italian immigrants predominated. In this downtown area there was no rigid residential separation, and the houses of prostitution as well as schoolhouses were desegregated, though without causing as much public excitement. Since nearly all of the schools in these districts were desegregated, one might assume that the character of the Latin or immigrant population explained everything. But this is not so. Negro residential areas were dispersed throughout the city, and some of the largest schools in the so-called American districts, the First and Fourth, contained Negro children. One of these, the Fisk School, contained "a considerable number." Below New Orleans proper, in the Fifth and Seventh Districts, the scattered settlements on both sides of the river contained some desegregated primary schools. Of the city's three public high schools, two were desegregated. At the Lower Girls' High School, desegregation proceeded peacefully for years, about one-fifth of the students being colored. At the Central Boys' High several Negro pupils attended after 1875, and a Negro was professor of mathematics there for two years, until after the end of Reconstruction.

Desegregation caused only a temporary decline of enrollment in the schools as a whole and in the mixed schools themselves. Enrollment dropped from 24,892 to 19,091 in the first year of desegregation, but then rose steadily to 26,251 in 1875, which was higher than at any other time in the nineteenth century. The report that 21,000 of these were white and 5,000 colored indicates that there were actually more white pupils in the public schools during desegregation than either before or after.

In the desegregated schools the same trend was evident. The Fillmore Boys' School in the Third District, for example, was desegregated in 1871, when its enrollment was 377, and soon contained 100 colored pupils. In 1873 the conservative New Orleans *Times* reported 700 enrolled, "wonderful" attendance, and good discipline. Fillmore School was the largest in the city, crowded to capacity. In 1874 its enrollment reached 890, and the following year more of its graduates qualified for the high school, through competitive examinations, than those of any other boys' school. Other mixed schools with large Negro enrollments had similar records of increasing enrollment and high academic standing. At the Bienville School, where attendance was cut in half in 1871 by desegregation and a river flood, both enrollment and average attendance by 1874 exceeded the levels prior to desegregation. It sent more of its graduates to high school in 1873 than any two other boys' schools.

Why would desegregated schools be so crowded in a community as race conscious as New Orleans? The explanation seems to be that the quality of instruction was higher in those schools than in most of the others, because of the system of classification of elementary schools. Nearly all the mixed schools were classified as Grammar A schools, which had more teachers and a higher salary scale, and sent more graduates to the high schools than the Grammar B schools and Primary schools. Apparently this was why Negro children chose to enter them and why whites also attended them regardless of color, so that their enrollment steadily increased. Most of the Negro schools were Grammar B, and, according to report, "the mixed schools are the best in the city, and the colored schools the poorest—the poorest in quarters, furniture, text-books, and in every way."

Desegregation of the public schools caused enrollment in private and parochial schools to increase, but not enough to damage the public schools. The most ambitious plan of the period, "an elaborate design for the establishment of schools by private enterprise," was presented to a mass meeting of citizens of the Second and Third districts by former state superintendent Robert M. Lusher. It temporarily evoked much enthusiasm, but Lusher later wrote: "The failure of the Canvassers appointed to raise means for making the plan effectual, to collect a sufficient amount, unfortunately caused the plan to be abandoned." No coordination of private school efforts was ever developed.

Existing Catholic parochial schools, new Presbyterian and Episcopalian parochial schools, and the old and new private schools all expanded. Enrollment in these schools rose from about ten thousand in 1869 to seventeen thousand in 1873, but then declined to fourteen thousand the next year and subsequently even further. "Parochial schools on the pay system are virtually a failure," confessed Father Abram J. Ryan, editor of the local Catholic weekly; the reason he gave

was economic: "Poor families who have three or four, sometimes eight or ten children . . . cannot possibly send them to
the parochial schools at the rate of $2 or even $1 per month,
each." This consideration applied with even greater force to
the private schools, where tuition was normally twice as high.

Predicted racial violence and tax resistance did not materialize, and after experimenting with walkouts from mixed
schools and with private schools, the people of New Orleans
learned to live with the change. For three years, from the fall
of 1871 until the fall of 1874, the tumult and the shouting
diminished. At the risk of oversimplification, two explanations
may be suggested. First, desegregation was administered with
such skill that the opposition was disarmed, but foremost, for
reasons largely political, thousands of New Orleans whites
and the leading newspapers actually sought to win the Negro's vote on a basis of recognizing his civil rights.

Though statesmanlike qualities are not generally attributed
to Reconstruction leaders, and the school officials were certainly not plaster saints, they administered the New Orleans
schools efficiently and without major scandal. "If an irrational
prejudice is exhibited on one side of this question," said Superintendent Conway, "let it not be met by an equally irrational
precipitancy on the other side. This great question of education for the people . . . should not be imperiled by injudicious
action, even in behalf of a principle confessedly just and
equitable." Though rewarded with diatribes for their pains,
Conway, his Negro successor William G. Brown, and City
Superintendent Charles W. Boothby pursued a "firm and yet
moderate course" and conducted a school system good
enough to win loyalty from the teachers and even occasional
compliments from the opposition.

The complex reasons why many New Orleans whites embraced or acquiesced in Negro civil rights between 1871 and
1874 have been treated elsewhere by T. Harry Williams and
can only be outlined here. The central fact was that Louisiana

Negroes had a majority of the votes and were protected against intimidation by federal troops. As Reconstruction continued in Louisiana after its demise in other states, native whites realized that they had to win a substantial segment of the Negro vote if they hoped to oust the carpetbaggers. The Negroes were ably led, not so much by the white carpetbaggers as by their own well-educated New Orleans persons of color and Negro carpetbaggers. It was to these colored leaders that the white conservatives made overtures when the inevitable conflicts of interest developed between the white and colored wings of the Radical Republicans.

In 1871 and 1872 New Departure Democrats and new parties that abandoned the Democratic label partly because of its unpopularity among Negroes made bids for Negro votes by platform promises of recognition of civil rights and by parading a few Negro speakers at their rallies. The vague commitments were insufficient to win the Negro vote in the election of 1872, and this failure led to the specific commitments of the unification movement of 1873. Simply stated, the unification movement proposed a fusion of the native white and Negro voters in which the Negroes would promise to assist in ousting the carpetbaggers and cutting the taxes and the whites would guarantee the Negroes full civil rights: suffrage, office holding, desegregated transportation and places of public resort, and mixed schools. Confederate General P. G. T. Beauregard, the merchant Isaac N. Marks, and a thousand other New Orleans citizens of both races signed a unification manifesto endorsing desegregated schools in unmistakable terms and presented it for endorsement to cheering crowds. In this atmosphere it is understandable that the press and pulpits ceased to thunder against desegregation. After Marks had read the school clause of the manifesto to a mass meeting and a voice interrupted to ask, "Will you send your children to the public schools?" that is, to desegregated schools, the question was greeted with "hisses and other demonstrations" and an invitation to leave the hall. The unification movement failed to achieve the interracial political alliance it sought, because of the reluctance of many whites, particularly in the rural areas, to concede so much to the Negroes, and because of Negro suspicion that the white unificationists would be unwilling or unable to make good their commitments. The movement did give desegregation a breathing spell, however, and its spirit continued to animate some New Orleans whites. Marks, stating his freedom of racial bias, took a seat on the city school board and helped to administer school desegregation. In 1875 George W. Cable sent carefully reasoned arguments for mixed schools to a New Orleans paper, and in the same year David F. Boyd, president of the state university, tried to publish a proposal to desegregate his school.

To most New Orleans whites, however, the failure of unification was the signal for a change in policy and leadership. If Negroes could not be persuaded to vote with the whites, then enough Negroes had to be kept from the polls to ensure a white majority. The White League arose in 1874, spread quickly from the rural parishes to New Orleans, staged a three-day *coup d'état* in September until the arrival of federal troops, and installed a Conservative city government in December. In the same period the position of mixed schools was weakened by the removal from the congressional civil rights bill of the school desegregation clause. The stage was set for the well-known school riots of December, 1874, which reflected the momentary political climate of that period as clearly as the acquiescent mood of the previous three years reflected an opposite policy.

During three days of rioting, mobs often described as high school boys or "boy regulators" rudely ejected from mixed schools colored children who had been peacefully attending for years, insulted teachers, beat and threatened to hang the city superintendent. What is not generally understood is that the White League and its newspaper supporters instigated and directed the mobs, which were composed mostly of men and adolescents not enrolled in the high schools, using a handful of high school rowdies as fronts. Moreover, the riots failed to achieve their objective. Sober citizens persuaded the White League to call off "the boys," and the schools reopened after the holidays on a desegregated basis, remaining so for another two and a half years, until after Reconstruction.

Even after the end of Reconstruction, it appeared at first that desegregation might survive the change. The schools remained mixed through the remainder of the term, and Negroes were appointed to the school boards. But when the city school board voted to segregate the schools the following fall, the governor gave a Negro delegation neither aid nor comfort. Resort to the state and federal courts proved equally futile. The Negroes lost three test cases despite the mandatory provisions of the state constitution, and the constitution itself was rewritten in 1879 to permit separate schools and in 1898 to require them.

An obvious conclusion is that the southern devices of evasion and resistance broke down, largely through their own internal weaknesses. On the other hand, New Orleans whites never really surrendered their concept of the public school as a sort of private club. The chief significance of the New Orleans experiment with desegregation, however, centers around the fact, which was not merely incidental, that it occurred in a deep southern state with a large Negro population.

It was really universal suffrage—Negro suffrage protected by strong federal sanctions—that produced the mixed schools and sustained them through the years of trial. Negro votes in the constitutional convention secured the mixed school clause, and Negro votes elected school officers who would carry it out. Negro votes were the consideration for which whites were willing to bargain acquiescence in desegregation. And when the compromise of 1877 removed the federal sanctions for Negro suffrage, the mixed schools were an early casualty. Desegregation was only part of a broader social struggle in which the ballot was the primary lever of power.

New Orleans desegregation is not entirely explained by Negro votes, however, since the Negro majority was in rural Louisiana, where schools were only rarely desegregated. In the adjacent rural state of Mississippi, the Negro majority permitted separate schools to be established by a local-option school law. It would seem that any rural effort at mixed schools in the lower South was foredoomed by the weak economic position of Negro sharecroppers, the lack of demand for educated labor in the cotton fields, and the desire of white planters to maintain racial segregation as a means of social control. In southern states outside of the cotton belt, of course, the Negro minority was too weak politically to win desegregation against almost unanimous white opposition.

If the key to desegregation was to be found in the city, then why was the New Orleans experience so different from that of Charleston, South Carolina? The South Carolina constitution of 1868 also required desegregation, and that state also had a Negro majority of voters. Yet the state officials successfully opposed desegregation, and neither the Negro legislators nor the Charleston Negro community pressed the issue. Explanation of the difference between these two urban centers involves consideration of such intangible but very real influences as the singular character of New Orleans and the structure of leadership in the New Orleans Negro community.

With a population of 200,000, New Orleans was metropolitan in size and in the radiating influence of its river trade and railroad connections. Linked with continental Europe by its Creole tradition, its large and diverse immigrant population, and the cultural ties of more recent French *émigrés*, and linked by trade with racially complex Latin America, it was in many respects the nation's most cosmopolitan city. Travelers, immigrants, and clients frequently reminded New Orleans citizens that southern racial attitudes and practices were not widely accepted.

In many other ways New Orleans was unique among southern cities. Desegregated worship in the Catholic churches, which claimed about half of the city's population, possibly modified racial attitudes. The colored population was residentially dispersed throughout the city and was only about one-fourth of the total population; it was not so large as to induce in whites the fear of being engulfed if racial barriers were lowered. The city had opposed secession and was part of the Confederacy less than two years, whereas it underwent Reconstruction for almost nine years prior to desegregation and for some fifteen years in all. The interest of many New Orleans leaders in sugar protection and in federal subsidies for river and harbor improvement and railroads made them ideologically more amenable to Whiggish Republicanism than the cotton planters of the Charleston area. The prominence of New Orleans merchants in the unification movement of 1873 suggests that many of them were more concerned with economic development than with social control. They were willing to compromise on racial issues in order to free themselves from a political regime on which they blamed the city's economic plight. Thus political polarization by race was incomplete and ephemeral.

The vigorous and ambitious leadership of the New Orleans Negro community was also a powerful stimulus to desegregation. The basis for the high quality of this leadership was laid during the slavery period, when the free Negroes of New Orleans enjoyed a status "probably unequaled in any other part of the South." Whereas the Charleston free Negroes formed a truncated social pyramid in which artisans were the highest large class, the New Orleans *gens de couleur* included a number of substantial merchants, cotton factors, caterers, doctors and lawyers, even newspaper editors and poets. Ne-

groes also had much social freedom in cosmopolitan New
Orleans. "The whole behavior of the Negro toward the
whites," says Joseph G. Tregle, "was singularly free of that
deference and circumspection which might have been expected in a slave community." Though the social weather
became stormier in the last years of slavery, the colored elite
regained self-confidence during the Union occupation, serving as officers in the Union army and eventually as officeholders in the state government. Soon after the war they won a
crucial struggle for desegregation of streetcars against almost
the same arguments and dire predictions later used to obstruct
school desegregation.

The light-skinned New Orleans Negroes, abandoning an
early effort to be classed legally as whites, merged their lot
with that of the Negro masses and forged an impressive
Negro solidarity on racial questions. Since New Orleans was
the state capital in this period, they were able to incorporate
the darker-skinned rural political leaders into their upper-class
circle. There is little evidence in the Reconstruction period
that the colored bourgeoisie of New Orleans was as isolated
from the Negro masses as E. Franklin Frazier has found the
same class in the mid-twentieth century. Well educated in
private schools, in the North, and in France, they maintained a
highly articulate newspaper press and an efficient if opportunistic political organization. They held about half of the seats
on the city school board and protected the desegregation
experiment against occasional desertion and failure of nerve
on the part of their white colleagues. Sharing with most professional men the belief that "knowledge is power," these
Negro leaders pressed their own children steadily into desegregated schools in search of equal educational opportunities.

New Orleans desegregation, then, achieved its successes in
the 1870's through a unique conjunction of circumstances. A
political coalition was temporarily created between the rural
Negro majority, the urban Negro minority, and northern

Republicans in control of federal and state governments. New Orleans was a metropolitan and cosmopolitan, not merely polyglot, center, in which the southern rural mores were challenged by other traditions, values, and interests. The prior development of a free Negro elite in New Orleans provided the leadership and steadfastness which outsiders could not furnish. Such a fortuitous convergence, however, depended too heavily on one *sine qua non,* the temporary sojourn of federal power in the South. Not until the whole region came more closely to resemble New Orleans, not until an urban South and a more strongly based Negro community emerged, could the experiment be renewed auspiciously.

16

THE NEGRO AND POLITICS

1870–1875

Vernon Lane Wharton

The role of the Negro in the southern Radical
governments remains one of the most neglected
aspects of Reconstruction history. Much has been
written about how white men manipulated Negroes
during this period but little attention has been paid
to the development of Negro leadership and independent action. The efforts of "revisionist" historians to correct the erroneous notion of "Negro
domination" during Reconstruction have tended to
create the impression of a passive and leaderless
black electorate. Among the first attempts to evalu-
ate the extent and quality of Negro participation in
Reconstruction politics were Alrutheus A. Taylor's
state studies, DuBois' *Black Reconstruction,* and
Vernon L. Wharton's *The Negro in Mississippi.*

The Republican party which took control of the politics of
the state in 1869 included in its membership at least ninety
percent of the more than one hundred thousand registered
Negro voters. It also included at times from fifteen to twenty
thousand of the seventy to eighty thousand white voters. In
the beginning, these white Republicans were largely a poverty-stricken element who had been Unionists during the war.
There was also an element of planters and businessmen which

increased rapidly in numbers until 1874. Many of these men had been Whigs before the war, and they regarded the Democratic party as the organ of their enemies, the small farmers.

The Republican leadership in Mississippi contained an unusually large number of prominent white men who were old residents of the state. The names of J. L. Alcorn, H. F. Simrall, J. L. Wofford, J. F. H. Claiborne, Joshua Morris, R. W. Flournoy, Jason Niles, and R. W. Millsaps will serve as examples. The motives which caused these men to enter the party were many and varied. Colonel R. W. Flournoy, who before the war was the largest slaveholder in northeastern Mississippi, was essentially a humanitarian. For him, the protection and elevation of the Negro was a project that sprang out of deep Christian convictions. To a certain extent, this was also true of Major Millsaps, but he represented especially the rising commercial and financial element that saw the Republican party as the promoter of its interests both in the nation and in the state. Judge W. W. Chisholm of Kemper County was an example of a fairly large group who carried personal feuds into politics. The mortal enemies of his clan, the Gullys and the Balls, were Democrats. Where they went, Chisholm and his friends and relatives could not go. Even less respectable were those native whites, a relatively small group, who became Republicans entirely for the sake of personal advantage. The prominent Dr. William M. Compton of Marshall County furnished an excellent example. A leader of the irreconcilable anti-radicals in the convention of 1868, a "nigger-hater" of high degree, and an organizer of Ku Klux Klans, he later entered the Alcorn faction, and became superintendent of the state insane asylum.

Among the "carpet-baggers" there was the same variety of types. Adelbert Ames, absolutely honest, and to a large extent unselfish, had become more and more impressed with the needs and possibilities of the Negroes. Almost forty years later, as a cynical old man, he said: "My explanation may seem ludicrous now, but then, it seemed to me that I had a mission with a large M." His constant refusal to sell out the interests of the freedmen made him their idol; one terrified Negro in 1875 addressed him as "Gov. Ames Dar Father of the State." There were other able and honest Republican leaders from the North who had little sympathy for the Negroes, and regarded their presence in the party as a necessary evil. Among such men were H. R. Pease, R. C. Powers, and George C. McKee. Finally, there were some unscrupulous "carpet-baggers" who sought only personal advantage and profit, and held to no principle. The white leader of the corrupt Negro-Republican Vicksburg ring, for example, neatly leaped the divide in 1875 and remained a prominent figure in the equally corrupt Democratic machine in that city.

Whatever the motives or character of these white Republicans might be, to the Democratic press and to the growing mass of white-liners, they were all scoundrels, carpetbaggers, and scalawags. Thus Jason Niles, described by Charles Nordhoff as "a man of singular purity of character, a quiet scholar, and an old resident of the State," was the subject of constant abuse. Colonel Flournoy was so bitterly attacked that J. W. Garner has spoken of him as "the most extreme and obnoxious radical in the state." Yet the Democratic historian of his home county, of which he was the wealthiest and most distinguished old citizen, wrote that he was "highly respected and beloved." He took an active part in church affairs, and gave freely to all charities. "The ideas he advocated [among them complete equality for Negroes] were the mistakes of his life." On the other hand, almost no "carpet-bagger" was too vile to shift to the Democratic party and become a "respectable citizen." Thus C. E. Furlong, a Northern white who took heavy profits from the Vicksburg ring, received high state offices after changing parties, and in 1877 was suggested for the governorship by one of the leading Democratic papers.

Mississippi was extremely fortunate in the character of her more important Negro Republican leaders. In the words of Alexander K. McClure:

Mississippi is exceptionable also in the reputable character of her most prominent colored leaders. In all the other southern States the negro leaders have rivaled the white adventurers in reckless and bewildering robbery, but they have not done so in Mississippi. Three black men have here reached national fame as leaders of their race, and they are all esteemed as honest men.

. . . .

These three men . . . have maintained the manhood that should be the pride of every race, and, much as Mississippi has suffered from the carpet-bag and colored rule, there has not been a tithe of the demoralization and waste here that has dishonored the reign of the black man in the Carolinas and the Gulf States. That much of this comparatively good record of a bad domination is due to Revels, Bruce, and Lynch, who successfully breasted the wave of corruption, is a fact that should be confessed and justly appreciated.

Hiram Rhodes Revels, the least important of the three named by McClure, was the first Negro to serve in the United States Senate, in which body he completed the unexpired term of Jefferson Davis. Born of free parents in Fayetteville, North Carolina, September 27, 1827, he received his early education in a school taught by a Negro woman. The desire to continue his studies caused him to leave North Carolina and go to Indiana, where he attended a Quaker seminary. After further work at a Negro seminary in Ohio, he completed his training at Knox College, in Galesburg, Illinois. After his ordination as an African Methodist Episcopal preacher, Revels taught, lectured, and preached in Indiana, Illinois, Ohio, Missouri, and Maryland. During the war, after assisting in the organization of Negro regiments in Maryland and Missouri, he went to Mississippi, where he organized churches, lectured, and attempted to organize schools. An interlude of two years in

Kansas and Missouri was followed by his return to Mississippi, where he settled in Natchez as presiding elder of the Methodist Episcopal Church. Immediately, and almost entirely against his will, he was drawn into politics.

After a term of service on the city council of Natchez, Revels was persuaded by John R. Lynch to enter the race for the state senate. His election to that body opened the way for his advancement to a much higher office. It had been agreed that the short term available in the United States Senate should go to a Negro. So impressive was the prayer with which Revels opened the proceedings of the upper house that he immediately became the candidate of the Negro legislators.

In Washington, Revels naturally attracted a great deal of attention. Tall, portly, dignified, and an excellent speaker, he delighted those who had worked for the elevation of his race, and to some extent eased the misgivings of those who had opposed it. His actual accomplishments as a new man in the short session of the Senate were few. None of the bills introduced by him was passed. He did, however, speak effectively on several occasions, and in his speaking and voting he showed intelligence and moderation. His support of a bill for the general removal of the political disabilities of southern whites was especially effective. In his work outside the Senate, he succeeded in obtaining the admission of Negro mechanics to work in the United States Navy Yard.

Upon his return to Mississippi Revels was appointed to the presidency of Alcorn University, the new state college for Negroes. His work there was complicated by unruly elements in the faculty and student body, but in his appearances outside the college he gained the approval of most of the leading whites. After one of his speeches, the editor of a Democratic paper wrote: "As everywhere and on other occasions he impressed those who saw and heard him as a good man, honestly intent upon doing his people real good and quieting so far as he is able the bitterness between the races. In this work he will have the sympathy and encouragement of the white people." So thoroughly did Revels gain the "sympathy and encouragement of the white people" that he soon lost the confidence of the masses of his own race. Essentially a timid man, more of a scholar than a leader, and anxiously desirous of peace, he came more and more to be dominated by white Democrats. After a brief term as acting secretary of state, he returned to the presidency of Alcorn, only to be ousted from the office by Governor Ames. He worked with the Democrats in the election of 1875, and once more received the presidency of the university from Governor J. M. Stone. After his retirement from that office on account of poor health, he continued to be active in church work until his death at a Methodist Episcopal conference in 1901. In spite of his extreme caution and timidity, Revels throughout his career was a credit to his race. Had there been more like him, both white and black, some compromise would have brought peace in Mississippi.

A much more prominent figure than Revels was Blanche Kelso Bruce, the only Negro ever to serve a full term in the United States Senate, and the man described by Benjamin Brawley as "probably the most astute political leader the Negro ever had." A light mulatto, born in Prince Edward County, Virginia, March 1, 1841, of a mother who was the slave of a wealthy planter, Bruce knew few of the burdens of slavery. He received his early education from a private tutor. Nominally a slave, he was carried before the war to Missouri, where he studied the printing trade, and later dealt in books and papers. Soon after the opening of the war, he went to Hannibal, Missouri, where he organized the first Negro school in the state. In 1868, after two years at Oberlin College, Bruce moved to Mississippi, and almost immediately began his political career. After brief experience as election commissioner and as sergeant-at-arms of the state senate, he became assessor, and then sheriff and tax collector of the rich Delta county of Bolivar. His experience also included service as county superintendent of schools and as levee commissioner. During this time he was gaining wealth as a planter. By 1874, after a long campaign in his favor by the Floreyville *Star*, Bruce was ready to make his bid for election to the Senate. In this, with the backing of Governor Ames and of the Negro leader James Hill, he obtained an easy victory.

Upon his entrance to the Senate in March, 1875, Bruce immediately made a favorable impression. A man of magnificent physique and handsome countenance, he was described by a contemporary Mississippi Democrat as possessing "almost the manners of a Chesterfield." Through the influence of Roscoe Conkling, he obtained good committee appointments, and after his first session he became active on the floor. His chief interests lay in the improvement of the Mississsippi River, the establishment of a more enlightened policy toward the Indians, the development of interracial harmony, and the clearing up of the affairs of the Freedmen's Bank. On the floor of the Senate, he was often surrounded by a circle of friends similar to those which centered around Blaine, Edmunds, Bayard, and Lamar; while in his home, he and his cultured wife entertained a distinguished group which included the wives of Supreme Court justices and other officials. With the Democrats of the Mississippi delegation, Bruce maintained surprisingly pleasant relations, being especially close to his colleague L. Q. C. Lamar.

After the close of his senatorial term, Bruce was suggested for a place in Garfield's cabinet, receiving the unqualified endorsement of such Mississippi Democrats as Senator Lamar and Congressmen Chalmers, Money, Muldrow, and Singleton. Instead, however, he received an appointment as register of the treasury. Under Harrison, he served as recorder of deeds for the District of Columbia, and with the election of McKinley he once more became register of the treasury. While holding this office he died, March 17, 1898. To the end of his distinguished career, Bruce was always the gentleman, graceful, polished, self-assured, and never humble. He scorned the use of the phrase "colored man," often declaring "I am a negro, and proud of my race."

Equally remarkable was the career of John R. Lynch. The son of a slave mother and a wealthy white planter, Lynch was born near Vidalia, Louisiana, September 10, 1847. After the death of the father, both mother and son were sold and were taken to Natchez, where the boy became the favored body servant of one of the leading citizens. Upon the occupation of the city by federal troops, Lynch began to attend night school. Later he continued his studies through wide reading and work with tutors. After a brief term as a justice of the peace, he resigned to become, at the age of twenty-two, a member of the state legislature. There he made a remarkable impression. In spite of his youth, and in spite of the fact that there were only thirty-two Negroes in the House, he was elected speaker in 1872. Democrats and Republicans alike praised his ability and impartiality. In November, 1872, he was elected to Congress, and in December, 1873, he entered that body as its youngest member.

On the floor, Lynch showed himself to be perfectly at ease, making his first formal speech within eight days of the opening of the session. Of a distinctly aristocratic appearance, slender and active, with a very light complexion and regular features, he spoke fluently, tersely, and correctly. Franklin A. Montgomery wrote that he had few, if any, superiors as a stump speaker. His effective delivery and ready wit appealed to blacks and whites alike. Montgomery advised Democratic speakers to avoid clashing with him in debate. Serving in the Forty-Third, Forty-Fourth, and Forty-Seventh Congresses, he probably possessed as much influence at the White House as any Negro has ever had, being frequently called for consultation by Grant and Garfield. Throughout his public career, no scandal ever touched him, and by 1880 the Jackson *Clarion* was calling him "the ablest man of his race in the South."

Refusing offers from Lamar and Cleveland of appointments based on his retirement from politics, Lynch remained in the Republican party, serving as the temporary chairman of its national convention in 1884, and as fourth auditor of the treasury under Harrison. After studying and practicing law, he entered the army in 1898, and served until 1911, when he retired with the rank of major. He then opened law offices in Chicago, and became a power in the Republican organization in that city. In the meantime, he wrote three books on Reconstruction and his political experiences. Two of these, along with a number of articles, have been published. Shortly before his death in November, 1939, at the age of ninety-three, he reported that he was "taking life quite easily." In view of the few advantages he had in his youth, and of the distinguished career which he achieved in the face of difficulties, he must be judged worthy of the honors and comforts that came to him in his declining years.

To McClure's list of the outstanding Negro leaders in Mississippi one more must be added. James Hill, a light mulatto, was born July 25, 1846, on the plantation of one J. Hill, near Holly Springs. He received his early education from two daughters of his master, and continued it while working as a youth in the railroad shops at Holly Springs. He received no formal training, although he recognized its value and sent his younger brother Frank to Oberlin. For James Hill himself, study and work were serious businesses. He had no time for any diversions. He possessed none of the brilliance or oratorical ability of Bruce or Lynch, but for the larger part of the period he was probably a more influential factor in the politics of the state than either of his much more famous colleagues.

After a year as sergeant-at-arms of the house of representatives, Hill entered that body as a member in 1871. By the latter part of 1872, he was powerful enough to promise Bruce that he would be elected senator in 1874. For himself, Hill chose the office of secretary of state, which he filled quietly and efficiently for three years after the overthrow of 1875. Against him there was never any charge of dishonesty. After the close of his term, he was postmaster at Vicksburg for a time, and then collector of internal revenue. In 1882, he waged a hopeless campaign for a place in Congress. After that year, he centered his attention on business, and acquired a modest fortune as a successful land agent for the Louisville, New Orleans & Texas Railroad. He closed his career as receiver for the Federal Land Office in Jackson, as an active leader in the African Methodist Church, and as sponsor of other projects looking toward the advancement of his race. His career was at times mysterious and hard to explain. He stood very high in the favor of all of the Republican administrations at Washington. With the exception of the brief periods of his apparently useless campaigns for Congress, the white Democrats of the state seen almost never to have attacked him, and indeed to have worked with him as a colleague. He engaged in large business enterprises, and in projects for the aid of Negroes, almost as quietly and obscurely as he aided the family of the white man who had formerly been his master. The Democratic historian of Marshall County wrote, "He was extremely well thought of by the citizens, and is remembered as a good negro." He was also "extremely well thought of" by the Negroes, who have named their largest public school in Jackson for "Jim Hill."

Mississippi was not so fortunate in the two other Negroes, A. K. Davis and T. W. Cardozo, who held high offices in the state. Both these men were obscure local politicians, and little can be learned of their background. Davis, who served as lieutenant-governor from 1874 until his impeachment in 1875, was weak, treacherous, and apparently dishonest, although he was cleared in a criminal court of the charge of bribery on which he was convicted by the legislature. He had practically no influence outside his home district of Noxubee County.

Cardozo, superintendent of education from 1874 until his resignation under threat of impeachment in 1876, was an educated mulatto from New York. Nominated as a result of pressure from the Vicksburg machine, he was almost unknown outside Warren County before his election. Although both Ames and Lynch testify as to his intellectual and educational qualifications, neither of them defends his character. He was undoubtedly involved in the corruption at Vicksburg, and was shown to have embezzled more than two thousand dollars of the funds of Tougaloo University. After this episode, he returned to the obscurity from which he came.

LOCAL LEADERS AND THE LOYAL LEAGUES

Even more remarkable than the rise of Bruce, Lynch, and others to prominent positions in the state and nation was the amazingly rapid development of efficient local leaders among the Negroes. There is something fascinating about the suddenness with which, all over the state, they emerged from the anonymity of slavery to become directors and counselors for their race. In general, it can be said that they were not Negroes who had held positions of leadership under the old regime; the characteristics which made a man a slave driver or foreman were not those which would allow him to organize a Loyal League. Almost none of them came from the small group who had been free before the war. Such men, as barbers, artisans, or small farmers, had depended too long on the favor of the whites for the maintenance of their existence. Servility had become a part of them. Most of this group became Democrats, although a number of the younger element in the comparatively liberal region around Natchez gained prominence in the Republican organization.

A large portion of the minor Negro leaders were preachers,

lawyers, or teachers from the free states or from Canada. Their education and their independent attitude gained for them immediate favor and leadership. Of the natives who became their rivals, the majority had been urban slaves, blacksmiths, carpenters, clerks, or waiters in hotels and boarding houses; a few of them had been favored body servants of affluent whites. Most of them were more intelligent than the mass of their fellows, and had picked up some smattering of education, at least to the point of being able to read and write. There was a general tendency for them to combine preaching with their politics; as Sir George Campbell has said, they were rather preachers because they were leaders than leaders because they were preachers. The death rate of these local organizers, both during and immediately after Reconstruction, was alarmingly high.

The organ through which the local leaders worked was the "Loyal League." This body, an outgrowth of a northern patriotic organization established during the war, continued to maintain a very vague national connection. The state setup was equally sketchy. The local groups, of which there was at least one in almost every Black Belt community, were extremely active, especially during periods immediately preceding elections. Given a start by whites and Negroes from the North, they made an immediate appeal to the freedmen, and quickly came to rival the churches as centers of social activities. With their elaborate rituals, their multiplicity of offices, and their sashes and badges, they performed a function which later was taken over by the Negro lodges. The general practice in Mississippi was for the leagues to hold a social gathering twice each month. At these meetings, the Negroes danced and played games, and discussed local affairs, their churches, and their schools. As a rule, the gatherings took place in church or school buildings except in times of violence, when the members collected secretly in secluded spots in the woods.

The clubs also had a political significance, which at times of elections became pre-eminent. The oath taken by the initiate generally included a section similar to that in the ritual of Tarbell Council no. 4, at Morton: "Furthermore, that I will do all in my power to elect true and reliable Union men and supporters to the Government and none others, to all offices of profit or trust, from the lowest to the highest in Ward, Town, County, State and General Government. And should I ever be called to fill any office, I will faithfully carry out the objects and principles of this L. [*sic*]" Local or visiting speakers urged the Negroes to protect their freedom and their rights by voting for Republican nominees, and in some of the leagues a majority vote bound all of the members to vote for the candidates chosen. It was also in the leagues that preparations were made for gathering the Negroes in large groups early on the morning of election days. With their courage thus bolstered, they monopolized the polls during the early hours, and left them to the white Democrats in the afternoon.

These clubs also provided political banquets and barbecues, and arranged political processions that were most attractive to the freedmen and annoying to the white Democrats. These activities involved the wearing of sashes and badges, the building of floats, and the loud beating of drums. At a night parade in Holly Springs, the Negroes wore red oilcloth caps with red feathers, red sashes, and enormous red and blue badges. Torches and transparencies completed the equipment. At a barbecue in Lawrence County, the members of the league formed into a large procession and marched in double file around the courthouse and under a cross of blue cloth, bowing as they passed beneath it.

These activities, and especially the pompous processions, aroused the wrath of the white Democrats. Conditions in Oktibbeha County were typical:

In the early seventies the Democratic political organizations made it a point to intimidate and if necessary to whip the leaders of the negro drum companies and break up the meetings of these organizations. If possible the drums were always secured and destroyed and threats made of more drastic treatment if any further meeting, marching or drumming was attempted. These measures of expediency were not always carried through without bloodshed.

This development of a symbolic significance for the use of drums by the Negroes gave an excuse for violent attacks by white Democratic organizations. In 1876, Negroes in De Soto County published an announcement that in order to avoid further trouble they would entirely abandon the use of drums and fifes. This move, although largely ineffective, became a general policy throughout the state.

Democratic efforts to break up the leagues also involved the use of white "detectives" and Negro spies to learn the meeting places of the groups, and especially to identify their leaders. With this information, "the Ku Klux Klan lost no time in getting rid of the chief offenders and leaders." After the successful revolution of 1875, the leagues rapidly disappeared, and lodges and benevolent societies gradually took their places.

Negro Officials in County and Municipal Governments

By a provision of the new constitution of the state, the terms of all local officials expired with the readmission of Mississippi to the Union. Appointments to local offices were then to be made by the governor with the advice and consent of the senate. Thus there were no municipal or county elections in the state until the fall of 1871. The governor, J. L. Alcorn, as an old and relatively conservative citizen of the state, made appointments that at least were up to the usual standard for such officials. In some cases, the entire county lists were made up of Democrats or old Whigs. Alcorn's selections for the judiciary were made up almost entirely of leading members of the state bar. Altogether, the total of his appointments included 247 Republicans, 217 Democrats, and 72 members of other opposition groups. So far as possible, Alcorn avoided the appointment of Negroes. It appears that no member of that race except Robert H. Wood of Natchez was made mayor of any town. With the possible exception of Coffeeville and Greenville, no town had a Negro majority on its board of aldermen.

Even after the election of 1871, a Negro majority in a municipal government seems to have been unknown. The city of Jackson, with a powerful Republican machine that maintained its control for thirteen years after the overthrow of the party in the state, only once had more than one Negro on its city council of six members. The one exception followed the election of 1874, when two Negroes became aldermen. In Natchez, where the Negroes held an enormous majority, they placed only three members on a council of seven. Efforts of the Negro majority to gain control of the board in Vicksburg in 1874 lost the support of the white members of their party, and with it the election.

The chief complaint against the participation of the freedmen in the government of the towns grew out of their appointment as policemen. The presence of such officials helped to bring on the Meridian riot in 1871, and furnished the central theme of the attack on the Republican government in Jackson. The general attitude of the whites, as expressed by Ethelbert Barksdale, was that "negroes ought not to be put in a position to discharge constabulary functions which it is proper for white men to exercise." Law enforcement implied domination, and as Barksdale said, the white race was "not in the habit of being dominated by the colored race."

In general the few towns which had Republican governments as late as 1874 overthrew them before the state government fell in the fall of 1875. The Democrats took Vicksburg in August, 1874, and Columbus in December. Yazoo City was captured in April, 1875, and Okolona in August. The methods generally used in this process, combining persuasion, intimidation, economic pressure, and violence, were similar to those used later in the state campaign. For towns which had Negro majorities, the legislature assured the continuation of Democratic control by excluding from the corporate limits large portions of the Negro residential sections. The one important exception to the overthrow of Republican municipal governments in the years 1874 and 1875 was the city of Jackson, where a peculiar situation and a large number of white votes maintained that party in power until 1888.

Very little information is available as to the participation of the Negroes in the various county governments. More than half of the counties held white majorities, and most of these naturally eliminated in the elections of 1871 the few Negro officials appointed by Alcorn in 1870. In the elections of 1873, the Democrats carried thirty-nine of the seventy-four counties, and in 1875 sixty-two of the seventy-four. Of course, in several of the predominantly white counties, black votes at times elected one or two supervisors or justices of the peace. Yalobusha, Scott, and Lawrence counties, as examples, generally had one Negro supervisor on the board of five. Such Negroes were almost entirely without influence, and generally found it to their advantage to be "very quiet, good negroes," to use the description given of those in Lawrence.

Even in the minority of the counties which had Negro and Republican majorities, the freedmen seldom obtained many of the offices. By 1873, however, they became assertive enough to take control of a number of counties in which the white population was small. In Marshall County, for example, three of the five supervisors were Negroes who could barely read and write. The three on the board in Yazoo County, the three in Warren, four of the five in Madison, and all five in Issaquena were described as "illiterate." In these counties, there were also varying numbers of Negro justices of the peace, few of whom were capable of carrying out properly even the simple duties of their office. There were also a small number of Negro chancery and circuit clerks varying in ability from an "illiterate" in Yazoo to the highly cultured L. J. Winston, who remained as circuit clerk in Adams County, under white Democratic control, until his appointment as collector of the port of Vicksburg in 1897. According to John R. Lynch, "Out of seventy-two counties in the State at that time, electing on an average twenty-eight officers to a county, it is safe to assert that not over five out of one hundred of such officers were colored men." This statement seems to be approximately correct.

The most important office in the counties, both in responsibilities and in financial returns, was that of sheriff. According to Lynch, not more than twelve Negroes in Mississippi ever held this office. Available material supplies the names Blanche K. Bruce of Bolivar, J. J. Evans of De Soto, John Brown of Coahoma, Winslow of Washington, Sumner of Holmes, Merrimon Howard of Jefferson, Peter Crosby of Warren, William McCary and Robert H. Wood of Adams, W. H. Harney of Hinds, Scott of Issaquena, and Joe Spencer Watkins of Monroe. In regard to Sumner and Watkins, there is almost no information. Of Blanche K. Bruce, it is sufficient to say that his handling of the office of sheriff fully merited the confidence of the white planters who supplied his bond of $120,000. The offices of Evans and Winslow seem to have been managed very largely by the whites who supplied their bonds. Charges of embezzlement against Evans, an ex-slave who was described as a good, sound Negro, seem to have been entirely unjustified. Scott, judged by his testimony before the Boutwell Committee, was a man of intelligence and ability who, although he was elected by the votes of Negroes, was completely under the control of white Democrats. Almost exactly the same description applies to Merrimon Howard of Jefferson, although he at times showed a bit more independence than Scott. John Brown, run out of Coahoma County after a "race riot" during the campaign of 1875, six years later was declared to have embezzled a large sum for which his sureties were liable. Peter Crosby, whose violent expulsion by white leaguers led to the Vicksburg riots of 1874, was a member of the infamous ring of that city. Yet, strangely enough, subsequent examination of his accounts disclosed them to be entirely in order. Nordhoff's statement that he was illiterate is incorrect. W. H. Harney of Hinds County was a Canadian Negro of some education and ability. He was popular with whites and blacks alike until the development of the bitter campaign of 1875. Charges that he was from twelve to twenty-one thousand dollars short in his accounts occupied the courts for five years. Newspaper reports of the settlement are confusing and contradictory. William McCary and Robert Wood were intelligent members of families who had been free and respected residents of Natchez for several generations. Their conduct seems to have given general satisfaction.

In regard to the quality and activity of county governments between 1870 and 1875, a few generalizations may be drawn. As compared with the period before the war, this was one of greatly increased activity. Bridges, roads, and public buildings destroyed or allowed to go to pieces during the war had to be reconstructed. In addition, the greatly increased business of country stores, the rapid growth of small towns, and expanded social and political activities called for the building of new roads. Under the new system of public education, there were schools to be built and a great number of teachers to be employed. The admission of the freedmen to the courts more than doubled their business. Then too, there was a great burst of enthusiasm for the building of railroads. County after county and town after town made contributions for this purpose after overwhelmingly favorable votes by whites and blacks, and Democrats and Republicans alike. All of this implied an enormous increase in county expenditures, and a proportional increase in taxation. Furthermore, the burden of this increase fell directly on the owners of real estate. The large revenue from the head tax on slaves was no longer available, and the Republican party, made up largely of propertyless Negroes and of business and professional men, quickly lightened the heavy levies that formerly had been made on artisans, professional men, and commercial enterprisers.

Interestingly enough, there seems to be no correlation at all between the rate of taxation and the political or racial character of the counties. In 1874, at the height of Negro-Republican control, the average rate for the thirty-nine Democratic counties was 12 7/13 mills. That for the thirty-four Republican counties was 13 7/17—a difference of less than one mill. The county tax in the Democratic units ranged from 6.2 mills in Pontotoc to 20.3 in Chickasaw. In the Republican counties, the range was from 5.3 in De Soto to 23.2 in Colfax. Negro influence was probably greatest in Madison, Issaquena, Amite, Washington, Warren, Yazoo, Wilkinson, and Hinds. As compared with a state average of 13, the rates in these counties were, respectively, 11, 16, 11, 13½, 14, 10, 19, and 11.4 mills. Warrants in counties with heavy Negro populations were running at from forty to seventy-five cents on the dollar. On the other hand, those in Lee County, where no Negro or Republican of any kind ever held office, fell to thirty cents. The conclusion must be drawn that everywhere in the state a large part of the increase in expenditures was unavoidable. Then too, the wave of extravagance which was sweeping the nation did not fail to touch Mississippi. To a certain extent, the situation probably reflects the new feeling of self-importance and the new influence that had come to the poor whites.

The question of how much fraud existed in the various counties is difficult to answer. Charges, in general terms, were frequently made in the Democratic press. The leading Republican paper assembled the available evidence, and attempted to show that a great deal more dishonesty had been uncovered in

Democratic than in Republican counties. With the exception of J. H. Jones, who charges graft in Wilkinson, it is the general conclusion of the few students who have investigated individual counties that while there was some extravagance, there is no evidence of open fraud. Their conclusions are hard to reconcile with the many charges which were prevalent at the time.

There can be little doubt that there was a rotten situation in Vicksburg, a city which seldom knew an honest government before the war, and has almost never had one since. City expenditures were enormous. Most of them went for improvement of streets and wharves, and other projects which were really necessary for a town that was rapidly becoming a city, but if half of the charges of extravagance and graft were true, the city was getting little for its money. In this exploitation, Democrats and Republicans shared alike. It is also true that the enormous grants to railroads met almost no opposition at the polls. It is therefore difficult to say just how much of the extravagance and corruption was real, or how much of it should be charged to Negroes and white Republicans.

The Vicksburg ring also controlled the government of Warren County, and there can be little doubt, in spite of the curious fact that Sheriff Crosby's accounts were found to be in order, that several of the county officials, Negroes and whites, were engaged in extensive embezzlement through such methods as the forgery of warrants. Unfortunately, it must be recorded that the thrifty black and white taxpayers who joined the violent white "Modocs" in overthrowing the Republican city government in 1874, and the county government in the following year, saw control pass into the hands of the least desirable element of the whites. The result was that conditions in city and county became worse rather than better.

In conclusion it may be stated that although Negroes formed a majority of the population in thirty counties in Mississippi, they almost never took advantage of their opportunity to place any large number of their race in local offices. Of those who did hold offices, the twelve sheriffs were moderately satisfactory; most of them were at least capable of exercising the functions of their office. No Negro in the state ever held any higher judicial office than that of justice of the peace, and those who held that office seem generally to have been incompetent. Among the small number of chancery and circuit clerks there was a wide range of ability; most of them were not suitable men for their positions. Negroes who gained election to the boards of supervisors of the various counties, even in those cases where they formed a majority, generally were dominated by white Republicans, either natives or northerners. Although many of the Negro supervisors were ignorant and incompetent, little difference can be discovered in the administration of their counties and that of counties under Democratic control.

NEGROES AND STATE GOVERNMENT

The first legislature under the new constitution assembled in Jackson in January, 1870. Of the 107 men in the house of representatives, twenty-five were Democrats and eighty-two were Republicans. The number of Negro representatives, originally thirty-one, was immediately reduced to thirty by the death of C. A. Yancey of Panola County. Thus, in a state which held a large Negro majority, members of that race made up less than two-sevenths of the total membership of the house, and less than three-eighths of the Republican majority. Their representation in the senate was even smaller. In the total membership of thirty-three, and in a Republican group of twenty-eight, only five were Negroes.

Of the thirty Negroes in the house, eight had served in the constitutional convention. A dozen or more of the group, either by education or unusual native ability, were entirely capable of meeting their obligations as legislators. Among these were H. P. Jacobs, Henry Mayson, J. F. Boulden, M. T. Newsome, Merrimon Howard, John R. Lynch, J. Aaron Moore, H. M. Foley, J. J. Spelman, and J. H. Piles. All of these men made distinguished records in fields other than politics. Almost as capable were Albert Johnson, Nathan McNeese, A. K. Davis, Doctor Stites, Emanuel Handy, Richard Griggs, and W. H. Foote. The other fourteen members were inclined to be self-effacing, and took little part in the formation of policy.

Of the five members of the senate, three, Charles Caldwell, Hiram Revels, and T. W. Stringer, have already been discussed.* Robert Gleed, of Columbus, was a man of fair education, good character, and some financial ability, although he

* Charles Caldwell . . . from Hinds County . . . exercised some influence in the convention [Constitutional Convention of 1868]. A mulatto, he had been a slave blacksmith in Clinton, and had picked up a smattering of education. A Democratic leader declared he was "far above the average negro in intelligence." Although he was no orator, he was a natural leader. Later, as state senator, he helped to guide his party, and, as "the Warwick of the administration," became one of the strongest supporters of Governor Ames. Unlike the great mass of Negroes of the time, in or out of politics, he was absolutely fearless. Although he used his power for the maintenance of peace between the races, in the crisis of 1875 he led a unit of militia through Clinton, and for this he was marked for death. One night about a month after the overthrow, he was literally riddled with bullets on a street in that town.

By far the most influential Negro in the convention [Constitutional Convention of 1868], and the most powerful political leader of his race in the state until 1869, was T. W. Stringer of Vicksburg. A former resident of Ohio, he came to Mississippi as general superintendent of missions and presiding elder for the African Methodist Church, of which he had almost complete control for many years. The man had a genius for organization. After a distinguished career in religious and fraternal organizations in Ohio, he led in the development of the African Methodist Episcopal Church in Canada before his move to Mississippi. Wherever he went in the state, churches, lodges, benevolent societies, and political machines sprang up and flourished. His influence upon the constitution of 1868 was as great as that of any other man in the convention.

had been a slave until the close of the war. An excellent speaker, he was employed by the Democratic administration after the overthrow of the Republican regime to lecture to the Negroes of the state on educational and agricultural matters. The fifth senator, William Gray of Greenville, was a young Baptist preacher of some education and much natural cleverness. A leader in the demands for civil rights for Negroes, he was lacking in tact, and was probably at times guilty of double-dealing both in politics and in religious affairs.

The election of a new house of representatives in 1871, for the term of 1872 and 1873, brought a heavy reduction of the Republican majority. Of the 115 members, the Republicans claimed sixty-six. Actually, however, several of the white members of their group, calling themselves independents, generally voted with the Democrats and against the administration. Negro membership rose to thirty-eight, but R. R. Applewhite of Copiah was completely under Democratic control, and later announced himself a member of that party. The Negroes now had a theoretical control of the Republican caucus in the lower house, but actually any attempt to press their advantage was generally blocked by the desertion of a number of their white colleagues. It was only after Alcorn urged it as a political necessity that John R. Lynch received enough white Republican votes to gain the speakership.

It may therefore be said that during the first four years of Republican control the dominant group in both houses of the legislature was a combination of native and northern white Republicans, who were influenced by the desires of their Negro constituents, but were also attentive to the large white element in their party, an element whose numbers they earnestly desired to increase. Their leader until late in 1871 was Governor Alcorn, an old Whig with Hamiltonian sentiments and a dream of bringing into the Republican party of the state men in the Democratic and Conservative groups who shared his beliefs. When Alcorn resigned in November, 1871, to take his place in the United States Senate, he was succeeded by R. C. Powers, a man of the same sentiments. Both of these men wished to carry out a program which they considered to be for the best interests of whites and blacks alike. Both of them, like many of the white Republicans in the legislature, avoided social contacts with the Negroes as much as possible, and were absolutely opposed to any real control of their party by the Negroes.

In this situation, the Negro minority in the legislature generally followed the lead of the white Republicans, with whom, in matters of routine legislation, they were usually naturally in accord. In such routine business, the more able Negroes, including Stringer, Boulden, Jacobs, Spelman, and Lynch, were about as prominent as any of the white leaders. In fact, when the proportion of their numbers is kept in mind, a survey of the *Journals* reveals little difference between the whites and Negroes in attendance, in service on committees, or in activity on the floor. Negro members almost never suggested legislation to obtain special privileges for their race. The more able Negroes either recognized the weakness of their position or had no desire to gain undue advantage. The few who would have gone futher received no encouragement or support.

In his inaugural address, in January, 1870, Governor Alcorn outlined clearly the two basic problems faced by the Republicans. "The obligations resting on us under the new order of things," he said, "extend very greatly the breadth of duty of the State Government. The 'patriarchal' groupings of our society in the days of slavery, confined the work of our political organizations, to a very great extent, to the heads of what we called 'families.'" Under the new regime, every individual had become a distinct entity. In addition to the great increase in the number of individuals concerned, a large increase in the *amount* of government was contemplated. The costs of the new administration must be much greater than those of the old. He would therefore urge the legislature to take advantage of every opportunity for economy. In regard to the state's new citizens, he said: "In the face of memories that might have separated them from me as the wronged from the wronger, they have offered me their confidence. . . . In response to that touching reliance, the most profound anxiety with which I enter my office . . . is that of making the colored man the equal, before the law, of any other man. . . ." Thus, in the beginning, Alcorn presented the problems that doomed the Republican regime. There were many whites who were alienated by the extension of the powers of the state, and even more by the increase in costs and taxes. A larger group, including, to a certain extent, Alcorn himself, absolutely refused to accept the implications of Negro equality before the law. Such revolutions, unless maintained by overwhelming force, cannot be accomplished in a decade.

With a treasury balance of about fifty dollars in cash and five hundred dollars in negotiable paper, the Republicans entered upon the program that was to reconstruct the state. During the next four years, they set up, organized, and maintained at state expense a biracial system of common school education which, although it did not approach the national average in facilities or expense, was an amazing advance beyond anything the state had known before. They gave state support to normal schools at Holly Springs and Tougaloo, and established Alcorn as a Negro counterpart to the state university. They completely reorganized, coordinated, and centralized the state judiciary, and gave to it a new code of laws. Old public buildings were renovated and enlarged and new ones were constructed. State hospitals were set up and supported at Natchez and Vicksburg, and the facilities of the state asylums for the blind, deaf and dumb, and insane were greatly expanded. All racial discrimination was eliminated from the laws of the state. Finally, after much disagreement, the legislature granted to the Negroes in 1873 a civil rights bill, which in theory guaranteed to them equal access to all places of public entertainment.

Although much of this legislation was expensive, and almost all of it was controversial, a partial acceptance of the program and a loss of faith in the Democratic party produced a sweeping victory in 1872, and the election of Republicans to five of the six congressional seats. By the summer of 1873, the Republican party had reached the height of its power in the state. In this very strength, however, there was a great weakness. The breakdown of Democratic opposition, in the state as in the nation, opened the way for a struggle among the discordant elements in the dominant party. Between 1867 and 1872, it had appeared that this struggle, when it came, would involve a choice by the Negroes between northern and native whites as their leaders. In spite of efforts of the Democrats to aggravate differences on this basis, it had greatly declined in importance by 1873. The great line of division had come to be the question of the extent to which Negroes were to be allowed to hold offices and to dominate the councils of the party.

This became apparent in the state and county conventions in the summer of 1873. The Negroes, after six years of domination of the party by whites, now declared that they must have a larger share of the offices. Although, in general, their demands were not yet proportional to their party membership, the Negroes overestimated their ability to supply suitable candidates. This became evident when, after Bruce's refusal to accept the lieutenant-governorship, that office went to the weak A. K. Davis. Matters became worse when the Vicksburg ring, threatening violence and secession, secured the post of superintendent of education for Cardozo. This left James Hill, candidate for the office of secretary of state, as the only really acceptable candidate offered by the Negroes for the three state positions which they demanded. Similar weaknesses were to be found in many of the men whom they chose for places in the legislature and in the county governments. The most important point at issue, however, was the fact that it was now clear that actual domination of the party by the mass of its Negro membership would probably come in the near future. By thousands of white members of the party, and by a majority of its white leaders, such a development could not be accepted.

J. L. Alcorn, already repudiated by the Negroes, undertook to lead the opposition, and announced his candidacy for the governorship in opposition to Adelbert Ames. With him went most of the Republican leaders who were native whites, and a number of those from the North. To this group, calling itself the "Republican Party of Mississippi," the Democrat-Conservative organization immediately threw its support.

In an election in which the color line was rather sharply drawn, Ames defeated Alcorn by a vote of 69,870 to 50,490. Seventy-seven of the 115 members of the lower house were Republicans of either the Alcorn or the Ames faction. Fifty-five were Negroes, but one or two of these were Democrats. In a senate of thirty-seven members, twenty-five were Republicans, including nine Negroes. All of the seven state officers were regular Ames Republicans, and three of them, the lieutenant-governor, the secretary of state, and the superintendent of education, were Negroes. Furthermore, a Negro from Warren County, I. D. Shadd, soon became the none-too-competent speaker of the house.

In his inaugural address, Governor Ames made a good impression. After pledging himself to work for economy and reform, he turned to the race problem, analyzed the causes of conflict, and called for tolerance and a mutual recognition of rights and interests. Thus, as Alcorn had done four years before, Ames recognized the two great problems which neither of them could solve. The elevation of the Negro involved a rapid expansion of state services which were inconsistent with the old ideas of economy. The readjustment of the relationship between the races was a matter beyond the power of the governor or the legislature.

The heavy increase in the number of Negroes in the government of the state did not greatly decrease its efficiency or change its character. The secretary of state was both competent and honest, and the superintendent of education at least was competent. The Negro legislators, as a group, were fairly capable of handling their duties, and probably represented their race more worthily than did the Negroes in any other southern legislature. Visiting the state in 1874, Edward King wrote:

. . . [Negroes] lounge everywhere, and there are large numbers of smartly dressed mulattoes, or sometimes full blacks, who flit here and there with the conscious air which distinguishes the freedman. I wish here to avow, however, that those of the negroes in office, with whom I came in contact in Mississippi, impressed me much more powerfully as worthy, intelligent, and likely to progress, than many whom I saw elsewhere in the South. There are some who are exceedingly capable, and none of those immediately attached to the government at Jackson are incapable. In the Legislature there are now and then negroes who are ignorant; but of late both branches have been freer of this curse than those of Louisiana or South Carolina.

A visit to the Capitol showed me that the negroes, who form considerably more than half the population of Mississippi, had certainly secured a fair share of the offices. Colored men act as officials or assistants in the offices of the Auditor, the Secretary of State, the Public Library, the Commissioner of Emigration [sic], and the Superintendent of Public Instruction. The Secretary of State [James Hill] who has some negro blood in his veins, is the natural son of a well-known Mississippian of the old regime, formerly engaged in the politics of his State; and the Speaker of the House of Representatives at the last session was a black man. The blacks who went and came from the Governor's office seemed very intelligent, and some of them entered into general conversation in an interesting manner.

In spite of Ames' evidently sincere interest in economy, he and his legislature found it very difficult to make any substantial reduction in the expenses of the state government. Under the Republican administration, expenses had grown to what the Democrats declared were fantastic proportions. As a matter of fact, when the abnormal years of the war are omitted, the figures of the state auditors do give the impression that the Republican administrations were extravagant:

Year	Democratic Administrations	Year	Republican Administrations
1856 through		1870	$1,061,249.90
1860—average	$ 767,438.78	1871	1,729,046.34
1865	1,410,250.13	1872	1,596,828.64
1866	1,860,809.89	1873	1,450,632.80
1867	625,817.80	1874	1,319,281.60
1868	525,678.80	1875	1,430,192.83
1869	463,219.71		
1876	518,709.03		
1877	697,018.86		
1878	707,022.46		
1879	553,326.81		
1880	803,191.31		

Thus the average yearly cost of the state government under the six years of Republican control was $1,431,205.35, or almost twice the normal expenditure of the years immediately preceding the war. Even more spectacular, however, had been the increase in taxation of real estate. For many years, real property had been practically exempt from taxation in Mississippi. In 1869, the last year of Democratic control, the rate on this class of property was only one mill, or a tax of only twenty dollars a year on a plantation assessed by its owner at twenty thousand dollars and worth perhaps fifty thousand. The great sources of revenue were a tax of a dollar a bale on cotton, and privilege and license taxes which seem to have been inordinately high. The Republican regime reversed this system; after abolishing the tax on cotton and almost entirely eliminating the privilege taxes, the Republicans placed almost the entire burden of the support of the state on real and personal property. The result was a rate that rose from five mills in 1871 to fourteen in 1874. However pleasing such a system might be to the advocate of the single tax, there can be no doubt that it brought wrath to the landowners in a period of agricultural depression.

So strong had the protest of the landowners become by the spring of 1875 that the legislature could no longer afford to overlook it. Governor Ames insisted that changes were necessary, and the representatives undertook the problem. The reductions for which they provided, like those made later by the Democrats, were more apparent than real. For a centralized government in a state of more than a million people, it was a simple fact that a cost of $1,400,000 per year was not extravagant. To meet the situation, the legislature put back on the counties the cost of jury, witness, and inquest fees that had been assumed by the state. Thus, at one blow, an item of $200,000 a year was chopped from the cost of the government of the state, but it was added to that of the counties. In addition, the legislature presented to the people a constitutional amendment to provide for a great reduction in the number of the circuit judges. It also reduced printing costs by cutting down the number of the legislative journals, and by eliminating the publication of departmental reports. Then, against the opposition of about half of the Negro members, it reduced the salaries of the governor and other state officials, and provided for biennial rather than annual sessions of the legislature. Appropriations to the state universities were reduced, and scholarships were abolished. Another amendment to the constitution provided for the distribution of income from state lands, fines, and liquor licenses rather than their incorporation in the permanent school endowment fund. The ratification of this amendment was to allow a heavy reduction

in the state school tax. Finally, turning to the system of taxation, the legislature reduced the *ad valorem* levy to nine and
one-fourth mills, placed a tax on railroads, and made a partial
return to the use of privilege taxes. Ironically enough, the
effect of most of these reforms could not become apparent
until the following year, at which time their benefits were
easily claimed by the triumphant Democrats. Their adoption
went almost unnoticed in the midst of the tumultuous movement toward the revolution of 1875.

Unlike the Republican administrations in most of the other
southern states, those in Mississippi financed their enterprises
almost entirely through taxation. When the party assumed
control in January, 1871, the state had an empty treasury and
a debt of $1,178,175.33. When the Democrats returned to
power in January, 1876, they found $524,388.68 in the treas-
ury and a debt of $3,341,162.89. With the deduction in each
case of permanent funds which the state owed to itself, and
consideration of the treasury balance, the payable debt in
1876, as in 1871, was approximately half a million dollars, a
negligible amount.

Furthermore, the Republican state regime left a remarkable
record of honesty. The conclusion of J. W. Garner seems to
be approximately correct:

So far as the conduct of state officials who were entrusted with
the custody of public funds is concerned, it may be said that there
were no great embezzlements or other cases of misappropriation
during the period of Republican rule. . . . The treasurer of the
Natchez hospital seems to have been the only defaulting state
official during the administration of Governor Ames. He was a
carpet-bagger, and the amount of the shortage was $7,251.81. The
colored state librarian during Alcorn's administration was charged
with stealing books from the library. The only large case of
embezzlement during the post-bellum period was that of the
Democratic treasurer in 1866. The amount of the shortage was
$61,962.

It may be added that the next embezzlement of any importance was that of the Democratic "redemption" treasurer who
was elected in 1875. His shortage was $315,612.19.

Altogether, as governments go, that supplied by the Negro
and white Republicans in Mississippi between 1870 and 1876
was not a bad government. Never, in state, counties, or towns,
did the Negroes hold office in proportion to their numbers,
although their demands in this direction were undeniably increasing. The Negroes who held county offices were often
ignorant, but under the control of white Democrats or Republicans they supplied a form of government which differed
little from that in counties where they held no offices. The
three who represented the state in the national Congress were
above reproach. Those in the legislature sought no special
advantages for their race, and in one of their very first acts
they petitioned Congress to remove all political disabilities
from the whites. With their white Republican colleagues,
they gave to the state a government of greatly expanded
functions at a cost that was low in comparison with that of
almost any other state. The legislature of 1875 reduced that
cost to some extent, and opened the way for further reductions by the passage of constitutional amendments. It also
removed some of the apparent injustices in the system of
taxation. But one situation it did not alter. The Republican
party had come to be branded as a party of Negroes, and it
was apparent that the Negroes were more and more determined to assert their right to control that party. It is also true
that many of the Negroes, probably a majority, favored a
further expansion of the functions of the state, entirely at the
expense, according to the whites, of white taxpayers. The
way was open for the formation of a "white-line" party.

17

SOCIAL AND ECONOMIC FORCES IN ALABAMA RECONSTRUCTION

Horace Mann Bond

The major contribution of Horace M. Bond's study of post-Civil War Alabama is to underscore how the Reconstruction experience could vary so considerably from state to state. What emerges from this study are some significant insights into the benefactors of corruption (the bribe giver as well as the taker) and the extent to which rival economic interests could determine the nature of political development.

The story of Reconstruction in Alabama, more than a twice-told tale, has become a commonly accepted pattern for the historical description of the South. In the definitive work of Walter Lynwood Fleming, the central figures and facts are set forth with a conviction, and documentation, that for thirty years has closed the subject to further investigation.

The central figures in this stereotype are the shiftless, poor white scalawags; the greedy carpetbaggers; the ignorant, deluded, sometimes vicious Negroes; and the noble, courageous and chivalrous southrons who fought and won the battle for White Supremacy. The accepted facts are: the imposition of a corrupt carpetbagger-Negro regime on a proud state; the accumulation of a debt of $25,503,593; the final victory of honesty; and the shouldering of this immense debt by a war-

SOCIAL AND ECONOMIC FORCES IN ALABAMA RECONSTRUCTION

ridden, despoiled people who toiled for generations under the
incubus of fearful interest payments. . . .

Whatever Reconstruction meant to Fleming, we may now
agree that it involved social, economic, and political redefini-
tion of the status of varied economic and racial groupings.
The shape of future institutions was to be moulded, super-
ficially by the partisan elements, fundamentally by the social
and economic forces which gave those elements strength and
direction. . . .

Social Forces in Alabama Reconstruction

The Native Whites: The Aristocracy of Tradition.

At the end of the Civil War, as we are likely to forget, the
sponsors of varied policies were actuated by an acute realism.
No one can forget, as Garfield did not, that to expect "seven
million men to change their hearts on the issue of a battle" is
an absurdity. It is clear that the former slaveholders never
intended to accept the "freedom" of Negroes without the
reservation that members of the race should continue to be the
wards, and under the tutelage, of the class which had owned
them before the war. The slaveholders were realistic enough,
and those who now view the figure of Thaddeus Stevens with
such horror forget that, like the slaveholders, the Pennsylvanian was just as realistic, and pursued precisely the only
course which he saw would nullify those firm reservations
as to Negro status. In his inaugural address of December 13,
1865, Governor Patton, newly elected provisional governor,
said: "We shall not only extend to the freedmen all their
legitimate rights, but shall throw around them such effectual
safeguards as will secure them in their full and complete
enjoyment. At the same time it must be understood that politically and socially ours is a white man's government." The
Negro, continued Governor Patton, "must be made to learn
that freedom does not mean idleness and vagrancy." A cynic

[3 7 1]

might have retorted that this is what freedom, precisely defined, *does* mean. A charge to a jury in Pike County is quoted by Fleming to show the "sentiments of the judiciary officers and members of the bar as well as jurists." The charge was apparently an acceptance of freedom for the Negro; but it was *freedom* as conceived by Alabama planters:

> We deplore the result as injurious to the country and fatal to the Negroes, but we are in honor bound to observe the laws which acknowledge their freedom . . . Nominally free, he (The Negro) is beyond expression helpless by his want of self-reliance, of experience, of ability to understand and appreciate his condition. . . . (We must) convince the world of our good faith, get rid of the Freedmen's Bureau, . . . secure the service of the Negroes, teach them their place, and convince him (*sic*) that we are their best friends.

Fleming could have selected no better document to show prevailing "sentiments."

The restrictive legislation of the Provisional Assembly, and the numerous "Black Codes" of municipalities, are of the same nature. We need not concern ourselves here, as so many historians have done, with the "right" or "wrong" of these provisions. For our purposes, they are documentary evidences as to a state of mind; they are exhibitions of attitudes which had force to motivate human action. The "aristocrats" had a tradition of righteous paternalism toward the Negro; and the issue of the battle had not changed the force of that tradition perceptibly. Indeed, many of those kindly disposed toward Negroes could not understand why their former slaves deserted their masters for the Yankees. It was, they reflected bitterly, final proof of an unregenerate, animalistic lack of gratitude. . . .

The Negroes.

The role of the Negro during Reconstruction has been given as many different interpretations as there are theories of racial psychology. No esoteric explanation of their behaviour is needed in this essay; it may be helpful to remember that the Negroes were ex-slaves, and we know what the institution of chattel slavery consciously designed to produce as its labor force. That the masses were ignorant goes without saying; that they were disorganized and restless was inevitable.

And yet these masses—these ignorant and restless ex-slaves —knew exactly what they needed. Their slogan has been ridiculous for nearly seventy years, and probably will be so for eternity. What they asked of the government which had set them free was, indeed, a monstrosity. They asked for a subsistence farmstead—for forty acres and a mule.

The leadership of this mass of ignorance was more important than the mass itself in directing its energies. This leadership has been alternately blamed and praised by partisans. Unfortunately, they left no documents which would help us understand what kind of men they were. We do know that they were frequently persons with an education equal or superior to that of the white politicians of their day, and that they had the same economic point of view.

The Mobile Creole community sent Ovide Gregory to the Constitutional Convention of 1867; John Carraway, a prominent politican, was also from Mobile. James T. Rapier was a mulatto of planting antecedents, a well-educated man with a cultural background probably unsurpassed in Alabama among his contemporaries, whether white or black.

A significant fact about the Negro leadership prevalent during Alabama Reconstruction is that few were actually identified, in economic position, with the great mass of landless, utterly penniless Negro ex-slaves whom they purported to represent. The economic ambitions of the Negro leaders are reflected in Rapier's self-conscious pride in the ownership of a large plantation in north Alabama. The Negro leaders of a "radical" party had little reason to advocate the economic radicalism of agrarian Republicanism. They were bent on achieving, within the economic framework which favored them, the social and political privileges which were the dower of the white Conservatives whom they publicly opposed.

The Negro masses were in a revolutionary mood, willing to accept ideas because they were not articulate enough to force the ideas which were their own. That they were not as utterly impassive as many writers on the period have insisted is shown by the fervor with which they sloughed off their apparent loyalties to their former masters, who, in bitter disappointment, promptly called them "fickle." Governor Lindsay, elected as a Democrat in 1870, gives an exceedingly valuable picture of the disposition of the Negroes to change from docility as soon as they learned that they were "free."

> They were disposed (he said) to get into a drunken disposition —I use that expression not in its literal sense—to assert their rights, thinking that such assertion was necessary to their maintenance. . . . (They would) rush right into a church, without any change having taken place, where the white people were sitting; not that they had no place to sit (i.e., the Negro pew) but simply to show their equality.

One Democrat protested bitterly that his female servant refused to milk the cows after her husband began to vote, and generally began "to put on airs around the house."

Negroes were even reported as striking white men, an offense punishable by death under the code in force less than a decade before. At Selma the Negroes were alleged, by the Democrats, to have lynched a white man who had assassinated a Negro policeman. At Tuskegee a Negro politician was shot by a masked band, and another band, this time composed of Negroes, started out from Montgomery to retaliate.

In this troublous time the Conservatives still felt themselves to be "the best friend of the Negro," but they insisted on preserving caste lines in dealing with him. General Clanton was bitter because the Negroes in Montgomery refused to attend "a large barbecue got up of whites and blacks," the idea being to "harmonize and prevent a war of races." He emphasized the fact that "the whites were going to march in to one table and the Negroes the other." Yet he expressed the utmost scorn for the Republican tactics by which the sheriff of Montgomery county solicited the Negro vote; the sheriff "went out to a Negro baptizing about five miles from town, took a bottle of whiskey, let the Negroes drink first, and then drank."

We have said that the Negro masses were agreed on the need for an agrarian reform that would assure them of control of the land. The notion of "forty acres and a mule" appears to have had its origin in the Homestead Act of 1862, when Thaddeus Stevens brought into the debate on the measure the possibility of confiscating the estates of those in the "rebellious states" and dividing the land among the Negroes. This was western agrarianism applied to the South. The creation of a Bureau for Refugees and Abandoned Lands in 1864 had implicit in it the idea of resettlement for stranded white and black populations upon land sequestrated by the government from former enemies.

In Georgia Sherman, following the example of other federal commanders along the seacoast of Carolina, had assented to taking over the Sea Island plantations abandoned by their owners, and had allotted parcels to the Negroes for cultivation. The first Freedmen's Bureau Bill of 1866 provided that unoccupied lands in Florida, Mississippi, Arkansas, Alabama, and Louisiana (not exceeding 3,000,000 acres of good land) should be set aside for refugees and for freedmen. Allotments to individual families were not to exceed forty acres. Andrew Johnson vetoed the bill. In the subsequent debate, Stevens and Trumbull expressed the opinion that the provision of "forty acres and a mule" was more important than the right of the franchise. Stevens said, "Forty acres of land and a hut would be more valuable to him (the Negro) than the immediate right to vote." Trumbull agreed: "I believe a homestead is worth more to these people than almost anything else."

We quote again from Fleming, who used the incident to give point to his story of the brutish ignorance and ridiculous hopes of the recently emancipated Negroes. During the canvass for the Constitutional Convention of 1867, a Negro voter at Selma ". . . held up a blue (Conservative) ticket and cried out, 'No land! no votes! slavery again!' Then holding up a red (Radical) ticket he shouted 'Forty acres of land! a mule! freedom! votes! equal of white man!' "

Our seventy years of perspective may lead us to wonder as to whether the Negro, or Fleming, who ridiculed him, was the wiser advocate of human betterment in the South and in the nation. . . .

There is precedent for linking the long-favored figures of the Reconstruction history to the less romantic forces by which ". . . the planting class was being trampled in the dust —stripped of its wealth and political power—(while)—the capitalist class was marching onward in seven league boots." With an eye to what happened in Alabama, Russ says that the process of disfranchisement in the South "played an important part in producing modern Industrial America," through keeping the "ex-leaders of the South" out of Congress until it was too late to change the new industrial order which had become firmly entrenched in the interim." Whether these grand motives affected policy in Alabama, so far as internal politics was concerned, may be doubted.

What is doubtless is the value of the point of view for interpreting the record of Reconstruction in Alabama, for Alabama was more likely to witness the working of unsuspected economic forces than any other southern state. Its natural resources were unique in the South; and, in an age when coal was power, and iron the other necessity for industry, it was already known that the northern hill country of Alabama had both in unexampled proximity. The bankers in

Philadelphia and New York, and even in London and Paris, had known this for almost two decades. The only thing lacking was transportation.

We propose to examine here the thesis, that the most important elements involved in the Reconstruction of Alabama were the economic factors incident to the state itself and to the times.

The Economic Disaster of War.

Sensational accounts of political and racial struggles during Reconstruction are inducement, frequently, to forget that the Civil War was in itself a first-class economic disaster. If we can imagine France after the Versailles of 1871, or Germany after that of 1919, we may not need to rely too heavily upon the stock figures of carpetbagger or Negro to explain the resulting social and economic prostration of the South. The plantation system of cotton culture, disrupted during the war, was not cured by peace. In Alabama the planters turned from cotton to corn in the declining days of the struggle, when markets had become invisible. Much of the desertion of the fields by Negroes was a response to the internal decay of an economy which no longer had use for a labor force. The recruiting—in most instances by force—of Negro labor by contesting armies was another factor. One is inclined to suspect that planters, Negroes, and governmental agencies were alike helpless and ineffective, not so much as a result of their own failings, but because the entire system had lost its structure. . . .

Local capital was almost annihilated by the war. Vast sums of money were lost through railroad investments charged off to depreciated Confederate currency, although stock holdings in these early lines became the nucleus for many of the bitter political struggles waged by conservative Democrats. The emancipation of Negroes wiped out a class of capital investment estimated at $200,000,000 in 1860, a sum equal to one-half the assessed valuation of property in the entire state. Banks were either ruined at the beginning of the war, or found their capital impaired by compulsory accumulations of Confederate currency.

An assessment in 1860 of state property in the amount of $432,193,654 included the item of $152,278,000 for slaves. The white counties, prior to the War, had forced the levy of heavy taxes upon slaves so that this form of property paid most of the taxes in 1860. In 1865 property was assessed at $128,846,475, and in 1870 at $156,770,387. Taxation for the support of state government in 1860 was $530,107; for county purposes, $309,474; and for towns and cities only $11,590, a total of $651,171 for all taxes levied for the support of state, county, and muncipal government in Alabama in that year. The state expended for common schools in 1860, $272,211, or slightly more than one-half of its total budget.

To maintain state or local expenditures in 1870 on the relatively simple scale of 1860 would have required the levying of taxes nearly three times as high as those collected in the former year. But the expense of maintaining new services set up by the Reconstruction government required a state budget for education alone which exceeded the total revenues of the state in 1860, when three times as much taxable property was assessed. With a 74 percent decrease in assessed valuations, state levies increased 178 percent, county levies 252 percent, and town and city levies 3,385 percent.

Both Democrats and Republicans during Reconstruction were fond of telling the people of the state that taxation in Alabama was, even at Reconstruction rates, lower than existing levies in other parts of the country. However true this may have been, it gave little comfort to the Alabama taxpayers of 1870 who were still in a position to remember their status in 1860.

Reconstruction loses something of its apparent simplicity as an entirely racial or sectional problem in view of but two aspects of this destroyed economic structure: (a) the possibility of tax exemption for various interests, or sectors of interests; and (b) the possibility of exploiting the only source of new wealth available in the state, i.e., its natural resources. To understand this is to understand how transportation became the most important single factor in Reconstruction politics.

Capital in Alabama—Railroads, Coal, and Iron.

In 1850 the "Little Giant," Stephen A. Douglas, visited Alabama, spending most of the time in Mobile. The result of his visit was eminently successful; the Alabama congressional delegation, which in 1848 had been unanimously opposed to the railroad bill of that year as introduced by Douglas, in 1850 furnished the small majority by which it became law. One reason for the change was that the 1850 bill made possible, with later enactments, a grant of 3,077,373 acres to various Alabama roads, in a compromise addition to the terms of the 1848 bill which specified a grant to the Illinois Central. The Alabama roads thus favored were the Mobile and Ohio, planned to make a juncture with the Illinois Central at Cairo; the Selma, Rome, and Dalton; the Alabama and Chattanooga; the South and North Alabama; and the Mobile and Girard.

In 1852 a young man named Jabez Lamar Monroe Curry "traversed the counties of Talladega, Calhoun, and Randolph, making speeches, and obtaining rights of way and subscriptions" for the Alabama and Tennessee River Railroad Company, in which his father was a prominent stockholder. In 1853 this young man was elected to the state legislature from Talladega County, and was immediately appointed chairman of the Committee on Internal Improvements. He held membership also on the Committee on Education. Curry sponsored legislation to give state aid to railroads from his Committee on Internal Improvements. Two measures which had more relationship than one might imagine were also sponsored by Curry; one became the basis for the foundation of the first

[379]

public school system in Alabama, and the second authorized the appointment of a state geologist whose duty it was to survey "the mineral resources, their location, and the best means for their development" in the interests of the state of Alabama.

A fellow member of the legislature of 1853–54 was one Luke Pryor, who had been elected from Madison County. He was "pledged to the work of securing authority to subscribe two hundred thousand dollars to the capital stock of the Tennessee and Alabama Central Railroad, at Nashville and Decatur, and secured the bill raising that tax, enacted over the veto of Governor Winston." Curry's biographers give him the same credit: "His influence in the legislature, *or other undisclosed causes*, served to pass the State aid bills over the Governor's vetoes."

The power behind Luke Pryor was James W. Sloss, described by Armes as Pryor's "side partner in railroad and commercial ventures." Sloss's name is unheralded and unsung in the more romantic annals of Alabama Reconstruction, and yet his influence, on close inspection, will be found connected with every important industrial and commercial enterprise in the state during the latter half of the nineteenth century. Like Curry's father, Sloss had accumulated capital for investment in railroads, not from planting, but from storekeeping. If the ventures of men like Sloss were less spectacular than those of the great planters of the Black Belt, and of his own Tennessee Valley, and if they are less known to history, it is because this was the southern version of the new class of capitalists and industrialists, manipulating great affairs of state in the obscurity of public inattention while public officials basked in the outward gaze of the multitude.

In 1855 Sloss was president of the Tennessee and Alabama Central Railroad, and it was for this line that Luke Pryor "was sent to the State Legislature." Meanwhile, some five hundred miles to the north of Sloss's smaller principality,

James Guthrie, president of the Louisville and Nashville Railroad, "was establishing that road as the political control of the State" of Kentucky. The L. & N. early had visions of extending its empire to the South, and James Sloss's enterprise in Alabama stretched northward toward Nashville, in the same direction which expansion for the L. & N. would, of necessity, involve. It was, perhaps, no accident that James Guthrie, president of the L. & N., in 1860, came into bitter conflict with the supporters of the "Little Giant" at the Charleston convention. In 1860 the candidate for a presidential nominaton was still the former protagonist of the Illinois Central and the Mobile and Ohio Railroads. Could the feud, even this early, have involved the ultimate goal of tapping Alabama's mineral wealth?

The Civil War left Alabama's railroads in poor condition; rolling stock, tracks, bridges, and other equipment were indiscriminately destroyed by contending armies in the ebb and flow of the tide of battle. Such disaster, however, does not seem to have overcome the fortunes of the north Alabama capitalists and politicians who were the associates of James Sloss. Robert Patton, a member of the Sloss north Alabama coterie, had a brother-in-law, J. J. Griers, who was in constant communication with General Grant during the war. Patton was later provisional governor under the short-lived Johnson regime, and during his tenure of office worked in close cooperation with the Sloss interests. George Houston, who became Luke Pryor's law partner in 1866, had a most uncertain record of loyalty to the Confederacy. Samuel Noble, later associated with Sloss in developing the mineral resources of north Alabama, and an ally of William "Pig-Iron" Kelley, traded through the lines with the connivance of Confederate and Federal officials.

The Louisville and Nashville Railroad also emerged from the war with enhanced prospects. As the direct carrier between North and South of the immense federal business, the line had extraordinary profits during the War, and its "wonderful prosperity" then attained continued until 1870. By the end of the war Sloss's railroad interests were already inextricably bound up with the L. & N. In 1865 three small roads in north Alabama, including the Tennessee and Alabama, combined under Sloss's leadership. In 1866 Albert Fink, general superintendent of the L. & N., spoke in his report to the directors as though the Sloss roads were already a part of the L. & N. system, as, indeed, they probably were: ". . . *Decatur and Montgomery Railroad*. This road, when completed, will, by connecting Decatur with Montgomery, Alabama, form a most important link, in the through line from Louisville, to Montgomery, Mobile and Pensacola, and open to the enterprise of Louisville the rich country tributary to the above cities."

By 1867 the L. & N. had come to terms with the Mobile and Ohio, negotiating a ten-year lease of the property. But at Nashville the L. & N. found a strong competitor for the Alabama mineral regions' trade, in the Nashville and Chattanooga. The struggle between the competing interests may be simplified as follows: Should the L. & N. affiliates, by way of the Nashville and Decatur and the proposed Montgomery and Decatur (later the North and South Railroad) have access to Alabama's coal and iron, or should the Nashville and Chattanooga, and its controlling capitalists, win the field through extending a line from Chattanooga to the southwestward along the Tennessee River Valley?

Railroads and Reconstruction: First Phase.

Officially, in the public eye and that of later historians, the actors in this dramatic struggle were, respectively, Republicans and Democrats, fighting for the slogans of "White Supremacy," on the one hand, or "Equal Rights" on the other. Not apparent on the political stage, but working powerfully behind the scenes, were such men as James Guthrie, Albert Fink, and James Sloss of the L. & N.; and V. K. Stevenson, the principal apparent owner of the Nashville and Chattanooga. These men in turn had their masters. A local, but not altogether a minor capitalist, was Josiah Morris, a Montgomery banker, who is listed as a large stockholder and a director of all the Sloss railroad affiliates.

V. K. Stevenson is said to have been supported by "Boston Financiers," made visible in the person of Russell Sage. The L. & N. was financed largely by local Louisville capital, with frequent and sizable contributions from the municipality itself. The name of August Belmont—and this suggests, not only the activity of the chairman of the national Democratic party, but also of the omnipresent and almost omnipotent Rothschilds, of whom he was the American agent—was also linked to the financing of the L. & N., especially in enterprises connected with the opening of Alabama coal fields.

Sam Tate, a prominent figure in Tennessee railroad building and politics, was also a factor in Alabama. Tate was the builder and president of the Memphis and Charleston, a road traversing north Alabama from the Mississippi line, on the west, running just south of the Tennessee River to Decatur, where a bridge had been built, and terminating at Stevenson, with a connecting line from that point to Chattanooga. Like Albert Fink, of the L. & N., Tate had the same vision of the possibilities of exploiting Alabama's mineral resources:

Decatur to Montgomery is another important connection, feeding your entire line with an abundance of iron and coal, with seventy-five miles of your line, from which tonnage for local consumption would alone be profitable, to say nothing of the immense amount of western produce you would carry over your lines to feed the thousands of operatives that will be employed in developing the vast resources of mineral wealth in the mountains south of Decatur. Your fostering aid and care should be extended to this road, too, as early as practicable, as it will be one of its most productive arteries.

Indeed, at this time (1866) a close cooperation was in effect between the L. & N., represented by Fink, and the Memphis and Charleston, as represented by Tate. Fink rebuilt the bridge for the Memphis and Charleston at Decatur which had been destroyed during the War. Tate got the contract for building the road he and Fink had proposed.

By act of February 19, 1867, the General Assembly of Alabama embarked on the adventure of giving the state endorsement to railroad bonds of certain extant companies, in the amount of $12,000 a mile. This legislation was enacted in the face of impending congressional reconstruction. This was the provisional assembly, with Governor Robert Patton, north Alabamian, and associate of Sloss, in control; and the endorsements included only those roads which were controlled by the coterie associated with Sloss. The South and North, the Montgomery and Eufaula, the Montgomery and Mobile, the Northeast and the Southwest, and the Wills Valley roads were the beneficiaries. An examination of the directorates of these railroads will show the presence of Sloss, of Pryor, of Houston, of Morris; i.e., the leading politico-capitalists who figured in the Democratic (Conservative) party during Reconstruction.

When a Republican General Assembly was convened on July 13, 1868—the work of railroad endorsement had been done hurriedly in the waning days of the provisional assembly, when pending bills in Congress assured Republican control by the next year—a brief period ensued during which strange industrial and capitalistic bedfellows made political peace for mutual profit.

The Wills Valley and the Northeast and Northwest roads were combined and incorporated as the Alabama and Chattanooga. The formal date of the merger was October 6, 1868. In a series of acts of the General Assembly during the session of 1868–69, the state endorsement for railroad bonds was increased from $12,000 to $16,000 a mile. The increased endorsement was not a "Republican" grab; for a brief period Sloss enjoyed a paramount interest in the South and North, and the Alabama and Chattanooga, which became the particular beneficiaries of the raised endorsement. Robert Patton, his associate in politics and business, and formerly governor under the provisional government, became a vice-president of the new Alabama and Chattanooga road, whose bonds he had aided in endorsing shortly before as governor. John T. Milner, engineer of the South and North, and John C. Stanton, who held a like responsibility with the Alabama and Chattanooga, joined in bribing members of the assembly. A history of industrialization in Alabama, bearing the official approval of the Birmingham Chamber of Commerce, has this account of the manner in which the finances of the South and North were rescued under Republican rule: "Mr. John T. Milner, Engineer of the Road, said that John Whiting, a Montgomery cotton factor, President of the South and North Railroad, told him 'he spurned the idea of getting among these Yankees at all, much less of paying them for their votes,' but he said that 'I might do so if I felt like it. So I went.'"

Milner's ventures were financed principally by Josiah Morris, the Montgomery banker. Stanton was the field agent of Russell Sage. The South and North, as an extension of the main line of the Louisville and Nashville, through 1868–69 apparently had a working agreement with the Alabama and Chattanooga, through which the two lines were to be connected at a strategic point in the mineral region where a great industrial city would be built. The legislators were generous both with the South and North, planned to run from Montgomery to Decatur and there to connect with the L. & N., and with the Alabama and Chattanooga, which was planned to run from Chattanooga across the state to Meridian, and from there, eventually, to New Orleans. In 1868 the South and North received the 2 and 3 percent funds as a loan from the state. By February 5, 1870, the Alabama and Chattanooga was loaned $2,000,000 by the state.

A recounting of the liabilities assumed for these two railroad systems shows that between 1867 and 1871–under, first, a provisional, "Conservative" government, and, later, under a "Radical" Republican government—the state incurred what have been called *debts* of approximately $17,000,000 in endorsements and loans. Of this amount L. & N. affiliates (the South and North, the Montgomery and Eufaula, etc.) accounted for $7,000,000; while obligations assumed for the Alabama and Chattanooga, and railroads represented in this merger, equalled approximately $10,000,000. Since the Alabama "debt" at the end of Reconstruction has been estimated at a maximum of $30,000,000, and $9,000,000 represented ante-Reconstruction obligations, it is obvious how largely the manipulations of these two railroad systems alone entered into the final financial picture of the period.

The apparent cooperation of the two groups of capitalists —the L. & N. group, on the one hand, and the Alabama and Chattanooga (Russell Sage) on the other—came to an end in November, 1870. The Democratic candidate for governor, Lindsay, was elected over his Republican opponent, with a Democratic lower house and a Republican hold-over senate. An agreement had been reached between the sponsors of the lines financed by the Louisville and Nashville, and the Alabama and Chattanooga, to locate the crossing of the railroad at a certain site in Jefferson County. The Stanton brothers, of the Alabama and Chattanooga (agents for Russell Sage), had taken options on the land surrounding the proposed crossing. A group of Alabama capitalists, including Josiah Morris, W. S. Mudd, F. M. Gilmer, James W. Sloss, and others, took options on a new site, and, unknown to the Stantons, changed the route of the South and North so that it intersected with the Alabama and Chattanooga through the area which they controlled.

The triumph of the local capitalists threatened to be of but brief duration. V. K. Stevenson and Russell Sage had acquired a majority of the $2,200,000 worth of bonds issued by the state in endorsing the building of the South and North. They now (1871) threatened to foreclose on their mortgage, demanding as an alternative that the South and North, already constructed from Montgomery to the Alabama and Chattanooga crossing, be turned over to the latter railroad for operation.

In this crisis Albert Fink, said already to have had an agreement with James Sloss, "and at all times a helper and cooperator, along with Luke Pryor and George Houston, of the South and North," met the backers of the L. & N. at a hastily convened conference in Louisville. Perhaps ratifying a convention already in force, the L. & N. agreed to take open and complete control of the South and North, averted Russell Sage's threatened foreclosure, and dated the agreement as of May 19, 1871.

The point of these intraindustrial feuds to our discussion is that they dominated every political maneuver that took place in the state during these troublous times. The Democratic and Republican parties in Alabama, viewed from this angle, seem to have been only the obverse aspects of the L. & N. Railroad on the one hand, and the Alabama and Chattanooga Railroad on the other. The political tactics developed during this struggle were strikingly similar to contemporary developments in other states.

In Kentucky and Tennessee the L. & N. was said to "hide behind the City of Louisville" in its classic feud with Cincinnati. Promoters in the latter city proposed to build a road from Cincinnati to Chattanooga which would become the natural competitor of the L. & N. Unable to obtain capital elsewhere, the promoters managed to get a grant of $10,000,000 from the city of Cincinnati itself. The L. & N. "ably supported Louisville in this fight," against the threatened competition from the sister city on the Ohio. When proposed legislative aid to the Cincinnati-sponsored road was pending in the Kentucky Legislature, ". . . it was claimed by the friends of the bill that this gigantic corporation (i.e., the L. & N.) was the main source of opposition, trying to hide behind the City (Louisville)." The L. & N. adopted as its principal tactical weapon in Kentucky, identification with the political, social, and ideological pattern of the stricken South. "Isaac Caldwell, who was one of Louisville's stanchest defenders, accused Cincinnati of helping to vote Negro suffrage upon Kentucky, and then immediately coming and asking a special favor for doing so." Louisville (i.e., the L. & N.) hired merchants ". . . to go South and appeal to the disloyalty of their political record to seduce custom, and when they find that the South demands a better market than she affords, it again appeals to the more sectional feeling at home to prevent the South from getting to that market." If there is any truth in this partisan accusation, it is the suggestion that capital—as represented by the L. & N.—preceded the politicians in appealing to racial and sectional interests. The fact that the L. & N. in Alabama was closely identified with local capitalists, while the Alabama and Chattanooga had such men as the "Stantons of Boston" in the chief place of prominence in operations there, is an important key to politics in the state during the crucial years of Reconstruction. . . .

Industrial Conflict and Debt, 1871–76.

With this background, both political and industrial conflict in Alabama during the latter stages of Reconstruction becomes understandable. Reference has been made above to the close cooperation existing between the officials of the affiliated lines of the L. & N. in Alabama, and the Democratic administration elected in the fall of 1870. According to the terms of state endorsements, the state was liable for interest payments in the event of defaults by the roads. The Alabama and Chattanooga defaulted payment of interest due immediately after the new Democratic administration went into office, as of January 1, 1871. Governor Lindsay did not take over the road at that time, stating that to do so would acknowledge the validity of the grants to the road, which his faction rejected as the corrupt malpractice of the prior Republican administration. When the railroad made its second default in June, 1871 (two weeks after the Louisville and Nashville had contracted to take over the South and North), Lindsay had different advice from his supporters; and he seized the road for the state, and appointed Colonel Gindrat and James H. Clanton as receivers. Clanton was, at the time, chairman of the Democratic State Executive Committee. He was also a director of the Montgomery and Eufaula road, soon to become officially an affiliate of the L. & N. system. Among his fellow directors were Josiah Morris, of Montgomery, and Bolling Hall, politician, director of the South and North, and one of the founders of the Elyton Land Company.

Clanton is frequently quoted in Fleming's work on Reconstruction as a paragon of pure political motive. The Montgomery and Eufaula railroad, with the Alabama and Chattanooga, was a beneficiary of the extensive endorsements and state loans negotiated during the prior period. In 1871 Clanton was killed in a brawl in Knoxville by one Nelson, who was employed by the Stanton, or Alabama and Chattanooga interests. There is a certain irony in Fleming's eulogy of Clanton: "He was killed in Knoxville by a hireling of one of the railroad companies which had looted the state treasury and which he was fighting."

The Alabama and Chattanooga dragged through a long period of litigation during the next few years. From July, 1871, to October, 1872, it was operated by the state. The interest on the A. & C. bonds alone amounted to $500,000 a year.

In 1872 David P. Lewis, Republican, was elected governor of Alabama. Lewis immediately took steps to relieve the state of the devastating interest payments which had accumulated with successive defaults, following that of the Alabama and Chattanooga. By an agreement negotiated in the spring of 1873, the railroad companies, through an act known as the "$4,000 a mile law," agreed to turn in their $16,000-a-mile bonds, and to receive back $4,000-a-mile straight state bonds, thus reducing the state liability by 75 percent. In December of 1873, Governor Lewis stated that all of the roads involved had filed notice of their acceptance of the act.

It is strange that but little attention has been given to the effect of the Panic of 1873 upon the course of Reconstruction in the South. The failure of Jay Cooke removed from the scene, not only a heavy investor in southern railroads, but also an "angel" of the Republican party in the section; and left supreme in the field of these investments the combined forces of the Drexels and the rising Junius S. Morgan. While these circumstances may be of speculative interest here, they are worthy of study.

The majority of the Alabama and Chattanooga bonds had passed into the hands of a "group of English capitalists." The accumulation of defaulted interest payments reached a peak in 1873, in the financial panic of that year. Even the L. & N. was completely prostrated. An operating deficit of $568,362 for the entire system in 1873 was laid at the doors of the South and North. "The prostration of the iron industries has greatly retarded the development of the rich mineral resources along the lines of that road, which had been greatly relied upon for supplying it with a profitable business." The result was that the L. & N. went into bankruptcy and the ownership of the line passed finally and completely from whatever local capitalists had shared in its major control before into eastern and European hands.

The financial crisis made the election of 1874 of paramount importance to the persons involved, who saw an opportunity to rescue from the general wreckage whatever salvage might be had. Industrial conflict, accordingly, was sharply focused in political conflict. The strictly racial and sectional interpretation of the period by Fleming is likely to suggest that all of the corruption visible in Alabama was an outcome of Black Republican thievery. We may say that the basic economic issue of the campaign of 1874 in Alabama was to determine which of the financial interests involved would be able to make the best possible settlement with a state government bankrupted by the earnest efforts of both. Certain facts add piquancy to the general notion that Reconstruction in Alabama was a tightly drawn struggle between Virtue, as represented by the Democrats, and Vice, as represented by the Republicans.

Henry Clews, an associate of Jay Cooke, and a heavy investor in southern issues, was among the most prominent of the bankers holding the Alabama railroad bonds which lay in the scale of battle. Clews boasted of having negotiated Dix's nomination as governor of New York, which, he believed, made Grant's renomination certain. His interest in Alabama, he said, was motivated by a noble-hearted impulse "to help the South and to help develop its resources." He added, almost as an afterthought, that he had considered Alabama as the most profitable place for investment on account of its manifest industrial advantages over the North in the years immediately after the war. Writing of the "repudiation" of Alabama issues owned by him, after the final victory of the Democrats, he laid it to "political manipulation." In addition to investments in state issues, Clews was associated with Samuel Noble and William D. "Pig-Iron" Kelley in financing the Oxford Iron Works at Anniston, which lay along the right-of-way of the Alabama and Chattanooga, and was a director of the Selma and Gulf Railroad (projected to run from Selma to Pensacola), advertised as forming "the most practicable route from the coal fields and valuable deposits of iron from Alabama, to the harbor of Pensacola."

The election of 1874 determined the fate of the Republican party in Alabama. George Houston, poetically represented in Democratic literature and in Fleming's account as "The Bald Eagle of the Mountains," and as the defender of "White Supremacy," was elected by a large majority. Neither the campaign literature nor Fleming referred to his close cooperation and participation in the Sloss and L. & N. enterprises. Almost too innocently, Fleming states that: "The campaign fund was the largest in the history of the State; every man who was able, and many who were not, contributed; assistance also came from Northern Democrats, and Northern Capitalists who had investments in the South or *who owned part of the legal* bonds of the State." * As the "legality" of the bonds had not been determined at the time when these gentlemen made their contributions, the discrimination seems doubtful. Obviously the "Northern Capitalists" who contributed to the Democratic fund did so *in the hope that with Democratic victory the bonds they owned would be declared legal by the new government.* Nordhoff, a witness whose verdict was uncompromisingly against the Republican regime, said that "where conspicuous financial jobbery took place (in railroad legislation) Democrats have, oftener than not, been parties in interest." Let us not forget what has already been noted: that as a specific effect of the Panic of 1873, it was the misfortune of the Republicans to enter the election of 1874 a year after the house of Jay Cooke had drawn Henry Clews with it to failure.

There is a final incident to this industrial epic that may or may not have had a connection with the end of Reconstruction in Alabama in 1874, and in other states soon thereafter. On December 21, 1874, at Macon, Georgia, was formed what has been described as the "most efficient railroad pool in the

* Italics added.

United States, largely owing to the genius of Albert Fink as manager."

Sharp competition first appeared after prostration by the Civil War, when it was soon discovered that there were more roads than available traffic. Agreements to restore and maintain charges alternated for a time with the most destructive rate wars. . . . Bankruptcy and ruin in railroad affairs were widespread. Permanent success was finally wrought out of such chaos by the first General Commissioner, who perfected an agreement in 1875 which proved lasting.

The pool rejoiced in the innocent name of "The Southern Railroad and Steamship Company." It allayed competition and facilitated the growth of several great systems where the highly individualistic small lines had flourished theretofore. Coincident with the formation of this pool, it is interesting to note certain changes in the directorates of many of the southern lines as reported for 1875–76, and contrasted with the same lists for 1868–69. J. Pierpont Morgan, in 1875–76, appears as a director for several of the Alabama and Georgia lines, including the Mobile and Montgomery, an L. & N. affiliate. Josiah Morris appears as a member of the directorate of the Mobile and Montgomery, the Western Railroad of Alabama (a Central of Georgia affiliate), and the South and North (L. & N. affiliate). H. B. Plant, founder of the Plant system, appears as director of the Western Railroad of Alabama.

The election of Governor Houston in 1874 provided an opportunity for the settlement of the "debt" of Alabama, as pledged by the winning party. The debt settlement is supposed to have been framed by a state senator, Rufus W. Cobb, "and others." Cobb, according to a biographical sketch, "devised the plan of readjustment for the state debt which Governor Houston submitted to the legislature after elaboration. He was the friend and admirer of Governor Houston during his administration." Cobb was also president of the Central Iron and Coal Works at Helena, which was subsidized by the L. & N. In addition, he was a local attorney for the L. & N.

Governor Houston began his administration with the expressed desire of settling the "debt." It should be kept in mind here that "debts" are either paid or repudiated; and those who, following Fleming, state that the "Reconstruction Debt" in Alabama amounted to from $25,000,000 to $30,000,000, need to ask themselves how a "debt" of this size, existing at the accession of Houston in 1874, could become a "debt" of less than $10,000,000 through his adjustments without actual repudiation. Certainly the Alabama "debt" was adjusted; but there was no repudiation. It will appear in the following paragraphs that the Alabama "debt" of $25,000,000 to $30,000,000 was not, at any time, an actual "debt," but always a potential one; and that if it had been, or become, an "actual debt," the state would have owned all of the railroads endorsed by it as compensation for the "debt" assumed. The long-heralded triumph of Governor Houston's "debt settlement" actually will be seen to have consisted in relieving the state of its "potential debt," and the railroads of the threat of state foreclosure on mortgages held by it, on grounds highly advantageous to the railroads; or, at least, to those railroad systems with which the leadership of the Alabama Democracy was on a fairly intimate basis.

As his "debt commissioners" Governor Houston appointed Levi W. Lawler, T. B. Bethea, and himself as *ex-officio* chairman. T. B. Bethea does not appear as a director or stockholder in any published records of these facts. Levi W. Lawler was reported in 1868 and 1870 as a director of the Selma, Rome, and Dalton, a competing road to the Alabama and Chattanooga; Peter Hamilton, listed with Rufus Cobb as one of the men responsible for the debt settlement in preliminary negotiations, is recorded as a Mobile and Ohio (an L. & N.

subsidiary) director in 1868, and in 1870–71. Houston was a director of the Nashville and Decatur (an L. & N. affiliate) in 1868 and 1870; his law partner, Luke Pryor, whom he followed to Washington as United States Senator from Alabama, was a director of the South and North (an L. & N. subsidiary) in 1870 and in 1875.

The Report of the Debt Commissioners prefaced an analysis of the nature of state obligations by saying that the "direct and contingent indebtedness of the State is $30,000,000." For political purposes, these obligations had been talked about during the campaign as though they were a "direct" debt; and the historians have not distinguished between the two classes. As suggested above, the greater part of this "debt" was "*contingent*"; that is to say, it would become a direct debt only in the event that the state foreclosed its mortgages upon the railroad property, leaving the state in debt, indeed, to bondholders, to the amount of the endorsements and loans, but at the same time possessed of the valuable railroad properties as compensation.

The Debt Commission divided the said "indebtedness" into four classes. Class I was defined as including:

. . . bonds issued or loaned to railroad companies (consisting) of bonds bearing five, six, and eight per cent interest; bonds issued for temporary loans; bonds hypothecated with and sold by the New York Guaranty and Indemnity Company, on account of a temporary loan; bonds hypothecated with and sold by agencies appointed by the United States District Court, in bankrupt cases; State obligations, bearing eight per cent interest; State Certificates, known as "Patton money"; Trust funds, and some small claims against the State.

This class of indebtedness amounted to $11,677,470, including $1,050,000 of unpaid interest. The great portion of this debt had accumulated prior to Republican rule in 1868; when this party had taken over control in 1868, the state bonded debt was $6,848,400, with $2,494,654.87 of additional state funds which had been dissipated, but still involved the state in interest payments. Obligations in Class I which might be laid to "Reconstruction extravagance" therefore accounted for approximately one million of the total.

Class I debts were "settled" by a refunding operation by which the state was granted a lower rate of interest and the cancellation of past due interest payments.

Class II amounted to $1,156,000. They represented the liability of the state for railroad endorsements compromised under the law of 1873, in Governor Lewis' administration, when the railroads had exchanged $4,000-a-mile bonds for the prior bonds valued at $18,000-a-mile. By this means the state had, by 1874, reduced its liability by retiring $5,103,000 worth of endorsed bonds.

Class II debts were "settled" by exchanging endorsement bonds for one-half of their face value; in other words, admitted the commission, the "State accepted a clear loss of one-half." The roads so favored were the (James Sloss-George Houston-Luke Pryor) L. & N. affiliate, the South and North; the Grand Trunk; and the Savannah and Memphis.

Class III debts are called by Fleming "the worst of all." They totalled $2,573,093. These obligations included $600,000 of claims rendered by the South and North, of which Governor Houston's law partner, Luke Pryor, was a director, and in which, as we have seen, the omnipresent James W. Sloss had been from the first a prominent figure. Governor Houston himself had been a director of the affiliated L. & N. company, the Nashville and Decatur, in 1868 and in 1870. The South and North claims were actually L. & N. claims, since the company was a subsidiary of the greater line.

Regarding these claims, the Debt Commission, of which, it will be remembered, Governor Houston was chairman, stated: "It is not our province to make any suggestion in regard to the claim of the South and North . . . . They are not connected in any way with the bonded debt of the State, and do not come within the scope of our investigation and adjustment."

But this $600,000 had been included in the "debt" as originally claimed by the Democrats, and as quoted by later historians. To disregard it was one of the simpler devices for "settlement" and "reduction" adopted by the Debt Commission.

The commission dealt less kindly with $1,464,689 of obligations which involved the banking house of Henry Clews & Company. Clews, we have observed, was a banking associate of Jay Cooke, and in Alabama had investments at Anniston in the Oxford Iron Works along with Samuel Noble, erstwhile trader-between-the-lines, and William D. "Pig-Iron" Kelley. Clews's interests had been with the Alabama and Chattanooga, the Russell Sage, Republican sponsored road that was intent on invading the Alabama Mineral District from the direction of Chattanooga as the L. & N. was similarly bent on tapping this region from the North.

Mr. Clews's autobiography states simply, but eloquently, that the Debt Commission was motivated by "political manipulations" in disposing of his claims. This was their solemn pronouncement regarding the Clews obligation: "The State is liable only for the amount of the debt which was due to Clews and Co., amounting to about three hundred and ten thousand dollars, with interest. This amount is all that we recommend to be arranged by the State; and as to which of the claimants it belongs we do not undertake to decide." It was in this manner that another million of the "debt" was settled.

Class IV "debts" amounted to $14,641,000. They consisted of endorsed bonds on the basis of $16,000 a mile which had not been compromised under the $4,000-a-mile law. The total obligation, on inspection by the commission, was scaled down to $11,597,000, excluding $3,024,000 in loans due from the Alabama and Chattanooga and the Montgomery and Eufaula with unpaid interest. The "scaled down" figure of $11,597,000 included $5,300,000 worth of endorsements at $16,000-a-mile for the Alabama and Chattanooga, $3,474,000 worth of unpaid interest, and a $2,000,000 loan from the state to the Alabama and Chattanooga.

It has been pointed out above that Governor Lindsay, Democrat, had thrown the Alabama and Chattanooga into the hands of the state in 1871. Extensive litigation had resulted, the bondholders, most of whom were English, claiming that the state had deliberately wrecked the road. Considering the fact that Clanton, whom Lindsay appointed as one of the receivers, was also executive chairman of the State Democratic Committee, as well as a leading figure in the competing L. & N. affiliates, the complaint had at least plausibility. The Debt Commission compromised the claims of the English bondholders by (a) paying them $1,000,000, thus disposing of the alleged $9,000,000 of indebtedness charged against the state in this connection, and (b) transferring to the owners of the railroad's first mortgage bonds more than a half million acres of land, in the heart of the rich mineral region, and which later became the scene of extensive industrialization in Alabama.

The remaining items of endorsement, involving the Montgomery and Eufaula, the East Alabama and Cincinnati, the Selma and Gulf, the Selma, Marion and Memphis, and the New Orleans and Selma, were in litigation at the time of the committee report. The commission stated that the action of the court would probably result in nullifying the purported liability of the state, and that the interests of the bondholders would best be served by "their acceptance of a transfer of the lien of the State created by statute, and giving to the State a full discharge from those pretended claims against it." In other words, the Debt Commission itself denominated as "pretended claims" large amounts which it afterward proudly claimed to have "settled," and which historians have accepted as the "Alabama Debt."

The final report of the Debt Commission stated that: "the volume of indebtedness of the State, including State obligations, will be reduced to about $9,500,000 *exclusive of trust funds.*" Since the commission had begun its first report by stating that the debt amounted to more than $30,000,000, this immense reduction was hailed as a triumph of Democratic honesty over Republican extravagance. It has been so regarded by practically all historians. More interesting still, the myth of an immense debt of $30,000,000, crushing the people of Alabama for two generations, has persisted along with the paradoxical belief that the Democratic party, immediately on its return to power, rescued the state from an immense load of debt. To all intents and purposes, the debt existed for purposes of Democratic propaganda in the election of 1874; it ceased to exist in 1875–76 for the purpose of showing Democratic honesty; but it has always existed to show how great was the ruin wreaked upon the state by the Republican Reconstruction government.

Fleming's conclusion to a discussion of the debt situation remains in evidence as *the* perfect document:

There was not an honest white person who lived in the State during Reconstruction, nor a man, woman or child, descended from such a person, who did not then suffer or does not still suffer from the direct results of the carpet-bag financiering. Homes were sold or mortgaged; schools were closed, and children grew up in ignorance; the taxes for nearly twenty years were used to pay interest on the debt then piled up. Not until 1899 was there a one-mill school tax (until then the interest paid on the Reconstruction debt was larger than the school fund), and not until 1891 was the state able to care for the disabled Confederate soldiers.

Knight states that one of the reasons for the backwardness of Alabama in education was the fact that "upon Alabama was heaped a debt of $18,000,000." Cubberly states, similarly, that the Reconstruction government caused backwardness in the schools through "wasting of resources."

These statements may be seen to be exaggerated and incorrect, especially when they lay blame for immense "debts" upon "Negro," "Republican" regimes in Alabama. There was no "Negro" government; no such debts were left after Reconstruction; and what debts were created resulted from the activities of various capitalists working through both Republican and Democratic party channels. The debt settlement of 1876 left the residual obligations of the state government, including both bonded debt and the various trust funds for which the state was responsible, at approximately $12,000,000. It has been shown, above, that these same obligations in 1868, when the Reconstruction government took control, amounted approximately to $9,500,000.

What is true is that in the negotiations leading up to the refunding of the debt the holders of various state obligations drove a hard bargain with the Debt Commission regarding future tax policy. The Constitutional Convention of 1875 was in session while the debt negotiations were being held, and the articles adopted on taxation and finance were dictated by the arrangement with the bondholders. Considering their financial affiliations, it can be readily imagined that Governor Houston and his fellow-committeemen were all too eager to comply. On October 16, 1875, the convention was reported on the verge of complete repudiation; a combination of Black Belt Conservatives, not in the "ring," with hill country "radicals," were all for making trouble for the Debt Commission and its mission. The Committee on Taxation of the convention reported that they had advised with General L. W. Lawler and Colonel T. B. Bethea, two of the three debt commissioners. These men were sanguine that the "debt" could be "reduced" from $30,000,000 to $10,000,000 through their negotiations, and advised the convention to limit state tax levies to a maximum impost of .0075 on the dollar. If this were done, the debt commissioners believed that "capital, seeing that our debt is reduced and our taxing power limited, will seek investment in our cheap lands, and population, always following capital, will fill up our waste places . . . . Capital (will see) that our property will enhance in value."

In a letter written by the debt commissioners to the bondholders, dated December 30, 1875, it is revealed that the latter had made various suggestions regarding ways in which the expenses of the state could be cut, so as to allow payment of interest due on state obligations. One method suggested was to cut the size of appropriations made to the schools. A second was to save money by cutting down the expenses of feeding prisoners. In fact, the two fundamental antisocial weaknesses in Alabama's state government to comparatively modern times, i.e., poor schools and the convict lease system, were specifically suggested by the bondholders as possible sources of needed revenue.

During debate in the Alabama House on a proposed tax bill, the estimate of the Debt Commission was taken as a guide for the House Committee. The Debt Commission estimated a total income of $1,066,000 would derive from a seven and one-half mill levy. State expenses were estimated:

State Government	$400,000
Interest, Trust Fund	100,000
Appropriation, School	100,000
Interest, Univ. Fund	24,000
Interest, A. & M. Bonds	20,280
Interest, State Obligations	54,000
Total	$698,280

This would leave $367,720 to pay interest on the various debts. The refunding arrangement operated so that on several classes of obligations the interest began five years from the date of settlement, while on others interest was set at a low figure for the first few years. The only provisions made for the support of schools were (a) the "Interest on the Trust Fund"; this meant that the interest upon the fictitious literary fund which had been dissipated in the failure of the state bank twenty years before, would be appropriated by the legislature yearly to the support of the schools; and, (b), a yearly appropriation of $100,000 from the state treasury. The constitution imbedded in the organic law of the state a fixed state tax levy maximum. This, together with the graduation of interest payments to increase over a period of years, and the constitutional prohibition of local taxation for schools, effectually estopped any major increases in appropriations for schools so long as the constitution of 1875 remained in force.

CONCLUSION

The story of Reconstruction, as viewed in the foregoing pages, admittedly needs elaboration; it concerns itself unduly neither with whites, nor with blacks; with the state legislature, nor with the senate; with carpetbaggers, nor with scalawags; nor even with the senators, congressmen, governors, legislators, and other factotums usually accorded major attention.

Our story has sought to identify great social and economic forces whose working in Alabama during Reconstruction gives to the period the quality of inevitable, inexorable pressure and response, action and reaction. These forces are none the less significant because they lack tangible form, and frequently defy exact statistical description.

We have seen that the land—Mother Earth—attracted and repelled different social and economic classes of white migrants, and so moulded the shape of institutions, and the ecology of their distribution. We have seen, further, that man-made institutions could become the source of attitudes which reciprocally reinforced the strength of the institution. The geography of Alabama determined the boundaries of the plantation system of cotton culture, and, together with the source of the migrants, defined the structure of chattel slavery in the state. The institution of chattel slavery in turn required the development of an elaborate set of mental attitudes bulwarking its structure. Social and economic classes among white persons depended for their form upon the nature of the land and the nature of the institution of Negro slavery, as well as upon "natural" principles of economic stratification. Each of these diversifying factors affected the institutions maintained, and, consequently, the attitudes derivative from them.

The natural endowment of the state with resources for an industrial civilization attracted capital bent on exploiting this mineral wealth. Our perspective enables us to perceive that accumulations of capital, and the men who controlled them, were as unaffected by attitudinal prejudices as it is possible to be. Without sentiment, without emotion, those who sought profit from an exploitation of Alabama's natural resources turned other men's prejudices and attitudes to their own account, and did so with skill and a ruthless acumen. Meanwhile, there were men of sentiment who had a mixed vision of another kind of social structure—the northern humanitarians, the landless whites and the landless Negroes. Reconstruction in Alabama, during its first stages, was affected by nineteenth century humanitarianism, as it was finally determined by nineteenth century capital expansion and exploitation. A decadent and paralyzed agrarian structure founded on chattel slavery, in combination with political and economic forces working on a nationwide scale, witnessed the defeat of the humanitarian ideal and the triumph of the capital investor. Since, politically, humanitarianism, as it had power to affect the government of the South, died with Thaddeus Stevens in 1868, Reconstruction after that date may be signalized as a struggle between different financiers. The Panic of 1873, and the collapse of one of the contestants as a result, paved the way for the general peace that came in the period from 1874–76.

In this retrospect such institutions as the Louisville and Nashville Railroad, the Alabama and Chattanooga Railroad, the Union League (considered as an instrument of northern capital), the banking houses of the Cookes, of Russell Sage, of the Morgans and the Drexels loom more significantly in Alabama Reconstruction than do the time-honored figures of the history books. Such personalities as James W. Sloss, Josiah Morris, Albert Fink, Henry Clews, Jay Cooke, William Kelley, Luke Pryor, Russell Sage, and V. K. Stevenson assume larger proportions than all of the governors and legislators of whom such full account has been taken in the past.

We may even be tempted to conclude that the carpetbaggers, the scalawags, "Nigger domination," and even the Ku Klux Klan, were not the principal heroes, or the villains, of the Reconstruction period in Alabama.

18

SOUTHERN RECONSTRUCTION:
A Radical View

Jack B. Scroggs

By utilizing the hitherto neglected correspondence of southern Radicals, Jack B. Scroggs has illuminated the internal workings of Reconstruction, the nature of the factional disputes, and the relationship between the state Republican parties and the national leadership.

The advent of Radical Republican leadership in the reconstruction of the recently rebellious states of the South in early 1867 resulted in sweeping changes in both the form and substance of government in this conquered area. Of revolutionary political significance, this shift brought to the fore a new group of leaders gathered from Negroes, the heretofore politically submerged class of native whites, and recently arrived northerners. The fortunes of this unusual alliance, especially during the early phase of Reconstruction, depended largely upon the success of the Radical party in Congress, a circumstance which led to widespread efforts by state leaders to establish a close liaison with the national party. Correspondence from the southern Republicans to congressional Radicals discloses many of the problems which they encountered and presents Reconstruction from a point of view frequently ignored by many historians. Here is found an intimate record of local political leaders striving to revamp southern political institutions despite the determined opposition of southern spokesmen trained in the school of conservatism. This task, ambitious at best, was made increasingly difficult by intraparty factionalism on the state and local level and by the failure to maintain close cooperation between the national Republican leadership and the Radical party in the South. A cross section of regional Radicalism, based on the voluminous correspondence from the South Atlantic states—Virginia, North and South Carolina, Georgia, and Florida—clearly reveals these difficulties inherent in the organization of state parties dedicated to radical reform within the framework of a national party rapidly evolving as the agent of conservative interests.

The return to power of traditional political leaders in 1865 and 1866 touched off an initial storm of protest from southern Radicals. Union men vigorously charged that these former rebels continued to be hostile toward the government and could not be trusted with the job of reconstructing the economy, politics, and society of the South. From North Carolina and Virginia came complaints that rebels held the offices of "trust, honor, or emolument" to the exclusion and proscription of men loyal to the Union. An observer in North Carolina asserted that "the feelings of by far the larger proportion of the people of this State are disloyal to the Govt—and enamored by the bitterest hatred towards the North." He expressed the view that the duplicity of southern leaders led observers like General Grant to form hasty and erroneous opinions of their loyalty. Thaddeus Stevens, Radical leader in the House, received a report from Georgia that the rebellious spirit in that state was greater than when the state seceded from the Union. Former rebels were accused of tampering with the mails and practicing discrimination in the courts; one North Carolinian expressed fear of mob violence should the rebels discover that he had written to Charles Sumner.

Initially this proscriptive attitude was displayed most prominently toward southerners who had resisted the Confederacy, but northerners and freedmen complained of similar treatment. The assistant superintendent of the Freedmen's Bureau at Harpers Ferry declared that "to be an Officer of the US is to subject one to continual insult, without the power of redress." Protesting against the action of the Georgia convention of 1865 in requiring two years prior residence for voting, a recent immigrant to that state wrote to Thaddeus Stevens: "The loyal men thousands in number now residing in Georgia appeal to you to save them from this rebel act which has been passed to disfranchise them because they are loyal." The former rebels were accused not only of being unwilling to extend any considerable rights and privileges to the Negroes, but also of subjecting them to abuse and refusing to encourage them to labor for themselves. A Georgia correspondent, refuting the claim that the Negro was indolent, maintained that "the Southern people as a whole, are not faithful or true exponents of the negroe's [sic] character or his ability." Negro testimony in a similar vein came from freedmen at Halifax, North Carolina, who requested aid from Elihu B. Washburne in collecting a fund to allow them to emigrate to Liberia. They complained that landowners would not let land to black men and they were unable to collect their wages, in arrears for two years. Seeing no hope for freedom in the South, they lamented: "There is nothing in this country for a blackman that has comon sence but cruelty starvation & bloodshed." Also from North Carolina came the warning that the "protection afforded on account of property interest, and the social attachments of Master & Slave are destroyed, and now God have mercy on the blacks, if they are turned over to the government of their old masters, who seem determined to prove emancipation a curse." Southern Radicals argued that Congress should remove the ex-Confederates from office and place Reconstruction in the hands of loyal Union men. Although not wholly responsible for the changing attitude of Congress, these pleas undoubtedly exerted considerable influence in crystallizing congressional action against the relatively lenient policies of President Johnson.

With the overthrow of the Johnson-supported state governments by the Reconstruction Acts of 1867, the three factions of southern Republicans saw no further impediment in the path toward reform and personal aggrandizement. The exuberant Radicals suggested that the incumbent state officers be immediately dismissed and replaced by loyal Republicans. Although congressional Radicals refused to aid southern Republicans to this extent, the influence of Radicals in the South began to show a remarkable growth. Negro meetings called by southern Conservatives tended to evolve into Radical rallies. The freedmen, safely under the control of carpetbag leadership, refused to respond to Conservative overtures, preferring to remain with the party which promised to preserve their political and civil rights.

Armed with the twin weapons of Negro enfranchisement and partial white disfranchisement, southern Radicals faced the convention elections of the autumn of 1867 with unbounded confidence. From Augusta, Georgia, a local Republican wrote: "We are going to carry Ga for a Convention and frame a Radical Constitution with a *Liberal disfranchising* clause for rebels." John T. Deweese, a leading carpetbagger in North Carolina, anticipated carrying the convention election by twenty or thirty thousand votes and declared that the Republicans could carry the state for either Grant or Salmon P. Chase in the 1868 presidential election. From Florida carpetbaggers came optimistic predictions along with requests for campaign funds. Only from Georgia were there complaints of bitter opposition by the Conservatives. One Radical in Augusta wrote that the Conservatives "talk confidently of the 'near approach of the day when all the Yanks & white niggers will have to leave the South' "; another reported from Savannah: "Our enemies *here*, are as *Savage as rattlesnakes*."

True to pre-election predictions, the people of the South voted for conventions and returned large Republican majorities in each of the South Atlantic states, but exultant reports of victory from southern Radicals were intermingled with their charges of fraud by the Conservative opposition. A carpetbagger in Florida announced that "God is good and the 'radical team' has triumphed . . . in opposition to all the rings Cliques and Statemakers in the State." Declaring that the convention would be "extremely radical," he boasted: "We have secured the confidence of the masses so that we do not much fear opposition." From Georgia came complaints of Conservative fraud; one writer maintained that "Disloyalty was as rampant here during said election in *spirit* as I have seen it at any time during the Rebellion." Forecasting future difficulties for the Republicans, a Georgia carpetbagger wrote: "The white people of Georgia have thrown off their 'masterly inactivity,' of which they boasted so much during the canvass and election for delegates . . . and are going to work in earnest to *defeat the constitution, whatever it may be!*" John C. Underwood, carpetbag leader in Virginia, complained that the state judiciary was "most unrelenting in the persecution of every white or colored voter who is favorable to the Republican party." He further alleged that "thousands have been discharged for the avowed reason that they voted the Republican ticket in October."

Faced with heightening Conservative opposition, southern Radicals became more insistent upon assurances from Congress of continued support during this inchoate period of their new governments. In Virginia, Underwood wrote of threats "that if the colored and poor laboring people continued to vote against the land holders . . . they would find themselves between the upper & nether mill stones & would be ground to

[409]

powder." A Conservative member of the Virginia constitutional convention was charged with declaring that no such voter could live upon his land and that he "would sooner see it all grow up in broom sedge & scrub pine." Underwood declared: "These threats are made boldly & defiantly by those who hold all the offices with very rare exceptions & who are at heart just as rebellious as when they were in arms against us." Faced with these threats to the rising power of the Radicals, Underwood asked, "Can Congress save us from annihilation?" From Georgia John Sherman received urgent pleas for firm action by Congress with the prophecy that if the South were to go Democratic "the poor negroes will have no rights and I may truthfully say will not be allowed even to exist except as the nominal slaves of the landed aristocracy of this section." A member of the Georgia convention told of being "grossly insulted . . . for being a member of a 'Yankee and negro Convention,'" and warned that if Congress should take a backward step the cause would be lost. A Florida carpetbagger expressed fear that the Supreme Court might declare the Reconstruction Acts unconstitutional and precipitate another struggle in which "hopes for the 'lost Cause' would be revived and the hot breath of these infernal fiends would make this Southern country anything but comfortable."

Despite such warnings of tightening opposition, the constitutional conventions which met to reform the state governments were safely in the control of the Radicals, and reports received by congressional leaders were optimistic of the ultimate success of the Republican party in the South. Although the South Carolina group contained a Negro majority, congressional Radicals were assured by a leading white member that "we have now a convention composed of better material than any other Southern state." Urged by Elihu B. Washburne to finish the Florida constitution in time to get it ratified before the Chicago Republican convention, a Radical leader from that state predicted early agreement on the new frame of government. Virginia Radicals wrote for advice on the further disfranchisement of rebels; many Virginia Republicans favored disfranchisement but hoped to avoid anything that would injure the Republican party or "impede its glorious march toward human freedom." North Carolina leaders were optimistic, but Albion W. Tourgée, outstanding carpetbag leader in that state, advised congressional Radicals to defer action on Sherman's Alabama Bill until after all the state elections in order to lull the Conservatives into a continuation of their policy of inaction.

Relative harmony attended the deliberations in all the constitutional conventions except that of Florida. In that state the Republican organization, much to the delight of the Conservatives, broke into three factions, each of which was led by carpetbaggers. The regular Republicans, under the leadership of Daniel Richards, Liberty Billings, and William U. Saunders, reflected the opinions of the Republican national committee, and their power rested upon the political potentialities of the Union Leagues, which they controlled. A more moderate group, led by Harrison Reed, from Wisconsin, and O. B. Hart, a local Union man, possessed some capital and was supported by the businessmen in the party. The third faction, of lesser power and significance, was led by T. W. Osborn, formerly of Massachusetts. A vivid, partisan description of this dissension is to be found in the regular reports forwarded to Washburne by Daniel Richards.

In the struggle for control of the convention, scheduled to meet in Tallahassee on January 20, 1868, the Billings-Richards wing of the party made the initial move. A week before the assembling of the convention, Richards reported that the regular Republicans had rented a house and spent four or five hundred dollars converting it into a "mess" for fifteen or twenty delegates in order to keep them from being subjected to corrupting influences. This action was countered by similar activity on the part of the Reed forces, whereupon Richards claimed that the Johnson officeholders were behind the move and accused them of "running a hotel free of expense and . . . pouring out money and whiskey most profusely to try and break up the organization of the Convention." He further asserted that Reed, who was the administration mail agent for Florida and Georgia, had authority to draw upon Postmaster General A. W. Randall for $13,500 for campaign expenses. The affluence of the Reed forces constituted a threat to the other factions in their struggle for delegates. Richards reported: "Probably ¾ of them [delegates] had to borrow money to come with and of course all those of easy virtue soon fall a prey to these minions of the devil and A. Johnson who have plenty of money."

On February 11, Richards reported that Johnson men had continued to ply members with money, whiskey, and offers of office until a test vote on eligibility revealed that the Radical wing of the party controlled a majority of one. With all hope of controlling the convention gone, the minority left the city, adjourned to a meeting place twenty-five miles away, and set up a rival constitutional convention. The rump convention in Tallahassee, in perfect harmony, then adopted a constitution extremely Radical in character. In spite of the fact that the seceding delegates returned in mass, broke into the convention hall around midnight of February 10, organized, and requested recognition as the lawful convention, Richards maintained: "We feel quite certain that our Constitution will be popular with our people and acceptable to Congress."

Richards' optimism was premature. With the support of General George G. Meade, military commander of the district, the seceders did gain recognition as the legal constitutional assembly and drafted a more restrictive document than that proposed by the ousted rump convention. Even with the solid support of the Negroes, the Radicals in Florida were defeated, and their constitution was never presented to the people for ratification.

The campaign for ratification of the new state constitutions revealed a growing Conservative opposition which gave rise to another flurry of protests from southern Republicans. A Savannah resident wrote that organized clubs of Conservatives were using all sorts of spurious promises to win Negro support and by the use of threats were making freedom of speech impossible. Merchants in Savannah were reportedly advertising that they did not want any further trade from Radicals. Another Georgia observer declared: "There are parties of rebels now going about through the state murdering loyal citizens in their houses at night and shooting them from bushes during the day. . . . These murdering parties are said to be chiefly composed of slave holders sons." Virginia Republicans complained of social ostracism of Yankees and animosity toward further settlement of northerners; a Richmond Republican informed Stevens that "the Southern white man has become so demoralised in the late rebellion that very few can be trusted politically or in honorable business transactions." A North Carolinian reported that Conservatives in his state bitterly opposed the new constitution because it required the payment of the interest on the state debt, thus increasing taxation. Thaddeus Stevens was urgently requested to curb further the power of President Johnson as a requisite to victory in South Carolina.

The ratification contest also brought a renewal of party strife in Florida, and both factions of Republicans sought congressional support. An adherent of the "Johnson" Republicans wrote: "The rebel element is powerless in Florida before a *united* Republican party, but in the event of disaffection among ourselves and a consequent division of our strength, a Conservative (rebel) ticket will *inevitably* be put in the field and the hazard of our success would be very great." Washburne's faithful reporter, the carpetbagger Richards, warned that "a perfect reign of terror is most imminent." He pointed out that Klan outrages were applauded in

Florida, and that "threats of violence against all those who dare oppose the adoption of the Rebel Constitution come from high quarters so that we are not permitted to question their purposes." Richards later reported that "the rebels are organizing rapidly and will all support the Constitution," and that their leaders were sponsoring Reed meetings. The Conservatives not only used threats and intimidation, but the Reed Republican faction boasted of their employment of force and their control of the election boards. And yet, even though the Negro leader Saunders deserted them, the Radicals remained optimistic of a shift in the tide.

Despite internal party divisions and growing Conservative opposition, the ratification elections resulted in Republican victories in each of the states except Virginia, where the election was postponed. A combination of factors contributed to this victory, but Republican reports particularly stressed the value of the Union League organizations in achieving ultimate victory.

Meanwhile disaffection continued among the Republicans of strife-torn Florida. Lamenting Reed's victory in that state, Daniel Richards charged that the Reed party had controlled the newspapers, telegraph, mail, and railroads, had used the school fund for campaign purposes, and had perpetrated "enormous and startling frauds" to secure the adoption of their illegal constitution. He reported that General Milton S. Littlefield, notorious lobbyist from Pennsylvania, had been active in buying up votes for the Reed group; and Richards lamented: "If hell has not turned out all its imps against us then it must be a big and roomy place." Liberty Billings also complained of fraud by the Reed faction; he asked: "Is not Congress bound to see that the people of these States are likely to have a loyal government of equal rights in the future secured by decisive and trustworthy majorites? . . . Give us another opportunity, & we will see that the State is reconstructed upon a basis that will secure permanent peace, progress and prosperity."

Assuring congressional Radicals that Reed was preparing to sell out Radical Republicanism to the Democrats, the Florida extremists pleaded for the rejection of the Florida constitution by Congress. Richards warned: "They have swindled and cheated the people and now they mean to try it on with Congress, and defy their wishes and choice in the matter." Liberty Billings referred to the "Rebel Herods and Johnson office-holding Copperhead-Pilates combining to crucify Radical Republicanism," and predicted that the acceptance of the constitution by Congress would ruin the Republican party in Florida. Charges that the constitution was the result of a compact between Reed and the rebels were mingled with requests for a new provisional government and summary rejection by Congress of the Reed constitution.

To all pleas from the Florida extremists for congressional action national Radicals turned a deaf ear. On June 8, 1868, Governor Reed was sworn into office, and seventeen days later a bill passed over Johnson's veto admitted Florida's representatives to Congress. Apparent party harmony settled over the political scene in Florida, although one prominent Tallahassee Radical described this harmony as "the concord of a gang of slaves lashed by the whip of the enormous appointing power of the Governor." Congressional Republicans, however, apparently chose to accept the Reed constitution in preference to risking the loss of the state electoral vote in the forthcoming presidential election.

With an apparent victory won in the battle for state reorganization, congressional and local Radicals began to show increasing concern over the approaching presidential election. For a time there was some doubt among southern Radicals as to whether they should support Grant or Chase for the nomination. Grant's nomination by the Chicago Republican convention resolved this doubt, but left the Radicals to face the twin difficulties of Conservative opposition in the South and dissension within their own state organizations. A moderate Republican of Florida reported to national party secretary William E. Chandler: "The Rebels are thoroughly organized and are using every means to intimidate and prevent the loyal people black and white from a free expression & exercise of their political rights. . . . It is evident that . . . the Rebels intend to take forcible possession of these State Governments." North Carolina Republicans, blessed with relative party harmony, caused no worry to the national leaders, although a correspondent from Smithfield informed Washburne that "the rebels are more industrious than the bee & the vote on the constitution is not significant of the presidential vote." Virginia Radicals, although unable to participate in the election, expressed an anxiety over the outcome, predicting that "if [Horatio] Seymour & [Francis P.] Blair should be elected, we are satisfied all loyal men would have to leave the State."

Political conditions in South Carolina during the presidential campaign became so chaotic as to justify the dispatch of a special Radical agent and observer to that state. This observer, John M. Morris, reported that the Democrats were very active and well supplied with money—the "rich rebels coax with one breath and threaten with the next." As to intimidation by the Democrats, Morris declared: "All that is said in the North is true. It is not safe for me to go alone unarmed into the up country here. Negroes are daily shot dead or wounded. Nobody is convicted because no adequate testimony is found or the magistrates don't prosecute. . . . I fear that thousands of voters will be kept away or driven away from the polls." The carpetbag leadership in the state reported that the malignancy of the Democrats was growing and that they were openly proclaiming that no Negro would be allowed to approach the polls. Governor Robert K. Scott warned: "The rebels did not misrepresent the fact when they said they were not whipped but only overpowered." Nor was evidence lacking to corroborate these charges. In Abbeville County, B. F. Randolph, colored state senator and chairman of the Republican state central committee, while on a speaking tour was murdered by a group of undisguised whites. A congressional representative from the state reported: "Three members of the General Assembly and one member of the late Constitutional Convention have been murdered secretly." He added that the "whole upper portion of the State is said to be in such a condition that it is regarded as unsafe for Republicans to go there to speak." It was impossible, he said, to punish the murderers because of the sympathy of their white neighbors.

Faced with this determined Democratic opposition, Morris was concerned over the prospects of a divided state machine. He reported: "There is yet small *party discipline* and self control. . . . Every man nominated by the State Convention was heartily cursed and shamelessly abused by those he defeated." The colored element, the majority in South Carolina, Morris described as "shrewd—but not educated politically. They have not experience and sagacity." Such lack of party harmony in a northern state would lead to inevitable defeat. "But here," Morris observed, "I think all can be quieted . . . and a victory won."

The position of the party in Georgia caused further anxiety to the national Radicals. The Negroes of that state were of doubtful value to the Republicans, and the white members of the party were hopelessly at odds. The Democrats, on the other hand, were well organized. Ex-Governor Joseph E. Brown predicted a difficult campaign to swing the state to Grant, and, in a plea for funds, declared that all the money in Georgia was concentrated in the hands of the Democrats. John H. Caldwell, national Republican committee member from Georgia, reported that the Democrats were spending vast sums on barbecues to lure the colored vote to the Seymour ticket. He believed that the position of the party would improve when Governor Rufus B. Bullock assumed charge of the patronage; but another prominent Republican informed Chandler that the "sadly demoralized" condition of the party was caused by the action of the constitutional convention in nominating Bullock instead of calling a state Republican convention. He wrote: "In order to secure his nomination and to allay opposition to such action by the Cons'l Conv'n Gov. B. had recourse to bargain and sale of all the prominent offices in the State mainly amongst the members of the Convention, which bargains are now being carried into effect in his appointments to the great mortification and disgust of the prominent Republicans of the State."

The success of the Democrats in the newly elected Georgia legislature served to heighten the anxiety of the Radicals. Close division not only made it impossible for the Republican administration to carry out an effective program, but ultimately led to the expulsion of the Negro members of both houses by the Democrats, and thus to an absolute Democratic majority. The Radicals hoped that this move would "arouse the colored race to sense of their danger, and . . . stimulate them in the cause of their own defense, and that of the Republican party." Actually, Democratic assumption of control in the legislature caused talk of calling a "white man's" constitutional convention. A Republican observer declared: "It is manifestly the intention of the Rebel leaders, to defy the power of the U.S. Govt. and to set at naught the laws of Congress."

Democratic success in Georgia brought an increased volume of Republican protests against frauds, violence, and intimidation. An Atlanta Radical informed Chandler that the colored vote could not be trusted:

The Negroes are too dependent upon their employers to be counted upon with certainty. They are without property, and cannot sustain themselves, but a few days at most, without being fed by their Masters; they are without education or sufficient intelligence to appreciate the power the *Ballot* gives them, add to which a system of intimidation persistently practiced by the Rebels, appealing to their fears through their superstitions, and you have a mass of poverty, ignorance, stupidity, and superstition under the influence of fears both real and imaginary, to organize and control, upon whom but little reliance can be placed.

Joseph E. Brown feared that the Negroes would be driven from the polls either by intimidation or by force. In the event of a free election the state would go Republican by a ten thousand majority, but, Brown declared: "There is . . . a reign of terror and violence in some parts of the state, and Republicans cannot hold meetings and discuss the questions involved in the canvass without actual violence or such threats of it as drive off the timid from the meetings." Foster Blodgett, notorious Georgia scalawag, echoed the former governor's observations. "The rebellious spirit is more intense and bitter now than in 1860 and 1861," he said. "Negroes are killed almost every day while white Republicans are threatened [with] abuse and maltreated to an extent that is alarming." John H. Caldwell, Republican candidate for Congress, reported that Democratic methods in Georgia included "bribery, threats, and when they can do so unmolested, actual violence, as well as fraud in the election."

When it became increasingly obvious that the Republican organization lacked the strength to carry Georgia for Grant, Radicals begged Congress to intercede. From Dalton came the assertion: "The present Rebellious spirit is greater here now than it was before the late War. Congress have been too lenient toward the Rebels. Give them an inch and they will take a mile. Active measures must be enacted or we are Butchered up and Law & Constitution trampled under foot." Chandler was warned that further congressional inaction would lead to civil war in the state. Blodgett suggested that Georgia be given another provisional government with Bullock as governor and with six regiments of infantry and one of cavalry to support him. When the election returns confirmed the fears of the Republicans, additional charges of corruption were accompanied by pleas for the overthrow of the "rebel" government and the disallowance of the Georgia electoral vote.

The election resulted in a Grant victory in three of the five states. Through intimidation of the Negroes and a tightly-knit white organization the Democrats secured the ascendancy in Georgia; Virginia, not yet readmitted to the Union, was not entitled to a vote.

With the Republicans in control in North Carolina, South Carolina, and Florida, and the status of Virginia and Georgia not fully decided, correspondence between the Radicals of the South and congressional Republicans began to dwindle. No longer were southern Republicans entirely dependent upon northern arms for their support. And, with Grant safely elected, congressional Radicals were largely content to allow their southern colleagues free sway in the former rebellious states—their electoral votes would not be required again until 1872.

Only in Virginia and Georgia did southern Radicals still urgently petition congressional aid. In a bid for further help, a prominent Georgia Republican, early in 1869, reported that "There is no split in the Republican Party of Georgia. . . . There has never been a question as to whether Georgia is reconstructed." His solution of the problem called for the convening of the old constitutional convention to complete the work of reconstruction. The strife in Georgia led Congress, after a year of vacillation, again to impose military rule in that state. Even so, the state Radicals were still unable to cooperate, and a combination of anti-Bullock Republicans and Democrats brought about the overthrow of the Radical administration in the state election of December, 1870. In Virginia, the disputed sections on disfranchisement in the 1868 constitution delayed the ratification vote until 1869, when a

combination of conservative Republicans and Democrats secured the defeat of these provisions and elected a compromise
governor and a Democratic legislature.

The presidential election of 1872 brought another attempt
to affect a liaison between national Radical leaders and southern Republicans to assure the re-election of Grant. Southern
Republicans again poured forth tales of Democratic violence
and intimidation and bemoaned the dissension within the Radical group of the South. From North Carolina came an early
request for protection from the outrages of the Ku Klux Klan.
A New Bern Republican wrote Benjamin F. Butler: "I can
Say to you With Safity that a Union man Chance is slender
hear in North Carolina." A prominent carpetbagger of
Greensboro wrote:

The old aristocracy and slave owners of the South are sore-
headed; thus far they have refused to be comforted by any
sanctifying grace flowing from republican sources. Their hostility
to the republican party and their hatred of the U.S. government
drove them into the Ku Klux organization. They hoped that by
means of that wicked order they would get undisputed control of
the South, and with the assistance of Tammany they would walk
into the White House in 1873.

On the other hand, Joseph C. Abbott, former carpetbag senator from North Carolina, telegraphed from Raleigh that
"prospects looks [sic] bright if fraud can be Prevented we
think success certain." The Radicals of South Carolina bitterly complained of their lot. A prominent Republican editor
of Columbia, protesting continued Klan activity, declared:
"There has never, during my four years residence here, been a
more intolerant and vindictive spirit manifest than is exhibited
now. The threat is openly made, that if Mr. Greeley is elected
President the northern men will all be driven out of the state,
the negroes degraded from office, and all the old Southern
rebel element put into power again." Despite the seriousness
of a growing party schism in South Carolina, however, na-

tional Radicals refused to intercede in aid of either group. William E. Chandler informed Franklin J. Moses that local politics were of no concern to the party leadership so long as the state was won for Grant.

Radical reports from Georgia expressed a more optimistic view of the chances of the party in that doubtful state. In spite of the activity of the Ku Klux Klan and the poll tax requirements for voting—a newly inaugurated Democratic device—informed Republicans were increasingly hopeful of a Democratic party split in the state. The carpetbag president of the local Union League Council reported to Chandler: "Hostility to the Federal Government and dread of 'negro supremacy,' constitute the cement that holds together the discordant elements of the Democratic Party. The refractory are tamed and whipped in by the fear of 'nigger equality'; but for this kind of pressure the Democratic Party would fall in pieces, and the whites would be about equally divided." The development of the "straight-out" Democratic movement in Georgia in opposition to Horace Greeley was a concrete illustration of internal Democratic strife. Georgia Republicans anticipated aid from the "straight-outs" in preventing the intimidation of Negroes at the polls, and an Atlanta Radical reported that "where they make no nomination, the agreement is, that they will support our man or else remain neutral."

Republican hopes for the capture of Georgia were dissipated by the results of the state election in August. Democrats again asserted their power. One Radical, reporting to Chandler, declared: "To say that the election was a farce, fails to express the truth; it was a mob, controlled by the Democratic bullies, and ended in *crime*." The "straights," he complained, either stayed at home or were bullied into the Democratic ranks. A South Carolinian observing the Georgia election reported:

Never since the formation of this government was there a more shameful outrage upon free suffrage than the one just perpetrated in Georgia in the name of democracy. The colored men were intimidated and driven away from the polls by the hundred and one devices of the democrats, and where words would not do, bloody deeds soon taught the negroes that to vote against the wishes of their white employers and neighbors was to risk death.

Despite internal Republican dissension, the political picture in Florida was cause for Radical optimism. A Tallahassee carpetbagger wrote of the improving political sagacity of the Negro: "The opposition may talk of the everlasting 'nigger' but it is beginning to learn that it has in the black man a foe whose opinions are born of honesty and whose native instincts assisted by six years' education in the exercise of the suffrage, and his naturally Christian heart, make him at this time their most formidable enemy, and the finest and most progressive friend of the Republican party." By mid-summer of 1872 the party had begun to recover from the effects of attempts to impeach Governor Reed, and the relative harmony displayed at the August state convention gave further hope of continued Radical success. Although Reed continued to press for the support of the national Radicals, his influence steadily declined. Republicans in Florida became more concerned over President Grant's removal from federal office of District Attorney H. Bisbee and Marshal Sherman Conant, two leading carpetbaggers, than with the contentions of Reed. Radicals protested that these removals "cast a damper upon the *honest Republicans* here and the Democrats are in great glee"; and the chairman of the state executive committee informed Chandler that this action would probably throw the state to the Democrats. So insistent were the state leaders that Grant was persuaded to reinstate the two carpetbaggers, a move hailed by the state Radical leadership as responsible for the revival of party harmony.

Notwithstanding the favorable turn of events in Florida, and continued strong Radical influence in North and South Carolina, Republican prospects generally were not thought to be as bright as in 1868. Indeed, a Savannah correspondent declared that the Republican victory of 1868 had brought about the ultimate decline of the party by the elevation of unworthy and corrupt individuals to positions of trust. A South Carolina Radical wrote that the main hope of a Grant victory must rest on the northern states, for "Southern States like Southern chivalry are mighty uncertain." A North Carolina carpetbagger suggested an astute political move by which national Radicals could improve the party position in the South. He proposed that a bill be drawn up for the assumption of the southern state debts and sent through the House with a great deal of fanfare. Then it could be held in the Senate until after the election, at which time it could be killed or passed as desired. Thus could favorable sentiment be created for the Republicans by subterfuge. More optimistically, the secretary of the National Union Council informed Chandler that with "the Union League in full blast all over the South and South West . . . we can rally all our forces, and control the black vote for Grant" even though there were persistent reports of organized attempts to mislead the Negro.

Doubtless these local Radical apprehensions had a salutary effect upon the activities and contributions of national Republicans, for the efforts of the Democrats and "straight-outs" to recapture these southern states were in vain except in Georgia. In that state, although it was a center of insurgent Democratic activity, the regular Democrats produced a sizable majority for Greeley.

After the re-election of Grant in 1872, the tie between the congressional Radicals and southern Republicans rapidly deteriorated. Southern Radicals, gradually losing power throughout the South Atlantic states, discovered that Congress was reluctant to act except during periods of national party crisis, and their complaints and pleas gradually lessened. Indeed, when in 1874 the Democrats captured the lower house of Congress, Radical congressional action was no longer possible.

As the election of 1876 approached, Democratic leaders displayed a determination to oust the Republicans regardless of methods. A Florida Radical, despairing of victory with two Republican electoral tickets in the field, informed Chandler that the strong opposition was composed of young men who had grown up in postwar conditions and who blamed all the ills of the South on Yankees and Negroes, and a Virginia observer told John Sherman that there was great danger of open revolt in the South if the Democrats failed to win the election. In South Carolina, Governor Daniel H. Chamberlain, candidate for re-election, faced Wade Hampton's formidable "red-shirts," undergoing personal abuse and even threats on his life. Chandler received a report that at one Republican rally in Barnwell County six hundred mounted Democrats had taken over the meeting and heaped abuse upon the carpetbaggers and scalawags. The governor was denounced as "a Carrion Crow, a Buzzard who has come down here to prey upon our people and steal from them their substance," and amidst frequent rebel yells it was suggested that the crowd hang him and his entourage on the spot. An observer of the affray declared that the Republicans of the state were no longer willing to undergo such punishment unless the North came to their aid. An Atlanta Republican suggested that northern speakers be sent South: "The ignorant masses here (mostly Republicans) require instruction in their political rights and duties as free citizens, and encouragement to stand up like men for their rights."

The determination of southern Democrats plus the dissension within the southern Republican party ultimately led to the defeat of the Radicals in each of the South Atlantic states by 1876. Contested election returns from both South Carolina and Florida for a time beclouded the political scene, but the repudiation of the Radical state leaders by the Hayes administration brought a quick collapse of the remaining Radical organizations.

Although southern Radical Republican correspondence necessarily presents a distorted picture of the full process of southern Reconstruction, it is nevertheless an invaluable source for a study of that much-disputed period of American history. From no other source is the historian able to secure so complete a picture of the motives, emotions, and reactions of the members of the three factions who composed the southern wing of the postwar Republican party. This correspondence, along with other contemporary sources, reveals a much more complex social, economic, and political evolution than is found in partisan accounts by historians who neglect material prejudicial to their sectional sympathies.

Several factors of primary importance are disclosed by these Radical letters from the South. In the first place they reveal a problem of adjustment of interests which plagued the party until its overthrow in 1876—a problem which undoubtedly contributed much to that downfall. A contemporary North Carolinian phrased the difficulty thus: "The problem of adjusting the balance between the three constituent elements of the Republican party South is certainly one pregnant with danger, therefore claiming imminent solution from the hands of the national leaders of our party." That the national leaders were either unable or unwilling to undertake this task is evidenced by the inability of the state organizations to follow consistently a policy of cooperation.

These communications further reveal a lack of close cooperation between the leading Radicals of the South and the congressional Radicals. Most frequently the correspondence was from less influential Republicans often in opposition to dominant groups. The urgency of pleas and complaints from these southern Radicals obviously was important in helping to shape the opinions of congressional leaders, but, after 1868, the pleas received a favorable response only when the strength of the national party was threatened. Intrastate party difficulties were, in the main, left to the solution of local leaders;

national leaders refused to become involved in party splits such as occurred in Florida and South Carolina. Central direction was difficult to achieve, particularly as the southern Radicals became increasingly a burden and an embarrassment to the national party. Personal ambition and differences in ideology worked to produce antagonistic groups within the party in each of the southern states, and astute Conservative politicians proved to be adept at widening the gaps. This intraparty division ultimately proved disastrous to the Republicans in all of the South Atlantic states, especially in South Carolina, Georgia, and Florida, where conflicting groups struggled for power throughout the Reconstruction years.

Southern Radical correspondence further reveals the effectiveness of the campaign developed by the Redeemers in their struggle to capture control of the state governments. Radical accounts of intimidation, fraud, and violence, while undoubtedly exaggerated, demonstrate an early reinvigoration of local political leadership. The evidence indicates that state Radicals, especially the carpetbag leaders, grossly underestimated the abilities and strength of this Conservative leadership in all of the South Atlantic states. The immigrants from the North seized upon the Reconstruction Acts as an opportunity to revamp southern political and social standards, but their methods were revolutionary in character and took little account of past development and of national trends in political economy. Ultimately cultural forces of the past, and long-standing mores, in league with newly evolving economic combinations, led to repudiation of southern Radicalism by the national party leaders and the emergence of conservative whites of the South as the stronger force.

19

BLACK RECONSTRUCTION

W. E. B. DuBois

The pioneering role of W. E. B. DuBois in Reconstruction historiography has already been made
evident. In 1935, with the publication of *Black Reconstruction*, DuBois elaborated upon the thesis he
had advanced in *The Souls of Black Folk* (1903)
and in his 1909 address to the American Historical
Association. The major shift in his approach was the
attempt to place Reconstruction in a Marxist framework. Whatever the shortcomings of this massive
work, it remains the most ambitious attempt to assess the role of the black man in Reconstruction.

It had been insistently and firmly believed by the best thought
of the South: (1) that the Negro could not work as a free
laborer; (2) that the Negro could not really be educated,
being congenitally inferior; (3) that if political power were
given to Negroes it would result virtually in the overthrow of
civilization.

Now, it is quite clear that during the period we are studying, the results failed to prove these assumptions. First of all,
the Negro did work as a free laborer. Slowly but certainly the
tremendous losses brought on by the Civil War were restored,
and restoration, as compared with other great wars, was comparatively rapid. By 1870, the Cotton Kingdom was re-established, and by 1875, the South knew that with cheap labor and
freedom from government control, it was possible for individ-

uals to reap large profit in the old agriculture and in new industry. . . .

With regard to education, the testimony is equally clear. Grant that the Negro began as almost totally illiterate, the increase in schools and education, largely by his own initiative, is one of the most extraordinary developments of modern days. . . . It is enough to say here that the question as to whether American Negroes were capable of education was no longer a debatable one in 1876. The whole problem was simply one of opportunity.

The third problem, of the Negro's use of his political power, was not so clear because it involved matters of norm and ideal. Whose civilization, whose culture, whose comfort, was involved? The Negro certainly did not attempt to "overthrow civilization" in the sense of attacking the fundamental morals and habits of modern life. Sir George Campbell said in 1879:

During the last dozen years the Negroes have had a very large share of political education. Considering the troubles and the ups and downs that they have gone through, it is, I think, wonderful how beneficial this education has been to them, and how much these people, so lately in the most debased condition of slavery, have acquired independent ideas; and, far from lapsing into anarchy, have become citizens with ideas of law and property and order. The white serfs of European countries took hundreds of years to rise to the level which these Negroes adopted in America. Before I went South I certainly expected to find that the Southern States had been for a time a sort of Pandemonium in which a white man could hardly live. Yet it certainly was not so. . . . When I went to South Carolina I thought there at least I must find great social disturbances; and in South Carolina I went to the county of Beaufort, the blackest part of the State in point of population, and that in which black rule has been most complete and has lasted longest. It has the reputation of being a sort of black paradise, and *per contra*, I rather expected a sort of white hell. There I thought I should see a rough Liberia, where blacks ruled roughshod over the whites. To my great surprise I found exactly the contrary. At no place that I have seen are the relations of the two races better and more peaceable. . . . All the best houses are in the occupation of the whites—almost all the trades, professions, and leading occupations. White girls go about freely and pleasantly as if no black had ever been in power. Here the blacks still control the elections and send their representatives to the State Assembly. . . .

In Mississippi alone did I find politicians silly enough to talk about the superiority of the Caucasian race, and the natural incapacity of the Negro for self-government; but even there the best Republicans told that these noisy Democratic demagogues were but a small, though aggressive and not unpowerful, minority.

Sir George Campbell, however, makes one interesting observation: "Not only is the Negro labor excellent, but also there is among the Southern proprietors and leading men accustomed to black labor, and not so used to whites, a disposition greatly to rely on black labor as a conservative element, securing them against the dangers and difficulties which they see arising from the combinations and violence of the white laborers in some of the Northern States; and on this ground the blacks are cherished and protected by Democratic statesmen, who now hold power in the South."

If we include in "morals" and "culture" the prevailing manner of holding and distributing wealth, then the sudden enfranchisement of a mass of laborers threatens fundamental and far-reaching change, no matter what their race or color. It was this that the South feared and had reason to fear. Economic revolution did not come immediately. Negro labor was ignorant, docile, and conservative. But it was beginning to learn; it was beginning to assert itself. It was beginning to have radical thoughts as to the distribution of land and wealth.

If now it is true that the enfranchisement of black labor in the South did not crush industry but gave the South a working class capable of being trained in intelligence and did not disturb the essential bases of civilization, what is the indictment—the bitter and deep-seated indictment brought against the Negro voter?

The indictment rests upon this unquestioned fact: Property in the South had its value cut in half during the Civil War. This meant that property was compelled, after the war, not simply to attempt to restore its losses, but to bear a burden of social expense largely because of the widened duties of the state and the greatly increased citizenship due to emancipation and enfranchisement. The bitter conflict, therefore, which followed the enfranchisement of Negro labor and of white labor, came because impoverished property holders were compelled by the votes of poor men to bear a burden which meant practically confiscation of much of that property which remained to them and were denied opportunity to exploit labor in the future as they had in the past. It was not, then, that the postbellum South could not produce wealth with free labor; it was the far more fundamental question as to whom this wealth was to belong to and for whose interests laborers were to work. There is no doubt that the object of the black and white labor vote was gradually conceived as one which involved confiscating the property of the rich. This was a program that could not be openly avowed by intelligent men in 1870, but it has become one of the acknowledged functions of the state in 1933; and it is quite possible that long before the end of the twentieth century, the deliberate distribution of property and income by the state on an equitable and logical basis will be looked upon as the state's prime function.

Put all these facts together and one gets a clear idea, not of the failure of Negro suffrage in the South, but of the basic difficulty which it encountered; and the results are quite consistent with a clear judgment that Negro and white labor ought to have had the right to vote; that they ought to have tried to change the basis of property and redistribute income; and that their failure to do this was a disaster to democratic government in the United States.

To men like Charles Sumner, the future of democracy in

America depended on bringing the southern revolution to a successful close by accomplishing two things: the making of the black freedmen really free, and the sweeping away of the animosities due to the war.

What liberalism did not understand was that such a revolution was economic and involved force. Those who against the public weal have power cannot be expected to yield save to superior power. The North used its power in the Civil War to break the political power of the slave barons. During and after the war, it united its force with that of the workers to uproot the still vast economic power of the planters. It hoped with the high humanitarianism of Charles Sumner eventually to induce the planter to surrender his economic power peacefully, in return for complete political amnesty, and hoped that the North would use its federal police power to maintain the black man's civil rights in return for peaceful industry and increasing intelligence. But Charles Sumner did not realize, and that other Charles—Karl Marx—had not yet published *Das Kapital* to prove to men that economic power underlies politics. Abolitionists failed to see that after the momentary exaltation of war, the nation did not want Negroes to have civil rights and that national industry could get its way easier by alliance with southern landholders than by sustaining southern workers. They did not know that when they let the dictatorship of labor be overthrown in the South they surrendered the hope of democracy in America for all men. . . .

The basic difficulty with the South after the war was poverty, a depth of grinding poverty not easily conceivable even in these days of depression. In the first place, it goes without saying that the emancipated slave was poor; he was desperately poor, and poor in a way that we do not easily grasp today. He was, and always had been, without money and, except for his work in the Union Army, had no way of getting hold of cash. He could ordinarily get no labor contract that involved regular or certain payments of cash. He was without clothes and without a home. He had no way to rent or build a home. Food had to be begged or stolen, unless in some way he could get hold of land or go to work; and hired labor would, if he did not exercise the greatest care and get honest advice, result in something that was practically slavery. These conditions, of course, while true for the mass of freedmen, did not apply to workers in the army, artisans or laborers in cities and others who had exceptional chances to obtain work for cash at something like decent rates.

The white worker, in the mass, was equally poverty-stricken, except that he did usually hold, as a squatter, some land, and emancipation gave him better chance to hire his labor in cities. Finally, there were the impoverished planters, merchants and professional men who came out of the war with greatly reduced income and resources. In this setting of poverty, as nearly universal as one could have under modern conditions, must come the effort to set up a new state, and it is clear to the unprejudiced observer that no matter who had conducted that state, if there had been no Negro or other alien elements in the land, if there had been no universal suffrage, there would have been bitter dissatisfaction, widespread injustice, and vast transfer of wealth involving stealing and corruption.

The freedman sought eagerly, after the war, property and income. He believed that his condition was not his own fault but due to Theft on a mighty scale. He demanded reimbursement and redress sufficient for a decent livelihood. . . . By far the most pressing of his problems as a worker was that of land. This land hunger—this absolutely fundamental and essential thing to any real emancipation of the slaves—was continually pushed by all emancipated Negroes and their representatives in every southern state. It was met by ridicule, by anger, and by dishonest and insincere efforts to satisfy it apparently.

The Freedmen's Bureau had much Confederate property in its possession. But the seizure of abandoned estates in the

South came as a measure to stop war and not as a plan for economic rebirth. Just as the slaves were enticed from the South in order to stop the aid which they could give to rebels, in the same way the land of masters who ran away or were absent aiding the rebellion was seized; and this large body of land was the nucleus of the proposal to furnish forty acres to each emancipated slave family. The scheme was further advanced when Sherman, embarrassed by the number of Negroes who followed him from Atlanta to the sea and gathered around him in Savannah and South Carolina, as a war measure settled them upon the abandoned Sea Islands and the adjacent coast.

Confiscated property was in some cases condemned or sold on order of the federal courts for unpaid taxes, and the title vested in the United States. Thus the Freedmen's Bureau came into possession of nearly 800,000 acres of farm land with control over it, except the right of sale. This land was in Virginia, Georgia, South Carolina, Louisiana, North Carolina, Kentucky and Tennessee. There was very little in Alabama and Florida and none in Texas. The bureau intended to divide up this land and allot it to the freedmen and the white refugees, but much of it was tied up with leases, and, after all, despite the large amount, there was never enough to give the freedmen alone an acre apiece.

A million acres among a million farmers meant nothing, and from the beginning there was need of from 25 to 50 million acres more if the Negroes were to be installed as peasant farmers. Against any plan of this sort was the settled determination of the planter South to keep the bulk of Negroes as landless laborers and the deep repugnance on the part of northerners to confiscating individual property. Even Thaddeus Stevens was not able to budge the majority of northerners from this attitude. Added to this was the disinclination of the United States to add to its huge debt by undertaking any large and costly social adjustments after the war. To give land to free citizens smacked of "paternalism"; it came directly in opposition to the American assumption that any American could be rich if he wanted to, or at least well-to-do; and it stubbornly ignored the exceptional position of a freed slave.

Indeed it is a singular commentary on the attitude of the government to remember that the Freedmen's Bureau itself during the first year was financed not by taxation but by the toil of ex-slaves: the total amount of rents collected from lands in the hands of the bureau, paid mostly by Negroes, amounted to $400,000, and curiously enough it was this rent that supported the Freedmen's Bureau during the first year!

Surprise and ridicule have often been voiced concerning this demand of Negroes for land. It has been regarded primarily as a method of punishing rebellion. Motives of this sort may have been in the minds of some northern whites, but so far as the Negroes were concerned, their demand for a reasonable part of the land on which they had worked for a quarter of a millennium was absolutely justified, and to give them anything less than this was an economic farce. On the other hand, to have given each one of the million Negro free families a forty-acre freehold would have made a basis of real democracy in the United States that might easily have transformed the modern world.

The law of June 21, 1860, opened public land in Alabama, Mississippi, Missouri, Arkansas and Florida; but comparatively few of the freedmen could take advantage of this offer. The bureau gave some assistance in transporting families, but most of the Negroes had neither stock nor farm implements, and the whites in those localities bitterly opposed their settling. Only about four thousand families out of nearly four million people acquired homes under this act.

The Sherman order gave rise to all sorts of difficulties. The Negroes were given only possessory titles. Then the owners came back and immediately there was trouble. The Negroes protested, "What is the use of giving us freedom if we can't stay where we were raised and own our own house where we were born and our own piece of ground?" It was on May 25, 1865, that Johnson in his Proclamation of Pardon had provided easy means whereby all property could be restored, except the land at Port Royal, which had been sold for taxes. General Howard came to Charleston to make arrangements, and the story is characteristic—"At first," said a witness, "the people hesitated, but soon as the meaning struck them that they must give up their little homes and gardens and work for others, there was a general murmuring of dissatisfaction."

General Howard was called upon to address them, and to cover his own confusion and sympathy he asked them to sing. Immediately an old woman on the outskirts of the meeting began "Nobody Knows the Trouble I've Seen." Howard wept.

The colored landholders drew up an illiterate petition to Andrew Johnson, the poor white, expressing "sad feelings" over his decree, and begging for an acre and a half of land each; but naturally nothing came of it; for President Johnson, forgetting his own pre-war declaration that the "great plantations must be seized, and divided into small farms," declared that this land must be restored to its original owners and this would be done if owners received a presidential pardon. The pardoning power was pushed and the land all over the South rapidly restored. Negroes were dispossessed, the revenue of the bureau reduced; many schools had to be discontinued. The bureau became no longer self-supporting and its whole policy was changed.

In December, 1865, the bureau had 768,590 acres of land; in 1868, there were only 139,644 acres left, and much of this unimproved and unfertile. For a long time there still persisted the idea that the government was going to make a distribution of land. The rumor was that this was to be made January 1, 1865, and for months before that Negroes all over the South declined to make contracts for work and were accordingly accused of laziness and insubordination. The restoration of the lands not only deprived Negroes in various ways of a clear path toward livelihood, but greatly discouraged them and broke their faith in the United States government. . . .

What the Negro needed, and what he desperately sought, was leadership in knowledge and industry. In knowledge he wanted through his own irrepressible demand for education to become an intelligent citizen; and a start toward this he received through the splendid and unselfish cooperation of the northern social workers connected with the federal dictatorship and through their allies, the teachers who came down to man the Freedmen's Bureau schools. By straining his political power to the utmost, the Negro voter got a public school system and got it because that was one clear object which he understood and which no bribery or chicanery could seduce him from advocating and insisting upon in season and out.

On the other hand, in economic leadership, in the whole question of work and wage, he was almost entirely at sea. His higher schools based on New England capitalism and individualism gave little training for an economic battle just dawning in the world and far from the conception of leaders in southern industry. Even his later industrial schools were tied hand and foot to triumphant capitalism unhampered by a labor vote.

He had, then, but one clear economic ideal and that was his demand for land, his demand that the great plantations be subdivided and given to him as his right. This was a perfectly fair and natural demand and ought to have been an integral part of emancipation. To emancipate four million laborers whose labor had been owned, and separate them from the land upon which they had worked for nearly two and a half centuries, was an operation such as no modern country had for a moment attempted or contemplated. The German and English and French serf, the Italian and Russian serf, were, on emancipation, given definite rights in the land. Only the

American Negro slave was emancipated without such rights and in the end this spelled for him the continuation of slavery.

Beyond this demand for land, economic leadership for the Negro failed. He appealed to his former master. The best of the planters, those who in slavery days had occupied a patriarchal position toward their slaves, were besieged not only by their own former slaves but by others for advice and leadership. If they had wished, they could have held the Negro vote in the palm of their hands. The Negroes would have followed them implicitly, and it was this that poor whites from Andrew Johnson down feared. But they forgot that the planters were estopped from this program by their own lack of capital; by the new and confiscatory taxation which the Negroes' demands entailed even under the most frugal and honest administration; by their own singular lack of knowledge of the methods of capitalistic democracy throughout the world, which was based on those very concessions to labor of which they could not conceive. They kept insisting on hard, regular toil, vague and irregular wages, and no exercise of political power; all this in a day when labor the world over demanded shorter hours, a definite high wage contract, and the right to vote.

To this attitude of the planters must be added the bitter jealousy, not only of the worst and more vicious and selfish of the planters, but of the poor whites. And when there was added to this the fact that they themselves were being supplanted as advisers of Negroes by the new white northern capitalist, willing to grant labor's demands at the expense of the state, they, in most cases, utterly refused to lead Negro labor, and thus threw the Negroes back on the carpetbag capitalists for advice and leadership. Thither, too, Negroes were attracted by a trust that naturally grew out of the fact that these people represented their emancipation. They represented Abraham Lincoln and his government, and Negroes were naturally strongly inclined to do anything that this leadership told them to, even when the advice was dishonest and unwise. Thus were the freedmen landed in piteous contradiction and difficulty.

The Negro's own black leadership was naturally of many sorts. Some, like the whites, were petty bourgeois, seeking to climb to wealth; others were educated men, helping to develop a new nation without regard to mere race lines; while a third group were idealists, trying to uplift the Negro race and put them on a par with the whites. But how was this to be accomplished? In the minds of very few of them was there any clear and distinct plan for the development of a laboring class into a position of power and mastery over the modern industrial state. And in this lack of vision, they were not singular in America. Where else in the land, even among labor leaders, was there any such fixed and definite program of action?

The fight for the domination of the new form of state which Reconstruction was building took the direction of using the income for new forms of state expenses; and for that, public investment for private profit was the widespread custom in the North. The South had entered only to a small extent into such schemes and tended to regard them as outside the function of the state. Even the forms of expenditure for education, and the help of indigents, were kinds of expenditure to which the southern taxpayers had not been used and in which for the most part they did not believe. There were consequently fierce outcries against the "waste" of such expenditures.

When in addition to that, there came widespread and deliberate investment of public funds in railroads and corporations where the profits went to speculators and grafters, the protest of landed property was intensified.

The results of this form of stealing bore hard upon the impoverished landholder and were particularly detestable to him because, monopolizing the government before the war, he had largely escaped taxation and had tried to transfer it to the shoulders of the small businessman. Now the small businessman, re-enforced by the carpetbagger and black voter, was returning it to the landholder. Assessments were increased and the gradual disestablishment of the landed aristocracy became imminent.

Here is the crux of the matter: It was this large and, for the day and circumstances, overwhelming loss that lay at the bottom of the extraordinary charges of extravagance and stealing that characterize the Reconstruction controversy. For had there been no further loss, and no necessity nor effort to increase the customary taxation of the past, the planter would have felt hurt to his heart by the disappearance of the bulk of his capital. But when to this was added a new taxation for uplifting Negroes and enriching northerners, he raised his protest to a shriek of bitterness.

When we try to get to the details of the southern states' debts after the war and during Reconstruction, we are faced by the fact that there is no agreement among authorities. The reasons for this are several: First, What is a debt? Is it the amount which a state actually owes, or is it the amount for which a state may become liable in the future, by reason of present commitments and promises? In this latter case, for how much does it actually become liable?

A careful examination of such facts as seem established shows that the increase of debts under the Reconstruction régime was not large. In eleven southern states there was little over $100,000,000 of debt in 1860, which rose to $222,000,000 on account of war. When the Confederate debt was repudiated, the recognized debts in 1865 stood at $156,000,000. To this should be added certain railroad liabilities of Alabama, which brings the total debt at the beginning of Reconstruction to $175,000,000. In 1871, this debt had increased nearly 100 percent to $305,000,000; but $100,000,000 of this debt consisted in contingent and prospective liabilities due to the issue of railway bonds, which confuses the whole issue with regard to Reconstruction debts. The whole increase of debt, during 1860–1871, amounted apparently to less than 100 percent. What now did this increase of debt due to the railway bonds mean? It meant that southern and northern men, Republicans and Democrats, had united to put the credit of the state back of their railway investments. The only way in which nine-tenths of Negro voters came into this matter was as their representatives were bribed by both parties to support this legislation for private profit. Such bribery undoubtedly was widespread. But it was widespread not only among Negro voters, but among white voters, and among all the voters of the United States, and among members of all legislatures and members of Congress. It could hardly be argued that in this respect, new and largely ignorant Negro voters should show a higher public morality than the rest of the country.

On the other hand, the wrath of the landholders against this increase in debt was the wrath of agrarian capitalists against the new industrialism; and yet they were unable to prosecute those who stole the state's money through the issue of railway bonds because there were too many southern people, and southern people of prominence, involved. This was shown in North Carolina, where despite the extravagant investment in railways, the hope of wide immigration and rapid development was disappointed, and the landholders put the commercialists out of power; but they did not dare prosecute them. In Mississippi, on the other hand, where the Negro was as powerful as in any state, there was no increase of debt, because from the first the landholders and Negroes refused to loan the credit of the state to railroads.

If the money raised by taxes had been spent carefully and honestly upon legitimate and necessary matters of restoration and government, the increase is not unreasonable. Or in other words, there is nothing on the face of the figures that proves unusual theft.

Over $150,000,000 of this debt was repudiated by the reactionary governments which came into office after 1876. John F. Hume claims that to this should be added $120,000,000 of debts repudiated before the Civil War, showing that the South was not unused to dealing in this way with borrowed funds.

This indebtedness must also be interpreted by considering the price of gold. South Carolina's debt of twenty-two million in 1871 was made when paper money was at 70 and was therefore equivalent to fifteen and a half million in 1860. Indeed the curve of the price of gold explains to some extent the curve of alleged extravagance.

The debt of these states between the time when it reached its highest point and 1880 was scaled down to $108,003,974. This meant that a sum of $155,525,856 was repudiated and it will be noted that this is almost exactly the increased indebtedness which the Reconstruction régime incurred in order to meet the increased burden of the state—public school education, charitable institutions, the restoration of public buildings, and increased social responsibilities.

There can be no possible proof that all of this increased indebtedness represented theft; nor is there any adequate reason for believing that most of it did. What happened in southern repudiation after the war was that the southern states proceeded to punish people who had dared to loan money to the southern states under Negro suffrage, by confiscating the sums which they had loaned. This was what they had threatened to do, and they did it with vengeance.

There are certain other considerations. White southerners were in practically complete control during the Reconstruction régime, in Virginia and Tennessee; yet in these two states, an indebtedness of $52,000,000 in 1860 increased to $88,000,000 before 1880, and $34,000,000 of this was repudiated. This could hardly be charged to Negro suffrage. Then, too, in North Carolina, Georgia and Alabama, the ex-Confederate South never lost all control, and was early restored to full control. Yet in these states, an indebtedness of $19,000,000 in 1860 reached $81,000,000 before 1880. And of this $56,000,000 was repudiated. A part of the blame of this may be shouldered on white northerners, but very little of it could possibly be attributed to Negroes.

In the case of Florida and Mississippi, the debt was negligible, and on the face of it, absolutely defensible. Yet large amounts were repudiated by the reform party. In South Carolina, the debt stood at nearly $6,000,000 in 1865, before Reconstruction. It reached at its highest point, before 1880, nearly $25,000,000. And of this $17,000,000 was repudiated. If any large proportion of it represented theft, it represented as much the illegal graft of northern moneylenders as the theft of money actually received by the state. Arkansas, under a government in which the Negro had almost no part, repudiated $12,000,000 out of $18,000,000 of indebtedness.

The whole debt transaction of the South after Reconstruction seemed to show that many of the accusations of unreasonable debt, and the haste at repudiation, were a blow aimed at northern finance, rather than a proof of Negro extravagance. It was openly said in Louisiana that it was fitting that "the Northerners who tore down the basis of our former prosperity should share some of the ills."

Sir George Campbell said: "All the Carpet-bag Governors are, as a matter of course, accused of the grossest personal corruption; and as soon as they fall from power it is almost a necessity that they should fly from criminal prosecutions instituted in the local courts under circumstances which give little security for fair trial. . . .

"On the whole, then, I am inclined to believe that the period of Carpet-bag rule was rather a scandal than a very permanent injury . . . ; and there was more pilfering than plunder on a scale permanently to cripple the State."

Indeed, in most cases, the testimony concerning stealing and corruption in the South during this time was either given by bitter political opponents who constituted themselves judge, witness, and jury or by criminals who were clearing their own skirts by accusing others.

Note well the character of the stealing in the South. In the first place, when money was appropriated even extravagantly, it was appropriated for railroads, which the South needed desperately, and it was appropriated under the same terms that had enabled the North and the West to get their railroads; it was appropriated for public institutions; it was appropriated for the buying of land in order to subdivide the great plantations; it was appropriated for certain public services.

In all cases the graft and dishonesty came in the carrying out, the fulfillment of these needs, and this was not only in the hands of white men, but southern white men as often as northern; and northern white financial agents and manipulators in Wall Street helped to make the bond sales of South Carolina, Alabama, Mississippi and Florida. To charge this debt to the Negroes is idiotic. It was not so charged at the time, but this came to be a popular version of southern corruption when it became unpopular to accuse the northerners.

In the original charges of graft and corruption made by the southerners, Negroes were mentioned only as tools. It was the carpetbaggers and scalawags, northern and southern white men, who were continually and insistently charged with theft and corruption.

Then as the carpetbaggers lost the power of military dictatorship, and as the prospect of alliance with the poor whites showed the planters a way of re-securing the government, they turned and with the poor whites concentrated all their accusations of misgovernment and corruption upon the Negro, in order to deprive the Negro of his political power.

Southern corruption was not the exclusive guilt of scalawags and carpetbaggers, nor were all carpetbaggers and scalawags thieves. Some carpetbaggers were noble-hearted philanthropists. Some scalawags were self-sacrificing benefactors of both Negroes and whites. Some of the scalawags and carpet-baggers lied and stole, and some helped and cooperated with the freedmen and worked for real democracy in the South for all races. Indeed in graft and theft the skirts of southern whites of all classes were not clear before or after the war.

Before the war, the South was ruled by an oligarchy and the functions of the state carried on largely by individuals. This meant that the state had little to do, and its expenses were small. The oligarchic state does not need to resort to corruption of the government. Its leaders, having the right to exploit labor to the limit, receive an income which makes them conspicuously independent of any income from the government. The government revenues are kept purposely small and the salaries low so that poor men cannot afford to enter into government service.

On the other hand, when the oligarchy is broken down and when labor increases its power, revenue is raised by taxing the rich, and then the temptation to bribery and stealing increases according to the amount of poverty. The corruption in the South before the war did not usually touch the state governments. The income there was too small to be tempting; yet in Mississippi, after two receivers of public money had defaulted for $155,000, a United States treasury agent recommended that the last one be retained since another would probably be as bad. Other southern states had defaulting officials, and shamelessly repudiated their public debts.

For thirty years, during 1830–60, the South was ruled by its own best citizens and yet during that time there were defalcations in Tennessee, Mississippi, Georgia, Louisiana, Texas, Alabama and Arkansas among postmasters, United States marshals, collectors and surveyors, amounting to more than one million dollars.

How far, then, was postbellum corruption due to Negroes? Only insofar as they represented ignorance and poverty and were thus peculiarly susceptible to petty bribery. No one contends that any considerable amount of money went to them. There were some reports of show and extravagance among them, but the great thieves were always white men; very few Negro leaders were specifically accused of theft, and again seldom in these cases were the accusations proven. Usually they were vague slurs resting on the assumption that all Negroes steal. Petty bribery of members of Reconstruction legislatures, white and black, was widespread; but Wallace in Florida shows the desperate inner turmoil of the Negroes to counteract this within their own ranks; and outstanding cases of notably incorruptible Negro leaders like Lieutenant-Governor Dunn of Louisiana, Treasurer Cardozo of South Carolina, Secretary of State Gibbs of Florida, and Speaker Lynch of Mississippi, are well known.

Certainly the mass of Negroes were unbribable when it came to demands for land and education and other things, the beneficent object of which they could thoroughly understand. But they were peculiarly susceptible to bribes when it was a matter of personal following of demagogues who catered to their likes and weaknesses.

The mass of Negroes were accused of selling votes and influence for small sums and of thus being easily bought up by big thieves; but even in this, they were usually bought up by pretended friends and not bribed against their beliefs or by enemies. To the principles that they understood and knew, they were true; but there were many things connected with government and its technical details which they did not know; in other words, they were ignorant and poor, and the ignorant and poor can always be misled and bribed. What made the Negro poor and ignorant? Surely, it was slavery, and he tried with his vote to escape slavery.

As Dunning says:

As to corruption under the Negro government of the South, this must be noted: first, the decade when the Negroes were ushered into political life, from 1867 to 1877, was probably the most

corrupt decade in the history of the United States, and of all parts
of the United States.

The form and manner of this corruption, which has given so
unsavory a connotation to the name 'reconstruction,' were no
different from those which have appeared in many another time
and place in democratic society. At the very time, indeed, when
the administrations of Scott, in South Carolina, and Warmoth, in
Louisiana, were establishing the Southern high-water mark of
rascality in public finance, the Tweed ring in New York City
was at the culmination of its closely parallel career.

"When we come to examine them, the charges made by such
men as Rhodes, Oberholtzer, Dunning, Bowers, etc., even if
taken at their face value, which they assuredly should not be,
are charges that might with equal force be leveled against
every government, Federal, state and municipal, North and
South, Republican and Democratic, of the time—and against
the 'lily white' Restoration governments that followed in the
South with reaction. Only compare the public moneys stolen
by officers of the Reconstruction governments with the vast
sums that found their way into the pockets of the Tweed
Ring in the perfectly Conservative, Democratic, Copperhead
City of New York!"

It may be contended that the presence of a mass of unlettered and inexperienced voters in a state makes bribery and
graft easier and more capable of misuse by malign elements.
This is true. But the question is, is the situation any better if
ignorance and poverty are permanently disfranchised? The
whole answer of modern industrial conditions is—no, it is not.
And the only alternative, therefore, is the one continually
urged by Sumner, Phillips and Stevens: if ignorance is dangerous—instruct it. If poverty is the cause of stealing and crime,
increase the income of the masses.

Property involves theft by the Rich from the Poor; but there
comes a grave question; given a mass of ignorance and poverty, is that mass less dangerous without the ballot? The answer to this depends upon whose danger one envisages. They

[447]

are not dangerous to the mass of laboring men. If they are kept in ignorance and poverty and dominated by capital, they are certainly dangerous to capital. To escape such revolution and prolong its sway property must yield political power to the mass of laborers, and let it wield that power more intelligently by giving it public schools and higher wages. It is naturally easier for capital to do this gradually, and if there could have been a choice in 1867 between an effective public school system for black labor in the South and its gradual enfranchisement, or even beyond that, a property qualification for such laborers as through free land and higher wage had some chance to accumulate some property—if this had been possible, it would have been, without doubt, the best transition program for capital and labor, provided of course that capitalists thus tamely yielded power. But there was no such alternative. Labor, black labor, must be either enfranchised or enslaved, unless, of course, the United States government was willing to come in with a permanent Freedmen's Bureau to train Negroes toward economic freedom and against the interest of southern capital. This was revolution. This was force and no such permanent Freedmen's Bureau backed by a strongly capitalistic northern government could have been expected in 1867.

The essential problem of Negro enfranchisement was this: How far is the poor and ignorant electorate a permanent injury to the state, and how far does the extent of the injury make for efforts to counteract it? More than a million Negroes were enfranchised in 1867. Of these, it is possible that between 100,000 and 200,000 could read and write, and certainly not more than 25,000, including black immigrants from the North, could be called educated. It was the theory that if these people were given the right to vote, the state, first of all, would be compelled to discontinue plans of political action or industrial organization which did not accord with the general plans of the North, and secondly, in self-defense, it would have to begin the education of the freedmen and establish a system of free labor with wages and conditions of work much fairer than those in vogue during slavery.

How far was this a feasible social program? It was not possible, of course, if the South had the right to continue its industrial organization based on land monopoly and ownership of labor. Conceding the emancipation of labor, that emancipation meant nothing if land monopoly continued and the wage contract was merely nominal. If a wage system was to be installed, it must receive protection either from an outside power, like that of the federal government, or from the worker himself. So far as the worker was concerned, the only protection feasible was the ballot in the hands of a united and intelligently led working class. Could it be assumed now that the possession of the ballot in the hands of ignorant working people, black and white, would lead to real economic emancipation, or on the other hand would it not become a menace to the state so great that its very existence would be threatened?

It had been the insistent contention of many that the basis of the state was threatened between 1867 and 1876 and, therefore, the revolution of 1876 had to take place. The known facts do not sustain this contention and it seems probable that if we had preserved a more complete story of the action of the Negro voter the facts in his favor would even be stronger. As it is, it must be remembered that the proponents of Negro suffrage did not for a moment contend that the experiment was not difficult and would not involve hardship and danger. The elections for the conventions went off, for the most part, without upheaval, with intelligence and certainly with unusual fairness. The conduct of the Negro voters, their selection of candidates, their action in conventions and early legislatures, was, on the whole, sane, thoughtful, and sincere. No one can, with any color of truth, say that civilization was threatened or the foundations of the state attacked in the South in the years from 1868 to 1876.

Then, however, came a time of decisions. Did the South want the Negro to become an intelligent voter and participant in the state under any circumstances, or on the other hand was it opposed to Negro voters no matter how intelligent and efficient?

It may be said, then, that the argument for giving the right to vote to the mass of the poor and ignorant still stands as defensible, without for a moment denying that there should not be such a class in any civilized community; but if the class is there, the fault is the fault of the community and the community must suffer and pay for it. The South had exploited Negro labor for nearly two and one-half centuries. If in ten years or twenty years things could be so changed that this class was receiving an education, getting hold of land, exercising some control over capital, and becoming co-partners in the state, the South would be a particularly fortunate community.

If, on the other hand, there had been the moral strength in the South so that without yielding immediate political power, they could have educated and uplifted the blacks and gradually inducted them into political power and real industrial emancipation, the results undoubtedly would have been better. There was no such disposition, and under the profit ideal of a capitalist organization, there could not have been. That would have required, after the losses of war, an industrial unselfishness of which capitalist organization does not for a moment admit. Force, therefore, and outside force, had to be applied or otherwise slavery would have persisted in a but slightly modified form, and the persistence of slavery in the United States longer than it had already persisted would have been a calamity worse than any of the calamities, real or imagined, of Reconstruction.

Consequently, with northern white leadership, the Negro voters quite confounded the planter plan; they proved apt pupils in politics. They developed their own leadership. They gained clearer and clearer conceptions of how their political power could be used for their own good. They were unselfish, too, in wishing to include in their own good the white worker and even the ex-master. Of course, all that was done in constitution-making and legislation at this time was not entirely the work of black men, and in the same way all that was done in maladministration and corruption was not entirely the fault of the black man. But if the black man is to be blamed for the ills of Reconstruction, he must also be credited for its good, and that good is indubitable. In less than ten years, the basic structure of capitalism in the South was changed by his vote. A new modern state was erected in the place of agrarian slavery. And its foundations were so sound and its general plan so good that despite bitter effort, the South had to accept universal suffrage in theory at least, and had to accept the public school system. It had to broaden social control by adding to the landholder the industrial capitalist.

Indeed the Negro voter in Reconstruction had disappointed all the prophets. The bravest of the carpetbaggers, Tourgée, declared concerning the Negro voters:

They instituted a public school system in a realm where public schools had been unknown. They opened the ballot-box and jury box to thousands of white men who had been debarred from them by a lack of earthly possessions. They introduced home rule in the South. They abolished the whipping post, and branding iron, the stocks and other barbarous forms of punishment which had up to that time prevailed. They reduced capital felonies from about twenty to two or three. In an age of extravagance they were extravagant in the sums appropriated for public works. In all that time no man's rights of person were invaded under the forms of laws.

The Negro buttressed southern civilization in precisely the places it was weakest, against popular ignorance, oligarchy in government, and land monopoly. His schools were more and more successful. If now he became a recognized part of the state, a larger and larger degree of social equality must be granted him. This was apparent in his demand for a single system of public schools without discrimination of race—a demand that came for obvious reasons of economy as well as for advantages of social contact. It appeared also in the demand for equal accommodations on railroads and in public places.

Ultimately, of course, a single system of public schools, and state universities without distinction of race, and equality of civil rights was going to lead to some social intermingling and attacks upon the anti-intermarriage laws which encouraged miscegenation and deliberately degraded women. This was a possibility that the planter class could not contemplate without concern and it stirred among the poor whites a blind and unreasoning fury.

The dictatorship of labor in the South, then, with its establishment of democratic control over social development, education and public improvements, succeeded only at the expense of a taxation on land and property which amounted to confiscation. And it was accompanied by a waste of public funds partly due to inexperience, and partly due to the prevailing wave of political dishonesty that engulfed the whole country.

The singular thing about the wholesale charge of stealing and corruption during Reconstruction times is that when government was restored to the whites and to the Democratic party, there were so few attempts at criminal indictment or to secure any return of the loot. In North Carolina, for instance, wholesale theft was charged against the carpetbaggers, and yet when the governor and leader of the Republican party was impeached, no charge of stealing was in the indictment. He was impeached for using the militia to put down admitted and widespread disorder, and for the arrest of the men who openly and impudently encouraged the disorder.

In Mississippi, all that the restored government apparently wanted was to get rid of Governor Ames. They made no attempt to charge him with theft. In South Carolina, the restored government claimed to have documentary evidence of widespread stealing and graft, and they made a few indictments which were afterward quietly quashed. Why did not the fraud committee go into the courts which they now controlled, and find out where the money they alleged was stolen had gone, and who was now enjoying it? The conclusion is almost inescapable, that the fraud committee knew perfectly well that a large proportion of the thieves were now on the side of white rule, and that much of their theft had been designed and calculated to discredit Negroes and carpetbaggers.

These facts and similar ones show that the overthrow of Reconstruction was in essence a revolution inspired by property, and not a race war.

The echo of the northern reform movement was felt in the South. It encouraged the northern capitalists and the more intelligent Negroes to unite in a southern reform movement. This was shown by the Chamberlain government in South Carolina, the Ames government in Mississippi, and less clearly by the Kellogg government in Louisiana.

The carpetbag reformers moved toward an alliance with the planters with an understanding that called for lower taxes and the elimination of graft and corruption. Negro voters began to support this program, but were restrained by distrust. They feared that the planters still planned their disfranchisement. If this fear could have been removed, and as far as it was removed, the power of the Negro vote in the South was certain to go gradually toward reform.

It was this contingency that the poor whites of all grades feared. It meant to them a re-establishment of that subordination under Negro labor which they had suffered during slavery. They, therefore, interposed by violence to increase the natural antagonism between southerners of the planter class and northerners who represented the military dictatorship as

well as capital, and also to increase the fear of the Negroes
that the planters might try to re-enslave them. The planters
certainly were not disposed to make any permanent alliance
with carpetbaggers like Chamberlain. After all they were
northerners, recent enemies, and were responsible for the taxation that had gone before reform.

The efforts at reform, therefore, at first widely applauded,
one by one began to go down before a new philosophy which
represented understanding between the planters and poor
whites. This again was not an easy thing for the planters to
swallow, but it was accompanied by deference to their social
status, by eagerness on the part of the poor whites to check
the demands of the Negroes by any means, and by willingness
to do the dirty work of the revolution that was coming, with
its blood and crass cruelties, its bitter words, upheaval and
turmoil. This was the birth and being of the Ku Klux Klan.

Before the war, there had been violent southern anti-Negro
propaganda on racial lines; but that had been mainly for
consumption in the North. Northerners, traveling in the
South, were always astonished at finding it accompanied by
peculiar evidences of social equality and closer intimacies; in
other words, there was no deep racial antagonism except in
the case of poor whites, where it had a tremendous economic
foundation. After the war, the race division, so long as the
economic foundation was equitable, would have become less
and less pronounced had it not been emphasized with determination in the application of the "Mississippi Plan."

It is one of the anomalies of history that political and economic reform in the North and West after 1873 joined hands
with monopoly and reaction in the South to oppress and
re-enslave labor.

Every effort was made by careful propaganda to induce the
nation to believe that the southern wing of the Democratic
party was fighting the same kind of corruption as the North
and that corruption was represented in the South solely by

carpetbaggers and Negroes. This was only partly true in the South; for there labor too was fighting corruption and dishonesty, so far as land and capital, which were secretly abetting graft in order to escape taxation, would allow it to do so without disfranchisement. But the South now began to use the diplomacy so badly lacking in its previous leadership since the war. Adroitly it stopped attacking abolitionists and even carpetbaggers, and gradually transferred all the blame for postwar misgovernment to the Negroes. The Negro vote and graft were indissolubly linked in the public mind by incessant propaganda. Race repulsion, race hate, and race pride were increased by every subtle method, until the Negro and his friends were on the defensive and the Negro himself almost convinced of his own guilt. Negro haters and pseudo-scientists raised their heads and voices in triumph. Lamar of Mississippi, fraudulently elected to Congress, unctuously praised Sumner with his tongue in his cheek; and Louisiana solemnly promised to give Negroes full political and civil rights with equal education for Negro children—a deliberate lie which is absolutely proven by the revelations of the last fifty years.

The South was impelled to brute force and deliberate deception in dealing with the Negro because it had been astonished and disappointed not by the Negro's failure, but by his success and promise of greater success.

All this came at a time when the best conscience of the nation—the conscience which was heir to the enthusiasm of abolitionist-democracy—was turned against the only power which could support democracy in the South. The truth of the insistence of Stevens was manifest: without land and without vocation, the Negro voter could not gain that economic independence which would protect his vote. Unless, therefore, his political and civil rights were supported by the United States Army, he was doomed to practical re-enslavement. But the United States Army became in the seventies the representative of the party of political corruption, while its political opponents represented land monopoly and capitalistic reaction in the South. When, therefore, the conscience of the United States attacked corruption, it at the same time attacked in the Republican party the only power that could support democracy in the South. It was a paradox too tragic to explain and it deceived leading reformers, like Carl Schurz, into consenting to throw the poor, ignorant black workers, whom he had helped to enfranchise, to the lions of land monopoly and capitalistic control, which proposed to devour them, and did.

In the South, reform sought to follow the northern model and the carpetbag capitalists turned toward the purging of the civil service and the throttling of monopoly. In this, they gained the backing of many intelligent Negroes. But for one thing they could have got the bulk of the Negro vote, and that one thing was the Negro's distrust of the honesty of the planters' objects. Did the planter want reform or did he want re-enslavement of Negro labor? As a matter of fact, the planter got the beginnings of reform in the administration of government in South Carolina, in Mississippi, and even in Louisiana. But he was aware that if that movement went far, it would prove that the Negro vote could be appealed to and made effective in good government as well as bad. This he did not want. As the South Carolina Democratic convention said, April, 1868, in an address to the colored people: "It is impossible that your present power can endure, whether you use it for good or ill."

Back of this was the knowledge that honest labor government would be more fatal to land monopoly and industrial privilege than government by bribery and graft.

The white South, therefore, quickly substituted violence and renewal of the war in order to get rid of the possibility of good government supported by black labor votes.

There was not a single honest southerner who did not know that any reasonable political program which included a fair chance for the Negro to get an honest wage, personal protection, land to work, and schools for his children, would have received the staunch, loyal and unyielding support of the overwhelming mass of Negro voters; but this program, when ostensibly offered the Negro, concealed the determination to reduce him practically to slavery. He knew this and in his endeavor to escape floundered through bribery, corruption, and murder, seeking a path to peace, freedom, and the income of a civilized man.

The South has itself to blame. It showed no historic sign of favoring emancipation before the war, rather the contrary. It showed no disposition to yield to the offer of recompensed emancipation which Abraham Lincoln repeatedly made. It showed no desire to yield to emancipation with correspondingly curtailed political power as Congress suggested. It showed no disposition to reform democracy with the Negro vote. It relied on stubborn brute force.

Meantime, the leaders of northern capital and finance were still afraid of the return of southern political power after the lapse of the military dictatorship. This power was larger than before the war and it was bound to grow. If it were to be used in conjunction with northern liberals, it might still mean the reduction of the tariff, the reduction of monopoly, and an attack upon new financial methods and upon concentrated control in industry. There was now no sentiment like "freedom" to which the northern industrialists could appeal. It was, therefore, necessary for northern capital to make terms with the dominant South.

Thus, both the liberal and the conservative North found themselves willing to sacrifice the interests of labor in the South to the interest of capital. The temporary dictatorship as represented by the Freedmen's Bureau was practically ended by 1870. This led to an increase of violence on the part of the Ku Klux Klan to subject black labor to strict domination by capital and to break Negro political power. The outbreak brought a temporary return of military dictatorship, but the return was unpopular in the North and aroused bitter protest in the South.

Yet the end that planters and poor whites envisaged and, as the fight went on, the end that large numbers of the northern capitalists were fighting for, was a movement in the face of modern progress. It did not go to the length of disfranchising the whole laboring class, black and white, because it dared not do this, although this was its logical end. It did disfranchise black labor with the aid of white southern labor and with the silent acquiescence of white northern labor.

The white capitalist of the South saw a chance of getting rid of the necessity of treating with and yielding to the voting power of fully half the laboring class. It seized this opportunity, knowing that it thus was setting back the economic progress of the world; that the United States, instead of marching forward through the preliminary revolution by which the petty bourgeois and the laboring class armed with the vote were fighting the power of capital, was disfranchising a part of labor and on the other hand allowing great capital a chance for enormous expansion in the country. And this enormous expansion got its main chance through the thirty-three electoral votes which the counting of the full black population in the South gave to that section. It was only necessary now that this political power of the South should be used in behalf of capital and not for the strengthening of labor and universal suffrage. This was the bargain of 1876.

Reconstruction, therefore, in the South degenerated into a fight of rivals to control property and through that to control the labor vote. This rivalry between dictators led to graft and corruption as they bid against each other for the vote of the Negro, while meantime Negro labor in its ignorance and poverty was agonizing for ways of escape. Northern capital compromised, and southern capital accepted race hate and black disfranchisement as a permanent program of exploitation.

In a certain way this great struggle of a laboring class of five black millions was epitomized by the appearance of sixteen of their representatives in the federal Congress from 1869 to 1876. These are the men, their states and their service:

Hiram R. Revels, Senator, Mississippi, 1870–1871.

Blanche K. Bruce, Senator, Mississippi, 1875–1881.

Jefferson P. Long, Congressman, Georgia, 1869–1871.

Joseph H. Rainey, Congressman, South Carolina, 1871–1879.

Robert C. DeLarge, Congressman, South Carolina, 1871–1873.

Robert Brown Elliott, Congressman, South Carolina, 1871–1875.

Benjamin S. Turner, Congressman, Alabama, 1871–1873.

Josiah T. Walls, Congressman, Florida, 1873–1877.

Alonzo J. Ransier, Congressman, South Carolina, 1871–1873.

James T. Rapier, Congressman, Alabama, 1873–1875.

Richard H. Cain, Congressman, South Carolina, 1873–1875, 1877–1879.

John R. Lynch, Congressman, Mississippi, 1873–1877, 1881–1883.

Charles E. Nash, Congressman, Louisiana, 1875–1877.

John A. Hyman, Congressman, North Carolina, 1875–1877.

Jere Haralson, Congressman, Alabama, 1875–1877.

Robert Smalls, Congressman, South Carolina, 1875–1879, 1881–1887.

Several others, like Menard of Florida, Pinchback of Louisiana, Lee and others, had excellent titles to their seats, but did not gain them. Twelve of these men who were the earliest to enter Congress were ex-slaves or born of slave parents and brought up when Negroes were denied education. On the other hand the other four had received a more or less complete college education in the North and abroad. Five of the Congressmen were lawyers, and two, Elliott and Rapier, had unusual training and ability.

Rhodes sneers at these men: "They left no mark on the legislation of their time; none of them, in comparison with their white associates, attained the least distinction."

But Blaine, who knew them and served with most of them, said: "The colored men who took seats in both Senate and House did not appear ignorant or helpless. They were as a rule studious, earnest, ambitious men, whose public conduct . . . would be honorable to any race."

Most of the colored congressmen had had experience in state legislatures and in public office. When these men entered Congress, questions of Reconstruction and of the economic and social condition in the North and West were before it. These included the exploitation of public lands, the development of railroads, the question of money, and the relation of the races in the South. The Negro Congressmen, especially, had three objects: to secure themselves civil rights, to aid education, and to settle the question of the political disabilities of their former masters.

This last question became of paramount importance. Long of Georgia was in favor of removing disabilities if the southerners proved loyal to the new legislation. Revels supported amnesty, but Rainey felt that it had led to force and murder. Elliott protested against amnesty, saying that the men seeking relief were responsible for the crimes perpetrated against loyal men in the South, and that this proposal put a premium on disloyalty and treason.

All the Negro congressmen plead for civil rights for their race. It was here that Robert Brown Elliott made one of his greatest speeches in a dramatic situation seldom equaled in Congress. Forney describes the incident:

Mr. Stephens, the Vice-President of the Confederacy, of which slavery was the corner-stone, spoke January 6, 1874, and Mr. Elliott, the colored champion of the liberated race, followed him the next day. I cannot describe the House when the two men addressed it, especially when the African answered the Caucasian. Here we have a new history—a history that may, indeed, be repeated, but which stands alone in the novelty of all its surroundings, and in the eloquence of all its lessons. . . .

Mr. Elliott, the last speaker, is a full-blooded black, a native of Boston, Massachusetts, where he was born August 11, 1842. Educated in England, he was not of age when the Rebellion broke out; and in 1868, in his twenty-sixth year, was a member of the South Carolina Legislature, and elected to Congress from Columbia district in 1872. He received 21,627 votes, against 1,079 votes for the Democratic candidate, W. H. McCaw. Had any man predicted that this colored boy, while attending school in 1853, at High Holborn Academy, and Eton College, England, in 1855, would sit in Congress from the capital of the proud state of South Carolina in 1874, and would there confute the ablest apostle of the old slave power, he would have been pronounced a madman.

Elliott, defending against Stephens civil rights for Negroes, said:

Sir, it is scarcely twelve years since that gentleman shocked the civilized world by announcing the birth of a government which rested on human slavery as its corner-stone. The progress of events has swept away that pseudo-government which rested on greed, pride, and tyranny; and the race whom he then ruthlessly spurned and trampled on are here to meet him in debate, and to demand that the rights which are enjoyed by their former oppressors—who vainly sought to overthrow a Government which they could not prostitute to the base uses of slavery—shall be accorded to those who even in the darkness of slavery kept their allegiance true to freedom and the Union. Sir, the gentleman from Georgia has learned much since 1861; but he is still a laggard. Let him put away entirely the false and fatal theories which have so greatly marred an otherwise enviable record. Let him accept, in its fullness and beneficence, the great doctrine that American citizenship carries with it every civil and political right which manhood can confer. Let him lend his influence, with all his masterly ability, to complete the proud structure of legislation which makes this nation worthy of the great declaration which heralded its birth, and he will have done that which will most nearly redeem his reputation in the eyes of the world, and best vindicate the wisdom of that policy which has permitted him to regain his seat upon this floor.

In the matter of education, Rainey of South Carolina was one of the first Americans to demand national aid for education. Walls of Florida protested that national aid was not an invasion of state rights, and showed the discrimination in the distribution of state funds.

The colored congressmen advocated local improvements, including distribution of public lands, public buildings, and appropriations for rivers and harbors, in Alabama, Florida, Mississippi and South Carolina.

Aside from these more personal questions, Negro congressmen discussed national economic matters. Walls of Florida and Lynch of Mississippi asked protective tariffs for local products, including cotton, lumber and sugar. Walls voted for an appropriation for the centennial exposition of 1876, and urged the recognition of Cuba. Hyman championed relief of the Cherokee Indians. Bruce opposed the restriction of Chinese immigration, arraigned our selfish policy toward Indians, and especially advocated improving the navigation of the Mississippi and protecting life and property from its overflow.

The words of these black men were, perhaps, the last clear, earnest expression of the democratic theory of American government in Congress.

Congressman DeLarge of South Carolina said in 1871:

When I heard the gentleman from New York (Mr. Cox) on Tuesday last hurl his shafts against the members of my race, charging that through their ignorance they had brought about these excesses, I thought he should have remembered that for the ignorance of that portion of the people, he and his party associates are responsible, not those people themselves. While there may have been extravagance and corruption resulting from the placing of improper men in official positions—and this is part of the cause of the existing state of things—these evils have been brought about by men identified with the race to which the gentleman from New York belongs, and not by our race.

Congressman Rainey of South Carolina said in the same debate:

Sir, I ask this House, I ask the country, I ask white men, I ask Democrats, I ask Republicans whether the Negroes have presumed to take improper advantage of the majority they hold in that State by disregarding the interest of the minority? They have not. Our convention which met in 1868, and in which the Negroes were in a large majority, did not pass any proscriptive or disfranchising acts, but adopted a liberal constitution, securing alike equal rights to all citizens, white and black, male and female, as far as possible. Mark you, we did not discriminate, although we had a majority. Our constitution towers up in its majesty with provisions for the equal protection of all classes of citizens.

It was not, then, race and culture calling out of the South in 1876; it was property and privilege, shrieking to its kind, and privilege and property heard and recognized the voice of its own.

The bargain of 1876 was essentially an understanding by which the federal government ceased to sustain the right to vote of half of the laboring population of the South, and left capital as represented by the old planter class, the new northern capitalist, and the capitalist that began to rise out of the poor whites, with a control of labor greater than in any modern industrial state in civilized lands. Out of that there has arisen in the South an exploitation of labor unparalleled in modern times, with a government in which all pretense at party alignment or regard for universal suffrage is given up. The methods of government have gone uncriticized, and elections are by secret understanding and manipulation; the dictatorship of capital in the South is complete.

The military dictatorship was withdrawn, and the representatives of northern capital gave up all efforts to lead the Negro vote. The new dictatorship became a manipulation of the white labor vote which followed the lines of similar control in the North, while it proceeded to deprive the black voter by violence and force of any vote at all. The rivalry of these two classes of labor and their competition neutralized the labor vote in the South. The black voter struggled and appealed, but it was in vain. And the United States, re-enforced by the increased political power of the South based on disfranchisement of black voters, took its place to re-enforce the capitalistic dictatorship of the United States, which became the most powerful in the world, and which backed the new industrial imperialism and degraded colored labor the world over.

This meant a tremendous change in the whole intellectual and spiritual development of civilization in the South and in the United States because of the predominant political power of the South, built on disfranchised labor. The United States was turned into a reactionary force. It became the cornerstone of that new imperialism which is subjecting the labor of yellow, brown, and black peoples to the dictation of capitalism organized on a world basis; and it has not only brought nearer the revolution by which the power of capitalism is to be challenged, but also it is transforming the fight to the sinister aspect of a fight on racial lines embittered by awful memories.

It is argued that Negro suffrage was bad because it failed, and at the same time that its failure was a proof of its badness. Negro suffrage failed because it was overthrown by brute force. Even if it had been the best government on earth, force, exercised by a majority of richer, more intelligent, and more experienced men, could have overthrown it. It was not overthrown so long as the military dictatorship of the North sustained it. But the South proved by appropriate propaganda that Negro government was the worst ever seen and that it threatened civilization. They suited their propaganda to their audience. They had tried the accusation of laziness but that was refuted by a restoration of agriculture to the prewar level and beyond it. They tried the accusation of ignorance but this was answered by the Negro schools.

It happened that the accusation of incompetence impressed the North not simply because of the moral revolt there against graft and dishonesty but because the North had never been thoroughly converted to the idea of Negro equality. When, therefore, the North, even granting that all the South said of the Negro was not true, contemplated possibilities, it paused. Did the nation want blacks with power sitting in the Senate and in the House of Representatives, accumulating wealth and entering the learned professions? Would this not eventually and inevitably lead to social equality and even to black sons and daughters-in-law and mulatto descendants? Was it possible to contemplate such eventualities?

Under such circumstances, it was much easier to believe the accusations of the South and to listen to the proof which biology and social science hastened to adduce of the inferiority of the Negro. The North seized upon the new Darwinism, the "Survival of the Fittest," to prove that what they had attempted in the South was an impossibility; and they did this in the face of the facts which were before them, the examples of Negro efficiency, of Negro brains, of phenomenal possibilities of advancement.

Moreover, Americans saw throughout the world the shadow of the coming change of the philanthropic attitude which had dominated the early nineteenth century, with regard to the backward races. International and commercial imperialism began to get a vision. Within the very echo of that philanthropy which had abolished the slave trade, was beginning a new industrial slavery of black and brown and yellow workers in Africa and Asia. Arising from this, as a result of this economic foundation, came the change in the attitude toward these darker people. They were no longer "Brothers in Black"; they were inferiors. These inferiors were to be governed for their own good. They were to be raised out of sloth and laziness by being compelled to work. The whole attitude of Europe was reflected in America and it found in America support for its own attitude.

The great republic of the West was trying an impossible experiment. They were trying to make white men out of black men. It could not be done. It was a mistake to conceive it. The North and Europe were still under the sway of individual laissez-faire in industry, and "hands off" in government. It was easy, therefore, for the North to persuade itself that whatever happened politically in the South was right. If the majority did not want Negro rule, or Negro participation in government, the majority was right, and they would not allow themselves to stop and ask how that majority was made. They knew that an organized inner group was compelling the mass of white people to act as a unit; was pounding them by false social sanctions into a false uniformity.

If that part of the white South which had a vision of democracy and was willing to grant equality to Negroes of equal standing had been sustained long enough by a standing federal police, democracy could have been established in the South. But brute force was allowed to use its unchecked power in the actions of the whites to destroy the possibility of democracy in the South, and thereby make the transition from democracy to plutocracy all the easier and more inevitable.

Through the rift of the opposition, between votes for and against the Negro, between high and low tariff, between free land and land monopoly, plutocracy drove a silent coach and four.

What the South did in 1876 was to make good its refusal either to give up slavery or to yield the political power based on the counting of slaves.

And so the South rode the wind into the whirlwind and accomplished what it sought. Did it pay? Did it settle either the Negro's problem or any problem of wealth, labor, or human uplift? On the contrary, it made the government of the South a system of secret manipulations with lying and cheating. It made its religion fundamental hypocrisy. And the South knows today that the essential Negro problem is just as it was—how far it dare let the Negro be a modern man.

It was all so clear and right and logical. A nation could not exist half-slave and half-free. If it tried, either its mass of laborers would by force of competition sink into the depths of exploited, ignorant poverty, or rising in bloody revolt break the monopoly of land and materials and endow the mass with more equal income and more political power to maintain their freedom.

So in America came Civil War over the slavery of labor and the end was not peace, but the endeavor really and honestly to remove the cause of strife—to give the black freedman and the white laborer land and education and power to conduct the state in the interests of labor and not of landed oligarchy. Labor lurched forward after it had paid in blood for the chance. And labor, especially black labor, cried for Light and Land and Leading. The world laughed. It laughed North. It laughed West. But in the South it roared with hysterical, angry, vengeful laughter. It said: "Look at these niggers; they are black and poor and ignorant. How can they rule those of us who are white and have been rich and have at our command all wisdom and skill? Back to slavery with the dumb brutes!"

Still the brutes strove on and up with silent, fearful persistency. They restored the lost crops; they established schools; they gave votes to the poor whites; they established democracy; and they even saved a pittance of land and capital out of their still slave-bound wage.

The masters feared their former slaves' success far more than their anticipated failure. They lied about the Negroes. They accused them of theft, crime, moral enormities and laughable grotesqueries. They forestalled the danger of a united southern labor movement by appealing to the fear and hate of white labor and offering them alliance and leisure. They encouraged them to ridicule Negroes and beat them, kill and burn their bodies. The planters even gave the poor whites their daughters in marriage, and raised a new oligarchy on the tottering, depleted foundations of the old oligarchy, a mass of new rulers the more ignorant, intolerant and ruthless because of their inferiority complex. And thus was built a solid South impervious to reason, justice or fact.

With this arose a solid North—a North born of that North which never meant to abolish Negro slavery, because its profits were built on it; but who had been gradually made by idealists and laborers and freed slaves to refuse more land to slavery; to refuse to catch and return slaves; and finally to fight for freedom since this preserved cotton, tobacco, sugar, and the southern market.

Then this new North, fired by a vision of concentrated economic power and profit greater than the world had visioned, tried to stop war and hasten back to industry. But the blind, angry, bewildered South threatened to block the building of this new industrial oligarchy by a political power increased by the very abolition of slavery, until the North had to yield to democracy and give black labor the power with which white southern landholders threatened northern industry.

In return, northern capital bribed black and white labor in the South and white and black labor in the North. It thrust debt, concessions, and graft on the South, while in the North it divided labor into exploiting and exploited groups of skilled and highly paid craftsmen who might and did become capitalists, and a mass of ignorant, disfranchised, imported foreign slaves. The West transformed its laboring peasant-farmers into land speculators and investors and united its interests through railways to the Solid South in return for non-interference with big business. . . .

And yet, despite this, and despite the long step backward toward slavery that black folk have been pushed, they have made withal a brave and fine fight; a fight against ridicule and monstrous caricature, against every refinement of cruelty and gross insult, against starvation, disease and murder in every form. It has left in their soul its scars, its deep scars; but when all is said, through it all has gone a thread of brave and splendid friendship from those few and rare men and women of white skins, North and South, who have dared to know and help and love black folk.

The unending tragedy of Reconstruction is the utter inability of the American mind to grasp its real significance, its national and worldwide implications. It was vain for Sumner and Stevens to hammer in the ears of the people that this problem involved the very foundations of American democracy, both political and economic. We are still too blind and infatuated to conceive of the emancipation of the laboring class in half the nation as a revolution comparable to the upheavals in France in the past, and in Russia, Spain, India and China today. We were worried when the beginnings of this experiment cost $18,000,000, and quite aghast when a debt of $225,000,000 was involved, including waste and theft. We apparently expected that this social upheaval was going to be accomplished with peace, honesty and efficiency, and that the planters were going quietly to surrender the right to live on the labor of black folk, after 250 years of habitual exploitation. And it seems to America a proof of inherent race inferiority that four million slaves did not completely emancipate themselves in eighty years, in the midst of nine million bitter enemies, and indifferent public opinion of the whole nation. If the reconstruction of the southern states, from slavery to free labor, and from aristocracy to industrial democracy, had been conceived as a major national program of America, whose accomplishment at any price was well worth the effort, we should be living today in a different world.

The attempt to make black men American citizens was in a certain sense all a failure, but a splendid failure. It did not fail where it was expected to fail. It was Athanasius contra mundum, with back to the wall, outnumbered ten to one, with all the wealth and all the opportunity, and all the world against him. And only in his hands and heart the consciousness of a great and just cause; fighting the battle of all the oppressed and despised humanity of every race and color, against the massed hirelings of religion, science, education, law, and brute force.

PART V

THE COLLAPSE OF RECONSTRUCTION

The climactic scene in the motion picture *Birth of a Nation* shows white-robed Klansmen riding to save South Carolina civilization from certain disaster. Corruption and depravity in the South, it is alleged, had reached such a point that the white citizens finally lost their patience and were forced to strike back violently. There is some truth in this view of southern "redemption." That is, although a number of factors help to explain the collapse of Radical rule, it was essentially a triumph of force and violence. The bipartisan nature of corruption during Reconstruction, and the extent to which it persisted after the collapse of the Radical governments, also makes it clear that the fundamental objection of the white South was the participation of black men in their political life and the real possibility that Reconstruction might actually reconstruct southern society. "There was one thing that the white South feared more than negro dishonesty," DuBois wrote, "and that was negro honesty, knowledge, and efficiency." It was this understandable fear that determined the nature of the southern response to Reconstruction and led the "redeemers" to attack indiscriminately both honest and corrupt governments. Within ten years after Radical Reconstruction had begun, this significant experiment in democratic government had come to a violent end.

20

THE REVOLUTION
OF 1875

Vernon Lane Wharton

> To redeem their state from Radical rule and Negro
> political power, white Mississippians developed an
> elaborate pattern of pressures, intimidation, and
> violence. Vernon L. Wharton describes what came
> to be called the Shot Gun or Mississippi Plan.

From the beginning of Reconstruction, there were in Mississippi a large number of white men who insisted upon the
necessity of accepting the results of the war and of complying
with the requirements of the national government. This
group, made up largely of old Whigs, and generally men of
property, desired above all else order, prosperity, and harmonious relations within the Union. Guaranteeing to the Negro
those minimum rights set up in the amendments to the Constitution, they would seek to gain his confidence and his vote by
convincing him that their leadership was for the best interests
of both races. Such distinguished citizens as A. G. Brown,
C. C. Shackleford, H. F. Simrall, Amos R. Johnston, J. A. P.
Campbell, Joshua Morris, and J. L. Alcorn were by tempera-
ment members of this group, although some worked with the
Democratic party and some with the Republican. The essence
of their failure lay in the fact that almost none of them could
bring himself to deal with a Negro, however able or honest

that Negro might be, as a political or social equal. In later years, J. L. Alcorn often declared that he had never been a "negro Republican." Exactly the same was true of such northern leaders as H. R. Pease, George C. McKee, and R. C. Powers. By 1874, men of this class had to recognize either their failure to make Democrats of the Negroes, or the repudiation of their leadership in the Republican party. Given the assurance that the national government would not intervene, most of these conservatives were then ready to join the mass of the white Democrats in any methods they might use to drive the Negroes from power.

The majority of the white citizens, brought up on the belief that the Negro was an inferior creature who must be kept in subjection, found themselves unable from the beginning to endorse the program of the Conservatives. In December, 1869, the editor of the Columbus *Index* made a bid for the leadership of this group with the declaration: "We have given the negro a fair trial. He has voted solidly against us, and we hoist, from this day, the white man's flag, and will never take it down so long as we have a voice in the government of the State." The year 1870 saw the organization of a number of "White Men's Clubs" throughout the state. One at Bellefontaine, with 152 members, pledged its subscribers to a perpetual and uncompromising opposition to social and political equality of the white and black races, and to all measures tending thereto. Believing that Negro suffrage was "wrong in principle and disastrous in effect," they pledged themselves to labor unceasingly, from year to year, for the restoration of white supremacy in Mississippi and in the United States. A similar club at West Point agreed to follow a policy that would ignore the Negro as a voter and as an element in politics. The Columbus *Democrat*, advocating the union of these groups in a revitalized Democratic party, declared:

. . . Its leading ideas are, that white men shall govern, that niggers are not rightly entitled to vote, and that when it gets into power, niggers will be placed upon the same footing with white minors who do not vote or hold office.

There are professed Democrats who do not understand Democratic principles, that want the party mongrelized, thinking that the less difference between the two parties will give them a better chance for the spoils. They are willing for the niggers to vote, but not to hold office. . . .

Nigger voting, holding office and sitting in the jury box, are all wrong, and against the sentiment of the country. There is nothing more certain to occur than that these outrages upon justice and good government will soon be removed, and the unprincipled men who are now their advocates will sink lower in the social scale than the niggers themselves.

Here was sheer racial antagonism. There was no consideration of the undesirability of the participation of ignorant and poverty-stricken masses in the government of the state; the line was drawn on the basis of race.

In the face of the decrepitude of the Democratic party, and of the certainty of federal intervention in case of a statewide movement based on violence, the program was held in check during 1871, 1872, and 1873. But with the rejection of Alcorn in the election of 1873, and the great increase in office holding by Negroes after that election, the movement gained new strength. Native and northern whites whose leadership had been rejected by the Negroes now joined in the demand for white supremacy. The great financial depression of 1873 was reflected in the state by increased unpleasantness in political and social relations, and in the nation by a decline of interest in affairs of the South. Furthermore this financial collapse, along with the discovery of scandals in the federal government, served greatly to weaken the power of the Republican party in the nation. There were predictions of a Democratic president in 1876. When these predictions were strengthened by the great Democratic victories which gained control of the House of Representatives in 1874, conservative leaders in Mississippi at last agreed to abandon their caution. The word went out that the time for revolution was at hand, and the efforts of such men as A. G. Brown and L. Q. C. Lamar to halt the movement were of no avail.

Greater and greater numbers of white Republicans in Mississippi were now deserting the party and joining the opposing conventions. As Charles Nordhoff was told in the spring of 1875, the Democrats were making it "too damned hot for them to stay out." Economic pressure and threats of physical violence were used, but the most powerful force was that of social ostracism. Colonel James A. Lusk, a prominent native Republican, said to a Negro leader: "No white man can live in the South in the future and act with any other than the Democratic party unless he is willing and prepared to live a life of social isolation and remain in political oblivion." In consideration of the future happiness of his sons and daughters, he felt it necessary to announce his renunciation of all Republican connections. The Canton *Mail* published the names of those whites who must no longer be recognized on the streets, and whose attentions must be scorned by "every true woman."

At the same time that white Republicans were abandoning their party, more and more of the conservative Democratic leaders and newspapers were accepting the "white-line" program. The transition could be seen clearly in most cases. Editors who for several years had written of the Negroes in terms of sympathy, impatience, or friendly ridicule, and who had even praised them at times in an effort to gain their votes, came to speak of them during the summer of 1874 with open dislike, and finally with hatred. By May of 1875, such original color liners as the Vicksburg *Herald*, Columbus *Index*, Handsboro *Democrat*, Yazoo City *Banner*, Vicksburg *Monitor*, and Okolona *Southern States*, had been joined by the conservative Hinds County *Gazette*, Newton *Ledger*, Brandon *Republican*, Forest *Register*, and Jackson *Clarion*, and by the Republican Meridian *Gazette*.

The general charge made by papers and individuals in renouncing their former conservatism was that the color line had already been drawn by the Negro. As evidence, they offered the fact that almost none of the Negroes ever voted with the whites (Democrats), that in some of the counties the Negroes had taken most of the offices, that in the Republican convention of 1873 Negroes had absolutely demanded three of the seven state offices, and that, on such questions as the reduction of the tax for schools, Negroes in the legislature had voted almost as a unit against the whites. In making these charges, the Democrats ignored the fact that the Negroes had from the beginning welcomed the leadership of almost any white who would serve with them, that in so doing they had taken into their party from ten to twenty thousand white Mississippians and that they could not be expected to join in any numbers a party which had from the beginning opposed all of the rights upon which their hopes were built.

As time went on the attack became more and more bitter. The Forest *Register* carried at its masthead the slogan: "A white man in a white man's place. A black man in a black man's place. Each according to the 'eternal fitness of things.'" The Yazoo City *Banner* declared, "*Mississippi is a white man's country, and by the Eternal God we'll rule it.*" The Handsboro *Democrat* called for "*A white man's Government, by white men, for the benefit of white men.*" All of these papers justified their stand in editorials describing the depravity and innate bestiality of the Negro. These reached a climax in one published by the Forest *Register*.

A negro preacher is an *error loci*. God Almighty, in farming out his privileges to mankind, drew a line as to qualifications.
He never exacted from a nation or tribe an impossibility. . . . Does any sane man believe the negro capable of comprehending the ten commandments? The miraculous conception and the birth of our Savior? The high moral precepts taught from the temple on the mount?

Every effort to inculcate these great truths but tends to bestialize his nature, and by obfuscating his little brain unfits him for the duties assigned him as a hewer of wood and drawer of water. The effort makes him a demon of wild, fanatical destruction, and consigns him to the fatal shot of the white man.

Declarations by the rapidly dwindling group of conservative Democrats that the votes of the Negroes could be secured by treating them fairly and reasoning with them met the scorn of the white-liners. The editor of the Newton *Democrat* declared that he would just as soon try to reason with a shoal of crocodiles or a drove of Kentucky mules. From Colonel McCardle of the Vicksburg *Herald* came the answer: "The way to treat Sambo is not to argue to him or to reason with him. If you do that, it puffs his vanity and it only makes him insolent. Say to him, 'Here, we are going to *carry* this election; you may vote as you like; but we *are* going to carry it. Then we are going to look after ourselves and our friends; you can look after yourself,' and he will vote with you." Furthermore, when Lamar succeeded in inserting in the Democrat-Conservative platform a vague statement recognizing "the civil and political equality of all men," and inviting the Negroes to vote with the party for good government, the white-liners were quick to deny any allegiance. As a Democratic leader declared the following year, ". . . [The] only issue in the election was whether the whites or the blacks should predominate; there was no other politics that I could see in it. Men that had been republicans all their lives just laid aside republicanism and said that they had to go into the ranks then." In the words of J. S. McNeily, "It was part of the creed of a desperate condition, one easily understood, that any white man, however odious, was preferable . . . to any negro however unobjectionable individually."

Once the general policy had been adopted that Negro and Republican control of the state government was to be broken

at any cost, a number of methods were followed for its accomplishment. One of these involved the intimidation of those
whites who still worked with the Republican party. There
was a general understanding that in the case of the outbreak of
a "race war," carpetbaggers would be the first to be killed. As
early as December, 1874, the Hinds County *Gazette* declared
that death should be meted out to those who continued their
opposition. "All other means having been exhausted to abate
the horrible condition of things, the thieves and robbers, and
scoundrels, white and black, deserve death and ought to be
killed. . . . The thieves and robbers kept in office by Governor Ames and his robber associates . . . ought to be compelled
to leave the State, or abide the consequences." After the Clinton "riot," Colonel McCardle of the *Herald* urged that in
future cases of violence white Republicans be killed and the
deluded Negroes spared. At the same time, the editor of the
Columbus *Index* announced, "The White League is resolved
to kill hereafter only those white wretches who incite negroes
to riot and murder." According to J. S. McNeily, "There is
no doubt that this sentiment made for peace, in the campaign." There is also no doubt that as time went by the
Negroes found fewer and fewer white leaders at their meetings.

Against the Negroes themselves one of the most powerful
forces used was economic pressure. All over the state, Democratic clubs announced that no Negro who voted Republican
could hope for any form of employment the following year.
It was also urged that the boycott be extended to the wives of
Negro Republicans. In some cases, doctors announced that
they would no longer serve Negroes who did not vote the
Democratic ticket. Lists of Negroes who were pledged for or
against the party were prepared, and arrangements were made
for checkers to be present at the polls. After the election, the
names of Negroes marked for discharge were printed in the

various papers, along with the names of those who deserved special consideration for having refrained from voting or for having worked with the Democrats.

At the same time, except in the counties where the Democrats had a safe majority, strenuous efforts were being made to get the Negroes into the various Democratic clubs. For those Negroes who would take this step, and participate in the processions and other functions of the clubs, there were pledges of protection and of continued employment. There were also abundant supplies of flags, transparencies, uniforms, and badges. The Democratic badge in Lafayette County not only protected the wearer from physical violence, but also allowed him to "boss" other Negroes. There were numerous barbecues and picnics at which Negro bands and glee clubs furnished entertainment, and at which Negroes either volunteered or were hired to speak. In some of the counties, no expense was spared. In Monroe, the candidates for the legislature gave one thousand dollars each, and subscriptions from private citizens ranged up to five hundred dollars. In Panola, the Democratic committee supplied five thousand dollars in addition to subscriptions from individuals. According to one of the leaders in that county, "Our purpose was to overawe the negroes and exhibit to them the ocular proof of our power . . . by magnificent torchlight processions at night and in the day by special trains of cars . . . loaded down with white people with flags flying, drums beating, and bands playing, the trains being chartered and free for everybody."

However pleasing these affairs may have been to those who participated, they had little effect on the campaign. Negro attendance was usually disappointingly small. Most of the Negro speakers and entertainers either had to be hired, or were "Uncle Toms" who had no standing with their fellows. At many of the barbecues, the Negroes were placed at separate tables, and at others many of the whites felt that the whole affair was "ridiculous," and refused to enter into the spirit of the occasion. Of the two methods that were used by the more conservative Democrats to persuade the Negroes to vote away their political power, then, only that involving economic pressure had any appreciable success.

Much more successful was the use of threats and actual violence. It is not to be imagined that this campaign of violence involved all who called themselves Democrats. Many members of the party undoubtedly opposed it, and many more probably considered it regrettable but necessary. It did involve directly thousands of young men and boys of all classes, a large part of the poor white element, and many local political leaders of some importance. Furthermore, it must be admitted that the Democratic leaders of the state, while they often denied the existence of violence, or tried to shift the blame for it to the Negroes, never actually repudiated its use, and in some cases encouraged it. In the meantime, the Democratic press adopted the slogan, "Carry the election peaceably if we can, forcibly if we must." Urged on by newspapers and political leaders, young men all over the state formed militia companies, and Democratic clubs provided themselves with the latest style of repeating rifles. By September, 1875, the Hinds County *Gazette* could announce, "The people of this State are now fully armed, equipped, and drilled. . . ." As described later by the Aberdeen *Examiner*, the situation was well under control in Monroe County:

. . . the firmest word was "victory"—to be achieved by arms if necessary. When the central power made treaties in Jackson involving the laying down or stacking of arms, the people in this part of the state burnished their arms and bought more cartridges, and each county conducted the campaign upon its own plan . . . each looking to winning its own home fight in its own home way, and each ready and willing to support its neighbors physically and morally whenever the emergency demanded aid, as was not unfrequently the case.

. . . here and elsewhere in the dark counties we guaranteed peace by thoroughly organising for war; and . . . at the call of the County Executive Committee it was easy—as demonstrated on several occasions—to put seventeen hundred well-mounted horsemen into line, that could be transposed into a brigade of cavalry at a moment's notice, to say nothing of a thoroughly organized artillery company and a company of Infantry armed with needle guns, purchased by our citizens, for home service. In addition to this, our eight hundred square miles of territory was so thoroughly connected by courier lines and posts, that we could communicate with every voter within its borders within a few hours.

With this powerful military force at its command, the white Democracy was ready for its campaign against a mass of Negroes who were timorous, unarmed, and largely unorganized. The program involved extensive processions and drills, and much firing of cannon, at least one of which was owned by every club of any importance. As the campaign of intimidation went on, Negro Republicans were ostentatiously enrolled in "dead books." Negro political leaders were warned that another speech would mean death. Republican political meetings were broken up by violent attacks, or prevented by armed force. Committees of "active young men" waited on Negroes who tried to prevent others of their race from deserting their party. Negroes were prevented from registering by sham battles and the firing of pistols at registration points, or by armed pickets who met them on the roads. Democrats adopted a policy of appearing in force at all Republican meetings, demanding the privilege of presenting Democratic speakers, and compelling Republican speakers to "tell the truth or quit the stand."

In the political, economic, and social subjugation of the freedmen, the most effective weapon ever developed was the "riot." Because this fact was discovered in the Meridian riot of 1871, that incident deserves some attention. In the spring of 1871, Meridian, a rapidly growing railroad town in the eastern part of the state, was under the control of white Republicans appointed to office by Governor Alcorn, and of Negro leaders including J. Aaron Moore, William Clopton, and Warren Tyler. The population of this new town could best be described as "tough," and relations between the races were bad. For the purpose of discussing the situation, the Negroes were brought together in a mass meeting early in March, and were addressed by the three Negro leaders and William Sturgis, the white Republican mayor. While the meeting was going on, a fire alarm was heard, and it was discovered that a store owned by Sturgis was on fire. In the resultant excitement, there was further unpleasantness between the whites and the blacks. On the following morning, white citizens persuaded a lawyer who had not been present at the Republican meeting to prepare an affidavit to the effect that the speeches of Warren Tyler, Bill Dennis [Clopton], and Aaron Moore had been of an incendiary character. The trial of these men was held the following Sunday afternoon before Judge Bramlette, a native white Republican, in a crowded courtroom. According to the prosecutor, one of the Negroes, Warren Tyler, interrupted James Brantley, a white witness, to say, "I want three colored men summoned to impeach your testimony." Brantley then seized the city marshal's stick and started toward the Negro. Tyler, moving toward a side door, reached back as though to draw a pistol, and general firing immediately began in the rear of the courtroom. Although it seems that no one actually saw Tyler fire, and although Negroes stoutly denied that he did so, the available evidence indicates that he probably shot at the advancing Brantley and, missing him, killed Judge Bramlette. W. H. Hardy, a local Democratic leader, later wrote a description of the affair in which he attributed the shot that killed Bramlette to the Negro Bill Dennis. In this he was probably incorrect, but to the rest of his story there is general agreement.

As quick as a flash the white men sitting in the rear drew their pistols and fired upon Dennis. [Tyler had run through the side door and leaped to the ground from a second-floor veranda.] By the time the smoke cleared away the court room had but few people left in it. Judge Bramlette was found dead and Bill Dennis mortally wounded. The riot [*sic*] was on and white men and negroes were seen running in every direction; the white men to get their arms and the negroes in mortal terror to seek a place of hiding. Every man that could do so got a gun or a pistol and went on the hunt for negroes. The two men left to guard the wounded Bill Dennis in the sheriff's office grew tired of their job and threw him from the balcony into the middle of the street, saying that their services were needed elsewhere, and they could not waste time guarding a wounded negro murderer. Warren Tyler was found concealed in a shack and shot to death. Aaron Moore had escaped from the courthouse in the confusion and lay out in the woods that night, and the next day made his way to Jackson. . . . It was not known how many negroes were killed by the enraged whites, but the number has been estimated at from twenty-five to thirty. . . .

The mayor, Bill Sturgis, was thoroughly overcome with terror at the vengeance of the people and concealed himself in the garret of his boarding house. Being a member of the Odd Fellows' order he opened communication with a member of the lodge, and it resulted in a cartel by which Sturgis was to resign the office of mayor and was to leave the State in twenty-four hours. . . .

This affair marked the end of Republican control in the area surrounding Meridian. According to Dunbar Rowland, "The Meridian riot marks an epoch in the transition period of reconstruction, and was a forecast of the end of carpetbag rule in Mississippi." His opinion endorses that of W. H. Hardy:

It [the Meridian riot] demonstrated the cowardice of both the carpetbaggers and the negro, and that in danger, either real or imaginary, they took counsel in their fear. When the white people failed, after every reasonable appeal to argument, to reason, to justice, to a sense of the public weal, they brought into full play the lessons learned in the Meridian riot, and it proved efficient in the campaign of 1875.

The lesson learned was that the Negroes, largely unarmed, economically dependent, and timid and unresourceful after generations of servitude, would offer no effective resistance to violence. Throughout the period, any unpleasant incident was likely to produce such a "riot." During the bad feeling of 1874 and 1875 there were a great number of unpleasant incidents, and after each resulting riot Negro resistance to white domination in the surrounding area completely collapsed.

With the development of the white-line program in the summer of 1874, the newspapers began to carry a constantly increasing number of stories about clashes between the races. Some of these were reports of real incidents growing out of increasing bitterness; others seem to have been the product of exaggerated rumors, or of an effort to arouse feeling against the Negroes. Soon blood began to flow. In Austin, Negroes raised violent objections to the release of a white man who, in shooting at a Negro man, had killed a Negro girl. In the quarrel which followed, six Negroes were killed; no whites were wounded. In Vicksburg, where the white militia had overthrown Republican control in the municipal election, a number of Negroes prepared to come into town in answer to a call from the Negro sheriff. After they had agreed to go back to their homes, firing started. About thirty-five Negroes were killed. Two whites met death, one possibly by accident. This was in December, 1874. Three months later, the Vicksburg *Monitor* announced, "*The same tactics that saved Vicksburg will surely save the State, and no other will.*" In the same city, in the following July, the Republicans held a celebration of Independence Day. Trouble developed with white Democrats. Two Negroes were killed; no whites were wounded. Water Valley was disturbed by a rumor that Negroes were going to attack the town. An exploring party found a group of Negroes concealed under a cliff. An unknown number of Negroes were killed; no whites were wounded. In August, Negroes at a Republican meeting in Louisville "succeeded in raising a disturbance." "Result, two negroes wounded, no white men hurt. Will the negro never learn that he is always sure to be the sufferer in these riots?" Late in the same month, a group of whites near Macon, including more than a hundred horsemen from Alabama, were out looking for a Negro political meeting. After they had failed to find one, they were told by a runner that several hundred Negroes had gathered at a church, where they were preparing to carry aid to those of their race in Vicksburg, on the other side of the state. When the church was found, the Alabamians disobeyed the order of the deputy sheriff and fired into the crowd. Twelve or thirteen Negroes were killed; no white was hurt.

A few nights later, the Republicans endeavored to hold a meeting in Yazoo City. Their hall was invaded by a number of Democrats, led by their "rope-bearer," H. M. Dixon. In the confusion which followed, a native white Republican was killed, and several Negroes were wounded. The white sheriff escaped with his life by fleeing to Jackson. White militia then took charge of the county, and systematically lynched the Negro leaders in each supervisor's district. Three days later, Democrats obtained their customary division of time at a large Republican meeting and picnic at Clinton. Trouble developed between a Negro policeman and a young white who was drunk. In the shooting which followed, two young white Democrats and a white Republican were killed. The number of Negroes killed is unknown; estimates varied from ten to thirty. Two thousand Negroes in wild panic rushed to the woods or to Jackson. By nightfall, armed whites, including the Vicksburg "Modocs," had control of the entire area. During the next four days they scoured the surrounding country, killing Negro leaders. Estimates of the number killed varied between ten and fifty. On the day of the Clinton affair, white Democrats captured a Republican meeting at Utica and compelled a thousand Negroes to listen to Democratic speakers for several hours. There seems to have been no bloodshed. A few days later, there was a minor skirmish at Satartia in which one Negro was killed. Early in the following month, the Negro sheriff was run out of Coahoma County after an encounter in which five Negroes were killed and five wounded. One white was killed from ambush; another shot himself by accident. The final clash of the campaign came at Columbus, a large town with a heavy Negro majority, on the night before the election. A crowd of young whites rushed from a drug store to attack a Negro parade, cutting the heads out of the drums and scattering the marchers. About an hour later, two old sheds in the Negro section were found to be burning, and the rumor was spread that the blacks were trying to burn the town. The Columbus Riflemen and a large number of visiting Alabamians immediately took charge, and Negroes began to flee for safety. Those who refused to halt were fired upon; four men were killed, and several men and one woman were wounded. No whites were hurt.

Long before the day of the election, a Democratic victory was assured. In many of the counties, all efforts to hold Republican meetings were abandoned. In several of the black counties, the sheriffs had fled or were powerless. White military units held the towns, and pickets patrolled the roads. The Negroes, with many of their leaders either dead or in hiding, faced the proposition of voting with the Democrats or staying away from the polls.

Letters to Governor Ames revealed the panic of the Negroes. From Yazoo City came the plea, "I beg you most fulley to send the United soldiers here; they have hung six more men since the killing of Mr. Fawn; they wont let the republican have no ticket . . . ; fighting comemense just I were closuing, 2 two killed . . . help; send troop and arms pleas. . . . Send help, help, troops. . . . ." From Noxubee County came the cry:

Last Saturday, the 30th, the democrats was in Macon town in high rage, raring around and shooting of their cannons all up and down the street, and shooting all their pistols also, and which they have already sword to you for peace; and I don't think they act much in that way last Saturday, for there was Richard Gray shot down walking on the pavements, shot by the democrats, and he was shot five times, four times after he fell, and was said shot because he was nominated for treasurer, and forher more, because he made a speech and said he never did expect to vote a democrate ticket, and also advised the colored citizens to do the same.

From Warren County came a letter from 108 Negroes who could not and would not register and vote, "for we cannot hold a meeting of no description without being molested and broken up; and further our lives are not safe at nor in our cabins, and therefore we deem it unwise to make a target of our body to be shot down like dogs and have no protection. . . ." From Vicksburg came the plea, "The rebles turbulent; are aiming themselves here now to-day to go to Sartartia to murder more poor negroes. Gov., aint the no pertiction?"

There was not any protection. In January, the administration had endeavored to secure the passage of a bill to allow the governor to set up special police bodies in towns where they were needed. Passed in the house by a vote of forty to thirty-eight, it was killed on a color-line vote in the senate. In the desperate days of September, Governor Ames made the formal gesture of commanding the private military bands to disperse. From the *Clarion*, there came a scornful answer that was echoed all over the state: " 'Now, therefore, I, A.A., do hereby command all persons belonging to such organizations to disband.' Ha! ha!! ha !!! 'Command.' 'Disband.' That's good."

The governor then turned to the federal government, although he knew his request would be unpopular, even in the North. To Attorney-General Edward Pierrepont, he wrote: "Let the odium, in all its magnitude descend on me. I cannot escape. I am conscious in the discharge of my duty toward a class of American citizens whose only offense consists in their color, and which I am powerless to protect." The plea was hopeless. Negro suffrage, or even Negro freedom, had never been really popular with the masses in the North. Negro suffrage had appeared to be necessary, and had been accepted as such. It had been inaugurated to save a party that a majority of the voters in a number of the northern states now considered hardly worth saving. Its maintenance had proved to be a troublesome problem. Why should the Negro majority in Mississippi be constantly crying for help? The sending of federal troops into a state simply to prevent white men from ruling Negroes was distasteful to the average northern voter. In the final moment of his decision, Grant was visited by a delegation of politicians from Ohio, a pivotal state which was to have an election in October. Mississippi, these visitors declared, was already lost to the party; troops would arrive too late to save the state. Even worse, the order that sent troops to Mississippi would mean the loss of Ohio to the party. The Negroes must be sacrificed. Grant's answer to Ames was a statement that aid could not be sent until all local resources had been exhausted. In the midst of the negotiations, Pierrepont declared, "The whole public are tired of these annual autumnal outbreaks in the South." "This flippant utterance of Attorney-General Edward Pierrepont," wrote Adelbert Ames twenty years later, "was the way the executive branch of the National government announced that it had decided that the reconstruction acts of congress were a failure."

As a last hope, Ames turned to the organization of a state militia, placing at its head Brigadier General William F. Fitzgerald, an ex-Confederate who had become a Republican. It was the governor's idea to organize equal companies of whites and blacks, and at first many of the Democrats, under the leadership of J. Z. George, proclaimed their willingness to join. It quickly became apparent, however, that the great mass of the party was absolutely opposed to such a move. If the militia was to be formed, it must be made up almost entirely of Negroes. Difficulties rapidly increased. Democrats secured two blanket injunctions against any further use of the funds which the legislature had appropriated. In several places, state arms were seized by the White Leagues. The refugee sheriff of Yazoo County was convinced that an attempt to use the militia there would bring open war, and finally refused to recommend it. A caucus of the Republican legislators found the Negro members almost as a unit opposed to the plan. By October 15, only two companies, one of whites and the other of Negroes, had been organized. Both of these were at the state capital.

In the meantime, it had become apparent both to Governor Ames and to the Democratic leaders that any activity by a Negro militia would bring immediate conflict. Both parties were anxious to avoid this, Ames for the sake of the Negroes, and the Democratic commiteemen because they feared it would bring federal intervention. The result was a conference between the governor on one side and J. Z. George and his colleagues on the other. Out of this conference came an agreement that Ames should immediately abandon all efforts to form a militia. On their side, the Democratic leaders guaranteed a fair and peaceful election.

There are some aspects of this agreement that are difficult to understand. Ames's report to Pierrepont included the lines: "I have full faith in their honor, and implicit confidence that they can accomplish all they undertake. Consequently, I believe that we shall have peace, order, and a fair election." This does not ring entirely true. It seems more probable that the governor had fought a hopeless fight as long as he dared, and was ready to seize an opportunity for an honorable surrender. More genuine was his remark to George K. Chase, as report after report of breaches of the peace agreement continued to come in: "I wish you would go to see them [J. Z. George and Ethelbert Barksdale], and get this thing fixed, and see what it means, and let us have quiet anyhow; no matter if they are going to carry the State, let them carry it, and let us be at peace and have no more killing."

The Democratic guarantee of peace and a fair election is

also hard to understand. There can be little doubt that such men as J. Z. George, Joshua Green, and Frank Johnston were anxious for peace. They were convinced that intimidation had already been carried far enough to guarantee Democratic control of the legislature. Any further violence might serve to reverse Grant's decision in regard to the sending of troops. From telegrams sent by George before and during the election, it appears that he made a real effort to preserve order; although in some cases, notably in that of Yazoo County, he seems to have sought, for political purposes, pledges which he knew would not be carried out. The essential difficulty lay in the fact that leaders in some of the black counties were determined to gain redemption not only for the state but also for their local governments. They felt that the work must be carried on through the day of the election. As a result, a large section of the Democratic press immediately repudiated the peace agreement, and local White Leagues "burnished up their arms and bought more cartridges."

On the day of the election, a peculiar quiet prevailed in many of the counties. "It was a very quiet day in Jackson—fearfully quiet." According to a witness at Yazoo City, "Hardly anybody spoke aloud." In Columbus, where many of the Negroes were still in the swamps as a result of the riot on the preceding night, the Democratic mayor reported everything as "quiet as a funeral." Similar reports came from Bolton, Lake, and Boswell. At Holly Springs, about 250 Negroes voted with the Democrats, offering their open ballots as proof. At Meridian, the White League seized the polls, while the Negroes, "sullen and morose," gathered in a mass across the street. Any Negro who approached without a white Democrat at his side was immediately crowded away from the ballot box.

In other sections, the day was not so peaceful. In Scott County, Negroes who were carrying the Republican tickets for distribution at the polls were fired on "by accident" by

Democratic squirrel hunters. They fled, abandoning both the tickets and their mules. At Forest, the county seat, it was arranged for boys with whips to rush suddenly into the crowd of Negroes. The voters, already frightened and nervous, feared that this was the beginning of an outbreak, and left in a panic. In Monroe County, on the day before the election, the Negro candidate for chancery clerk saved himself and several friends by a promise to leave the state and not to return. At Okolona, the Negroes, with women and children, gathered at a church in the edge of town, intending to go from there to the polls in groups. The Democratic army marched up and formed near the church. When guns went off by accident, the Negroes stampeded, paying no attention to Democratic invitations for them to come back and vote. At Aberdeen, in spite of the fact that the heavy Negro population in the eastern part of the county was cut off by an open bridge and pickets along the Tombigbee, a large number gathered at the polls early in the morning. E. O. Sykes, in charge of the Democratic war department, posted the cavalry he had imported from Alabama, surrounded the Negroes with infantry, loaded a cannon with chains and slugs, and then sent a strong-arm squad into the crowd to beat the Negroes over the head. They broke and ran, many of them swimming the river in search of safety. The Republican sheriff, an ex-Confederate, locked himself in his own jail. The Democrats then carried the box "very quietly," turning a Republican majority of 648 in 1871 into a Democratic majority of 1,175.

At Grenada, trouble developed between a white and a Negro at the polls. While the Democrat was beating the Negro over the head with an axe handle, the Democratic captain called for the cannon, and his men ran for their guns, which they had left at a neighboring store. General E. C. Walthall quieted the crowd, but the Negroes had stampeded, and would not return. At Port Gibson, there was trouble between a young white man and a young Negro. General firing began, resulting in the death of "an old, inoffensive negro man," and the wounding of four or five others. The Negroes scattered, and few of them returned to vote. In general, however, it can be said that the election was quiet, as elections went in Mississippi, and that the Republicans polled a heavy vote in many sections.

The Democrats came very close to sweeping the state. In some places they used fraud, but this method was generally unnecessary. In Yazoo County, the center of an overwhelming Negro majority, Republican candidates received only seven votes. In Kemper they received four, and in Tishomingo twelve. They received two votes at Utica, in the black county of Hinds, and none at Auburn. Democrats carried the first, third, fourth, and fifth congressional districts. The second went to G. Wiley Wells, renegade Republican who was working with the Democrats. In the sixth, John R. Lynch, with much white support, held his majorities in the black counties of Adams, Jefferson, and Wilkinson to win by a slim margin over Roderick Seal. In the state senate, of which only half the members had been involved in the election, there were now twenty-six Democrats and ten Republicans. Only five, all of them holdovers, were Negroes. In the new house of representatives, there were twenty Republicans and ninety-five Democrats. Sixteen of the representatives were Negroes; of these, fifteen were Republicans and one was a Democrat. Sixty-two of the seventy-four counties elected Democrats as their local officials. In the only race for a state office, that for state treasurer, the Democrat, W. L. Hemingway, polled 96,596 votes to 66,155 for George M. Buchanan, a popular and widely known ex-Confederate who was his Republican opponent.

When the Democratic legislature met in the following January, it quickly completed the work by impeaching and removing the lieutenant-governor, and by securing the resignations of the governor and the superintendent of education.

Thus ended the successful revolution of 1875. In its preparation and execution, economic and political motives played a large part. Essentially, however, it was a racial struggle. This was expressed most clearly, twenty years later, by Adelbert Ames:

There was a time when policy made it advisable for the white men of Mississippi to advance "corruption," "negro mobs," anything and everything but the true reason for their conduct. That time has long since passed. There is no good reason why the truth should not be stated in plain terms.

It is this—they are white men, Anglo-Saxons—a dominant race—educated to believe in negro slavery. To perpetuate the then existing order of things they ventured everything and lost. An unjust and tyrannical power (from their standpoint) had filled their state with mourning, beggared them, freed their slaves and as a last insult and injury made the ex-slave a political equal. They resisted by intimidation, violence and murder. Excuses by the way of justification were given while the powerful hand of the national government was to be feared. Soon the national government and public opinion ceased to be dreaded. They then announced boldly that this is a white man's government and that the negro and ex-slave should, forever, form no part of it.

This determination has been proclaimed time and again and what is more to the purpose has been acted on. With an excess of 60,000 colored people Mississippi became the seat of a white man's government.

Altogether, it is well that the federal government did not intervene to protect the Negroes in 1875. The entire process would have been repeated a few years later, with increased animosity and violence. Social revolutions are not accomplished by force, unless that force is overwhelming, merciless, and continued over a long period. The Negro, returned to a status intermediate between that of slavery and that of full citizenship, now finds in education and hard work opportunities for slow but certain advancement. On the other hand, the dominant race, dominant through tradition, education, and superior economic and legal advantages, yields more and more to the promptings of humanitarianism and enlightened self-interest. With each generation there is less violence and injustice, and more recognition of interdependence and of common needs and interests. There are retrogressions, but it is easy to believe that a gradual, healthy progress will be maintained.

21

THE WANING OF
RADICALISM

W. R. Brock

What was significant about the Mississippi Plan
was not simply its success but the acquiescence of
the North and the unwillingness of President Grant
and the Republican party to undertake the kind of
intervention that might have preserved the short-
lived democratic governments of the South. W. R.
Brock seeks to explain the waning of Radicalism
and the decline in national concern for the civil
rights of Negroes.

It is comparatively easy to explain the waning of Radicalism
in terms of personal failure, evaporating enthusiasm, the urgent demands of business, and the tendency of all political
organizations to fall into the hands of professionals. It is easy
also to see how the challenge of the new age, with its manifest
problems of the relationship between private business and
public authority, had a divisive effect upon the Radicals—
turning Kelley into a fanatical protectionist, Schurz into a free
trader, Butler into a Greenbacker, and Donnelly into an
agrarian radical—while drawing together the main body of
Republicans around the citadel of American capitalism. But
the break-up of Radicalism may also reflect more profound
weaknesses in the position which it maintained.

It has argued that much of the Radical success was explained by the pressures from below which drove cautious politicians even further than they had intended, and that this pressure must be explained in ideological terms and not as the product of mere interest groups. The ideology had expressed in abstract but attractive terms certain propositions about man in society which, for a moment in time, seemed to epitomise the aspirations of the northern people. Racial equality, equal rights, and the use of national authority to secure both were living ideas in the Reconstruction era as they have since become, in some quarters, in the mid-twentieth century. For the first time these concepts were cast in the form of a political programme which could be achieved; but their success depended upon the response which they aroused from the northern people. After Reconstruction the ideas persisted but failed to rouse the same enthusiasm; their formal acceptance was a very different thing from the popular emotion which could push them forward despite the usual obstacles to policies which disturb complacency and refuse to let men rest in peace. The question remains whether the slackening of the pressure behind the Radical ideology should be explained by rival distractions and changing interests or by a weakness in the ideology itself. Examination will show that the generalities of the Radical ideology—so attractive at first sight—could not stand pressure. The weapons bent and broke in the hands of those who used them.

A belief in racial equality has never won universal assent and to the majority of men in the mid-nineteenth century it seemed to be condemned both by experience and by science. The literal equality between men of obviously different physiological characteristics was an abolitionist invention and it rested upon emotional conviction rather than upon rational proof; the comparison between intelligent Negroes and retarded poor whites proved little because the civilization of a few blacks did not redeem the mass from docile ignorance and the degradation of some whites did not detract from the high standards of the majority. The abolitionist argument was based largely upon pure *a priori* statements or upon experience with fugitive slaves; a mass of argument could be produced against the one, while the defiance of the occasional runaway did not prove that the mass of his fellows were not fitted by nature for a subordinate position. The behaviour of the Negro was obviously different from that of the whites and, though those who knew him best granted him some admirable traits, they would also maintain that he was sadly deficient in the capacity for industry, thrift, self-reliance, enterprise, sexual restraint and the whole galaxy of virtues esteemed by nineteenth-century civilization. The abolitionist argument that the Negro appeared "inferior" because he had lived in slavery for generations failed to carry weight because no free Negro society could be found to prove the proposition. Moreover there was an added complication in the mixed ancestry of so many of those who, like Frederick Douglass, were quoted as evidence of innate negro intelligence. This is not the place to enter upon the tangled problem of racial characteristics; it is sufficient to state that in the later nineteenth century racial equality was a hypothesis which was generally rejected. It was not accepted in the North any more than it was in the South and even abolitionists were anxious to disclaim any intention of forcing social contacts between the races and all shied away from the dread subject of racial amalgamation. An initial weakness of the Radical ideology was therefore its dependence upon a concept which was not self-evident, lacked scientific proof, and offended popular susceptibilities.

The usual weakness of equalitarian theory lies in demonstrating that people ought to be treated as equals in spite of natural inequalities, and this difficulty is acute when dealing with people of different races. While it is possible to argue, among men of the same race, that it is necessary to treat men as though they were equal, it is far harder to do so in the face of popular prejudice that men of a different race are marked at birth as "inferior." The conventional Republican argument was that men were unequal in capabilities but equal in rights, and in the American context this proposition rested mainly upon an appeal to the preamble of the Declaration of Independence; but the assertions of the declaration were not "self-evident" to most white Americans when applied to Negroes. Moreover there were some particular difficulties in equalitarian theory when applied to a mass of people, concentrated in a single region, and occupying from time out of mind a subordinate position in society. Equality demands protection of the weak against the strong and positive law to afford it; but it usually involves the assumption that given certain legal rights the due process of law will enable men to maintain their equality. With the Negroes this assumption could not be made: what was required was protection, maintained by enforceable law, at every point where the power of the dominant race was likely to impinge upon the weaker. With tradition, economic power, prejudice, social custom and, in most southern districts, numbers all entrenched on one side, protection could not be provided merely by changing the law and leaving its administration to the local authorities and courts. The concept of Negro equality demanded interference with the processes of local government on a scale never before contemplated in America or in any other nation. Would the northern majority be prepared to exert continuously this kind of pressure and provide this kind of protection? In the answer to this question lay the second great weakness of the Radical ideology.

Further difficulties lay in the complexities which sheltered behind the simple word "equality." Whatever the moral arguments the Negro was not, and could not be in the immediate future, an equal to the white man in economic life, in competition for the scarce educational facilities of the South, or in winning public office. Racial equality would have to be an artificial creation imposed upon southern society; the Negro would have to have guarantees which were not given to the white man, and the quest for equality would demand unequal incidence of the law. No other minority required special legislation to ensure equal status in the courts, or the care of a federal bureau, or the use of force to protect the right to vote. Negro equality implied that something must be taken from the whites, and this was explicit in two features of Radical policy: confiscation and disqualification. Stevens never wavered in his belief that Negro democracy must have an economic basis in Negro landownership; confiscation and redistribution were therefore cardinal points in his program. Yet the most passionate advocates of equality could not persuade the Republican majority to embark upon such a disturbance of property. Negro democracy would also be a sham if the former ruling class retained its grasp upon local and national office, and disqualification was necessary. This policy succeeded because it was supported by northern fear of restored southern domination at Washington, but it proved to be the most vulnerable and perhaps the least wise aspect of Reconstruction. Both confiscation and disqualification demonstrate the formidable difficulties which attend the imposition of equality upon a society in which it did not exist, and in which the beneficiaries of equalitarian policy were too weak, socially and economically, to stand upon their own feet. The price of equality was revolutionary change, vigilance and constant pressure, and who would pay the price when enthusiasm grew cold and the suspicion grew that the Negroes were not yet ready to exercise rights which could not be secured without the coercion of their fellow citizens.

It is in this context that the work of John A. Bingham assumes great significance. In his fight for the civil rights clause of the Fourteenth Amendment he cut equal rights free from Negro protection and made them national. The later perversion of this clause to protect the rights of corporations tended to obscure the significance of a measure which protected all citizens and all persons under the jurisdiction of the states, but once the importance of nationalized right was recognized the Fourteenth Amendment grew in stature. Conversely the Fifteenth Amendment was weak from the outset because it linked suffrage with race; it was a law for Negro enfranchisement and could be enforced only so long as some people had an interest in doing so. If the Fifteenth Amendment had declared in unequivocal terms that all males over the age of twenty-one who were citizens of the United States had the right to vote it might have been recognised as a cornerstone of democracy and attracted popular support. As it was the Fifteenth Amendment enacted "impartial" suffrage which meant that the states could impose any qualification they chose provided that it was not based on race; this meant that the white majority of the nation had no particular interest in its enforcement.

Beyond the major problem of equality by enforcement lay the vast and ramifying difficulty of definition. Was equality indivisible or if divisible which aspects were essential? The three classic definitions of equality—*in* the eyes of God, *under* the law, and *of* opportunity—each carried different implications. Equality in the eyes of God might well be an excuse for inequality on earth: Dives and Lazarus had both lived under the judgment of God, both received their deserts after death, and their inequality on earth was dramatic but irrelevant to their condition in eternity. Equality in the eyes of God implied some limitation upon the principle of subordination for it had been an essential part of the abolitionist case that the children of God should not be treated as less than human beings, but it provided no definition of the place of man in society. Many pious northerners saw no inconsistency between Christian conviction and racial discrimination, and the brotherhood of man in Christ was no barrier to the belief that equality on earth was no part of God's purpose. It was therefore necessary to supplement the Christian concept of equality in eternity with the purely secular arguments for equality on earth.

Equality under the law had deep roots in the Anglo-Saxon tradition but in its mother country it had not proved incompatible with aristocratic privilege, an established church, denial of suffrage to the masses, and the exploitation of low paid labor. The guarantee of equal status in the courts was a great and important addition to the rights of Negroes, but it would not of itself create a political and social revolution. Beyond the formal guarantee of equality under the law lay the intractable question of who should administer the law. The legal rights of Negroes might be recognized in southern courts but they were likely to be strictly interpreted; one could be confident that the white southern judge would administer the law scrupulously, but between the Negro and equal justice stood the white southern jury. Equality under the law was a grand sweeping theory, without which no other form of secular equality was possible, but it did not erase the notion that the Negro was an inferior man to whom only a grudging recognition was extended. It might be argued that, once the groundwork of legal equality had been laid, the progress towards equality in other fields would follow, yet one might doubt the certainty of this hypothesis. It was only in 1867 that the British Parliament was to decide after centuries of equality under the law that the agricultural labourer was entitled to a vote, and millions of simple Englishmen still went unlettered to their graves.

Equality of opportunity seemed to be a more positive demand. If the racial barrier could be removed from access to education, occupation and public office the Negro would have the right to compete on equal terms with the whites in most of the fields to which his aspiration might lead him. Yet equality of opportunity implied inequality of achievement and in the South its immediate result might be the confirmation of white supremacy. If the Negro was to be given a real chance of equal achievement he must be given positive aids which were not given to the white man, and one was brought back once more to the basic problem of equalitarian theory: that positive government was required to correct habitual inequality. This led on to the political difficulty that, in the climate of nineteenth-century opinion, sustained and purposeful government intervention was unpopular and improbable. The comparatively modest aims of the Freedmen's Bureau aroused intense hostility in the South and many doubts in the North; any further attempt to translate the commitment to equality into governmental responsibilities might wreck the whole structure of Reconstruction, yet without this the purpose of equalitarian Radicalism could not be achieved.

Many Republicans contended that it was unnecessary to embark upon the troubled sea of racial equality if one could stop in the safe haven of guaranteed rights. The Negro was a man, and as a man he had certain inalienable rights; if these could be secured the vexed question of equality could be deferred or perhaps dismissed. This theory of inalienable right had better prospects than any theory of equality. American tradition had long accepted as its cornerstone the idea of man as an atom in society, entitled to do all that was within his power provided that it did not impinge upon the rights of others. But American tradition had usually failed to recognize the fact that rights were not "inalienable," that the exercise of legal rights depended upon the consent of the majority, or that some rights of some men could always be denied by the sovereign power of the people. In Reconstruction, Americans were brought face to face with the problem of free men whose "rights" were denied by the local majority and could be secured only by external coercion. Moreover the whole attitude of Americans towards rights had been governed by their implicit acceptance of the idea of checks and balances. The rights of the people were a check upon the enlargement of authority, and to give some rights to some people at the expense of others had been damned by association with the idea of privilege. What was the intrinsic difference between rights conferred upon a chartered monopoly and rights conferred upon a weak minority? This conundrum had always been implicit in American political discourse but Reconstruction made it explicit.

Even if these pitfalls could be avoided there remained the knotty problem of which rights should be protected and how they could be distinguished from rights which were unprotected. The Declaration of Independence referred to the rights of life, liberty, and the pursuit of happiness, but these were *among* the inalienable rights and not an exclusive list; and even if one stopped short at the classic three the pursuit of happiness was so elastic an idea that it was little guide to an enumeration of rights which could be protected by law. There were three main attempts to distinguish the categories of right and to determine which could, and which could not be protected. The first was the distinction between civil rights and political rights, the second between those which were fundamental and those which could be left to the discretion of political authorities, and the third was that between public and private rights. The first proposal made by Thaddeus Stevens —that all laws, state and national, should apply equally to all persons—attempted to cut through this maze of difficulties. Later Sumner was to express the same idea when he said "Show me . . . a legal institution, anything created or regulated by law, and I will show you what must be opened equally to all without distinction of color." This was the true Radical argument. It recognized that private prejudice could not be legislated out of existence, but maintained that discrimination could be prohibited in every activity touched by the law. Stevens and Sumner would have left people to do what they liked in their homes or in private associations, but they would have outlawed discrimination at the polls, in public places, on public transport, and in education. Sumner even hoped to add churches, cemeteries, and benevolent institutions to this list. He resisted the argument of "separate but equal" by asserting that "equality is where all men are alike. A substitute can never take the place of equality." At the other end of the Republican spectrum was Lyman Trumbull who said the "civil rights" (which should be guaranteed by law) were "the right to his liberty, to come and go as he pleases, have the avails of his own labor, and not to be restricted in that respect." In other respects the legal rights of Negroes must depend upon the discretion of their political sovereign for these were "all matters of privilege." This attempted to treat the Negro as a free man without treating him as an equal man, and Trumbull even regarded the right to serve on a jury as one of these matters of privilege.

Before the Reconstruction controversy ended, moderate Republicans, including Trumbull himself, had moved significantly nearer to the Radical view of rights which ought to be guaranteed, but there remained a distinct cleavage between those who believed that wherever the law flowed it should carry with it equality of right, and those who believed that one soon reached a frontier at which a "right" became a "privilege" and could be withheld at the discretion of the legal sovereign. The extreme Radical position was unequivocal and relatively uncomplicated, but would require a large invasion of the traditional areas of state authority; the "moderate" position was clouded with difficulties of definition and separation but in the nature of things it was more likely to appeal to the majority of men who disliked sweeping logic and preferred to believe that the minimum of effort would produce the best results. Under the circumstances the best which the Radicals could obtain was probably the imprecise but traditional phrases which Bingham wrote into the Fourteenth Amendment. The "privileges and immunities" of citizens of the United States, "the equal protection of the laws," and "due process of law" were all expressions which could mean as much or as little as lawyers were prepared to read into them. They did not prevent the Supreme Court from legalizing segregation but they also provided ammunition for the court's later attack upon segregation. It is possible that Bingham's first suggestion, which would have given to Congress the responsibility for initiating measures to protect rights, would have obviated some of the difficulties inherent in judicial legislation; but Congress, even more than the Court, would be unwilling to act until there was sufficient public interest to support action. Once the northern majority had refused to accept the principle that wherever the law operated race must be forgotten, and had accepted the distinctions between rights which were rights and rights which were privileges, the whole idea of equality under the law was lost. Natural right became neither more nor less than the right which the majority was prepared to recognize and to protect.

Charles Sumner realized the dangers inherent in the attempt to split up the rights of man into various categories, and devoted the closing years of his life to a struggle for a measure which would have embodied the Stevens principle of equal incidence of national and state laws on all citizens. When he was accused of occupying the time of the Senate with arguments over access to hotel rooms or the exclusion of Negroes from benevolent institutions he replied that "every question by which the equal rights of all are affected is transcendent. It cannot be magnified. But here are the rights of a whole race, not merely the rights of an individual, not merely the rights of two or three or four, but the rights of a whole race." A year after Sumner's death Congress enacted some of the provisions of the bill for which he had fought and guaranteed to the Negroes equal rights in hotels, places of public entertainment, and public transport, but did nothing about education. In 1883 the Supreme Court found this act invalid on the ground that it was intended to protect "social" and not "civil" or "political" rights. In 1896 the Supreme Court upheld a state law requiring segregated facilities on railroads, and the tide of Radicalism which had once lashed so furiously against the ramparts was at its lowest ebb. Only a bold man could have predicted that the stone which the builders rejected was to become a cornerstone of liberal orthodoxy in the second half of the twentieth century.

The Radical solution to the dilemma of rights which were natural but which could only be secured by artificial means was Negro suffrage. With the vote the Negro would be equipped to protect his own rights, and there were Jeffersonian echoes in the idea that the cultivator of the soil would not only defend his personal rights but also act as a repository for political virtue. The voting Negro would protect himself against injustice and the Union against its enemies, but this concept of suffrage as a protective device proved inadequate when Reconstruction governments were compelled to assume the tasks of modern administration in a region where the best government had always been that which governed least. So long as the vote was merely protective the ignorance of the Negro was not a relevant argument because a poor man could understand what had to be defended as well as the best educated; but when Negro suffrage became the basis for an economic and social revolution guided by positive government it was relevant to ask whether the former slave was yet equal to his responsibilities.

The Radicals argued the case for Negro suffrage in the context of nineteenth-century liberal thought, and they can hardly be blamed for not having transcended the ideas of their age. Moreover they were inhibited by the political circumstances in which they had to operate. It was hard enough to convince northern public opinion that Negro suffrage was safe and just without complicating the question. In the summer of 1866 a Radical member of the Reconstruction Committee told Congress that "we may as well state it plainly and fairly, so that there shall be no misunderstanding on the subject. It was our opinion that three fourths of the States of this Union (that is of the loyal States) could not be induced to vote to grant the right of suffrage, even in any degree or under any restriction, to the colored race." Between this time and the passage of the Fifteenth Amendment a remarkable change took place in public opinion, but in order to foster it the Radicals were forced to rely less and less upon appeals to abstract justice and more and more upon the utility of the Negro vote to the party and to the Union. This stress led them to pass lightly over the tasks which Negro democracy might be called upon to perform, and to treat their votes merely as a counterweight in the political balance of the nation.

Radicals themselves hesitated at times over the problem of the vote. Was it one of the inalienable rights, or was it, as everyone else said, a political right which could be granted or withheld at the discretion of the political sovereign? Among the conservative Republicans, and particularly amongst the better educated, there was genuine hesitation about mass democracy, and if they turned one eye towards the Negroes of the South they turned the other to the foreign-born city vote which formed the electoral basis of Boss Tweed's New York ring. Reformers could join hands with the merely fearful in urging the case for universal literacy tests, and old Know-Nothings could make common cause with new Republicans against universal suffrage. Yet literacy tests which would exclude the mass of the southern Negro people, and could be manipulated by the ruling state authorities, were useless as a political solution in the South, and Radicals were pushed from their early caution on the suffrage question to an outright avowal of belief in universal suffrage. In a letter written for communication to a Republican meeting in New York in January, 1868, Thaddeus Stevens insisted that the right to vote was inalienable, and put natural right ahead of the argument from utility, but he went on to stress the other aguments in favour of universal suffrage.

True, I deemed the hastening of the bestowal of that franchise as very essential to the welfare of the nation, because without it I believe that the Government will pass into the hands of the loco-focos, and that such an event will be disastrous to the whole country. With universal suffrage I believe the true men of the nation can maintain their position. Without it whether their suffrage be impartial or qualified I look upon the Republic as likely to relapse into an oligarchy which will be ruled by coarse Copperheadism and proud Conservatism. I have never insisted that the franchise should be unjustly regulated so as to secure a Republican ascendancy but I have insisted and do insist that there can be no unjust regulation of that franchise which will give to any other party the power if the Republicans are true to themselves and do not fall into their usual vice of cowardice. The Republicans once beaten into a minority by the force of Negro prejudice will never again obtain the majority and the nation will become a despotism.

Six months before his death Stevens explained that after long reflection he had "finally come to the conclusion that universal suffrage was one of the inalienable rights intended to be inserted in (the Declaration of Independence) by our Fathers at the time of the Revolution and that they were prevented from inserting it in the Constitution by slavery alone." His reflection owed more to the exigencies of contemporary politics than to a knowledge of history, but there is no need to doubt the sincerity of his conclusion. Universal suffrage was the logical and complete answer; "impartial" suffrage was not. With Stevens dead, however, there was no one with the same influence who could put the case so clearly and the Fifteenth Amendment enacted impartial and not universal suffrage. The Radicals failed in the first instance because they did not or could not spell out what Negro democracy was to do, and in the second instance because they could not resist the modification of the right to vote which let in literacy tests, grandfather clauses, and poll taxes.

Paradoxically some of the Radical arguments for Negro suffrage tended to rebound. The idea that the vote would enable the Negro to protect himself provided an excuse for nonintervention, and for the belief that the southern question could now be treated as a local question. In 1880 James G. Blaine, writing in the *North American Review*, justified the grant of Negro suffrage by saying that "had the franchise not been bestowed upon the negro as his shield and weapon for defence, the demand upon the General Government to interfere for his protection, would have been constant, irritating and embarrassing. Great complaint has been made for years past of the Government's interference, simply to secure to the colored citizen his constitutional right. But this intervention has been trifling compared to that which would have been required if we had not given suffrage to the negro." It was thus easy to infer that having instituted Negro suffrage as an automatic regulator of the southern political mechanism northerners could turn their eyes away from what actually went on in the South. To be fair one should add that when Blaine wrote the extensive disenfranchisement of the Negroes had not taken place, and that in some districts he could vote freely provided that he voted for the Democratic ticket.

It is not suggested that equal participation by the Negro in southern politics would have been automatically secured if the Radicals had succeeded in establishing the suffrage as an "inalienable right," but an unequivocal statement that all adult males had the right to vote would have been easier to enforce and more difficult to evade. Nor is it suggested that universal suffrage would have done anything to solve the vexed and unexamined question of what the Negro was to do with his vote. What is suggested is that the Fifteenth Amendment was a weak compromise which failed to achieve the Radical aims and, in the long run, helped to discredit that freedom of state action which moderates wished to preserve. Under the Reconstruction Acts all "loyal" males had voted; the Fifteenth

Amendment allowed states to retreat from that position while the belief that the suffrage was secured on equitable terms allowed the northern majority to relax pressure at the point where it was most needed. The keystone of the Radical arch proved too weak to hold up the edifice. In a sense Negro suffrage was premature—though it could have been written into the law at no other time—but this was only in part the result of Negro immaturity. Beneath the surface of the suffrage question lay larger problems of the role of government in a democratic state and these American society as a whole was unwilling or unready to contemplate. By 1880 the *Nation*, which had earlier given somewhat lukewarm support to Negro suffrage while insisting that it should be impartial and not universal, was emphasizing that the *quality* of voters should be the primary consideration. For the intelligentsia who had, for the most part, thrown their influence behind Radical Republicanism, the great national problem was no longer the protection of Negro rights but the defense of public morality, social respectability, and economic orthodoxy against demagogues, bosses, agitators, agrarian Radicals, and mass ignorance.

It has been argued in the preceding pages that an essential weakness in the Radical program lay in its demand for national intervention to secure equality and protect rights, exercising a power which was unfamiliar and depending upon the support of public opinion which might well be apathetic or even hostile to its objectives. The arguments for enlarged national power were made clearly and forcibly, and there was no failure on the part of the Radicals to realize that their policy demanded the use of national authority not only on a greater scale than ever before but also upon new principles. The idea which had been presented in Sumner's "Freedom National" speech of 1852 had germinated and grown until it was possible to see the nation newly based upon equal right and abandoning the divided sovereignty of the past. "It certainly seems desirable," said the moderate Luke Poland in 1866, "that no doubt should be left as to the power of Congress to enforce principles lying at the very foundation of all Republican government if they be denied or violated by the States." This was a constant theme of the Republican party and one which brought forth the most bitter cries of anguish from their opponents. "The time was," said one Democrat in 1869, "when the suggestion of grave doubts of constitutional warrant would cause the advocates of pending measures to hesitate, to reflect. . . . Innovation and reform, however specious and desirable, were rejected at once and finally unless clearly sanctioned by constitutional authority." Six years later another Democrat expressed the common view of his party when he charged that Republican interpretation of the Constitution "freed from all verbiage and ambiguity . . . amounts simply to the assertion of a supreme power in Congress over every subject that concerns the life, liberty and property of any person within the United States; in other words over everything that is the subject of the law." The detached observer may well ask what was wrong with the exercise of such power, and why the national government should not remedy the deficiencies of the states. The Radicals did not wish to scrap the Constitution, but they thought that its failure in 1861 demonstrated the need for greater flexibility in interpretation and greater concentration of power at the center. This may appear to have been not unreasonable, but by and large the Democrats have had the best of the argument, and modern historians have echoed their criticisms though approving an extension of national authority during the New Deal which went far beyond the wildest expectations of the Radicals. It remains to ask why the concept of strong national government, which has proved so attractive to so many men in the twentieth century, did not gather the support which might have sustained it during the later nineteenth century.

Some of the explanations are obvious. The weight of tradition was against strong national government, and the word "centralism" was bogey enough to frighten large numbers of people who would not stop to ask what was being centralized, by whom, and for what purpose. Increased national authority might put power into the hands of those who were distrusted by the would-be reformers, and the professional politician might be the beneficiary from an attempt to provide the national government with a moral purpose. Roscoe Conkling had a telling point against the opponents of "centralism" when he said that "every civilized government may protect its citizens in the uttermost ends of the earth, but when the United States interposes to check murders, and burnings, and barbarities at which humanity shudders, perpetrated by thousands, and overawing all local authority, it is suddenly discovered that we are in danger of 'centralism.' " Yet for many people the argument against "centralism" was epitomized in the fear that it might increase the power of men like Roscoe Conkling; they could not ignore the fact that his vehemence against civil service reformers was as great as that against the perpetrators of southern atrocities.

In their presentation of the case for national power the Radicals were inhibited by conventional American and nineteenth-century political thought. While the old Whigs, whose ideas they inherited, had believed in more positive action by the national government than their Democratic opponents, they had never thought of writing a blank check for government intervention. What they wanted was federal responsibility for the performance of certain economic functions defined by the economic interests concerned, and since that time the concepts of *laissez-faire* had tended to narrow the sphere of action which business interests were likely to prescribe for government. Northern intellectuals who were attracted by the political aims of Reconstruction were precisely those who were equally attracted by the utopian elements in *laissez-faire*,

[513]

by the theory of natural harmony, and by the faith in betterment through individual enterprise. The government was therefore being asked to "secure the blessings of liberty" at the very time when it was being asked to contract its responsibility for "promoting the general welfare," and the hope of securing civil justice for the southern Negro was not coupled with the expectation of securing social justice for the northern farmer and worker. Thus the Radicals' concept of national power was too wide to satisfy conservative men but not wide enough to gather support from the nineteenth-century movements of protest.

Even if the concept of national power had not suffered from these inherent weaknesses it would still have had a precarious hold upon the nation. Radical Reconstruction declared certain principles of national responsibility but it did nothing to create the institutions of government which could give these principles a permanent place on the national stage. The Freedmen's Bureau was such an institution but even its friends recognized that its life must be limited. The Fourteenth Amendment left the door open for Congress to make laws which would enforce the civil rights clause, but it did not make it mandatory for Congress to do so and the assumption was that the law would be self-enforcing through the existing machinery of government and courts. The initiative remained with the traditional instruments of government—with the President, with the judges and with the states themselves—and no new instruments of government were brought into being. One can contrast this with the experience of the New Deal with its proliferation of governmental agencies; when enthusiasm receded the administrative achievement remained, and many Americans (ranging from highly paid government servants to the very poor) had acquired a vested interest in these new institutions. When Radical enthusiasm withered away it left behind it no such institutional bulwarks, and when the Freedmen's Bureau expired there remained no new government departments, no new government agencies, and no administrative doctrine to carry out those obligations to citizens of the United States of which so much had been heard.

The arguments which have been presented in the preceding pages have attempted to show why the ideology of Radical Republicanism, which appeared so powerful during the crisis of Reconstruction, failed to gather that momentum which could have carried it forward in the years which followed. It is of course exceedingly improbable that the Radicals of the Reconstruction period could have conceived their problems in any other way or that they could have gone on to produce the ideas and institutions which would have corrected the weaknesses in their edifice. Radicalism shared the weaknesses of all liberal bourgeois movements of the nineteenth century, and it would have required a far more profound revolution in thought and action to make them view their situation through the eyes of twentieth-century liberals. In their equalitarian sentiments, in their realization that individual rights might be incompatible with local self-government, and in their attitude towards national power they were prophets of the future; yet they remained children of their age and were bound by its assumptions and inhibitions. And even if their vision occasionally transcended these limitations they were unlikely to persuade the majority of their countrymen that the revolution which they had initiated ought to proceed to further innovation. The failure of Radicalism is thus a part of the wider failure of bourgeois liberalism to solve the problems of the new age which was dawning; but having said this it is important to remember that if the Radicals shared in the weaknesses of their age they also had some achievements which were exceptional. . . .

22

THE POLITICAL LEGACY
OF RECONSTRUCTION

C. Vann Woodward

The historians of Reconstruction no longer accept
the notion that this was "the most soul-sickening
spectacle that Americans had ever been called upon
to behold" or even Woodrow Wilson's conclusion
that southern Negroes had been "a host of dusky
children untimely put out of school." But there are
some who might still agree with Claude Bowers,
though for reasons altogether different, that this was
a "tragic era." In the estimation of C. Vann Woodward, Reconstruction was an age replete with both
ironic and tragic implications.

Of all the revolutionary proposals that eventually received the
sanction of law in the upheaval of Reconstruction, the proposal to give the freedmen the unrestricted right to vote was
one of the most difficult for contemporaries to accept, in the
North as well as in the South. Emancipation itself had been
repeatedly disavowed as a war aim until the war was well
under way. Civil rights for freedmen was another cautiously
advanced afterthought. Enfranchisement came in belatedly,
surreptitiously, almost disingenuously advanced by its proponents, grudgingly accepted by a North that moved under
duress and the argument of necessity and greeted with gloomy
forebodings of failure, if not disaster. These attitudes were

widespread, and they were not confined to copperheads, doughfaces, and mossback conservatives.

Representative of the skeptical and negative attitude of the time is the following pronouncement:

When was it ever known that liberation from bondage was accompanied by a recognition of political equality? Chattels personal may be instantly translated from the auction-block into freemen; but when were they ever taken at the same time to the ballot-box, and invested with all political rights and immunities? According to the laws of development and progress, it is not practicable. . . . Nor, if the freed blacks were admitted to the polls by Presidential fiat, do I see any permanent advantage likely to be secured by it; for, submitted to as a necessity at the outset, as soon as the state was organized and left to manage its own affairs, the white population, with their superior intelligence, wealth, and power, would unquestionably alter the franchise in accordance with their prejudices, and exclude those thus summarily brought to the polls. Coercion would gain nothing.

The author of these sentiments, written in 1864, was none other than William Lloyd Garrison of the *Liberator*, the man who swore to be "harsh as truth and uncompromising as justice." Nor was he alone among the abolitionists in these sentiments, for the Radicals themselves were divided on the matter of Negro suffrage. Even Senator Charles Sumner, one of the earlier and most powerful advocates of placing the ballot in the freedman's hands, was prepared in a Senate speech on February 5, 1866, to admit that educational qualifications for the suffrage would be advisable. At that time, of course, educational restrictions, even a literacy test fairly administered, would have limited the franchise to a small minority of the freedmen. Horace Greeley of the New York *Tribune*, an old friend of the slave, would "limit the voting privilege to the competent and deserving" and suggested such qualifications as ability to read and write, payment of taxes, or establishment in a trade. General O. O. Howard, head of the Freedmen's Bureau, hoped that the franchise would be limited "at least by an educational qualification." This far, of course, President Lincoln and President Johnson were prepared to go, and both in fact did unsuccessfully recommend to southern states such franchise laws.

To go further than that in 1866 or even later was to incur grave political risks, that even the most radical of Republicans were reluctant to assume. Only five states in the North, all with a negligible percentage of colored population, provided for Negro franchise. In 1865 Wisconsin, Minnesota, and Connecticut defeated proposals to allow the Negroes to vote, and the Nebraska constitution of 1866 confined suffrage to whites. New Jersey and Ohio in 1867 and Michigan and Pennsylvania in 1868 turned down proposals for Negro suffrage. Dr. W. E. B. DuBois, who contends that in 1861 "probably not one white American in a hundred believed that Negroes could become an integral part of American democracy," concludes that even by 1868 "the country was not ready for Negro suffrage."

Yet Negro suffrage did come. It came very quickly. In fact, by 1868 it had already come in the South. How it came and why are important determinants in the political legacy left the South and the American Negro by Reconstruction.

Thaddeus Stevens, foremost champion of the freedmen, master of the Republican House majority, and leader of Radical Reconstruction, was advocating some extremely radical measures. He was quite ready to disfranchise southern whites in great numbers and to confiscate great quantities of their land. "It is intended to revolutionize their feelings and principles," he declared. "This may startle feeble minds and shake weak nerves. So do all great improvements." To those who objected to humiliating the defeated foe, he replied: "Why not? Do not they deserve humiliation? If they do not, who does? What criminal, what felon deserves it more?"

But for all his radicalism, Stevens was not yet prepared to enfranchise the Negro freedmen. For one thing, of course, he knew that public opinion would not support it and that the majority of his own party was against it. But apart from political reasons he had other doubts about the wisdom of the measure, some of them similar to those expressed by Garrison, Greeley, Howard, and, for that matter, President Andrew Johnson.

On this vital matter Stevens, contrary to his reputation, can be classified as a moderate or conservative. For one thing he doubted that the freedmen were prepared for intelligent voting. The conditions and laws of slavery, he said on December 18, 1865, "have prevented them from acquiring an education, understanding the commonest laws of contract, or of managing the ordinary business of life." The following month, on January 31, 1866, while urging a constitutional amendment basing representation in the House on the number of qualified voters in a state, Stevens actually expressed hope that the southern states would not immediately grant the freedmen suffrage and thereby increase southern voting power in Congress. He assumed that the Negroes would fall under the political influence of their former masters. "I do not therefore want to grant them this privilege for some years," he said. "Four or five years hence, when the freedmen shall have been made free indeed, when they shall have become intelligent enough, and there are sufficient loyal men there to control the representation from those States," Negro voting would be safe enough. In fact, at this time, Stevens adopted a states' rights position: "I hold that the States have the right, and always have had it, to fix the elective franchise within their own States."

Stevens' solution to the freedmen's suffrage problem was to force upon the southern states the dilemma posed by the proposed Fourteenth Amendment. According to these terms the states would have to choose between excluding the freedmen from the ballot box, thus reducing their number of representatives to about forty-six, or on the other hand, enfranchising them, thereby increasing their representatives to about eighty-three but running the grave risk of losing control to the Republican party. To ensure the adoption of the amendment Stevens proposed that it be submitted only to the non-southern states and declared adopted when approved by three-fourths of these states, exclusive of the South. This solution was rejected by his party, and the southern states voted the amendment down when it was submitted to them along with the other states.

Still hesitant, still reluctant to accept immediate freedmen's suffrage and impose it by force, Stevens temporized with still another proposal. This was contained in a bill he introduced on December 13, 1866, for the reconstruction of North Carolina. In this he proposed to restrict the ballot to those of both races who could read and write or who owned real estate assessed at a value of a hundred dollars or more. Loyal men who had voted before (whites) were not to be disfranchised, but certain classes of Confederates were. There was at times, as Ralph Korngold has suggested, something of Lincoln's hesitant approach to emancipation about Stevens' approach to enfranchisement. Hesitation ceased, however, early in 1867, almost two years after the war. He now went the whole way of military rule, disfranchisement of large numbers of southern whites and immediate and universal Negro suffrage—full-scale Radical Reconstruction.

Reasons for the conversion of Thaddeus Stevens will always be debated. A few facts stand out, however, with inescapable clarity. President Johnson's plan of reconstruction would have increased the southern delegation in the House of Representatives by some thirteen members, since all the freedmen instead of three-fifths would have been counted in apportionment. Without Negro ballots it was probable that all the additional seats, plus all the rest of the seats of the eleven states, would be filled by Democrats and not Republicans. These same states would not only swell the opposition votes in

Congress but the electoral votes in presidential contests. About thirty-seven of the southern seats in the House would be accounted for by Negro population, who had no votes, and likely filled by sworn opponents of the party that took credit for Negro freedom. To ask an overwhelmingly Republican Congress—Radical or Conservative—to approve such a plan was to ask water to run uphill. Conservative Republicans were no more ready to commit political hara-kiri than Radical Republicans.

"Another good reason is," said Stevens in support of his plan, "it would insure the ascendancy of the Union [Republican] party. Do you avow the party purpose? exclaims some horror stricken demagogue. I do. For I believe, on my conscience, that on the continued ascendancy of that party depends the safety of this great nation. If impartial [Negro] suffrage is excluded in the rebel States then every one of them is sure to send a solid rebel [Democratic] representation to Congress, and cast a solid rebel electoral vote. They, with their kindred Copperheads [Democrats] of the North, would always elect the President and control Congress."

Stevens' follower, Roscoe Conkling of New York, was quite as blunt and more specific.

Shall one hundred and twenty-seven thousand white people in New York cast but one vote in this House and have but one voice here, while the same number of white people in Mississippi have three votes in three voices? Shall the death of slavery add two fifths to the entire power which slavery had when slavery was living? Shall one white man have as much share in the Government as three other white men merely because he lives where blacks out-number whites two to one? . . . No sir; not if I can help it.

In addition to "the party purpose" so frankly avowed by Stevens, there was another purpose which was not frankly declared. It was more often disavowed, concealed, deprecated.

This was the purpose of the business community. Although there were significant divisions within the community, a powerful group saw in the return of a disaffected and Democratic South a menace to the economic order that had been established during the absence of the seceding states from the Union. On nearly every delicate and disturbing economic issue of the day—taxation, the National Bank, the national debt, government bonds and their funding, railroads and their financing, regulation of corporations, government grants and subsidies to business, protective tariff legislation—on one and all the business community recognized in the unreconstructed South an antagonist of long standing. In combination with traditional allies in the West and North, the South could upset the new order. Under these circumstances, the northern business community, except for the banking and mercantile interests allied with the Democrats, put aside conservative habits and politics and threw its support to Radical Reconstruction.

Neither the party purpose, the business purpose, nor the two combined constituted a reputable justification with which to persuade the public to support a radical and unpopular program. But there was a purpose that *was* both reputable and persuasive—the philanthropic purpose, the argument that the freedmen needed the ballot to defend and protect their dearly bought freedom, their newly won civil rights, their welfare and livelihood. Of their philanthropic argument the Radicals could make a persuasive and cogent case. And it is undoubtedly true that some of the Radicals were motivated almost entirely by their idealism and their genuine concern for the rights and welfare of the freedmen. What is doubtful is that these were the effective or primary motives, or that they took priority over the pragmatic and materialistic motives of party advantage and sectional economic interests. It is clear at any rate that, until the latter were aroused and marshalled, the former made little progress. On the whole the skepticism of

Secretary Gideon Welles would seem to be justified. "It is evident," he wrote in his diary, "that intense partisanship instead of philanthropy is the root of the movement."

This ulterior motivation, then, is the incubus with which the Negro was burdened before he was ever awakened into political life. The operative and effective motives of his political genesis were extraneous to his own interests and calculated to serve other ends. If there ever came a time when those ends —party advantage and sectional business interests—were better served in some other way, even in a way destructive of the basic political rights of the race, then the political prospects of the Negro would darken. Another incubus was the strongly partisan identifications of his political origins. The major national party of opposition took no part in those origins, regarded them as wholly inimical to its interests, and consequently felt no real commitment to the movement nor to the preservation of its fruits. If there came a time when that party was in the ascendancy, even locally, the political future of the Negro again would darken. To these evil portents should be added the strong resistance to Negro suffrage in the northern states, the obvious reluctance and hesitance of Radical leaders to commit the party to that course, and the grudging acquiescence of the North in the coercive use of it in the South.

After enfranchisement was in full effect in the southern states, the Republican party felt obliged to give specific promise to the people of the North that they would be left free to keep the Negro disfranchised in their own states. In the Republican platform of 1868 appeared the following: "The guaranty by Congress of equal suffrage to all loyal men at the South was demanded by every consideration of public safety, of gratitude, and of justice, and must be maintained; while the question of suffrage in all loyal [non-southern] States properly belongs to the people of those States." Only after the presidential election was over and General Grant had won did

the party dare bring forward the Fifteenth Amendment denying the right of any state to disfranchise the Negro, and not
until 1870 was its ratification completed.

In the meantime a political revolution was underway in the
southern states, a revolution that is the first chapter in the
history of the Negro voter in America. The initial step under
military government, after the destruction of the old civil
governments, was the creation of the new electorate in 1867
and 1868. In all, more than 703,000 Negroes and some 627,000
whites were registered as qualified voters in the reconstructed
states. The processes of disfranchisement and enfranchisement were going on simultaneously. The number of whites
disfranchised is unknown and unknowable, but it is evident
from a comparison of population and registration figures that
the number was rather large in some states. While only two
states had a colored majority of population, five states were
given a colored majority of registered voters. The male population of voting age in Louisiana in 1860 was 94,711 whites
and 92,502 Negroes, but only 45,218 whites were registered as
against 84,436 Negroes. Alabama's voting age population in
1860 was 113,871 whites and 92,404 Negroes, but only 61,295
whites were registered against 104,518 Negroes. While some
states with white majorities in population were given colored
majorities in their electorate, others had their white majorities
drastically reduced, and the two states with a preponderance
of Negroes in population, South Carolina and Mississippi, had
overwhelming majorities of colored voters.

This new-born electorate of freedmen was plunged immediately into action by the election of delegates to constitutional conventions. They followed by electing legislative bodies, state and local officials, and by full-scale and continuous
participation in all phases and aspects of political life in a
period that was abnormally active in a political way. To
characterize the quality of the performance of this many people over a decade of time and in a multiplicity of activities

with sweeping adjectives, "good" or "bad" or "indifferent," would be to indulge in empty generalities. That the mass of these people had less education, less experience in public affairs, and less property of all sorts than the white voters is obvious. As for the more intangible endowments of status and inner security that the psychologists stress, their relative impoverishment was appalling, unprecedented among American or any other known electorates. Their very appearance at the polls in mass, wearing the rags of slave days and bearing the ancient stigmata of oppression, conjured up every gloomy prognostication of the fate of democracies from Aristotle to the Federalists. Not Athens, nor Rome, nor Paris at greatest turbulence had confronted their like. Here was the Federalist beast who would turn every garden into a pigsty. Here was old John Adams' shiftless and improvident Demos, pawn of demagogues and plutocrats and menace to all order. Here in the flesh was Hamilton's "turbulent and changing" mass who "seldom judge or determine right" and who made it necessary to give to "the rich and well born" that "distinct, permanent share in the government," which alone would insure stability. Here was the ultimate test of the democratic dogma in the most extreme form ever attempted.

The records left by that revolutionary experiment have been widely used to discredit both the experiment itself and democratic faith in general. Yet those records need not put democracy out of countenance, nor are they wholly devoid of comfort for those of that faith. No red glow of anarchy lit up the southern horizon as a consequence of the revolution, and the enfranchised freedmen did not prove the unleashed beast of Federalist imagination. Moral pigsties undoubtedly developed, but they were oftener than not the creation of the other race, and more of them were to be found outside the South than within.

The new electorate of freedmen proved on the whole remarkably modest in their demands, unaggressive in their conduct, and deferential in their attitude. In no state did they hold place and power in anything approaching their actual numbers and voting strength. The possible exception was South Carolina, and there they held a majority of seats only in the lower house of the legislature. In the first legislature under the new constitution of Mississippi, the other state with a large Negro majority of population, Negro representatives constituted only two-sevenths of the membership of the house and an even smaller proportion of the senate. Freedmen of that state almost never took advantage of their numbers to seize control in local government, for a Negro majority in a municipal government seems to have been unknown. There was only one Negro mayor of a city in the state and a record of only twelve sheriffs. Only three Negroes were elected in the whole country to the Forty-first Congress, the first to which they were eligible, and there were never more than eight at one time out of a total of more than one hundred members from the southern states. In view of the subordinate role and the few offices that the freedmen took, no state in the South could properly be said to have been under Negro rule or "domination" at any time.

Yet in varying numbers and different states Negroes occupied all the varieties of public office in existence, up to but not including the governorship. They served as policemen and supreme court justices, recorders of deeds and lieutenant-governors, sheriffs and prosecuting attorneys, justices of the peace and state superintendents of education, mayors and United States senators. Without doubt some of them made awkward efforts and a few of them cut some grotesque capers, but upon the crude stage of frontier democracy comic figures had appeared before this time, and none of them could have been taken for colored minstrels before 1868. In an age of low public morals the country over, some of the neophyte politicians were as guilty of corruption as the old hands, but the neophytes rarely seem to have received their fair share of graft.

In retrospect, one is more impressed with the success that a people of such meager resources and limited experience enjoyed in producing the number of sober, honest, and capable leaders and public servants they did. The appearance of some of this sort in every state is the main comfort the record provides to the democratic faith. They give the impression of people struggling conscientiously under desperate odds to live up to a test such as no other people had ever been subjected to in all the long testing of the democratic theory. Their success varied from state to state. With regard to Mississippi the conclusions of Vernon Wharton are that

altogether, as governments go, that supplied by the Negro and white Republicans in Misissippi between 1870 and 1876 was not a bad government. Never, in states, counties, or towns, did the Negro hold office in proportion to their numbers. . . . The Negroes who held county offices were often ignorant, but under the control of white Democrats or Republicans they supplied a form of government which differed little from that in counties where they held no offices. The three who represented the state in Congress were above reproach. Those in the legislature sought no special advantages for their race, and in one of their very first acts they petitioned Congress to remove all political disabilities from the whites. With their white Republican colleagues, they gave to the state a government of greatly expanded functions at a cost that was low in comparison with that of almost any other state.

By the operation of a sort of historical color bar, the history of the Negro's political experience in Reconstruction has been studied too much in isolation and pictured as unique. There were unique features in that history, of course, but it does not constitute the only, nor the last, instance of the sudden enfranchisement of large numbers of politically inexperienced people. Nor does it support the stereotype of the Negro as the political tyro and neophyte of the western world, the laggard in the race for political maturity. After the Reconstruction episode was over, millions of people entered this country. Of the more than twelve million white immigrants who poured into the stream of American citizenship in the fifty years after 1880 from southern and eastern European countries, it is doubtful that more than a very small percentage had ever enjoyed any significant experience of direct political participation in the democratic sense. Their first taste of such experience came in the 1880's, the 1890's, or 1900's, or later when they took out citizenship papers. Here were the real political neophytes of the American electorate. They greatly outnumber the Negro population. They too were dominated by bosses and influenced by handouts and small favors. The record of the inexperience, naiveté, and ineptitude of these erstwhile peasants in the big city slums is written in the history of corrupt city bosses, rings, and machines, a history that can match some of the darker chapters of Reconstruction government. The Mugwump reformers turned against them, as they turned against the Radical Republicans, because of the corruption associated with their regimes. Eventually the immigrants learned the ropes, gained experience and assurance, helped clean up some of the messes their inexperience had created, and gained acceptance as respected members of the body politic.

The immigrants had their own handicaps of language and prejudice to deal with, but they never had anything approaching the handicaps against which the Negro had to struggle to gain acceptance. The prejudices that the immigrants confronted were nothing like the race prejudice with which the Negro had to cope. Nor was the white immigrant's enfranchisement accompanied by the disfranchisement of the ruling and propertied classes of the community in which he settled. Neither did the exercise of his franchise have to be protected by the bayonets of federal troops, nor did the gaining of his political rights appear to old settlers as a penalty and punishment inflicted upon them, a deliberate humiliation of them by their conquerors. Political leaders of the immigrants were not ordinarily regarded by the old settlers as "carpetbaggers," intruders, and puppets of a hostile government sent to rule over them; immigrants did not regard the old settlers as their former owners, any more than the old settlers looked upon the immigrants as their former slaves. The situation of the latest political neophytes was, after all, in many ways quite different from that of the neophytes of the seventies.

The time eventually came when the incubus of their political genesis returned to haunt the freedmen and destroy their future. That was the time when the two dominant operative motives of Radical Reconstruction, party advantage and sectional business interests, became inactive—the time when it became apparent that those mighty ends could better be served by abandoning the experiment and leaving the freedmen to shift for themselves. The philanthropic motive was still a factor, and in many minds still strong, but it was not enough without the support of the two powerful props of party advantage and sectional interests. The moment of collapse came at different times in different states, but the climax and consolidation of the decision came with the disputed presidential election of 1876 and the settlement that resolved it in the Compromise of 1877.

It would be neither fair nor accurate to place all the blame upon the North and its selfish interests. There had been plenty of willing cooperation on the part of southern whites. They had used craft and guile, force and violence, economic pressure and physical terror, and all the subtle psychological devices of race prejudice and propaganda at their command. But the southern whites were after all a minority, and not a strong minority at that. The North had not only numbers and power on its side, but the law and the Constitution as well. When the moment of crisis arrived, however, the old doubts and skepticism of the North returned, the doubts that had kept the Negro disfranchised in the North after freedmen's suffrage had been imposed upon the South. After the Fifteenth Amendment was passed, the North rapidly lost interest in the

Negro voters. They were pushed out of the limelight by other interests, beset by prejudices, and neglected by politicians. The northern Negro did not enjoy a fraction of the political success the southern Negro enjoyed, as modest as that was. Reformers and Mugwumps of the North identified corruption with the Radical wing of the Republican party, lost interest in the Negro allies of the Radicals, and looked upon them as a means of perpetuating corrupt government all over the nation as well as in the South. In this mood they came to the conclusion that the Negro voter had been given a fair chance to prove his worth as a responsible citizen and that the experiment had proved a failure. This conclusion appeared in many places, most strangely perhaps in the columns of that old champion of the race, the New York *Tribune* (April 7, 1877), which declared that the Negroes had been given "ample opportunity to develop their own latent capacities," and had only succeeded in proving that "as a race they are idle, ignorant, and vicious."

The North's loss of faith in its own cause is reflected in many surprising places. One example must suffice. It is of special interest because it comes from the supreme official charged with enforcing the Fifteenth Amendment and guaranteeing to the freedmen their political rights, the President whose administration coincided with Radical Reconstruction and the whole great experiment—General U. S. Grant. According to the diary of Secretary Hamilton Fish, entry of January 17, 1877: "He [Grant] says he opposed the Fifteenth Amendment and thinks it was a mistake, that it had done the Negro no good, and had been a hindrance to the South, and by no means a political advantage to the North."

During the present struggle for Negro rights, which might be called the Second Reconstruction—though one of quite a different sort—I have noticed among Negro intellectuals at times a tendency to look back upon the First Reconstruction as if it were in some ways a sort of Golden Age. In this nostalgic view that period takes the shape of the race's finest hour, a time of heroic leaders and deeds, of high faith and firm resolution, a time of forthright and passionate action, with no bowing to compromises of "deliberate speed." I think I understand their feeling. Reconstruction will always have a special and powerful meaning for the Negro. It is undoubtedly a period full of rich and tragic and meaningful history, a period that should be studiously searched for its meanings, a period that has many meanings yet to yield. But I seriously doubt that it will ever serve satisfactorily as a Golden Age—for anybody. There is too much irony mixed with the tragedy.